PATERNOSTER BIBLICAL MONOGRAPHS

Enabling Fidelity to God

Perseverance in Hebrews in Light of the Reciprocity Systems of the Ancient Mediterranean World

PATERNOSTER BIBLICAL MONOGRAPHS

A full listing of titles in this series and Paternoster Theological Monographs
appear at the end of this book

PATERNOSTER BIBLICAL MONOGRAPHS

Enabling Fidelity to God

Perseverance in Hebrews in Light of the Reciprocity Systems of the Ancient Mediterranean World

Jason A. Whitlark

Foreword by Charles H. Talbert

WIPF & STOCK · Eugene, Oregon

Wipf and Stock Publishers
199 W 8th Ave, Suite 3
Eugene, OR 97401

Enabling Fidelity to God
Perseverance in Hebrews in Light of the Reciprocity Systems
of the Ancient Mediterranean World
By Whitlark, Jason A.
Copyright©2008 Paternoster
ISBN 13: 978-1-60608-477-9
Publication date 02/02/2009
Previously published by Paternoster, 2008

"This Edition Published by Wipf and Stock Publishers by arrangement with Paternoster".

Series Editors

I. Howard Marshall, Honorary Research Professor of New Testament, University of Aberdeen, Scotland, UK

Richard J. Bauckham, Professor of New Testament Studies and Bishop Wardlaw Professor, University of St Andrews, Scotland, UK

Craig Blomberg, Distinguished Professor of New Testament, Denver Seminary, Colorado, USA

Robert P. Gordon, Regius Professor of Hebrew, University of Cambridge, UK

Tremper Longman III, Robert H. Gundry Professor and Chair of the Department of Biblical Studies, Westmont College, Santa Barbara, California, USA

PATERNOSTER BIBLICAL MONOGRAPHS

Series Preface

One of the major objectives of Paternoster is to serve biblical scholarship by providing a channel for the publication of theses and other monographs of high quality at affordable prices. Paternoster stands within the broad evangelical tradition of Christianity. Our authors would describe themselves as Christians who recognise the authority of the Bible, maintain the centrality of the gospel message and assent to the classical credal statements of Christian belief. There is diversity within this constituency; advances in scholarship are possible only if there is freedom for frank debate on controversial issues and for the publication of new and sometimes provocative proposals. What is offered in this series is the best of writing by committed Christians who are concerned to develop well-founded biblical scholarship in a spirit of loyalty to the historic faith.

To Jennifer, my lily among thorns

Contents

Foreword by Charles H. Talbert	xiii
Acknowledgements	xv
Abbreviations	xvii

Chapter 1
Introduction — 1
Two Means of Fidelity: Reciprocity and Enablement — 1
Benefaction and Patronage: Previous Applications
to Interpretation — 2
   Greco-Roman Benefaction and Pauline Studies — 2
   Greco-Roman Benefaction, Hebrews, and David A. deSilva — 6
Method: Reading with the Authorial Audience — 8
Plan — 12

Chapter 2
The Historical Context of Hebrews — 15
A Characterization of Reciprocity — 17
   Reciprocity is a Relational Bond — 20
      A COHESIVE DYNAMIC — 20
      A NON-COMMERCIAL BOND — 21
      A NON-LEGISLATED BOND — 22
   The Bond is Characterized by Fidelity — 25
      EXPRESSIONS OF FIDELITY — 25
      THE EXTENT OF FIDELITY — 36
      CONFLICTING LOYALTIES — 37
   The Bond is Characterized by Cooperation — 38
      THE OBLIGATIONS OF SYMMETRICAL RECIPROCITY
      RELATIONSHIPS — 38
      THE OBLIGATIONS OF ASYMMETRICAL RECIPROCITY
      RELATIONSHIPS — 40

The Bond is Characterized by Mutual Dependence	49
RECIPROCITY INVOLVES A MEASURE OF RISK	49
RISK ARISES FROM THE VOLUNTARY NATURE OF THE RECIPROCITY BOND	50
ASSUAGING THE RISK: εὔνοια	51
Conclusion	53
The Anthropological Assumption of Reciprocity	54
The Optimistic Assumption of the Preceding Characterization	55
Additional Proof: Emphasis Placed Upon Character	56
IN THE SELECTION OF BENEFACTORS/BENEFICIARIES	56
TOUTED IN THE HONORIFIC INSCRIPTIONS	58
INTRINSIC TO THE BENEFACTOR/BENEFICIARY	60
Additional Proof: Giving Produces Gratitude	62
Additional Proof: Optimistic Anthropology Made Explicit in Aristotle and Seneca	65
Conclusion	68

Chapter 3
The Religious Background of Hebrews

The Religious Background of Hebrews	71
Divine-Human Reciprocity Relationship in the Jewish Milieu	72
The Mosaic Covenant and the Suzerainty-vassal Treaty	72
A RELATIONAL BOND	74
FIDELITY: INDEBTED GRATITUDE	76
COOPERATION	81
MUTUAL DEPENDENCE	82
Josephus and Greco-Roman Patronage/Benefaction	85
A RELATIONAL BOND	85
FIDELITY: INDEBTED GRATITUDE	87
COOPERATION	89
MUTUAL DEPENDENCE	91
CONCLUSION	92
Reciprocity and Other Streams of Middle Judaism	92
Rabbinic Judaism and Reciprocity	96
Consequence of Anthropological Assumptions in the Jewish Milieu	97
Consequence of an Optimistic Anthropological Assumption	97
POSSIBILITY OF SUCCESS	98

REALIZATION OF FIDELITY	102
Consequence of a Pessimistic Anthropological Assumption	103
FAILURE OF THE RELATIONSHIP	104
SOLUTION TO INFIDELITY	116
THE FUNCTION OF GRATITUDE	121
Conclusion	125

Chapter 4
Fidelity in Hebrews

Fidelity in Hebrews	**127**
Hebrews and Its Milieu: Echoes of Benefaction in Hebrews	127
Conceptual Echoes	128
Lexical Echoes	132
The Religious Appropriation of Benefaction/Patronage: Two Models	134
Josephus	135
Paul	135
Interpreting Fidelity in Hebrews: A Critique of DeSilva's Reciprocity Model	138
DeSilva's Methodology	138
DeSilva's Appropriation of Ancient Reciprocity	139
A Preliminary Critique of DeSilva's Interpretation	142
Interpreting Fidelity in Hebrews: Divine Enablement and Anthropological Assumption in Hebrews	146
Election and Enablement	148
ELECTION MOTIFS	148
ENABLEMENT	152
Anthropological Assumption	163
UNIVERSAL NEED FOR PURIFICATION	164
SUBJECTION OF HUMANITY TO DEATH	164
THE HISTORY OF ISRAEL	165
The Paradox of Divine Enablement and Human Responsibility	166
The Paradox in Hebrews	166
Other Representatives of This Paradox	168
Conclusion	171

Chapter 5
Conclusion 173
Summary 173
Hebrews's Place in the Theological Tradition of the Church 176
Avenues of Future Research 178

Appendix 183

Bibliography 185

Indexes
Index of Subjects 199
Index of References 215

Foreword

How does one understand the saving activity of God in the life of an individual? Recent scholarship uses the language of covenantal nomism for Judaism and reciprocity for Greco-Roman sacrificial cults. The soteriological reality is the same in both. God or the gods act beneficently to initiate a relation with humans; humans then respond out of gratitude to keep the relation going. Lately, scholars like David deSilva have attempted to read Hebrews as a positive Christian adaptation of the Mediterranean system of reciprocity. In Whitlark's reading, however, Hebrews rather offers its auditors an alternative to the reciprocity rationale of benefaction. Within a New Covenant frame of reference, Hebrews sees human faithfulness to God in the period between conversion and departure from this life issuing not from human gratitude for past grace but from God's ongoing gracious enablement. This soteriological orientation the author of Hebrews shares with Paul, although their conceptual worlds and modes of expression are different.

This is a fresh and provocative new reading of Hebrews that moves the homily from the periphery of New Testament soteriology into the early Christian mainstream. This is an exercise in biblical theology not to be missed.

Charles H. Talbert
Baylor University
August 2007

ACKNOWLEDGEMENTS

A project of this magnitude is never just the work of one person. While I claim full responsibility for my work and any of its shortcomings are a reflection of my own scholarship, this work would not have been possible without the collaboration and support of group of people. This work was given its initial impetus from my advising mentor Charles H. Talbert. Both his rigorous scholarship and warm piety provided me a worthy model and inspired my own scholarly pursuits. His interest in exploring the various ways divine enablement is understood in the New Testament documents shaped the foundations of this study. If there is any clarity of thought in this dissertation, it is due to his always cheerful, diligent, and patient guidance of this project to its completion. I pray that this study provides a worthy contribution to his own pursuits of interpreting the New Testament documents.

I thank Mikeal C. Parsons who read my dissertation with interest and always provided insightful comments and suggestions that refined and strengthened my argument. His own interests in both ancient and modern rhetorical studies of the New Testament also helped me grasp the significance of Hebrews's key rhetorical feature, syncrisis. Also, I thank Jeffrey Hamilton in Baylor's History Department for serving as my outside reader for this study. I greatly benefited from his course on Roman history. Finally, this level of scholarship would not have been possible without the nurture of the New Testament faculty at Baylor University, who always demanded and modeled scholarly excellence. I also thank Nathan Carson who carefully read this manuscript and compiled its subject index.

I also owe a debt of gratitude to all those interpreters of Hebrews upon whose shoulders I have stood: William Lane, Paul Ellingworth, Harold Attridge, David Peterson, Ceslaus Spicq, H. –F. Weiss, P. E. Hughs, James Moffatt, Craig Koester, and F. F. Bruce. I also want to especially acknowledge my appreciation of David deSilva's contribution to the study of Hebrews. Though in this study I challenge him on a fundamental aspect of his interpretation of Hebrews, I have greatly benefited from his commentary on Hebrews. His commentary reflects serious scholarship, interpretive insight, clarity of thought, and a deep appreciation of Hebrews as a religious text for the faith and life of the Christian community.

I would be amiss not to acknowledge the loving support of my family and, above all, the gentle and patient support of my wife, Jennifer. She graciously and enthusiastically undertook the tedious task of compiling the reference index to this book. Her constant prayers and encouragement sustained me throughout this project. This work is her achievement as well. To her, I dedicate this dissertation, not because it is worthy of her but because she should have the first.

Jason A. Whitlark
Baylor University
August 2007

ABBREVIATIONS

Unless otherwise indicated below, the abbreviations in this book for biblical texts, the OT and NT Apocrypha, the OT Pseudepigrapha, Dead Sea Scrolls, and other ancient sources as well as modern journals, series, and technical abbreviations follow *The SBL Handbook of Style for Ancient, Near Eastern, Biblical, and Early Christian Studies* (Peabody: Hendrickson, 1999).

CEG	*Carmina Epigraphica Graeca saeculorum VIII-V a. Chr. n.*
CID	*Corpus des Inscriptions de Delphes*
CIG	*Corpus Inscriptionum Graecarum*
I.Cret	*Inscriptiones Creticae*
I.Delos	*Inscriptions de Délos*
I.Priene	*Inschriften von Priene*
IG	*Inscriptiones Graecae*
IGRP	*Inscriptiones Graecae ad Res Romanas Pertinentes*
OGIS	*Orientis Graeci Inscriptiones Selectae*
SEG	*Supplementum Epigraphicum Graecum*
SIG³	*Sylloge Inscriptionum Graecarum* 3d. ed.
Vit. Pyth.	*De Vita Pythagorica*
TAM	*Tituli Asiae Minoris*

CHAPTER 1

Introduction

Two Means of Fidelity: Reciprocity and Enablement

In the ancient Mediterranean world, the dynamic of reciprocity provided social cohesion to the fabric of society. Reciprocity permeated and governed relationships at all levels of society as well as the relationship between the divine and human realms. Moreover, "[r]eciprocity was at the heart of all forms of benevolence in the ancient Graeco-Roman world. The bestowal of gifts initiated the establishment of long term relationships that involved mutual obligation and clear status differentials between the transactors."[1] The primary reciprocity systems of the first-century world were benefaction and patronage. These systems significantly structured the relationships in society, defining and stabilizing these relationships. More importantly, the fidelity necessary for these "long term relationships" in the Greco-Roman world was sustained by the dynamic of reciprocity. Fidelity, likewise, is central to the message of Hebrews, whose first auditors lived in this Greco-Roman society shaped by the daily workings of reciprocity to secure long-term, mutually beneficial relationships. In light of this observation, certain questions arise when we attempt to interpret the first-century Christian document of Hebrews: What impact, if any, did the reciprocity rationale that governed relationships in the human and divine realms in the ancient world have on the message of Hebrews? Was there anything in the message of Hebrews and its auditors' experience of salvation through Jesus Christ that would have redefined the reciprocity rationale with which its original audience would have been inundated? More constructively, wherein does persevering fidelity lie in Hebrews? To answer these questions leads us to consider both the dynamic of reciprocity as it was understood in the ancient Mediterranean world and the message of Hebrews as it was heard within that context. Thus the thesis of this study is twofold: (1) With regard to the divine-human relationship in the ancient Mediterranean world, the belief in the reciprocity rationale to secure fidelity rested on an optimistic anthropological assumption. (2) Hebrews, on the other hand, belonged to a stream of Middle Judaism[2] within the Greco-

---

[1] Stephen Joubert, *Paul as Benefactor: Reciprocity, Strategy and Theological Reflection in Paul's Collection* (WUNT 2.124; Tübingen: Mohr Siebeck, 2000), 6.
[2] For this terminology see Gabrielle Boccaccini, *Middle Judaism: Jewish Thought 300 B.C.E. to 200 C.E.* (Minneapolis: Fortress Press, 1991), esp. 7-25.

Roman world that held to a pessimistic anthropological assumption and thus looked to the divine enabling of human fidelity and not reciprocity.[3] The implications of this thesis are far reaching concerning the soteriology of Hebrews, the author's and auditors' presumed experience of salvation in Jesus Christ, and how the message of the supremacy of Jesus Christ was heard in the context Hebrews presupposes.

Benefaction and Patronage: Previous Applications to Interpretation

Before I demonstrate my thesis, we need a sense of how scholars of the New Testament have applied the ancient reciprocity systems to their studies of the New Testament documents. More specifically, how have they understood ancient reciprocity and how has this influenced their interpretation of the biblical text. What we will see is that the reciprocity system of Greco-Roman benefaction has recently become a popular model for understanding aspects of Paul's writings and his relationship to his cultural milieu. Concerning our topic, one scholar has also attempted a thorough reinterpretation of the message of Hebrews and its summons to fidelity in the light of Greco-Roman benefaction and the reciprocity that defined that social system.

Greco-Roman Benefaction and Pauline Studies

In the mid-1970s, S. C. Mott provided an initial characterization of reciprocity associated with giving benefits in the ancient world in his article, "The Power of Giving and Receiving".[4] He concluded, "The relationship between a benefactor and his beneficiary...consisted of reciprocal obligations, composed of gratitude of the recipient to his benefactor resulting in obligation of the benefactor to the beneficiary who had expressed gratitude."[5] Mott was attuned to some of the complexities of ancient reciprocity, namely how the mutual obligations incurred in an exchange of benefits and gratitude balanced power in the relationship. Mott, however, did not apply his findings to the New Testament but to the modern welfare system. The application of the pervasive social system of

---

3 The terminology, optimistic and pessimistic anthropology, is taken from Timo Laato, *Paul and Judaism: An Anthropological Approach* (trans. T. McElwain; South Florida Studies in the History of Judaism 115; Atlanta: Scholars Press, 1995).

4 S. C. Mott, "The Power of Giving and Receiving: Reciprocity in Hellenistic Benevolence," in *Current Issues in Biblical and Patristic Interpretation* (ed. Gerald F. Hawthorne; Grand Rapids: Eerdmans, 1975). See also the earlier work by S. C. Mott, "The Greek Benefactor and Deliverance from Moral Distress" (Ph.D. diss., Harvard University, 1971), where he applies his findings to the Pastorals.

5 Mott, "The Power of Giving and Receiving," 72.

benefaction in the ancient world to New Testament studies received renewed impetus from Frederick Danker's publication, *Benefactor: Epigraphic Study of a Greco-Roman and New Testament Semantic Field*, in 1982.[6] In this work, Danker not only provides several translations of representative epigraphic evidence relevant to the topic of Greco-Roman benefaction, he also provides several suggestive correlations that his summaries of the evidence have for understanding various aspects of the New Testament documents. Thus, he attempts to show how deeply imbedded the language and expectations associated with benefaction were in the New Testament.[7] Subsequently, in the past twenty years, there has been a steady application of aspects of Greco-Roman benefaction and patronage to Pauline studies.[8] There has more recently been a concerted effort to interpret the writings of Paul in the light of Greco-Roman benefaction by Stephen Joubert (2000), James Harrison (2003), and Zeba Crook (2004).

(1) Stephen Joubert believes that the reciprocity that governed the benefactor-beneficiary relationship provides the appropriate social context for understanding the rationale behind the Jerusalem collection taken up by Paul among his predominantly Gentile churches. Joubert states that, in exchange for the recognition of Paul's "law free" gospel by the "pillar apostles" in the Jerusalem church, Paul would collect material assistance from his Gentile congregations for the impoverished church in Jerusalem. Thus, Paul and the Antioch church by taking up this collection would be repaying a debt of gratitude to the Jerusalem church for the recognition of Paul's Gentile ministry and "law free" gospel. The completion of this task would secure Paul's own honor as the "would-be" benefactor of the

---

6 Frederick W. Danker, *Benefactor: Epigraphic Study of a Greco-Roman and New Testament Semantic Field* (St. Louis: Clayton Publishing House, 1982).

7 More recently, Jerome H. Neyrey (*Render unto God: New Testament Understandings of the Divine* [Minneapolis: Fortress Press, 2004]) has attempted to identify a significant element of the "God-talk" in representative New Testament documents along the lines of benefaction. See esp. Appendix I.

8 Peter Marshall, *Enmity in Corinth: Social Conventions in Paul's Relations with the Corinthians* (WUNT 2.23; Tübingen: J.C.B. Mohr, 1987); Reggie M. Kidd, *Wealth and Beneficence in the Pastoral Epistles: A "Bourgeois" Form of Early Christianity?* (SBLDS 122; Atlanta: Scholars Press, 1990); John K. Chow, *Patronage and Power: A Study of Social Networks in Corinth* (JSNTSup 75; Sheffield: JSOT Press, 1992); Andrew D. Clarke, *Secular and Christian Leadership in Corinth: A Socio-historical and Exegetical Study of 1 Corinthians 1-6* (AGJU 18; New York: Brill, 1993); Bruce W. Winter, *Seek the Welfare of the City: Christians as Benefactors and Citizens* (Grand Rapids: Eerdmans; Carlisle: Paternoster Press, 1994); Gerald W. Peterman, *Paul's Gift from Philippi: Conventions of Gift-exchange and Christian Giving* (SNTSMS 92; Cambridge: Cambridge University Press, 1997).

Jerusalem Christians.⁹ Furthermore, not only would Paul be repaying his debt to the Jerusalem church for its beneficial recognition of the legitimacy of his ministry, but also the predominantly Gentile congregations would be repaying their debt to God by participating in the collection.¹⁰ James R. Harrison has criticized Joubert's thesis on two grounds: Paul would not have submitted himself or his message to the pillar apostles in the manner of a beneficiary to a benefactor and Joubert plays down the unilateral nature of God's grace that resists the reciprocity rationale.¹¹ Harrison emphasizes that God's grace empowers human beneficence for Paul, not reciprocity. Another weakness of Joubert's thesis is that he fails to sufficiently describe the complexities of ancient reciprocity that undergird the benefactor-beneficiary relationship. Moreover, by too narrowly focusing on the Jerusalem collection in Paul's letters, he has failed to take into account broader aspects in Paul's writings that may not be congenial to the reciprocity rationale that governed Greco-Roman benefaction.

(2) James Harrison has examined the language of grace (χάρις) that was prevalent in Greco-Roman benefaction and related his examination of the ancient evidence to Paul's language of grace.¹² Harrison examines a very broad array of ancient sources, but the strength of his analysis lies in the significant attention he gives to inscriptional evidence related to benefaction that pervaded the ancient Mediterranean world.¹³ Harrison demonstrates that Greco-Roman benefaction provides the primary context for understanding where Paul derives his language of grace. Harrison, however, argues that Paul shaped his message in surprising ways that undercut the "ethos of reciprocity" associated with Greco-Roman benefaction. There are three aspects about the unilateral nature of God's χάρις for Paul that oppose this "ethos of reciprocity": it rejects the *do ut des* rationale of reciprocity; being unilateral, it is incapable of repayment; and as stated above, Gods' χάρις "impels" human beneficence.¹⁴ Moreover, Paul rejects the merit-thinking typical of the rationale of reciprocity in Greco-Roman benefaction.¹⁵ Instead, "God operates on the basis of His overflowing grace over against the obligations of reciprocity."¹⁶ Love is the dynamic that transforms and subverts

---

9 Joubert, *Paul as Benefactor*, 114-15.
10 Joubert, *Paul as Benefactor*, 152, cf. 201, 217.
11 James R. Harrison, *Paul's Language of Grace in Its Graeco-Roman Context* (WUNT 2.172; Tübingen: Mohr Siebeck, 2003), 299-300 n. 37, 310 n. 80.
12 Harrison, *Paul's Language of Grace*.
13 Harrison, *Paul's Language of Grace*, 26-63.
14 Harrison, *Paul's Language of Grace*, 284-85.
15 Harrison, *Paul's Language of Grace*, 270-71.
16 Harrison, *Paul's Language of Grace*, 348.

reciprocity.[17] Harrison is right both to point to those aspects of Paul's language and rhetoric that intersect with Greco-Roman benefaction and to point to those aspects that Paul transforms with respect to the "ethos of reciprocity" typical of this social system. Harrison has given some attention to the ancient sources and especially the epigraphic evidence for characterizing the reciprocity that sustained Greco-Roman benefaction. He is particularly fond of pointing out the merit-thinking that is associated with ancient reciprocity. He has not, however, significantly engaged the way reciprocity was meant to sustain fidelity in the relationship nor has he undertaken a focused characterization of ancient reciprocity. Additionally, he has not discussed what the reciprocity rationale assumes about human capabilities—an aspect central to Paul's gospel. So while Harrison has made a start in addressing reciprocity in the ancient world and the way it was appropriated in Paul's teaching and mission, more can be said.

(3) The last and most recent of the works on Paul that will be discussed here is Zeba Crook's examination of Paul's conversion passages in the context of Greco-Roman benefaction.[18] Crook dismisses the Western psychological models used to interpret the commonly accepted autobiographical passages related to Paul's conversion experience. Instead she opts for the social model of Greco-Roman benefaction to "reconceptualize" Paul's own witness to his conversion.[19] From the sociological studies of Marshall Sahlins and E. W. Stegemann and W. Stegemann, Crook adopts the category of generalized reciprocity in order to describe Greco-Roman benefaction. Generalized reciprocity defines relationships between unequal partners where a benefaction is bestowed and then repaid with honor, gratitude, and loyalty, and these are relationships of some duration.[20] More specifically, she addresses the key issue of loyalty that the reciprocity systems of benefaction and patronage attempted to secure. In the case of Paul, his conversion did not involve a change of religion only a change in loyalty to the broker of God's benefits, namely Jesus Christ.[21] Moreover, Paul's mission to the Gentiles is a reflection of Paul's "client reciprocity" or repayment of his debt of gratitude for the benefaction of the revelation God gave him of Jesus Christ.[22] Crook's thesis, though, has some problems. First, her narrow focus on Paul's conversion passages rarely relates these passages to the

---

17 Harrison, *Paul's Language of Grace*, 331.
18 Zeba A. Crook, *Reconceptualizing Conversion: Patronage Loyalty, and Conversion in the Religions of the Ancient Mediterranean* (BZNW 130; New York: Walter de Gruyter, 2004).
19 Crook, *Reconceptualizing Conversion*, 13-150.
20 Crook, *Reconceptualizing Conversion*, 58-59.
21 Crook, *Reconceptualizing Conversion*, 155.
22 Crook, *Reconceptualizing Conversion*, 158-61, 168-69.

larger contours of Paul's thought that might modify her thesis. As Harrison has argued, Paul's gospel of God's super-abounding grace and love opposed the reciprocity rationale of Greco-Roman benefaction. Second, she gives no detailed analysis of ancient reciprocity and mainly relies upon two modern sociological studies for her definition. Third, she misspeaks when she says "loyalty motivated action" within a patronage relationship.[23] Strictly speaking, loyalty is not a motivation but is a goal of Greco-Roman benefaction and patronage. This statement should be modified, as we will later see, to say that "indebted gratitude motivated loyalty" between the benefactor and beneficiary. Fourth, consonant with the rationale of reciprocity but not necessarily to the thought of Paul, Crook states that the grace (i.e., the vision) God gave Paul is what God owed Paul for his honorable Jewish past. This is because Crook defines Paul's conversion and loyalty in terms of reciprocity.[24] Fifth, Crook believes that ancient loyalty secured through reciprocity was more concerned with external action than internal choice.[25] Because she fails to understand the true dynamic of the loyalty secured by reciprocity (i.e., indebted gratitude), she outstrips her evidence with her assertion. Finally, she fails to consider whether an assumption about human ability was commonly associated with ancient reciprocity and whether this assumption was congruous with Paul's own view of human ability and the need of salvation through Jesus Christ.

Greco-Roman Benefaction, Hebrews, and David A. deSilva

In this study, however, our concern will be with the interpretation of fidelity in the message of Hebrews. More specifically, how does the first-century Christian document of Hebrews, which places singular emphasis upon the necessity of ongoing fidelity to God, relate to its milieu? This milieu was permeated by the reciprocity rationale of Greco-Roman benefaction and patronage among other reciprocity relationships. One scholar, David deSilva, has recently attempted to answer the question in the affirmative. He has reinterpreted the message of Hebrews in terms of the expectations associated with Greco-Roman benefaction. For deSilva, the reciprocity rationale ubiquitous in the ancient Mediterranean world is the key for understanding, rhetorically, the exhortations to fidelity and warnings against infidelity in Hebrews.[26] For instance, in deSilva's published

---

23 Crook, *Reconceptualizing Conversion*, 250, cf. 255.
24 Crook, *Reconceptualizing Conversion*, 185-86.
25 Crook, *Reconceptualizing Conversion*, 184, 250, 253.
26 David deSilva, *Despising Shame: Honor Discourse and Community Maintenance in the Epistle to the Hebrews* (SBLDS 152; Atlanta: Scholars Press, 1995), 209-75; idem., *Perseverance in Gratitude: A Socio-Rhetorical Commentary on the Epistle "to the Hebrews"* (Grand Rapids: Eerdmans, 2000), 59-64. See also David deSilva,

dissertation, he writes, "[Christians] are to return χάρις for χάρις, to show gratitude to God for the many benefits God has provided in Christ....They are called to give a just return to God for God's benefits, which will also assure that they retain their standing in God's favor."[27] Even the title of his commentary on Hebrews remains indicative of this perspective—*Perseverance in Gratitude*. We will have opportunity to engage deSilva's thesis more thoroughly later on in this study. Concerning his assessment of Greco-Roman benefaction and reciprocity, deSilva has correctly identified the dynamic that sustained ancient reciprocity relationships—indebted gratitude. Two areas, however, have been overlooked in deSilva's application of Greco-Roman reciprocity to Hebrews. (1) DeSilva has overlooked in his study of Hebrews the anthropological perspective that is assumed by those who believed that the reciprocity dynamic could successfully secure fidelity between the divine and human realms. Consequently, deSilva does not examine whether the anthropological perspective in Hebrews is accordant with ancient reciprocity. In this regard, he has also failed to consider if there were other ways, in contradistinction to reciprocity, by which a person's fidelity to God might be secured. (2) DeSilva has also failed to recognize that the Jewish religious context was uneven in it own assessment of the success of reciprocity to secure fidelity. Among the streams of exilic and Middle Judaism that will be discussed in this study, two different perspectives concerning the success of reciprocity to secure the people's fidelity to God developed based upon different anthropological assumptions, that is, beliefs about what people were inherently capable of doing with respect to a relationship with God. The examination of these areas will not only call for a modification of deSilva's thesis but also discover the message of Hebrews to be particularly relevant to a culture that was so pervasively marked by a reciprocity rationale.

These studies represent a range of views and opinions about Greco-Roman benefaction and ancient reciprocity. All the studies to some degree recognize that reciprocity was the relational dynamic of Greco-Roman benefaction and patronage among other relationships. Harrison, however, is the only one who has recently pointed out some of the complexities of the

---

"Patronage and Reciprocity: The Context of Grace in the New Testament," *Ashland Theological Journal* 31 (1999): 53. DeSilva does state that patronage among Christians and thus reciprocity among Christians and Christian communities was transformed into a notion of stewardship (69). This article is reproduced in *Honor, Patronage, Kinship, and Purity: Unlocking New Testament Culture* (Downers Grove: IVP, 2000). See also Kenneth Schenk, *Understanding the Book of Hebrews: The Story Behind the Sermon* (Louisville: Westminster/John Knox Press, 2003), 65, who uncritically accepts deSilva's thesis.

27 DeSilva, *Despising Shame*, 273.

reciprocity dynamic in the ancient world that Paul either transformed or opposed in his preaching of the gospel of God's grace. None of these studies has suggested or argued what was typically assumed about human capability among those in the ancient world who believed that reciprocity could secure fidelity within a relationship. Further, no one has characterized the Middle Judaic context according to two models for fidelity: reciprocity and divine enablement. Whichever of the two perspectives was adopted was usually determined by the underlying anthropological assumption, whether optimistic or pessimistic.

What this study proposes to do is to offer a fresh characterization of reciprocity from the ancient sources from both Hebrews's historical context, the Greco-Roman world, and Hebrews's religious heritage, the Jewish subculture within that world. Also, from this characterization, this study seeks to determine if there is a common anthropological assumption (i.e., an assumption about intrinsic human moral ability) associated with the expectations of reciprocity to secure ongoing fidelity, especially between the divine and human realms. What I will demonstrate is that the fidelity that was secured through ancient reciprocity was principally motivated by indebted gratitude. Furthermore, it was synergistic, and it was undergirded by an optimistic anthropological assumption where there was belief in its potential to secure fidelity. We will find all these aspects in both the Greco-Roman and Middle Judaic contexts. We, moreover, will find an exilic and a Middle Judaic stream that held to a pessimistic anthropology and, therefore, looked to divine enablement and human transformation, not reciprocity, to secure fidelity to God. Against this backdrop and reexamination of ancient reciprocity, aspects of Hebrews's theological contours will be more clearly appreciated. Hebrews will be seen to belong to the stream of Middle Judaism that looked to God's ongoing enabling and transformation of the believer to secure fidelity to the divine-human relationship. Thus, Hebrews's message will be seen to be both sobering with its stern warnings against apostasy and liberating in a culture that was held together by the often burdensome demands of reciprocity.

Method: Reading with the Authorial Audience

As with any examination of ancient or modern texts, a methodology legitimizes the questions that are asked of a text and the way those questions are answered. The methodology that will be employed in this proposal is a literary critical method that may be called authorial audience criticism. The method is based upon Peter J. Rabinowitz's discussion of audiences in literary works. About the authorial audience he writes,

> The author...cannot write without making certain assumptions about his readers' beliefs, knowledge and familiarity with conventions. His artistic

choices are based upon these assumptions, conscious or unconscious....[W]e must, as we read, come to share, in some measure, the characteristic of this [authorial audience] if we are to understand the text.[28]

The authorial audience is different from what is typically taken to be the implied reader in narrative criticism. The implied reader is solely constructed from the text whereas the authorial audience is constructed from both the text and historical context. "To read as the authorial audience is to attempt to answer the question: If the literary work fell into the hands of an audience that closely matched the author's target audience in terms of knowledge brought to the text, how would they have understood the work?"[29] Hans-Josef Klauck writes that texts "tacitly presuppose the entire cultural knowledge of the period at which they were composed, so that a knowledge of the implied cultural codes is also necessary, if they are to be fully understood".[30] Consequently, primary sources are not utilized in an attempt to demonstrate genetic links between early Christian texts and their context, but they are utilized to help us best approximate the values and worldviews which the ancient auditors would have brought to the hearing of a text. Moreover, the interaction of the primary sources with the text under investigation will both demonstrate how that text assumed or articulated such values and expectations but also, equally important, how it transformed or defied those expectations.

So the methodological question that will be the focus of this proposal is: How did the original audience of Hebrews hear its message in light of the ancient Mediterranean reciprocity systems—both Greco-Roman and Jewish—that permeated these auditors' world?[31] This methodology, thus, calls for a description of both Greco-Roman and Jewish primary sources

---

28 Peter J. Rabinowitz, "Truth in Fiction: A Reexamination of Audiences," *Critical Inquiry* 4 (1977): 126. *Film* (Ithaca: Cornell University Press, 1978), 50. See also, idem., *Before Reading: Narrative Conventions and the Politics of Interpretation* (Ithaca: Cornell University Press, 1987); "Whirl without End: Audience Oriented Criticism," in *Contemporary Literary Theory* (ed. G. Douglas Atkins; Amherst: University of Massachusetts Press, 1989), 81-100. Cf. Hans Robert Jauss, "Literary History as a Challenge to Literary Theory," *New Literary History* 2 (1970): 7-37 and Seymour Chatman's discussion of verisimilitude, *Story and Discourse: Narrative Structure in Fiction and Film* (Ithaca: Cornell University Press, 1978), 50.
29 Charles H. Talbert, *Reading Luke-Acts in its Mediterranean Milieu* (Leiden: Brill, 2003), 15. For a fuller discussion of this methodology see pp. 14-18.
30 Hans-Josef Klauck, *The Religious Context of Early Christianity: A Guide to Graeco-Roman Religions* (trans. Brian McNeil; Minneapolis: Fortress Press, 2003), 2.
31 While at times I will mention the author when we discuss Hebrews from the perspective of the composition of the text, the author is also assumed to be a part of the original audience when I speak of the understanding of the author.

that will enable us to discern the way fidelity and reciprocity were understood in the historical context of Hebrews and the way a subculture, i.e., the religious heritage of Hebrews, imbibed and deviated from those expectations.

The focus of this authorial audience methodology is to put Hebrews in conversation with its context. The way the text addresses its cultural milieu can only be done through a close reading of the text and an understanding of its broader context. In order to communicate its declaration of the supremacy of Jesus Christ in the first-century Mediterranean world, Hebrews had to adopt conventional forms of language and interact with common expectations. This does not mean, however, that in all ways Hebrews imbibed or mirrored its broader culture. Hebrews and its audience were shaped both by its historical and religious heritage. Both of those heritages were already in conversation and these heritages were not always in agreement. Hebrews, as well, joins this conversation and offers its contribution. We should also allow for an authentic religious experience of the author and his audience that shaped and transformed conventional expectations and creatively adopted aspects of both their historical and religious heritage. Hebrews is thus a highly creative composition that embodies an authentically Christian religious experience, adapts its Middle Judaic religious heritage, and engages it larger cultural milieu.

Concerning Hebrews's historical and religious heritages, a sharp divide should not be made between the first-century Jewish world, even its specific Palestinian form, and the larger Greco-Roman world as though the Jewish world was somehow insulated from its larger cultural context. Clearly by the time of Jesus, Palestine had been shaped by the Hellenizing and Romanizing forces that were present there.[32] A Diaspora Jew like Philo demonstrates how a Jewish heritage was communicated within and not insulated from the Greco-Roman cultural context. Concerning the topic at hand, Harrison writes, "Jewish communities of Palestine and the Diaspora had sought legitimation for the reciprocity ideology of their milieu in the Mosaic law and in the LXX narratives, domesticating its more socially congenial practices, and critiquing many of the same benefaction *topoi* as the popular philosophers."[33] Thus there must be an equal consideration

---

[32] Martin Hengel, *Jews, Greeks, and Barbarians: Aspects of the Hellenization of Judaism in the pre-Christian Period* (trans. John Bowden; Philadelphia: Fortress Press, 1980). Also see Klauck, *Religious Context of Early Christianity*, 2-7 and deSilva, "Patronage and Reciprocity," 77 n. 65; John J. Collins and Gregory E. Sterling, eds., *Hellenism in the Land of Israel* (Christianity and Judaism in Antiquity Series 13; Notre Dame: University of Notre Dame Press, 2001); Erich S. Gruen, *Heritage and Hellenism: The Reinvention of Jewish Tradition* (Berkeley: University of California Press, 1998).

[33] Harrison, *Paul's Language of Grace*, 2.

given to both Greco-Roman and Jewish sources relevant for approximating the cultural values, assumptions, and conventional knowledge of the audience of Hebrews.

To this end Greco-Roman inscriptions from the Middle Judaic time period (300 B.C.E. – 200 C.E.), the treatises of philosophers and political figures, as well as influential extant literature during that time will be marshaled in order to characterize the dynamic of reciprocity. Moreover, Jewish religious texts will be considered in order to discern how these sources contribute to our understanding of fidelity to God and of reciprocity in the time of Hebrews. Specifically the question that will be asked of these sources will be what anthropological orientation (optimistic or pessimistic) is assumed or explicitly stated related to the effectiveness of reciprocity to secure fidelity. How else was fidelity secured in the divine-human relationship? With these cultural assumptions and conventional knowledge, we will "listen" to the early Christian sermon of Hebrews for how it understood the basis of fidelity to God in the context of ancient Mediterranean reciprocity systems.

I ought to address the increased application of modern sociology to the study of the New Testament, since sociology studies have sought to examine the phenomenon of reciprocity and benefactor-beneficiary relationships.[34] Craffert has pointed out that those who apply sociological models to the study of the New Testament advocate such an approach on the basis that we inevitably use models (literary, theological, sociological), whether consciously or unconsciously, to interpret the New Testament documents.[35] Moreover, there is an undemonstrated assumption in the implementation of the social-scientific method that models derived from the study of one culture are universal and commensurable to other modern and ancient cultures.[36] Thus has arisen what E. A. Judge designated the

---

[34] For a helpful introduction to social-scientific criticism in the New Testament see John H. Elliot, *What is Social-Scientific Criticism?* (Minneapolis: Fortress Press, 1993), especially 36-59; idem., "Social-Scientific Criticism of the New Testament: More on Methods and Models," *Semeia* 35 (1986): 1-33; David G. Horrell, ed., *Social Scientific Approaches to New Testament Interpretation* (Edinburgh: T & T Clark, 1999); Bruce J. Malina, *The New Testament World: Insights from Cultural Anthropology* (rev. ed.; Louisville: Westminster/John Knox Press, 1993); Bengt Holmberg, *Sociology and the New Testament: An Appraisal* (Minneapolis: Fortress Press, 1990), esp. 153-57 for a helpful and succinct assessment.

[35] P. F. Craffert, "More on Models and Muddles in the Social-Scientific Interpretation of the New Testament: The *Sociological Fallacy* Reconsidered," *Neot* 26 (1992): 217.

[36] Craffert, "The *Sociological Fallacy* Reconsidered," 218-19, 224. I would add that calling the method scientific leads to the assumption that the generalization is valid for all times. Much of scientific inquiry assumes that processes observed in the present have always operated in such a manner over time. In some scientific fields of

"sociological fallacy", that is, the model applied to the modern context and to the ancient context is addressing the same phenomenon. Craffert has helpfully distinguished between (1) non-historical deductive models that are used as "law-like" models or "iron matrixes" which are laid over the historical data and (2) historical inductive models that are measured on the basis of their heuristic value to explain the phenomena.[37] Craffert ends up advocating the second perspective in the use of sociological tools in the study of the New Testament, a perspective that is very similar to reading with the authorial audience. He writes, "In interpreting historical sources, the first step seems to be to create the mental world behind them." We must seek to think and read from the "native's" viewpoint.[38] Consequently, this study will not begin with some presupposed sociological model but will incorporate the insights of sociology when they are heuristically helpful in illuminating the data collected and synthesized from the ancient world. This study will seek to construct an understanding of fidelity, reciprocity, and the message of Hebrews from the "native's" viewpoint through an analysis of the relevant, extant ancient sources.

Plan

Reading with the authorial audience presupposes a certain logical order for demonstrating my thesis. First, chapter 2 of this study will be an examination of the historical context of Hebrews. Therefore, this chapter will provide a characterization of reciprocity and an analysis of its anthropological assumption in the Greco-Roman context. Much of the materials and syntax of the ancient Mediterranean reciprocity systems have already been collected and analyzed from different perspectives and in different fields of study. This chapter will offer a fresh synthesis and reexamination of the primary and secondary literature in order to construct a characterization of ancient reciprocity as it relates to fidelity. This examination will also focus on whether a typical anthropological assumption (optimistic or pessimistic) accompanied the anticipation of reciprocity to secure successfully long-term fidelity to a relationship. What I will demonstrate from the characterization of ancient Mediterranean reciprocity is that the perceived success of reciprocity to secure fidelity was undergirded by an optimistic anthropology.

Second, chapter 3 will consider the religious heritage of Hebrews. It will provide a characterization of reciprocity in the Middle Judaic context in light of the characterization of reciprocity in the Greco-Roman context. We

---

inquiry this seems to be a reasonable assumption, but this assumption claims too much in the field of sociology.
37 Craffert, "The *Sociological Fallacy* Reconsidered," 231.
38 Craffert, "The *Sociological Fallacy* Reconsidered," 233-34.

will look closely at the function of reciprocity for securing fidelity in the Mosaic covenant of the Tetrateuch, Josephus's biblical paraphrase, and the rabbinic literature. Also the literature will be examined for alternate understandings for the way fidelity between humans and God was secured. We will see that there was an exilic perspective, represented in the Deuteronomistic History, Jeremiah, and Ezekiel, that was critical of reciprocity. This perspective continued to be represented by the Qumran community and Paul. In light of this analysis, we will observe that a pessimistic or optimistic anthropological assumption led to two different rationales for how fidelity was successfully secured between God and humans: fidelity (1) by means of reciprocity or (2) by means of divine enablement. Moreover, we will examine what alternate function gratitude has in a context where divine enablement and not reciprocity is the means of human fidelity to God.

Third, after the examination of Hebrews's historical and religious heritages, we can commence in chapter 4 with "listening" to Hebrews's summons to fidelity in light of the Greco-Roman and variegated Middle Judaic perspectives toward the rationale of ancient reciprocity. We will see that there were at least two models among Hellenistic Jews and Christians for the appropriation of benefaction terminology and concepts to describe the divine-human relationship. One model maintained the rationale of reciprocity as the foundation of fidelity while the other model implicitly rejected this rationale. The latter model belongs to that Middle Judaic stream that held to a pessimistic anthropology and looked to divine enablement and human transformation to secure fidelity. Our examination of the cultic reinterpretation of the New Covenant and the soteriological pattern in Hebrews will demonstrate that Hebrews follows the latter model.[39] Therefore, Hebrews, though conventional in its understanding of God as the divine benefactor of the Christian community, advocates a different foundation and motivation for fidelity than the dynamic of reciprocity commonly associated with Greco-Roman benefaction.

In conclusion, this study will call for a reassessment of deSilva's understanding of fidelity in Hebrews. It also will call for a reassessment of our understanding of ancient reciprocity and its relationship to fidelity. We will see that, in light of the characterization of ancient reciprocity, differing anthropological assumptions (pessimistic or optimistic) determined the perceived success of reciprocity to secure fidelity. More positively, this study will show how Hebrews understood both the foundation of human

---

39 What I mean by "soteriological pattern" is in accordance with E. P. Sanders's now popular categories, i.e., how "getting in" and "staying in" and, I would add, getting in to the age-to-come was understood in the religious life of a community (*Paul and Palestinian Judaism: A Comparison of Patterns of Religion* [Philadelphia: Fortress Press, 1977], 16-17).

fidelity and its motivation via its cultic reinterpretation of the New Covenant and its eschatological framework. We will then be able to better locate Hebrews's much debated place in the broader theological streams of church tradition that have been shaped by two trajectories of early Christian thought, Pelagianism and Augustinianism. Also the results of this study will prove fruitful for future application in pastoral/practical theology and will raise questions related to the topic of canon.

CHAPTER 2

The Historical Context of Hebrews: A Characterization of Reciprocity and Its Anthropological Assumption in the Greco-Roman World

The historical context of Hebrews was the first-century Greco-Roman world where life at the personal, civic, political, and religious levels was often governed by the rationale of reciprocity.[1] Our question is, how would the authorial audience of Hebrews have heard the conventions of reciprocity in light of the general cultural values and expectations of a first-century Christian auditor who "lived and moved and had his or her being" in a Greco-Roman world? Accordingly, this chapter seeks to locate Hebrews in its broader historical context by defining the Greco-Roman cultural expectations and presuppositions concerning the dynamic of reciprocity through an analysis of Greco-Roman reciprocity systems.

The reciprocity systems of the Greco-Roman world included personal patronage and benefaction,[2] civic euergetism, hospitality, and friendship

---

1   When I speak of the Greco-Roman world, I am referring to the pagan element of the ancient Mediterranean world. I am not using pagan in a pejorative sense but to designate the non-Jewish and non-Christian milieu specifically. For example, Bart Ehrman (*Jesus: Apocalyptic Prophet of the New Millennium* [New York: Oxford University Press, 1999], 56) writes, "When historians use the term 'pagan,' it does not have derogatory connotation....Instead, it refers to anyone who followed any of the polytheistic religions of the ancient world—that is, anyone who wasn't either Jewish or Christian." I am thankful to my colleague, Andy Arterbury, for sharing this reference with me.
2   Stephen Joubert (*Paul as Benefactor: Reciprocity, Strategy and Theological Reflection in Paul's Collection* [WUNT 2 Reihe 124; Tübingen: Mohr Siebeck, 2000], 60-68) has recently attempted to argue that patronage and benefaction are not interchangeable concepts. The basic difference that Joubert sees is that patronage was personal and left the social status of the two parties unaffected while Greek euergetism or benefaction was collective and emphasized equality between the two parties. See also Stephen Joubert, "One Form of Social Exchange or Two? 'Euergetism,' Patronage, and Testament Studies," *BTB* 31 (2001): 17-25. Contrary to this argument, John Nicols ("Pliny and the Patronage of Community," *Hermes* 108 [1980]: 375, 380) has shown that Roman patronage extended to communities.

among others. Though each was recognized as a discreet social system, their conceptual and linguistic domains overlapped.[3] Evidence from the discussions and representations of all these reciprocity systems will be marshaled in an effort to trace the broad outlines of the dynamic of reciprocity in the Greco-Roman world. I have cast my nets widely, exploring evidence that includes Homer[4] along with texts and inscriptions

---

A. R. Hand (*Charities and Social Aid in Greece and Rome* [Ithaca: Cornell University Press, 1968], 15) believes there is little point in distinguishing between patronage and benefaction due to the Romans' adoption of much of Greek culture during their rise to prominence. E. S. Gruen ("Greek Πιστις and Roman Fides," *Athenaeum* 60 [1982]: 50-68, esp. n. 70) has demonstrated that the Greek concept of πίστις and the Roman concept of *fides*—both central to the system of patronage and benefaction—were not at variance. See also John Rich, "Patronage and Interstate Relations in the Roman Republic," in *Patronage in Ancient Society* (ed. Andrew Wallace-Hadrill; London: Routledge, 1989), 130-31. Additionally, Greeks conceptualized their relationship with the gods based on the benefactor-beneficiary model, in which, as Joubert claims for patronage, there was no change of status among the two parties (cf. S. C. Mott, "The Power of Giving and Receiving: Reciprocity in Hellenistic Benevolence," in *Current Issues in Biblical and Patristic Interpretation* [ed. Gerald F. Hawthorne; Grand Rapids: Eerdmans, 1975], 64). Joubert (*Paul as Benefactor*, 67-68) does finally concede that both patronage and benefaction were defined by the dynamic of reciprocity and so had overlapping functions and could be used interchangeably, e.g., the patronage of the emperor was understood in the euergetistic terms of the Greeks. See also the analysis and critique of Joubert's position by Zeba Crook, *Reconceptualizing Conversion: Patronage Loyalty, and Conversion in the Religions of the Ancient Mediterranean* (BZNW 130; New York: Walter de Gruyter, 2004), 60-66. In this chapter, I will follow the consensus of scholars who understand patronage and benefaction, especially in the Hellenistic period and during the Principate, as interchangeable concepts.

3   E.g., Richard Saller, *Personal Patronage under the Early Empire* (Cambridge: Cambridge University Press, 1982), who writes that "Romans continued to use words such as *beneficium* and *gratia* in their private lives to conceptualize social roles involved in man-god, familial and friendship relations" (26). Elsewhere Saller writes that the language of friendship (*amicitia/amicus*) was employed in representations of patron-client relationships (12). This overlap of terminology is also found in Polybius's *Histories*, see below.

4   On the status of Homeric materials in the Hellenistic world, see Ronald F. Hock, "Homer in Greco-Roman Education," in *Mimesis and Intertextuality in Antiquity and Christianity* (ed. Dennis R. MacDonald; Studies in Antiquity and Christianity; Harrisburg: Trinity Press International, 2001), 56-77; Rafaella Cribiore, *Gymanstics of the Mind: Greek Education in Hellenistic and Roman Egypt* (Princeton: Princeton University Press, 2001); eadem., *Writing, Teachers, and Students in Graeco-Roman Egypt* (American Studies in Papyrology 36; Atlanta: Scholars Press, 1996); Stan Harstine, *Moses as a Character in the Fourth Gospel: A Study of Ancient Reading Techniques* (JSNTSup 229; Sheffield, England: Sheffield

from the classical Greek period, the Hellenistic period, and the period of the Principate. I have organized the data from the primary sources around two related topics. First, a characterization of reciprocity will be supplied. The characterization will involve expositions of four related aspects of reciprocity from the ancient sources. Second, the predominant anthropological assumption suggested by the preceding characterization of the reciprocity systems in the ancient world will be set forth. The supposed success of achieving fidelity to the relationship by means of reciprocity in the Greco-Roman world was predicated on an optimistic anthropological assumption.

A Characterization of Reciprocity

Before we proceed with a characterization of reciprocity in the Greco-Roman world, we should establish a working definition of reciprocity. Modern scholars have developed various but compatible definitions of reciprocity. Stephen Joubert in his analysis of Greco-Roman patronage and benefaction writes that that the universal norm of reciprocity is based on the demand that people must reward those who have helped or benefited them.[5] Hans van Wees defines reciprocity as "the performance and requital of gratuitous actions [actions going beyond what is required]".[6] The sociologist Alvin Gouldner argues that reciprocity is a universal norm and its universal form is: "(1) people should help those who have helped them and (2) people should not injure those who have helped them."[7]

These definitions of modern scholars are shared by descriptions of relationships within generally-accepted reciprocity systems of the Greco-Roman world. For example, Aristotle closely reflects the modern definition

---

Academic Press, 2002), 132-33. Also, Simon Price (*Religions of the Ancient Greeks* [Key Themes in Ancient History; Cambridge: Cambridge University Press, 1999], 6-7) writes that Homer and Hesiod serve as the classic formulation of Greek ideas of which many were still alive in the second century CE. These formulations served as a stable system for a long time.

5   Joubert, *Paul as Benefactor*, 19.
6   Hans van Wees, "The Law of Gratitude: Reciprocity in Anthropological Theory," in *Reciprocity in Ancient Greece* (eds. Christopher Gill, Norman Postelthwaite, and Richard Seaford; Oxford: Oxford University Press, 1998), 20. Van Wees states that for a gift to be a gift it must be experienced as something extra, as something beyond obligation (19). I would add that what is required or beyond obligation refers to what is not officially enforceable. There were definitely expectations and obligations associated with the various reciprocity systems of the Greco-Roman world but were not officially enforceable.
7   Alvin W. Gouldner, "The Norm of Reciprocity: A Preliminary Statement," *American Sociological Review* 25 (1960): 171.

of reciprocity in his discussion on of the Graces:

> But in the interchange of services Justice in the form of Reciprocity is the bond that maintains the association...This is why we set up a shrine of the Graces [Χαρίτων] in a public place, to remind men to return kindness; for that is a special characteristic of χάριτος. (*Eth. nic.* 5.5.6-7 [Rackham, LCL]).

In a fuller sense, the Greco-Roman world understood the dynamic of reciprocity to establish long-term relationships maintained by the enduring feeling of indebted gratitude that seeks to repay kindness for kindness done. Two representative pieces of evidence, Homer's epics[8] and sources that discuss benefaction, demonstrate this typical Greco-Roman understanding of reciprocity. In one example from Homer's *Iliad*, Thetis requests that Hephaestus makes Achilles some armor. Because Thetis had earlier in Hephaestus's life cared for him in his lameness, Hephaestus declares his indebtedness or obligation to heed Thetis's request, saying, "And now has Thetis come to my house: so surely on me the need is great to pay to fair-tressed Thetis the full price for the saving of my life" (18.406-408 [Murray, LCL]). Elsewhere in the *Iliad*, Hera declares her undying gratitude to Sleep if Sleep will heed her request, vowing, "If ever you heard a word of mine...I will owe you thanks (χάριν) all my days" (14.234-35 [Murray, LCL]). This notion that reciprocity produces long-term relationships sustained by indebted gratitude is also born out in Seneca's discussion of benefit exchange. In typical Stoic fashion, he allegorizes the dance of the three Graces,[9] writing:

> Why the Graces are three in number and why they are sisters, why they have their hands interlocked, and why they are smiling and youthful and virginal, and are clad in loose and transparent garb. Some would have it appear that there is one for bestowing a benefit, another for receiving it, and a third for returning it....Why do the sisters hand in hand dance in a ring which returns upon itself? For the reason that a benefit passing in its course from hand to hand returns nevertheless to the giver; the beauty of

---

8   In the relationships of the Homeric epic narratives, reciprocity is commonly believed to play a significant role. Richard Seaford ("Introduction," in *Reciprocity in Ancient Greece*, 1) states that Homeric society was held together by "codes of reciprocity". Also Seaford (*Reciprocity and Ritual: Homer and Tragedy in the Developing City-State* [Oxford: Clarendon Press, 1994], 65) argues that a crisis of reciprocity is what drives the plot of the *Iliad*. For further discussion of this point see below.

9   Homer in the *Odyssey* briefly refers to the dance of the Graces when he writes about one of the Graces, Cytheraea, that "she goes into the lovely dance of the Graces [Charites]" (18.194 [Murray, LCL]).

the whole is destroyed if the course is anywhere broken, and the most beauty if it is continuous and maintains uninterrupted succession. (*Ben.* 1.3.2-4 [Basore, LCL])

Throughout his discussion on benefaction, Seneca repeatedly returns to this description of reciprocity as a never-ending circle of indebtedness that arises from favorable exchange: "I ought properly, to receive a benefit, then be indebted, then repay" (*Ben.* 5.9.4 [Basore, LCL]).[10] In the honorific inscriptions dedicated to benefactors, this circle of reciprocity is most clearly represented in the manifesto clauses.[11] The manifesto clause of an honorary inscription from 200 BCE is typical and reads:

Therefore, in order that the people might continue to be known for expressing appropriate appreciation for those who choose to be their benefactors and in order that physicians to come might show themselves all the more zealous in meeting the needs of the people.[12]

S. C. Mott succinctly sums up this ethos of reciprocity seen in these representative passages, writing: "The possibility of producing favorable action toward oneself from a political unit or from an individual by granting a benefit or by expressing gratitude for a benefit was an important factor binding Greco-Roman society together, especially vertically between units possessing different degrees of power."[13]

From this picture of reciprocity shared by both modern and, more importantly, ancient sources, we can discern four related aspects of reciprocity that will be more fully born out in the following discussion. (1) Reciprocity is a relational bond. (2) Ideally, the bond is long-term and maintained by each party's fidelity to the relationship by means of a sense of indebted gratitude. (3) The bond is a cooperative agreement where both

---

10   Cf. *Ben.* 1.4.3 and 2.18.5.
11   For this term see A. G. Woodhead, "Competitive Outlay and Community Profit: Φιλοτιμία in Democatic Athens," *Classica et Mediaevalia* 34 (1983): 63. Manifesto clauses were typical features of honorific inscriptions. The clause is introduced by ὅπως or ἵνα along with φαίνηται and the participle. The clause sets out the rationale for honoring the benefactor.
12   Frederick Danker, *Benefactor: Epigraphic Study of a Graeco-Roman and New Testament Semantic Field* (St. Louis: Clayton Publishing House, 1982), §2.
13   Mott, "The Power of Giving and Receiving," 67. George M. Masden (*Jonathan Edwards: A Life* [New Haven: Yale University Press, 2003], 3) writes that the eighteenth-century British worldview was "monarchical and controlled by hierarchies of personal relationships". Such would be an accurate description of the Roman world in the first century CE. See also James R. Harrison, *Paul's Language of Grace in Its Graeco-Roman Context* (WUNT 2.172; Tübingen: Mohr Siebeck, 2003), 1.

parties undertake specific obligations to maintain the relationship. (4) Cooperation entails mutual dependence with each party having to rely upon the other for the fulfillment of his or her specific obligations.[14] Each of these aspects will be explored in its turn.

Reciprocity is a Relational Bond

A COHESIVE DYNAMIC

In the Greco-Roman world, reciprocity systems created relational bonds, that is, a noncommercial,[15] nonlegislated cohesive dynamic in which each party voluntary undertook mutually beneficial obligations. First, reciprocity was a cohesive dynamic. Seneca writes, concerning benefaction, that the giving and receiving of benefits constitutes the "chief bond of human society" (*Ben.* 1.4.2 [Basore, LCL]; cf. 6.41.2). Aristotle writes, "But in associations (κοινίαις) that are based on mutual exchange the just in this sense constitutes the bond which holds the association together, that is, reciprocity (ἀντιπεπονθός) in terms of a proportion and not in term of exact equality in return" (*Eth. nic.* 1132 B31–1133 A5).[16] Gouldner contends that the norm of reciprocity is "a kind of plastic filler, capable of being poured into the shifting crevices of social structures, and serving as a kind of all purpose moral cement", thus providing stability to relationships—even to relationships within a well-developed system of specific duties.[17] Therefore, the dynamic of reciprocity is capable of

---

14 A relationship characterized by cooperation and mutual dependence in theological jargon is described as synergistic.
15 Cf. Richard Seaford, "Introduction," 3. See also Andrew Wallace-Hadrill, "Introduction," in *Patronage in Ancient Society* (ed. Andrew Wallace-Hadrill; London: Routledge, 1989), 3.
16 Unless specified, translations and citations of Aristotle's *Ethica nichomachea* follows: Aristotle, *Nichomachean Ethics* (trans. Martin Oswald; New Jersey: Prentice Hall, 1999). The Greek text consulted is based on John Burnet, ed., *The Ethics of Aristotle* (London: Methuen & Co., 1900). Hand (*Charities*, 32) cites a statement of Aristotle that is similar to Seneca's statement, "giving and returning is that which binds people together".
17 Gouldner, "The Norm of Reciprocity," 175. Cf. Ekkehard W. Stegemann and Wolfgang Stegemann, *Urchristliche Socialgeschichte: Die Anfänge in Judentum und die Christusgemeinden in der Mediterranen Welt* (Stuttgart: W. Kohlhammer 1995), 43. ET, *The Jesus Movement: A Social History of Its First Century* (trans. O. C. Dean, Jr.; Minneapolis: Fortress Press, 1999). They discuss four types of reciprocity: (1) *Familiäre Reciprozität*, household or clan, (2) *Ausgeglichene*, friendship or hospitality, (3) *Generelle*, between social unequals, (4) *Negative*, strangers and enemies. These observations affirm Gouldner's observation that reciprocity is a dynamic that operates in a variety of social relationships. I would

operating in a variety of social systems or relationships and should be conceptualized as the cohesive, stabilizing element in those relationships.

A NONCOMMERCIAL BOND

Second, reciprocity was a noncommercial bond. The focus of the exchange was not primarily upon the gifts or services exchanged but on the relationship that was established between the two parties. Two points highlight this aspect of the relational bond from the ancient sources: (1) the ideal goal of reciprocity and (2) what the exchange of gifts and services symbolized. First, the goal of reciprocity was friendship. Dio in his oration to the Rhodians states that those who do an act of kindness in giving a benefit were either repaying a former benefit or were taking the initiative to invite a person to be his or her friend (cf. *Or.* 31.39). For Seneca as well, benefaction was not primarily about commodity exchange; its goal was friendship (cf. *Ben.* 2.18.5; *Ben.* 6.16.2).[18] In fact, Seneca rebukes the recipients of a benefit who looked to repay the benefit as soon as possible in order to extricate themselves from the obligations of the relationship. In such a case persons consider themselves merely debtors and not friends (cf. *Ben.* 6.41.1-2).

Second, the gifts and services exchanged between the benefactor and beneficiary symbolized the goodwill each party had toward the other. Van Wees writes that the function of reciprocity is to "establish, cement, and symbolize amicable relationships".[19] The symbolic nature of a benefit derives from the notion that a benefit has its provenance in the mind. According to Seneca, what was most valuable in a benefit was "the goodwill of him who bestows it" (*Ben.* 1.5.2 [Basore, LCL]). He goes on to

---

not so much speak of four types of reciprocity but four basic social relationships in which reciprocity operates. See a concise summary of these categories in Crook, *Reconceptualizing Conversion*, 56-59.

18 Hand (*Charities*, 29-30) lists several sources that condemn getting just to get and so devalue the relational aspect of reciprocity in benefit exchange. Jan-Marten Bremer in discussing the terminology of reciprocity in the ancient world states that they are expressions of goodwill and friendship and not *do ut des* ("The Reciprocity of Giving and Thanksgiving in Greek Worship," in *Reciprocity in Ancient Greece*, 133). Cf. A.J. Festugière "'ΑΝΘ' "ΩΝ. La formle 'en échange de quoi' dans la prière grecque hellénistique," *Revue des sciences philosophiques et théoligiques* 60 (1976): 369-418.

19 Van Wees, "The Law of Gratitude," 25. He goes on to argue that the economics of reciprocity places emphasis on relationship. Wealth is acquired to create networks of friends and security (34-41). Cf. David deSilva, "Patronage and Reciprocity: The Context of Grace in the New Testament," *Ashland Theological Journal* 31 (1999): 46 (reproduced in idem., *Honor, Patronage, Kinship, and Purity: Unlocking New Testament Culture* [Downers Grove: IVP, 2000]).

write: "What is a benefit? It is an act of a well-wisher who...is inclined to do what he does from the prompting of his own will....A benefit consists...in the intention of the giver or doer" (*Ben.* 1.6.1 [Basore, LCL]). The tangible benefits were just "services through which the goodwill of a friend reveals itself" (*Ben.* 1.5.4 [Basore, LCL]).[20] For Seneca, where these feelings of goodwill were not a part of the exchange there was no bond forged. He relates an incident in the reign of Tiberius where Marius Nepos, a praetorian, had asked Tiberius to rescue him from the debt he had acquired. When Tiberius freed Nepos from his creditors, Seneca reports that Tiberius failed to "attach [Nepos] to himself" because Tiberius gave his benefit with reproach and admonition (*Ben.* 2.7.2 [Basore, LCL]). We also see benefits understood as expressions of goodwill and friendship in an inscribed letter from Attalus III in 135 BCE to Cyzicus commending Athenaeus for the priesthood in glowing terms: "I have decided to write to you, sending also the other decrees and benefactions which we have put in writing concerning him, so that you may know what affection we have toward him (φιλοστοργίας πρὸς αὐτόν)."[21]

A NONLEGISLATED BOND

Finally, reciprocity was not only a noncommercial bond but also a nonlegislated bond.[22] For instance, in the *Odyssey,* Laertes declares to Odysseus, who is posing as Eperitus,

> Stranger, know that you have come to the country of which you ask, but wanton reckless men now posses it. And all in vain did you bestow those gifts, the countless gifts you gave. For if you had found him [Odysseus] still alive in the land of Ithaca, then would he have sent you on your way

---

20 E. Vernon Arnold (*Roman Stoicism: Being Lectures on the History of Stoicism with Special Reference to Its Development within the Roman Empire* [Cambridge: Cambridge University Press, 1911; repr. New York: Humanities Press, 1958], 354) states that for Stoics, such as Seneca, virtue and vice lie in the inner disposition or intention of the agent. See also Ludwig Edelstein, *The Meaning of Stoicism* (Martin Classic Lectures; Cambridge: Harvard University Press, 1966), 1.

21 C. Bradford Welles, *Royal Correspondence in the Hellenistic Period: A Study in Greek Epigraphy* (Chicago: Ares Publishers, Inc., 1974), §66, lines 17-18.

22 Cf. DeSilva, "Patronage and Reciprocity," 43; S. N. Eisenstadt and L. Roniger, *Patrons, Clients, and Friends: Interpersonal Relations and the Structure of Trust in Society* (Themes in the Social Sciences; New York: Cambridge University Press, 1984), 48-49. Gruen ("Roman Fides," 54) states that *fides* "to be sure...stands outside the juridical realm". Crook (*Reconceptualizing Conversion*, 229) cites a couple of examples where legislation was proposed to regulate the loyalty between a patron and his or her freedperson, but Crook acknowledges this was the exception rather than the rule.

with ample requital of gifts (δώροισιν ἀμειψάμενος) and good entertainment; for that is the due (θέμις) of him who begins a kindness. (24.280-86 [Murray, LCL])

Homer uses the term θέμις to relate that one who initiates a positive reciprocal relation is owed return gifts or benefits. Θέμις is not an official law that is enforced by a magistrate but a law that is established by custom.[23] Eperitus has supposedly come to Ithaca to receive hospitality and gifts from Odysseus whom he had previously entertained. Eperitus will not be requited because the moral state of Ithaca is deplorable, and there are no hosts of honorable character who will bind themselves to the codes of reciprocity. Thus reciprocity that sustained the social convention of hospitality was understood as an internally regulated dynamic, and fundamental societal bonds and customs break down in the Homeric world where it is lacking.[24] Seneca emphasizes this nonlegislated aspect of reciprocity in the benefactor-beneficiary relationship when he writes, "In no state has the ungrateful man become liable to prosecution" (*Ben.* 3.6.2 [Basore, LCL]).[25] In fact, to legislate and thus enforce bonds forged by reciprocity was to destroy the relational aspect of that union altogether. To enforce gratitude by legislation was to transform a benefit into a loan[26] as well as remove anything praiseworthy when gratefully repaying a benefit (cf. *Ben.* 3.7.1-2). Andrew Drummand notes further the advantage of the nonlegislated character of patronage in the Greco-Roman world. He writes, "[T]he reciprocal obligations, and the bond itself, were never prescribed by legislation and hence were potentially flexible according to the status and

---

23 Cf. BDAG, "Θέμις."
24 Seneca reveals the importance he gave to bonds formed by reciprocity in *Ben.* 4.18.2-3 where he writes, "It is only with the interchange of benefits that life becomes in some measure equipped and fortified against sudden disaster....safety lies in fellowship...Fellowship has given to [humanity] dominion over all creatures." Concerning friendship, Aristotle writes that friendship is the greatest external good (*Eth. nic.* 1169 B10). In ancient rhetoric there were three types of goods: external goods, goods of the mind, and goods of the body.
25 In the note on p. 136 of the LCL edition of *De Beneficiis*, Basore mentions that Athens was an exception to this statement while Seneca goes on to mention that Macedonia was the exception to his assertion. John Rich ("Patronage and Interstate Relations in the Roman Republic," 118) writes that the patron-client relationship was "an essentially extra-legal relationship, imposing mutual obligations which were not legal but moral".
26 Seneca often refers to a benefit as a loan that must be repaid. In *Ben.* 4.12.1, Seneca clarifies this analogy, "When I use the term 'loan,' I resort to a figure, a metaphor...when I say 'loan,' a quasi-loan is understood" (Basore, LCL). In fact, in *Ben.* 2.18.5, Seneca states that the major difference between a loan and a benefit is that a benefit creates a durable personal relationship as opposed to a loan.

needs of the party concerned."[27] Seneca brings attention to the difficulty that such flexibility and ambiguity in the relational bond produce for enforcing gratitude by court order: "Since benefits may be given in one form and repaid in another, it is difficult to establish their equality" and so render judgment (*Ben.* 3.9.3 [Basore, LCL]).

Such statements make clear that reciprocity relationships—instead of being legislated by law and enforced by a third party—were voluntary. Seneca is explicit that benefaction (and thus reciprocity) was a voluntary act entered into willingly by both parties (*Ben.* 5.9.2).[28] John Rich cites Proculus, a first-century CE jurist, who states that in patron-client relationships though one member was superior (the patron) that does not mean that the inferior member (the client) was not free.[29] Moreover, the Greco-Roman city-states were financed on a voluntary basis. "[O]ne of the attractions [of the voluntary basis of public benefaction] for the wealthy man was that it enabled him...to publicize his worth...by his generosity. It allowed him to play the part of a truly free and liberal man instead of subjecting him to laws which called for a merely passive acquiescence in meeting the financial needs of the state."[30]

Ideally, once such amicable relational bonds of reciprocity—whether guest-friendship, patronage/benefaction, or friendship—were forged, these relationships were understood to be durable. About the long-term nature of the relationship established between a benefactor and beneficiary, Seneca writes:

> And so it is necessary for me to choose the person from whom I wish to receive a benefit; and, in truth, I must be far more careful in selecting my creditor for a benefit than a creditor for a loan. For to the latter I shall have to return the same that I have received, when I have returned it, I have paid all my debt and am free; but to the other I must take on an additional payment, and even after I have paid my debt of gratitude, the bond between us holds; for just when I have finished paying it, I am obliged to begin again, and the friendship endures; and as I would not

---

27   Andrew Drummand, "Early Roman *Clientes*," in *Patronage in Ancient Society*, 101.

28   David Konstan ("Reciprocity and Friendship," in *Reciprocity in Ancient Greece*, 279) writes, "As an elective association, friendship seems to be predicated on the voluntary exchange of benefits underwritten by feelings that are understood to be mutual." Concerning patronage, Wallace-Hadrill ("Introduction," 3) notes that Garnsey and Wolf add a fourth element to the generally accepted definition of patronage, namely, it is voluntary, not legally enforceable.

29   Rich, "Patronage and Interstate Relations," 117. See his quote from Proculus and the Latin text reproduced in n. 1.

30   Hand, *Charities*, 43.

admit an unworthy man to my friendship, so neither would I admit one who is unworthy to the most sacred privilege of benefits; from which friendship springs. (*Ben.* 2.18.5 [Basore, LCL])

Thus fidelity to the relationship was a central virtue. As we have already observed in Seneca's description of the dance of the Graces, the dance of reciprocity was to be a self-perpetuating dynamic securing long-term commitment to the relationship.

The Bond Is Characterized by Fidelity

For there to be an ongoing, voluntary bond between two parties there must be loyalty or fidelity to the relationship. According to Cicero, "[T]he first demand of duty is that we do most for him who loves us most; but we should measure affection...by its strength and constancy" (*Off.* 1.47 [Miller, LCL]). So how was this endurablity of the bond expressed in these various Greco-Roman reciprocity systems? And how did reciprocity create these long-term attachments? To what extent was fidelity to the relationship demanded? Did multiple relationships create a problem of conflicting loyalties? Each of these questions will be explored in this section.

EXPRESSIONS OF FIDELITY

There were three common ways fidelity was expressed in reciprocity relationships: (1) through the feeling of indebted gratitude, (2) by the remembering of benefits, and (3) in the concepts of πίστις/*fides*.

The primary way that reciprocity was expressed and understood to bind two parties together in these various reciprocity systems was by means of the feeling of indebted gratitude. Persevering in indebted gratitude was at the heart of reciprocity systems since there was not a set time for repayment or a third party to enforce repayment.[31] This expression, *feeling of indebted gratitude*, does not merely mean one is thankful but that one feels indebted. It is this sense of owing that binds the two people together where

---

31 Cf. *Il.* 18.406-408 above. I would note here that a secondary motivation, the fear of the gods, was sometimes employed to encourage a person to repay the debt of gratitude they owed. In Homer the gods are the chief guardians of positive reciprocal relations among humans and executed vengeance on those who violated the convention (*Il.* 13.625; *Od.* 7.165, 181; 9.269-71). Because of this, numerous imprecatory prayers are uttered in the *Iliad* and *Odyssey* (*Il.* 3.351-54; *Od.* 1.378-79; 2.144-45; 13.213-14). Fear of the gods is also a rationale offered for treating suppliants and strangers with kindness, and so commence a positive reciprocal relation when one may not be inclined to do so (*Od.* 14.388-89). See also Dio, *Or.* 31.97, where Dio relates the story of Theagenes to illustrate that the gods punish those who dishonor their benefactors.

reciprocity is the dynamic of the relationship.[32] The common rhetoric of debt or owing is pervasive in the ancient sources that touch on reciprocity. We have already observed in the *Iliad* that when Hera expresses her loyalty to Sleep from whom she has asked a favor, she says "I will owe you thanks (χάριν) all my days" (14.235 [Murray, LCL]).[33] James Harrison cites Pseudo-Demetrius, Τύποι Ἐπιστολικοί 21, who illustrates the model of a thankful letter:

> I hasten to show in my actions how grateful I am to you for the kindness you showed me in your words. For I know that what I am doing for you is less than I should, for even if I gave my life for you, I should not be giving adequate thanks for the benefits I have received. If you wish anything that is mine, do not write and request it, but demand a return (χάριν). For I am in your debt.[34]

Seneca intimately links gratitude and indebtedness when he writes "the one who is unwilling to be indebted is ungrateful" (*Ben.* 4.40.5 [Basore, LCL]).[35] Seneca elsewhere says that the one "who owes in good spirit, this man keeps his gratitude shut up in his heart" (*Ben.* 4.21.1 [Basore, LCL]). Consequently, paying back favor/gratitude was a common expression in the Greco-Roman world for fidelity to the relationship.[36] Pliny, in a letter to

---

32 See Peter Garnsey and Richard Saller, *The Roman Empire: Economy, Society and Culture* (Berkeley: University Press of California, 1987), 148, who write that the language of debt and repayment appears regularly in the discussion of patronage and friendship. Van Wees ("The Law of Gratitude," 26) states that "the sense of incurring debts to others in reciprocal relations is quite powerful". Gouldner ("The Norm of Reciprocity," 174) describes the time between the initial benefit and repayment as indebtedness. Furthermore, Gouldner assesses that "the value of a benefit and hence the debt is in proportion to and varies with—among other things—the intensity of the recipient's need at the time the benefit was bestowed...the resources of the donor...the motives imputed to the donor...and the nature of the constraints which are perceived to exist or to be absent" (171).
33 Cf. Plutarch, *Demetr.* 5.3, "Demetrius accepted the kindness and prayed to the gods that he might not long *become a debtor of favor/gratitude to Ptolemy* (ὀφειλέτην γενέσθαι Πτολεμαίῳ χάριτος) but might speedily make a like return (ἀμείψασθαι)" (Perrin, LCL [italics my own translation]); Iamblichus, *Vit. Pyth.* 38 (ὀφείλειν χάριν).
34 Harrison, *Paul's Language of Grace*, 69.
35 See further *Ben.* 2.22.1, "He who receives a benefit with gratitude repays the first installment on his debt"; 3.1.4, "continue in debt"; 3.12.2, "feels more indebted"; 3.17.4, "repays his gratitude" (Basore, LCL).
36 Χάρις was owed for χάρις. Cf. *Il.* 23.60 (τῶν δ' ἀντὶ χάριν); Dio, *Or.* 31.69, gratitude/favor in return for benefactions (τὰς χάριτος τὰς ἀντὶ τῶν εὐεργεσιῶν); Euripides, *Hel.* 1234 (χάρις γὰρ ἀντί χάριτος).

Apollinarus, seeks Apollinarus's support of Sextus's candidature. Pliny relates that his support of Sextus is in order to "repay my debt of gratitude (*referre gratium*)" he had incurred because of the benefaction he had received from Sextus's father and uncle (*Ep.* 2.9 [Melmoth, LCL]).[37] Among the evidence in Greek, χάρις and ἀντιδιδόναι (recompense) are ubiquitous in archaic, early classical, and Hellenistic dedicatory inscriptions, and χάριν ἀποδοῦναι is the general expression of gratitude in the archaic and classical period.[38]

Indebted gratitude was also the basis of a god's fidelity to his or her suppliant. In Ovid's *Metamorphoses*, Telethusa is given an order by her husband to kill her unborn child if it is a girl. Before she gives birth she has a vision of Isis who assures her, "You will not complain that you have worshipped an ungrateful deity" (9.700-701 [Miller, LCL]). An inscription in Istropolis (100 BCE) reads that Aristagoras took the duties and expenses of the priesthood of Zeus and Apollo in order to demonstrate "that there is gratitude from the gods and from men who receive benefits for those who conduct themselves in the life of the city with reverence and noble purpose".[39]

We cannot overestimate the value of indebted gratitude in the ancient world, precisely because it was the adhesive for mutually beneficial relationships. Seneca writes, "Nothing is more honourable than a grateful heart" (*Ep.* 81.30 [Gummere, LCL]). Cicero asserts that there is "no duty more imperative than that of proving one's gratitude" (*Off.* 1.47 [Miller, LCL]). He goes on to say:

> For if we do not hesitate to confer favours upon those who we hope will be of help to us, how ought we to deal with those who have already

---

37 See also *Ep.* 2.13 for a similar circumstance where Pliny speaks of "being indebted" or "under an obligation (*ego nemini lebentius debeo*)".

38 Robert Parker, "Pleasing Thighs: Reciprocity in Greek Religion," in *Reciprocity in Ancient Greece*, 112; cf. Bremer, "Giving and Thanksgiving," 129. See also *Diodorus Siculus* 1.86.3 (χάριν ἀποδιδιόντας); 1.86.5 (χάριν...ἀποδοῦναι); Dio, *Or.* 31.53, (ἀποδοῦναι χάριν); Aristotle, *Eth. nic.* 1124 B10-12; 1164 B26 (εὐεργέτῃ ἀνταποδοτέον χάριν). In Latin the corresponding expression was *referre gratiam*, e.g., Cicero, *Fam.* 10.11.1 and Pliny below. Also see Harrison's (*Paul's Language of Grace*, 180 n. 68) examples of this terminology from Aesop. Crook (*Reconceptualizing Conversion*, 99) mistakenly states that a benefit that belongs to a general reciprocity relationship was not to be repaid as was a gift in a balanced reciprocity relationship. The ancient sources do not support this assertion. Crook misses this point because she starts with modern sociological categories and organizes her evidence by these categories, and she also fails to discuss the language of indebtedness as a way of talking about loyalty to one's benefactor.

39 Hand, *Charities*, D9.

helped us? For generosity is of two kinds: doing a kindness and requiting one. Whether we do a kindness or not is optional but to fail to requite one is not allowable to a good man. (*Off.* 1.48 [Miller, LCL]).

Once a relationship was begun through the performance of a benefit or favor, incumbent on the recipient of the favor was to prove grateful, that is, faithfully to repay the favor with a favor to his or her benefactor or friend.

Thus ingratitude was among the chief vices in the Greco-Roman world, effectively dissolving mutually beneficial relationships. Ingratitude is everywhere denounced in the ancient sources because social cohesion breaks down where the dynamic of indebted gratitude is violated. For instance, in Homer's epic poems, the *Iliad* and *Odyssey*, a crisis of reciprocity or ingratitude drives their plots. The conflict that drives the plot in the *Iliad* is a crisis of reciprocity over the distribution of booty.[40] Agamemnon takes back Briseis who was Achilles's gift and booty from a battle in which he had participated. What this retraction of the gift precipitates is a dissolution of amicable relations between Agamemnon and Achilles, who refuses to go out with the Achaeans in battle (cf. *Il.* 1.292-303). The dissolution is caused by Agamemnon's ingratitude for the benefits he has enjoyed from having Achilles as a warrior. This is evident from Achilles's declaration in *Il.* 9.315-17, "It is clear there was to be no thanks (χάρις) for warring against the foe without respite" (Murray, LCL).[41] Midway through the *Iliad*, Agamemnon seeks to restore a positive reciprocal relation with Achilles by offering him vast gifts. But Achilles declares,

> Hateful in my eyes are his gifts; I count them at a hair's worth. (*Il.* 9.378-79 [Murray, LCL])

> Not even so will Agamemnon any more persuade my heart until he has paid the full price of all the outrage that stings my heart. (*Il.* 9.385-86 [Murray, LCL])

The refusal of the gift suspends positive reciprocal relations. Achilles declares he will not be satisfied until Agamemnon "will gnaw [his] heart within [him] in wrath that [he] did not at all honor the best of the

---

40 Seaford, *Reciprocity and Ritual*, 65.
41 Glaucus makes the same accusation against Hector when he fails to secure Patroclus's body so that Glaucus and the Lycians might exchange it for the body of Sarpedon. Glaucus threatens not to go out and fight because "there was to be no thanks (χάρις) for warring against the foe ever without respite" (*Il.* 17.147-48 [Murray, LCL]).

Achaeans" (*Il.* 1.243-44). Achilles has been stripped of honor,[42] and Achilles's dishonor because of Agamemnon's ingratitude has precipitated Achilles's *wrath*.

As in the *Iliad*, the plot of the *Odyssey* is driven by a crisis of reciprocity or a heinous display of ingratitude. The *Odyssey* opens up with the crisis already under way. Odysseus has been gone for almost ten years while for the past four years suitors have been flocking to Odysseus's court in pursuit of marriage to Penelope, who continues to put off the suitors with delaying tactics. Meanwhile the suitors consume Odysseus's property and possessions, which are Telemachus's inheritance, while waiting on Penelope. The suitors are portrayed throughout the epic as being inhospitable and treacherous, even devising death for Telemachus (cf. *Od.* 4.625-74). Nowhere is the violation of gratitude made more apparent than in Penelope's complaint to Medon that the suitors are forgetful of Odysseus's beneficial rule over Ithaca and so are acting ungratefully. She declares to Medon, "Nor is there in later days any gratitude (χάρις) for good deeds done" (*Od.* 4.694-95 [Murray, LCL]). The suitors' ingratitude has disrupted the positive reciprocal bond established by Odysseus with his own people. Consequently, the bond is broken and a new bond that is sustained by vengeance is forged between Odysseus and the suitors. As we observed in the *Iliad*, the wrath of Achilles is satisfied through the restoration of his honor, while in the *Odyssey* the house of Odysseus is restored when he slays the ungrateful suitors in his hall.

Also in the poetry of Theognis, the dynamics of the homosexual love expressed by a man towards his desired boy were founded upon reciprocity. Likewise, ingratitude from the boy effectively ended the mutually beneficial relationship with his elder partner. In lines 1263-66 of the Theognidean collection, the elder partner complains of his thwarted advances towards his desired boy:

> Boy, you who requite evil in exchange to one who has favored you,
> nor has there been any χάρις from you in return for good things given.[43]

---

42 The request of Achilles's mother, Thetis, to Zeus makes clear that Achilles's honor is at stake (cf. *Il.* 1.503-10). Cf. Bonnie MacLachlan, *The Age of Grace: Charis in Early Greek Poetry* (Princeton: Princeton University Press, 1993), 18-19. See also Norman Postlethwaite, "Akhilleus and Agamemnon: Generalized Reciprocity," in *Reciprocity in Ancient Greece*, 93. See especially Donna F. Wilson, *Ransom, Revenge, and Heroic Identity in the* Iliad (Cambridge: Cambridge University Press, 2002), 54-70, for an intricate and probing discussion of the conflict between Agamemnon and Achilles that demonstrates that central to this conflict are issues that revolve around honor and superiority.

43 Theognis, *The Elegies of Theognis and Other Elegies Included in the Theognidean*

"The lover berates the boy because he has not observed the conventions of reciprocity in their relationship. The elder partner invested not only money, in the form of gifts to the boy, but attention, providing the boy with protection and instruction."[44] In return, the boy was to grant sexual favor to his elder partner. The failure to reciprocate favor, that is, ingratitude, by the boy could arouse retribution, a withdrawal of favor, from the thwarted partner. In his frustration, the thwarted lover declares:

> I am released from the desire that comes from fair-garlended Cytherea;
> And for you, boy, there will be no χάρις from me. (1339-40)[45]

> If you experience some great good thing from me and don't acknowledge the χάριν may you come to my house next time and find yourself empty-handed. (957-58)[46]

In Pindar's *Pythionikai*, written to celebrate the victory of Hieron of Syracuse, he portrays the turpitude of ingratitude in the negative example of Ixion. Ixion was granted immortality by the gods but failed to show appropriate gratitude for the gift bestowed upon him by the gods when he attempted to seduce Hera. As a result, Ixion's ingratitude subjected him to the wrath of the gods. He was cast down to earth and his child was not blessed by the Graces (2.25-48). Pindar explicitly states at the beginning of this episode that the purpose of Ixion's example is to teach the lesson that one "should requite the benefactor with fresh tokens of warm gratitude" (2.24 [Sandys, LCL]).

Finally, discussions of benefaction/patronage decry the evils of ingratitude. Dio in his oration to the Rhodians decried their practice of marking out inscriptions on old statues dedicated to past benefactors and inscribing new inscriptions on them in order to dedicate them to the more recent benefactors of Rhodes. These actions were the height of ingratitude for Dio. Moreover, such actions of ingratitude not only endangered the Rhodians' relationship with past benefactors but also endangered relationships with any future benefactors. Dio forewarns, "Those who insult their benefactors will by nobody be esteemed to deserve a favor (χάριτις ἀξίους). Consequently, the danger for you is that you will no longer receive benefactions" (*Or.* 31.65 [Cohoon and Crosby, LCL]). In another

---

Sylloge: A Revised Text Based on a New Collation of the Mutinensis MS. With Introduction, Commentary, and Appendices by T. Hudson-Williams (London: G. Bell and Sons, Ltd., 1910), 164. The translation follows MacLachlan, *Age of Grace*, 69.

44 MacLachlan, *Age of Grace*, 69.
45 Theognis, *Elegies*, 168. The translation follows MacLachlan, *Age of Grace*, 70.
46 Theognis, *Elegies*, 149. The translation follows MacLachlan, *Age of Grace*, 79.

place, Dio denounced such acts more harshly, writing,

> For what is more sacred than honour or gratitude? Do you know that the majority of men regard the Graces as indeed goddesses? Therefore, if anyone mutilates their statues or overturns their altars, you hold this man guilty of impiety; but if injury or ruin is done to that vary grace from which these goddesses have derived their name by anyone's performing a gracious act in a way that is not right, but in ignoble, illiberal, and crafty manner [that is, rededicating old statues to new benefactors] showing rank ingratitude (ἀχαριστῶν) to his benefactors, can we say such a man has sense. (*Or*. 31.37 [Cohoon and Crosby, LCL])

Such dishonor through ingratitude was on par with the offense of Agamemnon in taking back his gift from Achilles. Cicero points out that ingratitude does not only affect present and future relationships for the ungrateful party, but was an evil that affected everyone. He writes, "For all men detest ingratitude and look upon the sin as a wrong committed against themselves also, because it discourages generosity; and they regard the ingrate as the common foe of all the poor" (*Off*. 2.63 [Miller, LCL]). Seneca puts ingratitude on par with sacrilege as did Dio (*Ben*. 1.4.4) and represents ingratitude as the most heinous of all moral violations. "Homocides, tyrants, thieves, adulterers, robbers, sacrilegious men, and traitors there will always be; but worse than all of these is the crime of ingratitude" (*Ben*. 1.10.4 [Basore, LCL]).

Another way fidelity to relationships defined by reciprocity was expressed in the Greco-Roman world was in the act of "remembering" benefits. The Homeric epics are full of this type of expression. The typical prayer formula, "if ever" often accompanied by "remember these things", was employed by suppliants to remind the gods of the favors they had received from the suppliant so that the gods would grant them a timely favor.[47] At the beginning of the *Iliad* after Agamemnon refuses Chryse's supplication to ransom his daughter, Chryse prays to Apollo,

> If ever (εἴ ποτέ) I roofed over a pleasing shrine for you, or if ever I burned to you fat thigh pieces of bulls of goats, fulfill for me this wish: let the Danaans pay for my tears by your arrows. (1.37-42 [Murray, LCL])[48]

In the *Odyssey*, after learning of the ruthless plot of the suitors to kill her

---

47 In a funeral oration of Lysias, Lysias identifies this practice as θυσιῶν ἀναμνήσεις, reminding of sacrifices (2.39 [Lamb, LCL]).
48 Seneca mentions this episode in *Ben*. 5.25.4. For other examples of this typical prayer or supplication in Homer see *Il*. 1.394-95; 15.372-75; 22.83-84; *Od*. 4.328-31; 15.54-55; 17.240-42.

son, Penelope prays to Athene for his deliverance: "If ever (εἴ ποτέ) resourceful Odysseus burned for you in his halls fat thigh pieces of heifer or ewe, remember these things now (τῶν νῦν μοι μνῆσαι)" (4.763-65 [Murray, LCL]). Also, when the gods showed favor to their suppliants, the gods were said to have remembered the honor the suppliants had shown them. Priam declares at the news that Hector's body will be returned by the Achaeans, "A good thing truly it is to give to the immortals such gifts as are due them, for never did my son...forget in our halls the gods...so they have remembered (ἀπομνήσαντο) this for him" (*Il.* 24.424-28 [Murray, LCL]).

Other examples abound in the ancient sources. In Sophocles's *Ajax*, Tecmessa, wife of Ajax, attempts to prevent Ajax from killing himself. She pleads with Ajax reminding him of the sexual χάρις she has brought Ajax as his wife:

> Think (μνῆστιν) of me also; gratitude is due
> From man for favors that a woman gives
> Kindness return for kindness e'er begets
> (χάρις χάριν γάρ ἐστιν ἡ τίκτους ἀεί)
> Who lets the memory (μνῆστις) of service pass
> Him will I ne'er with noble spirits rank. (520-24 [Storr, LCL])

In Diodorus's general history, Isis commands the priests to bury the body of Osiris, "after reminding them of the benefactions (τῶν εὐεργεσιῶν ὑπομνήσασαν) of Osiris" (1.21.6 [Oldfather, LCL]). In an inscription from 261 BCE, Antiochus II writes to Erythrae granting the city autonomy and tax exemption. He calls the citizens to loyalty by exhorting them to remember his benefits: "We summon you also...that you will remember (μνημονεύοντας) suitably those [by whom] you have been benefited."[49] In an inscription from 246 BCE, Seleucus II expresses his confidence in the loyalty of the citizens of Miletus:

> Whereas our ancestors and our father have conferred many great benefactions on your city because...of the gratitude (εὐχαριστίαν) of your people....We ourselves see that you preserve sincere and firm your esteem for your friends and that you remember (μεμνημένους) favors you have received, we both desired and considered it very important to raise [your city] to a more illustrious state and [to increase your present] privileges.[50]

Here we see that both gratitude and remembering benefits are brought together in the same text to express fidelity or loyalty to a relationship held

---

49   Welles, *Royal Correspondence*, §15, lines 30-35.
50   Welles, *Royal Correspondence*, §22.

together by reciprocity. Likewise, Seneca writes, "For only the man that remembers is able to repay gratitude" (*Ben.* 2.24.1 [Basore, LCL]). In fact, the cause of ingratitude is because the beneficiary forgets the benefit (cf. *Ben.* 3.1.1-5). Elsewhere, Seneca brings together the language of indebtedness and remembering to express the dynamics of fidelity within the reciprocity system of benefaction: "Those who owe persistently remember" (*Ben.* 1.4.5 [Basore, LCL]).

Finally, fidelity to the relationship in the reciprocity systems in that Greco-Roman world was also expressed in terms of πίστις/*fides*. Generally, these terms represented both the responsibility one undertook in a relationship and the trust one placed in the other to fulfill his or her responsibilities.[51] These concepts were both the goal of giving a benefit and the assurance that the debt of gratitude would be paid. First, πίστις/*fides* was the goal of giving benefits. Cicero relates an incident where Philip rebukes his son Alexander for attempting to secure the people's loyalty (*fides*) by means of paying them money. Though Cicero affirms this rebuke, he only disagrees with the type of benefit Alexander employed to obtain the loyalty of his people, not that giving benefits was the way a king was to secure the loyalty or fidelity of his subjects (cf. *Off.* 2.53). Polybius records that when Publius Scipio wintered in Spain that he sought the πίστις and φιλία of the Iberians. He did this by conferring a benefit, namely, releasing (ἀποδόσεως) his captives at the request of the Spanish prince, Edeco, and allowing them to return to their homes (cf. 10.34.1–35.3). Dio in his discourse on kingship argues that through the king's benefactions he is able to secure the loyalty of friends and thereby secure his throne:[52]

> Friendship, moreover, the good king holds to be the fairest and most sacred of his possessions, believing that lack of means is not so shameful or perilous for a king as the lack of friends, and that he maintains his happy state, not so much by revenues and armies and his other sources of strength, as by the loyalty (πίστει) of his friends. (3.86 [Crosby, LCL]).

Second, this virtue was also the assurance of the grateful repayment of a benefit. Aristotle writes that commercial relationships resemble a friendship when a delay of payment was κατά πίστιν (*Eth. nic.* 1126 B27-30). Seneca exhorts the benefactor to "look only to the good faith (*fidem*) of the recipient" not to a judge to enforce repayment (*Ben.* 3.14.2 [Basore, LCL]).[53]

---

51 Cf. David deSilva, *Perseverance in Gratitude. A Socio-Rhetorical Commentary on the Epistle to the Hebrews* (Grand Rapids: Eerdmans, 2000), 144.
52 Hand (*Charities*, 48) writes that the emperor depended on the "loyalty arising out of gratitude for benefits received and anticipated".
53 Cf. *Ben.* 7.19.2; 7.29.2. Joubert (*Paul as Benefactor*, 36) writes that the patron-

Furthermore, πίστις/*fides* embodied the notion of reciprocity when it took on the meaning of protection by a superior for an inferior and of the honor and submission of the inferior toward the superior. In Polybius's history of Rome, εἰς τὴν τῶν Ῥωμαίων πίστιν meant for a person or political entity to commit oneself to the protection of the Romans.[54] In 2.11.5 the Corcyreans accepted the "Roman's invitation to place themselves under their protection (εἰς τὴν τῶν Ῥωμαίων πίστιν)" which was the equivalent to the Romans admitting the Corcyreans "to their friendship (εἰς τὴν φιλίαν)" (2.11.6 [Paton, LCL]).[55] Moreover, Rome did not ignore the injuries done to those whom they had taken under their protection (πίστις; 3.29.8). For instance, Decius, a Campanian, led 4000 soldiers to Rhegium who had called for Roman protection against Pyrrhus and the Carthaginians. "He kept the city and their faith (πίστιν) for some time" (1.7.7 [Paton, LCL]). Decius, however, betrayed the trust and took the city. Upon being recaptured by the Romans they executed 300 men. Polybius writes of the Roman's actions that they were done "to recover as far as possible by this punishment their reputation for good faith (πίστιν) with the allies" (1.7.12 [Paton, LCL]). In fact, the Achaean leader, Philopomen, declared that the Romans were known for observing oaths, treaties, and πίστις toward their allies (24.13.3). The Romans undertook the obligation to protect their suppliants as long as they remained faithful to Rome. If one of Rome's allies broke their trust (as did Decius), the relationship was

---

client relationship was not regulated by legislation but was a *fides*-based relationship. D. Brendan Nagle (*The Ancient World: A Social and Cultural History* [5h ed.; Upper Saddle River: Prentice Hall, 2002], 299) relates that patrons and clients had "special ties of a nonlegal, fiduciary kind....[F]*ides* or 'faith,' bound clients and patrons together and though not expressed in the terms of a formal law, possessed great moral weight". See also Eisenstadt and Roniger, *Patrons, Clients, and Friends*, 48-49, 52-64, esp. 58: "The established relationship [between the patron and client] was considered to be a closed one, based on a moral base: patrons were assumed to be related morally (*in fide esse, in fidem vevire*). Obligations could then be loosely defined, and it was a mater of *fides* to state their scope; clients had no legal claims in law. Loyalty was considered essential to the link."

54 We read that the Aetolians commited themselves to the protection of the Romans (δόντες αὐτοὺς εἰς τὴν Ῥωμαίων πίστιν; 20.9.11). There has been much debate over this passage concerning whether Greeks understood Roman *fides* in terms of πίστις. See Gruen's ("Roman Fides," 50-68, esp. 52) excellent article that clarifies this passage as well as argues in the affirmative, i.e., Greek πίστις could be understood in terms of Roman *fides*.

55 Friendship in the ancient world could be understood to refer to relationships between equal partners or unequal partners. Cf. Aristotle, *Eth. nic.* 1158 B1 and I. E. M. Edlund, "Invisible Bonds: Clients and Patrons through the Eyes of Polybius," *Klio* 59 (1977): 136.

dissolved and the offending former ally was at the mercy of Rome.[56] Furthermore, "Romans envisaged that, unless it defected, a community which entered their *fides* remained there forever."[57] For example, in Livy's history of Rome (37.54.17), the Rhodians urge the Senate to liberate the Asian Greeks by arguing:

> You have undertaken to defend against enslavement to a king the liberty of a people of highest antiquity and renown...it behooves you to maintain for all time this *partocinium* [proctectorate] of a people received into your protection (*fides*) and clientela.[58]

Pliny demonstrates also a corresponding use of *fides*. He relates in a letter that the Baetici had requested that he undertake the prosecution of Caecilius. The Baetici had asked for Pliny's protection (*fidem*) in the presence of the Senate. Pliny states that his services will merit thanks (*gratiam*; *Ep.* 3.4), that is, loyalty. Homer also represents a similar conception in reciprocity relationships between unequals when he relates that Poseidon protected Aeneas in the midst of fighting because of the honor and loyalty he had received from Aeneas (cf. *Il.* 20.291-304). Gruen concludes that πίστις/*fides* in the Greco-Roman world was "a quality denoting the harmonious relationship and mutual obligations existing between superior and inferior powers".[59] This term identified both the inferior's submission to honor the superior while the superior undertook the protection of the inferior.

If ingratitude and forgetfulness are equally vicious vices, then we would expect that unfaithfulness would be viewed as equally hateful and destructive to the dynamic of reciprocity in mutually beneficial relationships.[60] In his oration to the Rhodians, Dio declares that one of the worst evils is that "there should be no confidence (ἀπίστως) which a city

---

56 Cf. *Polybius*, 20.9.7-10 that records the incident of the Aetolians' unfaithfulness to their mutual relationship with Rome. Andrew Wallace-Hadrill ("Patronage in Roman Society: From the Republic to Empire," in *Patronage in Ancient Society*, 64) cites Plautus's *Men.* 571ff., a play that demonstrates the ideal that a client should be marked by dependability, one to whom a patron can pledge his faith (*fides*).
57 Rich, "Patronage and Interstate Relations," 129. Cf. *Polybius* 3.15.5; 3.30.1.
58 Translation and Latin text in Rich, "Patronage and Interstate Relations," 125. See p. 128 for further discussion on the meaning of *fides* as protection.
59 See Gruen, "Roman Fides," 65, esp. 68, for πίστις being understood in this manner broadly in the Greco-Roman world. Cf. Konstan, "Reciprocity and Friendship," 287; Crook, *Reconceptualizing Conversion*, 204.
60 Seneca speaks equally of the virtue of *fides* as he does of gratitude: "Loyalty [*fides*] is the holiest good in a human heart" (*Ep.* 88.29 [Melmoth, LCL]).

bestows" upon its benefactors (*Or*. 31.25 [Cohoon and Crosby, LCL]). Cicero, likewise, writes that the mind without *fides* cannot be relied upon by friends (*Inv*. 1.47).[61] Furthermore, the semantic fields of ingratitude and infidelity overlapped.[62] In Polybius's history, Demetrios of Pharos (from the Corcyreans) aided the Romans in Illyria. Later he broke his alliance with Rome and turned to Philip of Macedon. Polybius writes that Demetrios was "oblivious to the benefits that the Romans conferred on him" and they would "rebuke [his] ingratitude (τὴν ἀχαριστίαν)" (3.16.2-4 [Paton, LCL]).

THE EXTENT OF FIDELITY

To what extent was fidelity to the relationship demanded? Seneca writes that "if you wish to return a favour, you must be willing to go into exile, or to pour forth blood, or to undergo poverty" (*Ep*. 81.30 [Melmoth, LCL]). An inscription from Antiochus to Ptolemy in 109 BCE affirms in nonspecific terms that the people of Seleucia in Pieria have demonstrated their "love" and loyalty "especially in the most desperate of times".[63] In Christopher Gill's discussion of Aristotle's *Ethica nichomachea*, he argues that, like Homer and Plato, Aristotle understands "a mutually-benefiting relationship may require that one party may have to give up something worthwhile for the sake of the other".[64] Eisenstadt and Roniger echo this

---

61 Zeba Crook ("BTB Readers Guide: Loyalty," *BTB* 34 (2003): 168) argues based on one of Cicero's comments that "loyalty consisted solely in appropriate actions". See also Crook, *Reconceptualizing Conversion*, 204, 205, 226. Elsewhere she says, "[B]ehaviour as individuals was governed less by internal than by external forces" (253). Crook repeatedly comments that when loyalty is the topic of discussion the focus is always upon the actions of the beneficiary. Crook is misguided. From the statement above, fidelity was a disposition of the mind. Additionally, Dio links πίστις with εὔνοια (*Or*. 31.113). Ideally, loyalty and trust were predicated upon the disposition of goodwill and beneficent intentions. Her unwarranted generalization fails to consider the larger semantic field for loyalty in the ancient world that includes the feeling of indebted gratitude. Furthermore, how else can dispositions and emotional states be measured except via actions? Crook gives only a couple of hypothetical examples (such as the abduction of girl who is then promised release by her abductor as long as she is loyal to him) where she imagines that loyalty is forced and there is disjunction between the disposition of the mind and the actions of a person (214). This disjunction was never ideal as represented by the ancient sources and was a perversion of reciprocity (much like the Cyclops-Odysseus exchange).
62 Edlund, "Invisible Bonds," 134.
63 Welles, *Royal Correspondence*, §71, line 8.
64 Christopher Gill, "Altruism and Reciprocity in Greek Ethical Philosophy," in *Reciprocity in Ancient Greece*, 322.

sentiment writing, "[T]he core characteristic of *amicitia* was the moral element of *fides* that people recognized and that brought *amici* to repay services even in circumstances, when it was no longer in the short-term interest to do so."[65] But what happened when a person's web of relationships sustained by reciprocity brought loyalties into conflict?

CONFLICTING LOYALTIES

We should not be surprised to find the dilemma when webs of relationships built upon reciprocity brought loyalties into conflict. In the reciprocity systems of patronage or benefaction, loyalty of one patron to one client was ideal. Cicero admits as much in *Fam.* 7.29 but also states that this is not a technical rule. Richard Saller cites inscriptional evidence that demonstrates that this ideal of the patron-client bond being exclusive, permanent, inheritable was undermined.[66] The potential for conflict, however, was real. The conflict stemming from webs of reciprocity relationships is an intriguing feature of the plot in the *Iliad*. Though Zeus admits to being greatly honored by the Trojans, Zeus's loyalty to the Trojans is compromised by his loyalty to Hera who seeks Zeus's assurance that Troy will be destroyed on the basis of the demands of reciprocity (*Il.* 4.42-49; 4.62). Again, Zeus is grieved over the fact that, though Hector had greatly honored Zeus during his life, Zeus could not protect him from Achilles because of the request that Achilles's mother, Thetis, had made of him on the basis of the demands of reciprocity (*Il.* 22.168-71; 1.394-95).[67] These few examples further demonstrate that there were clear expectations of each party in the reciprocity systems of the Greco-Roman world. Thus there were complaints and disappointments when these were not met. This leads us to the third aspect of reciprocity. The dance of reciprocity is a cooperative bond.

---

65 Eisenstadt and Roniger, *Patrons, Clients, and Friends*, 61.
66 Richard Saller, "Patronage and Friendship in Early Imperial Rome: Drawing a Distinction," in *Patronage in Ancient Society*, 53-55. Crook (*Reconceptualizing Conversion*, 215) observes that benefaction and patronage did not typically require exclusive loyalty. Exclusive loyalty was typical, however, of what Crook labels philosophical loyalty (235). Additionally, Rich ("Patronage and Interstate Relations," 127) points out that when Rome was the patron of client-kingdoms "there could be no other".
67 See Crook (*Reconceptualizing Conversion*, 205-6) who makes a similar observation about the potential conflicts in loyalty where multiple reciprocity relationships are held by one person. She cites the interesting dilemma in Sallust's *Bell. Jug.* 71 of Nabdalsa's slave who must choose between loyalty to his master or loyalty to his king.

The Bond Is Characterized by Cooperation

For there to be long-term mutually beneficial relationships there must be harmony through cooperation between the two parties. By cooperation, I mean that the bond of reciprocity is defined by specific obligations or expectations that are fulfilled by each party by means of the unique and/or timely resources each brings to the relationship. Occasionally, the obligations were open-ended or tempered by the two parties engaged. In the *Il.* 4.62, after Hera has requested of Zeus to end the truce between the Achaeans and Trojans so that the Achaeans might finally destroy the Trojans, she concludes by saying to Zeus, "I do for you and you do for me" (Murray, LCL). Zeus's obligation is clear but Hera leaves her obligation ambiguous as to whatever Zeus deems fit when he calls upon her repayment of the debt.[68] Often there were specific or anticipated obligations for each party to fulfill in the various reciprocity systems of the Greco-Roman world. I will examine in this section what expectations or obligations defined the cooperative bond in the various reciprocity relationships in the Greco-Roman world. We will look first at the obligations that defined the dance of reciprocity in symmetrical relationships and then those in asymmetrical relationships.

THE OBLIGATIONS OF SYMMETRICAL RECIPROCITY RELATIONSHIPS

In the symmetrical reciprocity relationship of guest-friendship, gifts were exchanged between the two individuals that symbolized the sealing of amicable relationships between them. The primary symmetrical relations in Homer are those of guest-friendship (ξεινηία). The symmetrical nature of the relationship is alluded to when Odysseus's deceased mother assures him that his son, Telemachus, "feasts at equal banquets" (*Od.* 11.185 [Murray, LCL]). In the exchange of gifts, often the host gave the initial gift, and at some future time, he or she could expect hospitality and a return gift from the guest. Odysseus's (who is posing as Eperitus) expectation best demonstrates this convention when he explains to Laertes that he as Eperitus had formerly hosted Odysseus and further declares "our hearts hoped that we should yet meet as host and guest and give one another glorious gifts" (*Od.* 24.313-14 [Murray, LCL]). Likewise, at the beginning

---

68 In the previous verses, Hera implies that she will yield cities that have honored her to Zeus' wrath if they should ever offend him just as Zeus is asked to give over Troy who has favored him. Also note the example above from the *Iliad* where Thetis comes to Hephaestus looking for a new suit of armor for Achilles. This was not the repayment anticipated at the beginning of this relationship. Hephaestus's debt of gratitude (i.e., obligation) was open-ended. Thetis simply counted on Hephaestus's enduring gratitude so that he would fulfill this timely favor in light of her past kindness.

of the *Odyssey*, Athene appears as a stranger to Telemachus who hosts her. After she gives favorable advice to Telemachus about finding out about the fate of his father, Odysseus, Telemachus insists on giving her a gift "as friends give to friends (ξεῖνοι ξείνοισι διδοῦι)" (1.311-13 [Murray, LCL]). Athene, as the stranger, declares that the gift "shall bring [Telemachus] its worth in return (ἀμοιβῆς)" (1.318 [Murray, LCL]). Sometimes the exchange of gifts occured at the same time. In a perversion of hospitality, the Cyclops declares he will give Odysseus the guest-gift of eating him last for the gift of wine Odysseus had just given to him (cf. *Od.* 9.355-70). And as we have already seen above in the *Iliad*, when a gift has been retracted, the favorable reciprocal relationship was put in jeopardy.

Another type of symmetrical reciprocity relationship can be found in the forensic speeches of Lysias. In some of these speeches wealthy citizens who were on trial appealed for a favorable verdict from the jury on the basis of the benefit the polis received and will receive from the performance of their liturgies. In the time of democratic Athens (fifth-fourth century BCE), wealthy citizens were expected to take upon themselves at their own expense liturgies (public services) for the benefit of the polis. The cooperation characteristic of reciprocity played a foundational role in the defense of wealthy citizens who were brought to public trial. In the twenty-first speech of Lysias part of the evidence presented in defense of the accused reads:

So the vessels that were saved were twelve in number; and two were brought away for you by myself,—my own warship, and that of Nausimachus.

After so many dangers encountered in your defense and after all the services that I have rendered to the city, I now request, not a boon for my reward, as others do, but that I be not deprived of my own property; for I consider it a disgrace to you also, to take it both with my will and against my will. I do not mind so much having to lose my possessions; but I could not put up with an outrage, and the impression that it must produce on those who shirk their public services,—that while I get no credit for what I have spent for you, they prove to have been rightly advised in giving up to you no part of their own property. Now, if you admit my plea, you will both vote what is just and choose what is to your own advantage. (11-12 [Lamb, LCL])

The defendant in this speech goes on to make a final plea saying, "In return I ask from you the grace that I deserve, and I expect that, since I have shown such regard for you in times of danger, you in your present security will set a high value on me" (24-25 [Lamb, LCL]). The benefit the defendant asks for is based upon his own merit, namely the benefit that he has brought to the polis undertaking liturgies with his own wealth and service. The benefits that the defendant has given to the polis he expects to be reciprocated with a favorable verdict by the jury, a favor, no doubt, that would be reciprocated with future beneficial returns to the polis. In the twenty-fifth speech of Lysias, the defendant explicitly states the reason why he undertook liturgies for the polis:

> But my purpose in spending more than was enjoined upon me by the city was to raise myself the higher in your opinion, so that if any misfortune should chance to befall me I might defend myself on better terms. Of all this credit I was deprived under the oligarchy; for instead of regarding those who bestowed some benefit on the people as worthy recipients of their favours, they placed in positions of honour the men who had done you the most harm. (13 [Lamb, LCL])

The defendant states that his excellence, evidenced by his record of liturgies, makes him worthy of a favorable verdict. A favorable verdict is the benefit that he considers an appropriate requital for the benefits he has rendered the polis.[69] The harmonious life of the polis continued as long as there was cooperation, that is, wealthy citizens continued their obligation, voluntarily undertaken, to fund public liturgies and the rest of the polis undertook the reciprocal obligation to take these acts of generosity into account whenever that citizen found himself or herself on trial in the court room.

THE OBLIGATIONS OF ASYMMETRICAL RECIPROCITY RELATIONSHIPS

Cooperation was also characteristic of asymmetrical reciprocity relationships. Concerning the cooperation characteristic of the asymmetrical benefactor-beneficiary relationship, Seneca employs the analogy of Chryssipus, namely that benefit exchange was like playing a game of catch. Seneca writes that the game "can only be carried on in a spirit of co-operation" (*Ben.* 2.17.5 [Basore, LCL]).[70] In fact the purpose of Seneca's treatise, *De Beneficiis*, was to outline the rules of the game, that is, the specific obligations benefactors and beneficiaries undertook (cf. *Ben.* 1.1.1). Seneca often gives paradoxical instructions, e.g., "The one should be taught to make no record of the amount, the other to feel indebted for more than the amount" (*Ben.* 1.4.3 [Basore, LCL]; cf. 2.16.1). Such paradoxical rules were not so much critiques of reciprocity but were instructions for maintaining the dance of reciprocity. These instructions ensured harmonious cooperation so that the two partners would not step on each other's feet.[71]

---

69 Cf. Hand, *Charities*, 80.
70 Plutarch also uses the analogy of throwing a ball to illustrate the cooperation that is characteristic of the benefactor-beneficiary relationship (*Mor.* 582F).
71 DeSilva, "Patronage and Reciprocity," 47-48. See also Aristotle, *Eth. nic.* 4.1.7, for

What were the general obligations of these asymmetrical reciprocity relationships? The benefactor bestowed the benefit looking for repayment from the beneficiary in the form of honor.[72] Aristotle affirms that these obligations define the cooperation between unequals. He writes that "the superior partner ought to be given a larger share of honor (τιμῆς) and the needy partner a larger share of profit" (*Eth. nic.* 1163 B2-3). Dio reflects a congruent sentiment, "[A] man who has proved himself good and worthy of gratitude (ἄξιος χάριτος) receives honour (τιμῆς) in return for (ἀντὶ) many noble deeds" (*Or.* 31.50 [Cohoon and Crosby, LCL]).[73] In another place, Dio declares:

> [T]here is nothing nobler or more just than to show honour to our good men[74] and to remember (μεμνῆσθαι) those who have served us well...and yet one may most clearly see in the principle also a practical advantage. For those who take seriously their obligations toward their benefactors and mete out just treatment to those who have loved them, all men regard as worthy (ἀξίους) of their favour (χάριτος), and without exception each would wish to benefit (ὠφελεῖν) them to the best of his ability; and as a result of having many who are well-disposed and who give assistance whenever there is occasion, not only the state as a whole, but also the citizen in private stations lives in greater security. (*Or.* 31.7 [Cohoon an Crosby, LCL])

Diodorus Siculus writes of the Egyptians in his general history written between 56-36 BCE that

> In general, they say, the Egyptians surpass all other peoples in showing gratitude (εὐχαρίστως) for every benefaction since they hold that the return of gratitude to benefactors (τὴν ἀμοιβὴν τῆς πρὸς τοὺς εὐεργέτας χάριτος) is a very great resource in life; for it is clear that all men will want to bestow their benefactions preferably upon those who they see will most honourably treasure up favors (χάριτας) they bestow. (1.90.2 [Oldfather, LCL])

The demonstration of gratitude in the form of honor was the way for a beneficiary to maintain the favorable, mutually benefiting relationship as well as secure new ones. The same rational and expectations are found in

---

a similar statement of paradoxical rules.

72 Cf. Hand, *Charities*, 49-61, on seeking honor through benefaction. Joubert (*Paul as Benefactor*, 57) writes that most benefits were given for the increase of honor and not for the alleviation of need. In the case when the benefit was supplying grain to a city, the alleviation of need and the pursuit of honor coincided.

73 Cf. Dio, *Or.* 31.27, 37.

74 That is, benefactors, cf. 31.8, 14, εὐεργέτας equals ἀγαθῶν ἀνδρῶν.

honorific inscriptions.[75] One inscription (c. 50 CE) reports the benefits of two brothers from Aigiale who rationed corn, provided for the sacrifices of Hera and Apollo, and funded the sacred festival for the city. The manifesto clause is typical and reads, "So that our city may be seen to honour men of ambitious spirit [*philotimioi*] and honest worth...honours are awarded for *arete, eunoia,* and *philitimia* towards the city, and for *eusebeia* (reverence) towards the gods."[76] The honorific inscription to Antiochus the Great from the town of Teos (c. 200 BCE) declares of the king and queen that they were "willing to bestow favor to the people and the guild of artisans of Dionysius". The people declare in the manifesto clause:

> So that therefore we also in everything are manifest as timely in repaying worthy gratitude to both the king and queen and surpassing them in tokens of honors for these thing in accordance with the benefactions that the people may show to everyone abundantly repayment for favor.[77]

---

75 Eiliv Skard (*Zwei religiös-politische Begriffe: Euergetes-Concordia* [Oslo: I kommisjon hos Jacob Dybwad, 1932], 14-15) writes that classical writers were indebted to the stereotyped formulae of honorific inscriptions. The quote from Dio, above, demonstrates a similar correspondence with honorific inscriptions in the first century CE.

76 Hand, *Charities*, D23 (*IG* 12.389). See manifesto clauses in D3, D10, D53, D64, D66, D67. See also the inscriptions from *I. Délos* 4.1519, *OGIS* 248, and *SEG* 11.948. Translations can be found in Harrison, *Paul's Language of Grace*, 30-31, 41, 51.

77 Translation from H. S. Versnel, "Religious Mentality in Ancient Prayer," in *Faith, Hope, and Worship: Aspects of Religious Mentality in the Ancient World* (ed. H. S. Versnel; Leiden: Brill, 1981), 58. He reproduces the Greek text which reads:

> θέλων χαρζεσθαι τῶι δε δήμωι καὶ τῶι κοινῶι τῶν περὶ τὸν Διόςυσος τεχνιτῶν...ἵνα οὖν καὶ ἡμῖς ἐμ [πα]ντὶ κα[ιρῶ] φαινώμεθα χάριτας ἀξίας ἀποδιδόντες τῶι τε Βασι[λεῖ]ῖ καὶ τῇ βᾱσιλίσσῃ καὶ ὑπερτιθέμενοι ἡαυτους ἐν ταῖς τ[ωμ]αῖς ταῖς πρὸς [τ]ούτους κα[τὰ] τας εὐεργεσίας καὶ φανερὸς ᾖ πᾶσιν ὁ δῆ[μος] εὐπόριστος διακίμε[ν]ος πρὸς χάριτος ἀποδιδοσιν.

See Harrison, *Paul's Language of Grace*, 39, for a discussion of the form of honorific decrees: (1) a preamble naming the magistrate under whom the resolution was proposed, the date of the proposal, and additional information (2) an announcement that the resolution had been passed, ἔδοξεν τῇ βουλῇ καὶ δήμῳ ("Resolved by the council and the people") (3) the proposer of the resolution named (identified by εἶπεν) (4) the resolution itself introduced by ἐπειδή ("whereas") followed by a series of clauses identifying the benefactor's honors (5) at the end of the eulogy, a manifesto clause introduced by ὅπως or ἵνα ("in order that") along with φαίνηται ("it may be manifest") (6) the wish of good fortune for the

The circle of reciprocity (giving [benefit], receiving, giving [honor]) continued as each, the benefactor and beneficiary, fulfilled his or her specific obligations (benefits for honor) of their mutually beneficial relationship. The "dynamic factor in the reciprocal benefactor relationship was the fact that expression of gratitude placed a valid claim for further benefits upon the benefactor."[78]

Honor had various expressions in the Greco-Roman world. First, let us examine the religious context, since the gods were just benefactors writ large in the ancient world.[79] In Homer, the gods received honor from their suppliants chiefly through sacrifice (*Il.* 9.497-500; *Od.* 3.58-59) but also through gifts and vows (*Il.* 23.193-95; *Od.* 3.380-83) and obedience (*Il.* 1.218). Twice in the *Iliad* Zeus declared,

> For never at any time was my altar lacking in the equal banquet, the drink offering, and the savor of burnt offering, for that is the privilege we gods have received. (4.48-49 [Murray, LCL])

> For in no way did he fail of gifts to me, for never at any time was my altar lacking in the equal banquet...for that we gods have received as our privilege. (22.168-70 [Murray, LCL])

In both of these instances, however, Zeus lamented that he was unable to spare Troy from destruction or Hector from death despite how richly he was honored in sacrifices and gifts by both. But Zeus was not indifferent or ungrateful for the honor he had received from the Trojans and Hector. He deeply lamented having to hand Troy over to Hera for destruction arguing that

> Of all the cities beneath sun and starry heaven in which men reared on earth have their abodes, of these sacred Ilios was most honored in my heart, and Priam, and the people of Priam of the good ashen spear. For

---

resolution's implementation following the honors to be given to the benefactor. Cf. A. G. Woodhead, *The Study of Greek Inscriptions* (London: Cambridge University Press, 1967), 38-39.

78 Mott, "The Power of Giving," 63. Cf. Versnel, "Religious Mentality in Ancient Prayer," 63: "It *is* a circle, for when ancient man 'thanked' his human or divine benefactor...he was reluctant to do so without also ensuring his future....The honorific decrees...regularly end with a so-called aphortative formula in which we find the following element: 'The city thus honors her *euergetes* to prove that she is grateful that she knows how to honor good citizens, so that these good citizens will have many imitators, to spur each man on to follow their example and to stimulate still greater devotion to the city.'"

79 Cf. Seneca, *Ben.* 2.29.5-30.2; 7.31.2. See also Crook, *Reconceptualizing Conversion*, 76-80.

never at anytime was my altar lacking in the equal banquet, the drink offering, and the savor of burnt offering. (*Il.* 4.42-48 [Murray, LCL])

Concerning Hector, Zeus lamented, "Truly a well-loved man...and my heart is grieved for Hector, who has burned for me many thighs of oxen" (*Il.* 22.169-71 [Murray, LCL]). As previously mentioned, Hector's gifts were not forgotten and, though not saving his life, achieved for him an honorable funeral (cf. *Il.* 24.424-28). Furthermore, failure to honor the appropriate god through sacrifice could arouse his or her wrath. Poseidon complains that after the Achaeans built their protective wall "they gave not glorious hecatombs to the gods—so that it might hold and keep safe their swift ships and great booty" (*Il.* 12.6 [Murray, LCL]). Again, Poseidon was not indifferent to the honor or, in this case, the lack of honor given to him by the Achaeans. Plato has Euthyphro confess that sacrifice to the gods is all a matter of "honour and praise, and...gratitude (χάρις)" (*Euthyphr.* 15A [Fowler, LCL]).[80] Hippocrates affirmed that the gods rejoice in being honored and adored by humans and for these things they repay favors (χάριτας ἀποδιδόασιν).[81] Aristotle writes of the value of honor, "[A]s the greatest external good we may posit that which we pay as tribute to the gods, for which eminent people strive, most, and which is the prize for the noblest achievements. Honor (τιμή) fits that description for it is the greatest of external goods" (*Eth. nic.* 1123 B17-21). Honor, especially by means of sacrifice, was what the gods greatly valued and what they could only obtain from humans made willing to give it through benefits bestowed.

Not only sacrifices but also votive gifts offered to the gods were another predominant way the beneficiary-supplicant expressed honor for divine favors received. Four dedicatory inscriptions are characteristic and were dedicated in order to stimulate the gods to continue their favorable relationship with the suppliant:

Maniklos dedicated me to the silver-bowed far-shooter from his tithe. Grant him, Phoebus, delightful recompense (χαρίϝεπαν ἀμοιβ[άν]). (*CEG* 326)

To Dionysus, who fulfilled his prayer, Neomedes dedicated this monument in return for good deeds. (*CEG* 332)

Maiden, Telesinos son of Ketis dedicated this image on the acropolis.

---

80 See also Theophrastus, Περὶ εὐσέβειας 24.1-5, who asserts that people sacrifice to honor the gods, to thank them, and to get something in return (cited in Harrison, *Paul's Language of Grace*, 189). Greek text reproduced in Versnel, "Religious Mentality in Ancient Prayer," 46.
81 Greek text reproduced in Versnel, "Religious Mentality in Ancient Prayer," 48.

Take delight in it, and allow him to dedicate another. (*CEG* 227)

Mistress, Menandros dedicated you this first offering in fulfillment of a vow, paying back a favour (χάριν)....Protect him, daughter of Zeus, (returning?) a favour (χάρ[ιν]) for this.[82] (*CEG* 275)

In fact the gods demanded that their miracles be inscribed as a reward for benefits: ἐκέλευσεν δὲ κὰ ἀναγράψαι ταῦτα (*IG* 4.955) and from a Delian hymn to Serapis, ἀνέγραψεν κατὰ πρόστιγμα τοῦ θεοῦ.[83] Cooperation in these complementary obligations—honor in the form of sacrifice and votive gifts for divine benefit—ensured the harmonious maintenance of the god-suppliant relationship. On the basis of such cooperation, Hesiod could write that gifts persuade gods (Δῶρα θεοὺς πείθει).[84] Similarly, one inscription reads, "Neomedes has put up this as a monument in honour of Dionysius who has fulfilled his prayer, in exchange for an excellent benefit (ἀντ' ἀγαθόν)."[85] Versnel observes that this cooperation in exchange "was fundamental in dealing with the deities". One of the most characteristic formulas in votive prayers was ἀνθ' ὧν, "in exchange for these things".[86] "Man gave and the gods had to answer with another gift and *vice versa*." In one example, a suppliant offered a simple gift and then adds, "If you (god) give something larger the recipient will also offer many times more gifts than he is giving today" (*Antholgreaeca* 6.152). As Versnel notes further, this attitude was also ubiquitous among the Romans.[87]

Another way suppliants repaid honor to the gods who had benefited them was through hymnic praise. Versnel points out that Greeks expressed gratitude in the form of praise (ἔπαινος/ἐπαινεῖν). He cites a Delian Serapis hymn, "We praise the gods by repaying worthy gratitude

---

82 Translations of epigraphic evidence follow Parker, "Pleasing Thighs," 110-11. See the evidence van Straten collects, "Gifts for the Gods," in *Faith, Hope, and Worship*, 71-73.
83 Greek text reproduced in Versnel, "Religious Mentality in Ancient Prayer," 55.
84 Greek text reproduced in Versnel, "Religious Mentality in Ancient Prayer," 56.
85 Greek text reproduced in Bremer, "Giving and Thanksgiving," 130 (*CEG* 332).
86 Bremer ("Giving and Thanksgiving," 131-32) also notes that several texts employ ἀμοιβή to relate the expectation of the gods' grant of a return gift for a gift offered by a suppliant. Cf. *CEG* 326, 359, 360, 227, 268, 375, 400.
87 Versnel, "Religious Mentality in Ancient Prayer," 56-57. Versnel demonstrates that a common habit was for a worshipper to make new requests at the same time he or she was gratefully fulfilling a vow for past benefits. Versnel cites a votive inscription to Athene Parthenos: "Telesinos has dedicated this show piece to you. Be content with it and grant that he may be able to dedicate another" (63, Greek text supplied).

(ἐπαινοῦμεν τουσ θεους ἀξίαν χάριν ἀποδίδοντες)."[88] Julian, in the fourth century CE, reflects the common sentiments of pagan religious dynamics. In *Or.* 4.158, he recites a hymn to Helios:

> But since I wish to compose a hymn to express gratitude to the god, I thought this was the best place in which to tell...of his essential nature. And so I think not in vain has this discourse been composed for the saying "to the extent of your powers offer sacrifice to the immortal gods", I apply not to sacrifice only, but also to praises that we offer to the gods. For the third time, therefore, I pray that Helios, king of all, may be gracious to me in recompense for this my zeal (ἀντὶ τῆς προθυμίας μοι ταύτης). (Wright, LCL)

Repayment of gratitude in the form of hymnic praise did not just fulfill the obligation of the supplicant for past benefits received from the divine, but was understood to place the deity under further obligations to continue to benefit his or her supplicant so as to maintain their praise among his or her worshippers. Thus the circular dance of reciprocity continued as each party (in these cases the divine and human partners) cooperated by continually fulfilling his or her obligations.

Honor for benefits was still the goal of the cooperative bond between human benefactors or patrons and their beneficiaries or clientele. Just as with the divine benefactors, honor toward human benefactors was expressed publicly in the form of hymns or poetry. In his *Pythionikai*, Pindar cites the example of Cinyras, priest-king of Cyprus, whose subjects praised him for his great benefactions: "For those praises are prompted by a gratitude (χάρις) which giveth reverential regard in requital for kindly deeds" (2.17 [Sandys, LCL]). Pindar, by commending the Cyprians, is upholding them as those who make appropriate responses to their benefactor-king. Bonnie MacLachlan points out that the tone of Pindar's ode suggests that the response of praise derives from a feeling of indebtedness and subservience when the relationship is asymmetrical as in the case of king-subjects or gods-worshippers. She goes on to say, "Pindar is voicing the specific obligation to render praise in return for actions undertaken by people of superior status."[89] Sometimes public praise was not in the form of a composed hymn or poem but simply in declaring one's indebtedness to one's benefactor. In *Ben.* 4.25.1, Seneca recommends a typical form for expressing one's gratitude publicly: "I shall never be able to repay to you my gratitude, but, at any rate, I shall not cease from

---

88 Versnel, "Religious Mentality in Ancient Prayer," 50 (Greek text provided). Bremer ("Giving and Thanksgiving," 134-35) points out that praise was the form of thanksgiving to the gods.
89 MacLachlan, *Age of Grace*, 122.

declaring it everywhere that I am unable to repay it" (Basore, LCL). Likewise, Pliny reports that the people of Tifernum "celebrate my arrival among them, express the greatest concern when I leave them, and rejoice over every preferment I attain that I might return their good offices (*referrem gratia*), I have built them a temple in this place" (*Ep.* 4.1 [Melmoth, LCL]).[90]

Honor for benefactors also took the form of crowns, statues, citizenship, and honorific inscriptions—thousands which have been found over the whole of the Greco-Roman world.[91] This leads to the related observation, namely, that benefactors sought durable honor.[92] Statues and inscriptions were fittingly utilized for this purpose. An inscription from Sestos affirms that the benefactor in giving his benefactions sought "to secure glory which would never be forgotten".[93] In an inscription of a will from Gytheion, the testator confesses, "My idea is to achieve immortality in making such a just and kindly disposal [of my property] and, entrusting it to the city, I shall not fail in my aim."[94] Diodorus points to this quest for immortal honor by benefactors:

> Of Osiris they say that, being of a beneficent (εὐεργετικὸν) mind, and eager for glory, he gathered together a great army, with the intention of visiting all the inhabited earth and teaching the race of men how to cultivate the vine and also wheat and barley; for he supposed that if he made men give up their savagery [cannibalism] and adopt a gentle manner of life he would receive immortal honours because of the magnitude of his benefactions (εὐεργεσίας). (1.17.1-2 [Oldfather, LCL])

The quest for immortal honor led ultimately to the deification of exceptional benefactors. Again Diodorus writes,

> On his [Osiris's] return to Egypt he brought with him the very greatest presents from every quarter and by reason of the magnitude of his

---

90 Cf. Nicols, "Pliny and the Patronage of Community," 369, 382-83.
91 For an example of crowns see *SEG* 1.366; for statues, Dio, *Or.* 31 (in fact, Rhodes to whom the oration is addressed, was famous for its honorary statues, c. 3000) and *IG* 7.190 and Welles, *Royal Correspondence*, §44, 19-20 (mentions both a crown and a statue); for citizenship, *SEG* 1.368 and *I. Cret.* 4.168. For other public honors such as front seats at the theater see *SEG* 11.948. See also, Aristotle, *Rhet.* 1.5.9. Crook (*Reconceptualizing Conversion*, 222-23) lists peculiar honors that were bestowed on the emperor, such as, coinage, buildings, and the naming of cities. Crook also lists the interesting category of proselytism as a way of honoring one's benefactor (112-16).
92 Cf. Versnel, "Religious Mentality in Ancient Prayer," 59-61.
93 Hand, *Charities*, D55 (*OGIS* 339).
94 Hand, *Charities*, D71 (*IG* 5.1, 1208)

benefactions (εὐεργεσιῶν) received the gift of immortality with the approval of all men and honour equal to that offered the gods in heaven. (1.20.5-6 [Oldfather, LCL])[95]

Commending his trade, Diodorus affirms that the great benefactors in effect did achieve immortality for their great deeds of beneficence because "history immortalizes their achievements" (1.2.4 [Oldfather, LCL]). Deification would have been the ultimate honor a human benefactor could achieve.[96] For instance, Augustus's reign was a time of unparalleled beneficence. Augustus's autobiographical aretology, *Res Gestae Divi Augusti*, is a staggering list of the benefits that he had bestowed upon the empire prior to his death. The peace that he brought to the empire and the lavish benefactions he gave caused him to be perceived as no less than divine by the populace.[97] Also, Plutarch recounts that upon Demetrius's liberation of Athens he and his father were declared σωτῆρα καὶ εὐεργέτην (*Dem.* 9.1) and σωτῆρας θεούς (*Dem.* 10.3).[98]

Finally, honor was expressed toward the benefactor (divine and human) in subservience.[99] In a previous example from Polybius, Edeco the Spanish prince sought to place himself, his friends, and relatives under the protection of the Romans (εἰς τὴν Ῥωμαίων πίστιν). In exchange, Edeco promised "he would be of the greatest service to [Scipio] both at present and in the future" (10.34.7 [Paton, LCL]). Those political entities that came under Roman protection were expected not only to give up their hostilities toward Rome but to aid Rome's efforts.[100] Seneca affirms that subjects of the king are able to render the king assistance even though he is preeminent in power because the power of the king "rests upon the consent and service of inferiors" (*Ben.* 5.4.3 [Basore, LCL]). Subservience was a way also to honor the divine benefactors. "Whoever obeys the gods, to him they gladly give ear" (*Il.* 1.218 [Murray, LCL]).

---

95 Cf. 1.31.1 that states that gods who were once mortal attained immortality like Osiris because of their good services rendered to humanity and 1.2.4 which recounts that Heracles performed great deeds "in order that he might confer benefits upon the race of man and thereby gain immortality" (Oldfather, LCL).
96 Hand, *Charities*, 54-55.
97 Robert Sherk, ed. and trans., *The Roman Empire: Augustus to Hadrian* (New York: Cambridge University Press, 1988), §31; Philo, *Legat.* 148.
98 Plutarch states, "And now that Demetrius had shown himself great and splendid in his benefactions, the Athenians rendered him odious by the extravagance of honor they voted him" (*Dem.* 10.2 [Perrin, LCL]).
99 Garnsey and Saller (*The Roman Empire: Economy, Society and Culture*, 149) write, "Since subjects could not repay imperial benefactions in kind, the reciprocity ethic dictated that they make a return in the form of deference, respect and loyalty."
100 Gruen, "Roman Fides," 53.

To conclude, cooperation was key to sustaining the ongoing dance of reciprocity in the various reciprocity systems of the Greco-Roman world. The obligations each party undertook were not rigidly defined and sometimes were open-ended in that an unspecified return favor would be expected at some future point. At other times basic obligations or expectations were defined. Honor, in its various forms, was the most common obligation an inferior undertook for benefits received from a superior. There was no guarantee, however, that such obligations would be fulfilled by either party, thus reciprocity is not only characterized by cooperation but also by the mutual dependence of each party to faithfully fulfill his or her obligations. Aristotle assumes as much: "The friendship of good men implies mutual trust (τὸ πιστεύειν)" (*Eth. nic.* 1157 A22). To the characteristic of mutual dependence we now turn.

The Bond Is Characterized by Mutual Dependence

RECIPROCITY INVOLVES A MEASURE OF RISK

Mutual dependence entails the reliance of each party in a reciprocity relationship on the other. This reliance involves a measure of risk in the relationship. Each party looks to the persevering gratitude or fidelity of the other to sustain the bond. Again, there are no guarantees that one or both parties would prove reliable and cooperate. Seneca readily admits to the risk. He writes that a benefit involves the potential of "one's own loss and risk" (*Ben.* 4.12.2 [Basore, LCL]). Furthermore, the benefactor cannot be paralyzed by the risk or uncertainty involved in giving a benefit; therefore, Seneca exhorts the benefactor, "We never wait for absolute certainty" in giving a benefit (*Ben.* 4.33.2 [Basore, LCL]). There will always be a measure of risk involved in choosing a beneficiary (and a benefactor). Seneca attempts to instruct beneficiaries to "do regularly their part, to encourage the belief in the possibility of repaying with gratitude" in order to assure benefactors that the risk they took was a wise one (*Ben.* 2.17.6 [Basore, LCL]). In a first-century honorific inscription, the risk of the relationship is implicit: "The People in gratitude agreed to vote to commend Iunia...and to invite her to extend her loyalty to the people in the certainty that in its turn our people will not show any negligence in its devotion and gratitude to her."[101] Even though the people of the inscription attempt to alleviate concern that they will always repay appropriate gratitude for benefits received, the fact that there is the need to alleviate this concern shows there was no guarantee that they or the benefactor would prove faithful to such a mutually beneficial relationship.

---

101 Translation from Harrison, *Paul's Language of Grace*, 50 (*SEG* 18.143).

This last example demonstrates that as there was risk in giving benefits, there was equally risk in securing benefits, especially from the divine benefactors. The risk involved in bonds forged from reciprocity was a great source of anxiety in divine-human relationships in the Greco-Roman world. Robert Parker argues that "without the ideal of reciprocity the whole rationality for Greek cult practices disappears. It was in consequence a prime source of anxiety for the ordinary believer: the fear that the gods might be ungrateful was a darker thought, perhaps, than the fear that they might be unjust."[102] Thus that sacrifices were described as pleasing or acceptable (κεχαρισμένα) was vital to entering and maintaining the dance of reciprocity with the gods.[103] In the *Iliad*, Poseidon argues that Aeneas should be spared from the wrath of Achilles because "he always gives acceptable (κεχαρισμένα) gifts to the gods" (20.298 [Murray, LCL]). In the *Odyssey*, Autolycus, Odysseus's grandfather, was given the "skill, to wit", from Hermes "for to him [Hermes] he burned acceptable (κεχαρισμένα) sacrifices of the thighs of lambs and kids; so Hermes befriended him with a ready heart" (19.396-99 [Murray, LCL]).[104]

On the other hand, we have already seen that sacrifices and gifts did not always secure the gods' favor in Homer's epic poems. Troy's sacrifices and honor of Zeus did not ward off its destruction nor was Zeus able to deliver his suppliant, Hector, from his death at the hands of Achilles, though Zeus lamented both of these outcomes. Further, in *Il.* 6.86-96, Hector instructs the older women of Troy to offer Athene the gift of a robe and to sacrifice twelve-year-old heifers in order to secure her favor, but we are told in 6.311 that Athene rejected their supplication with their gifts and sacrifices. Elsewhere, we are told that the Trojans sacrificed to the gods, "but the blessed gods partook not of it [sacrifices of the Trojans], nor were they minded to; for utterly hated by them was sacred Ilios" (*Il.* 8.550-51 [Murray, LCL]). In *Od.* 9.553-5, we read that Zeus did not heed Odysseus's sacrifice.

RISK ARISES FROM THE VOLUNTARY NATURE OF THE RECIPROCITY BOND

This risk and uncertainty involved in mutually dependent relationships

---

102 Robert Parker, "Pleasing Thighs," 103. See also the evidence he collects, 114-15. See the quote above from Ovid, namely that Telethusa will not find that Isis was an "ungrateful deity".

103 "If the gods do not 'receive' the sacrifice...then the supposed chain of reciprocal benefit is broken at the first link" (Parker, "Pleasing Thighs," 110).

104 For other references to pleasing sacrifices see Plato, *Euthryphr.* 14B (κεχαρισμένα τοῖς θεοῖς); Dio, *Or.* 3.97 (κεχαρισμένη); Plutarch, *Mor.* 355D (κεχαρισμένον), in this case what pleases the gods is not animal sacrifice but the offering of belief in their true nature.

arises out of the voluntary nature of the bond established by reciprocity.[105] As previously argued, the bond of reciprocity was a nonlegislated bond. Gratitude and beneficence have their provenance in the mind and cannot be legislated or enforced by a third party. The uncertainty due to the voluntary nature of the bond is most clearly illustrated in the rhetoric of a μεμπτική letter, that is, a letter written by a benefactor to a delinquent beneficiary to stimulate gratitude in the beneficiary by shaming him or her.[106] There are no threats of bringing in a third party to enforce the repayment of gratitude, only appeals to the beneficiary's own conscience and honor. Thus, in the case of benefaction, a benefactor had no recourse for repayment of his or her benefit from a delinquent beneficiary. Only if the beneficiary was willing to repay the favor was the relationship preserved. Seneca writes, "From the nature of such a trust we have the right to receive back only what is voluntarily returned" (*Ben.* 1.1.3 [Basore, LCL]). Congruently, a benefit is given "from the prompting of the [benefactor's] own will" (*Ben.* 1.6.1 [Basore, LCL]). Consequently, "we need to be taught to give willingly, to receive willingly, to return willingly" (*Ben.* 1.4.3 [Basore, LCL]). Seneca in *De Beneficiis* does not just rehearse the rules of benefit exchange but teaches the spirit of reciprocity. Emphasis is placed upon each party freely fulfilling their obligations in the relationship. In this way, Seneca draws our attention to the circle of reciprocity as a circle of dependence and thus risk.

ASSUAGING THE RISK: εὔνοια

Hence, the only assurance that neither party would be disappointed in his or her mutual dependence on the other was founded upon the mutual πίστις/*fides* or goodwill (εὔνοια) of each toward the other. We have already discussed the value of πίστις/*fides* in the reciprocity systems of the Greco-Roman world. As we have already observed from such sources as Seneca, in the reciprocity system of benefaction the benefactor should "look only to the good faith (*fidem*) of the recipient" for repayment of his or her benefit and not to a judge (*Ben.* 3.14.2 [Basore, LCL]). Let us then turn our attention to the value given to goodwill (εὔνοια) to assuage the risk

---

105 Seaford ("Introduction," 2) writes that reciprocity is voluntary. There is freedom not to requite and requital is expected but not enforced, i.e., there is a measure of risk in the relationship. Reciprocity is distinct from commercial exchange, which is voluntary but may be enforced by a third party. See Terry Johnson and Christopher Dandeker, "Patronage: Relation and System," in *Patronage in Ancient Society*, 221-24, 230, 233, for an excellent analysis on how voluntarism in the reciprocity system of patronage destabilizes it thereby creating a measure of risk in the patron-client/benefactor-beneficiary relationship. They conclude, "[P]atron competition and client choice ensure that this resource cannot be guaranteed" (233).
106 Cf. Ps. Demetrius and Ps.-Libanius cited in Harrison, *Paul's Language of Grace*, 70-71.

of mutual dependence.[107] Plutarch recounts in *Demetrius* that once Demetrius had freed Athens from the subjection of Cassander and Ptolemy, a friend of Antigonus argued that they should keep Athens under their control because of its strategic importance. Plutarch writes of Antigonus's response:

> But Antigonus would not hear of it; he said that the goodwill (εὔνοια) of a people was a noble gangway which no waves could shake, and that Athens the beacon-tower of the whole world would speedily flash the glory of their deed to all mankind. (8.2 [Perrin, LCL])

Furthermore, in *Romulus*, Plutarch discusses the traditional explanation for the rise of patronage in Roman history. Plutarch writes that Romulus "inspired both classes [patrons and clients] with an astonishing goodwill (εὔνοιαν) toward each other, and one which became the basis of important rights and privileges" (13.5 [Perrin, LCL]).[108] From these two examples in Plutarch's *Parallel Lives*, we see that the fulfillment of obligations rested upon goodwill, which inspired mutual dependence or trust. In his oration on kingship, Dio speaks of the importance of goodwill:

---

107 "Goodwill" or εὔνοια was another way to speak of fidelity in reciprocity systems and emphasized the favorable disposition (i.e., state of mind or emotions) each partner had for the other. Such a disposition, like the feeling of indebtedness, was the foundation for maintaining a long-term mutually beneficial relationship. It was an assuring quality that elicited trust from the other partner. Seaford ("Introduction," 3) makes the interesting observation that the factors that limit self-advantage in commercial exchange are external (e.g., official laws) whereas the factors controlling self-advantage in reciprocity depends upon the goodwill of each party. On the other hand, Konstan ("Reciprocity and Friendship," 288-90) discusses perversions of the reciprocity relationship where goodwill was feigned in order to exploit one of the partners. In the Hellenistic period discussion of friendship concerned predominantly unequal partners. While the classical concern was with a friend that did not help, the Hellenistic concern was with the imposter, false friend, and flatterer who exploit an individual for profit under the pretext of personal intimacy or goodwill.

108 In *Comp. Cim. Luc.* 2.3, Plutarch asserts that the task of government is to produce obedience through goodwill (εὐνοίας). In *Rom.* 13.5-6, Plutarch relates the duties of patrons and clients originally established by Romulus. Patrons were advisors and representatives in legal matters while clients held patrons in honor (τιμῶντες), but in cases of poverty, clients were to help patrons pay their daughters' dowries and their debts (though Plutarch points out that in later times it was looked upon as dishonorable and ungenerous to take money from those "more lowly"). For a further discussion of duties traditionally assigned to the patron-client relationship see Eisenstadt and Roniger, *Patrons, Clients, and Friends*, 57-58.

[N]o one, of and by himself, is sufficient for a single one of even his own needs; and the more and greater the responsibilities of a king are, the greater the number of co-workers that he needs, and the greater the εὐνοίας required of them, since he is forced to entrust (πιστεύειν) his greatest and most important interests to others. (*Or.* 3.87 [Crosby, LCL])

A king must depend upon others to secure his throne and that dependence is only ensured by the goodwill of those who assist him. This dependence assured by goodwill is acute for a king since a king "cannot look to the law for protection against betrayal of a trust (τὸ μὴ ἀδικεῖσθαι πιστεύσαντας) but must depend upon εὐνίοας....He has no other protection than their love" (*Or.* 3.88-89 [Crosby, LCL]). This need for goodwill to stabilize a king's rule is also found in the inscriptional evidence from Miletus where an inscribed letter from Ptolemy II (262/1 BCE) survives. The letter reports Ptolemy's praise of the city's loyalty and promises further support of the city. Lines 1-5 recount the past benefits of land and tax relief that he and his father bestowed on the citizens of Miletus. Lines 8-10 record that Ptolemy still seeks ongoing friendship, alliance, and the goodwill (εὐνοίας) of Miletus. He concludes his letter, "We shall try to requite you with benefactions, and we summon (παρακαλῶμεν) you for the future to maintain the same policy of friendship towards us so that in view of your faithfulness we may exercise even more our care for the city" (lines 11-12). Ptolemy could only rely upon the ongoing voluntary support of Miletus as long as he was assured of their goodwill.[109] Without the goodwill of the two parties involved in a reciprocity relationship, that relationship was unstable, and the risk either party took to initiate or maintain the relationship was amplified.

Conclusion

To this point our characterization of reciprocity has been defined by four related aspects. What we have observed is that reciprocity was meant to secure long-term amicable relationships of cooperative dependence. But what was the anthropological assumption that produced confidence in the success of the dynamic of reciprocity to create such favorable relationships? In the second major topic of this chapter we will explore the anthropological assumption of reciprocity that undergirds the belief in the success of reciprocal relationships to forge long-term, cooperative, mutually dependent bonds between two parties. We will see to what assumption this

---

109 Welles, *Royal Correspondence*, §14. Εὔνοια was ubiquitous among honorary inscriptions. Cf. §6, line 10; §25, line 28; §31, line 18; §45, lines 4, 9; §52, lines 41, 69; §66, line 11; §71, line 6.

characterization of reciprocity leads as well as examine additional proofs that support the initial claim. I will argue that the success of reciprocity relationships was predominantly built upon an optimistic anthropological assumption.

The Anthropological Assumption of Reciprocity

First, it is necessary to define what is meant by an optimistic anthropology.[110] This may be done by focusing on the difference between *can* and *should*, using one aspect of the benefactor-beneficiary relationship. A beneficiary *should*—in that a benefactor has moral expectations of the beneficiary—be gratefully indebted for the benefits he or she receives from his or her benefactor. Whether the beneficiary *can* be gratefully indebted and bear goodwill toward his or her benefactor for a benefit received is determined by the benefactor's belief in the intrinsic moral ability of the beneficiary. An optimistic anthropology says that what a beneficiary *should* do or be, that person *can* do or be. Additionally, an optimistic anthropology understands that a person's moral ability is intrinsic to the nature of all humanity. Persons, by virtue of being human, have the resources within themselves to do or be what is expected of them. Thus a pessimistic anthropology assumes that a person has no inherent ability to do what he or she should.[111] This nuance is important for my categories. For another way to talk about optimistic and pessimistic anthropologies is according to one's expectation of relative numbers of people to do what they should. In this scenario, optimism is understood as the expectation of the majority of people being or doing what they should while pessimism is the expectation of the majority not being or doing what they should. My use of these terms is not concerned primarily with numbers (though an optimistic anthropology is clear in the case when the vast majority of humans are expected to be or do what they should) but with assumption about intrinsic ability. Thus one could imagine scenarios when there is little expectation of people being or doing what they should but the belief that all humans intrinsically possess the ability to become what they ought if the right circumstances obtain. This according to my understanding of these categories belongs to an optimistic anthropology.[112] Furthermore, the

---

110 I am taking this terminology from Timo Laato, *Paul and Judaism: An Anthropological Approach* (trans. T. McElwain; South Florida Studies in the History of Judaism 115; Atlanta: Scholars Press, 1995).

111 One should not understand doing what one *should* in the realm of acts only but also in the realm of affections, feelings, and orientation.

112 Cf. Charles Talbert, *Romans* (Macon: Smyth & Helwys; 2002), 192-94, for a useful survey of both Pagan and Jewish literature demonstrating their range of

ultimate realm of my primary concern will be the presence of these assumptions in the divine-human relationship. Finally, when we are dealing with assumptions, the connection between whether what a person should do and what a person is able to do is not explicitly stated.[113] What we have to look for is whether the expectations from the ancient sources that touch on the various reciprocity systems of the Greco-Roman world demonstrate this belief that what persons should be or do, they can be or do.

The Optimistic Assumption of the Preceding Characterization

What we have observed in the foregoing characterization already suggests that when a relational bond is characterized by reciprocity, that is, long-term cooperation being grounded upon mutual dependence, belief in the success of such a relationship assumes that what persons should do or be, they can do or be. Again, reciprocity relationships did not look to third parties to enforce the bond but depended on the moral sensibilities of each other to sustain it. The relationship forged by the dynamic of reciprocity was destroyed once the obligations that define that bond had to be enforced by an outside authority. Thus the two parties, if they believed a relationship grounded upon reciprocity could be successful, believed each had the ability to be or do what he or she ought. In the remainder of this section we will look further at additional evidence that suggests an optimistic anthropology was assumed in these various reciprocity systems of the Greco-Roman world. We will see that, since the dynamic of reciprocity in the Greco-Roman world was characterized by a cooperative, voluntary bond of mutual dependence, which generated a measure of risk, great emphasis was placed upon the character of each party when entering into these various reciprocity relationships. Paradoxically, we will also see that the general belief was that the giving of benefits/favors could produce such dispositions of indebted gratitude and goodwill. Both of these observations indicate an optimistic anthropological assumption. We will also look at the explicit philosophical moral anthropology of Aristotle and Seneca that undergirds their ethical instructions on the reciprocity relationships of friendship and benefaction. What I will demonstrate here is that their philosophical systems held to an explicit optimistic anthropology that leads

---

anthropological assumptions. Talbert also recognizes the distinction in what he classifies as pessimistic anthropologies between those that have no hope in intrinsic human ability and those that understand the righteousness of the few as coming out of their inherent resources and ability. In my use of these anthropological categories, the latter will be classified as an optimistic anthropology.

113 Occasionally, what is assumed is made explicit in the primary sources. We will also highlight these places in the discussion that follows.

them to believe in the potential success of reciprocity to forge and sustain relational bonds.

Additional Proof: Emphasis Placed upon Character

IN THE SELECTION OF BENEFACTORS/BENEFICIARIES

The sources that describe the various reciprocity systems of the Greco-Roman world either emphasize the importance of character when selecting a partner, or they attribute the highest character and motives to each partner, thus guaranteeing the ongoing success of the bond established. For instance, Aristotle states that friendship is based upon the moral excellence (ἀρετή) of each person (cf. *Eth. nic.* 1162 B5-10). Moreover, one should not get into a reciprocal relationship with a bad person (cf. *Eth. nic.* 1165 A2-14). When selecting a benefactor, Seneca advises the beneficiary not to consider the magnitude of the benefits of which a benefactor was capable but to consider the greatness of his or her character (cf. *Ben.* 1.9.2). When selecting a beneficiary, Cicero advises, "we should take into consideration his moral character, his attitude toward us" (*Off.* 1.45 [Miller, LCL]). Seneca reasons, "For I choose a person who will be grateful, not one who is likely to make a return,...it is to the heart that my estimate is directed, consequently I shall pass by the man who, though rich, is unworthy; and shall give to one who, though poor, is good" (*Ben.* 4.10.4-5 [Basore, LCL]).[114] Once more, benefaction was not just about the actual tangible benefits exchanged but the relationship of goodwill that was symbolized by them. The benefit sought from the recipient is his or her goodwill while the benefit received was the favorable, beneficent intention of the benefactor (cf. *Ben* 1.5.1-4; 1.6.1).[115] Consequently, Seneca writes, "I shall choose a man who is

---

114 Cf. Cicero, *Off.* 2.71, "In conferring favours our decision should depend entirely upon a man's character, not on his wealth"; and 1.45, "[W]e should take into consideration his moral character, his attitude toward us when conferring benefits" (Miller, LCL). See also Hendrick Bolkestein, *Wohltätigkeit und Armenpflege im vochristlichen Altertum* (Morals and Law in Ancient Greece; Utrecht: A. Oosthoek, 1939; repr., New York: Arno Press, 1979), 107, who notes that beneficence was normally extended to good people, not to the poor in general, because only the good were able to reciprocate with gratitude and favor. Cicero's advice above is a modification of this generally accepted observation among scholars.

115 Cf. Cicero, *Off.* 2.63, "[T]he favour conferred upon a man who is good and grateful, finds its reward in such a case, not only in his own good-will but in that of others. For, when generosity is not indiscriminate giving, it wins most gratitude and people praise it with more enthusiasm, because goodness of heart in a man of high station becomes the common refuge of everyone" (Miller, LCL). Also see Aristotle, *Eth. nic.* 1155 B31-34, "When people wish for our good we attribute goodwill (εὔνους)

upright, sincere, mindful, grateful, who keeps his hands from another man's property, who is not greedily attached to his own, who is kind to others; although Fortune may bestow upon him nothing with which he may repay my favour" (*Ben* 4.11.1 [Basore, LCL]).[116] Likewise, Cicero argues,

> And so it is an easy mark, and one commonly made, to say that in investing kindness we look not to people's outward circumstances, but to their character....But we should observe more carefully how the matter really stands: the poor of whom we spoke cannot return a favour in kind...but if he is a good man he can do it at least in thankfulness of heart. (*Off.* 2.69 [Miller, LCL])

Cicero elsewhere writes that fidelity (*fides*) to the relationship is secured between the benefactor and beneficiary when each believes that the other possesses impeccable character (cf. *Off.* 2.33). Dio can conclude about the Rhodians that their many honorary statues "reveal the strength (ἰσχὺν) of your city and it character (ἦθος)", and thus they encourage both present and future benefactors to show them favor (*Or.* 31.149 [Cohoon and Crosby, LCL]).

Furthermore, impeccable character was not only a criterion of human benefactors in selecting a beneficiary but also of divine benefactors.[117] According to Cicero, "Worship and purity of character will win the favour of the gods" (*Off.* 2.11 [Miller, LCL]). Seneca writes, "Would you win over the gods? Then be a good man" (*Ep.* 95.50 [Gummere, LCL]). Dio thinks that the gods possibly do not require sacrifice "but in any event these acts are not ineffectual, because we there show our zeal and dispositions toward the god" assuring them that their favors will not go unrequited (*Or.* 31.15 [Cohoon and Crosby, LCL]). A votive gift from Erythrai (third-fourth century BCE) reads, "I, Simo...have preserved this image as both proof of my beauty (ἀρετῆς) and my virtue (ἐπίδειγμα) and wealth (ὄλβου), as an eternal memento ([ἀθ]άνατον μνήμην)." Van Straten writes that

---

to them [a disposition of the mind]...If goodwill (εὔνοιαν) is on a reciprocal (ἀντιπεπονθόσι) basis, it is friendship (φιλίαν)", and *Eth. nic.* 1167 A14-15, where goodwill (εὔνοια) is what is given in return for (ἀνθ' ὧν) a benefit.

116 For Aristotle, as well, moral excellence (ἀρετή or ἐπιείκεια) in a person is the fountain of goodwill (εὔνοια; *Eth. nic.* 1167 A19-21).

117 Harrison states "[T]he divinity looks more to the character of those sacrificing than the costliness or quantity of their sacrifice" (*Paul's Language of Grace*, 189). Elsewhere he writes of Plutarch's perspective in *The Parallel Lives* that Plutarch "highlights the way in which the gods recompense the καλοκαγαθοί for their display of ἀρετή in conducting the affairs of state. In each case, the presumption is that the gods reward with grace those who have demonstrated the requisite merit" (190-91).

worshippers' dedication of votive offerings was "primarily concerned with perpetuating the remembrance of their own excellence, their wealth, generosity, and piety".[118]

TOUTED IN THE HONORIFIC INSCRIPTIONS

In honorific inscriptions, the character of the beneficiaries is touted by the beneficiaries themselves. The common rhetoric was that because the beneficiaries have demonstrated they repay gratitude toward their benefactors, both present and future benefactors can be assured, based upon the beneficiaries' proven character, that the beneficiaries will show themselves faithful and cooperative should the benefactors decide to bestow more benefits on them. An honorary inscription from Pergea (60 BCE) reads, "In order that others may emulate such deeds for the advantage of the city, it was resolved...to commend Soteles...for his goodwill and generous spirit."[119] An inscription from Chalkis (second century BCE) reads, "In order, therefore, that the People may manifestly return the appropriate favours (τὰς καταξίας ἀποδιδοὺς χάριτας) to men who are fair and good and the rest, seeing the gratitude of the city to the benefactors, may be zealous imitators of the good men."[120] Examples could be multiplied but the phrasing is typical among honorific inscriptions.[121] As we have already cited from Diodorus's general history, the Egyptians placed prime importance on demonstrating their gratitude because such demonstrations of gracious character would stimulate other benefactors to bestow their favors upon them (cf. 1.90.2).[122] In this regard Dio reasons with the Rhodians that benefactors "without exception each would wish to benefit (ὠφελεῖν) them [those who prove themselves grateful] to the best of his ability" (*Or.* 31.7 [Cohoon and Crosby, LCL]). Therefore, "it is proper that good men should show themselves morally sound (ὑγιεῖς)...utterly free form deceit and baseness" (*Or.* 31.36 [Cohoon and Crosby, LCL]).

Not only do the honorific inscriptions represent the beneficiaries as having good character but also these inscriptions attribute moral excellence to the benefactors.[123] First, benefactors are typically referred to as "good

---

118 Van Straten, "Gifts for the Gods," 76 (Greek text provided).
119 Hand, *Charities*, D10 (*IG* 7.190).
120 Translation follows Harrison, *Paul's Language of Grace*, 42 (*IG* 12.9, 899).
121 Danker, *Benefactor,* 441. J. R. Harrison, "Paul, Eschatology and the Augustan Age of Grace," *TynBul* 50 (1999): 91.
122 Cf. Cicero, *Off.* 2.70, where a person's demonstration of gratitude, thereby good character, gives him or her a good credit report with future benefactors.
123 Joubert (*Paul as Benefactor*, 52) states that honorary decrees confirmed the elevated status of benefactors (καλοὶ καὶ ἀγαθοὶ ἄνδρες) and their elevated motives (καλοκαγαθία and φιλοτιμία). Eisenstadt and Roniger (*Patrons, Clients, and Friends*, 57) point out that the number of clients a patron had was an indication

men" (ἀνὴρ ἀγαθός) because they are full of virtue or moral excellence (ἀρετή).[124] In fact, one inscription from the first century CE goes so far as to declare that the benefactor's virtue is intrinsic to his nature, "Being a man, although possessed from birth of excellent moral qualities, has surpassed these in developing a character excelling his natural disposition".[125] Here, the beneficiary's anthropological assumption is made explicit, and clearly, in this example, we are dealing with an optimistic anthropology. Second, these inscriptions attribute noble motives or dispositions to the benefactors. Their benefactions are a demonstration of their goodwill (εὔνοια).[126] Also the inscriptions regularly attribute to their benefactors the love of honor (φιλοτιμία and φιλοδοξία) as their primary motivation in giving.[127] Hand points out that the Greeks believed a "good man" would seek honor.[128] All three of these qualities are listed together in the previously cited inscription from Aigiale (c. 50 CE), "honors are awarded for *arete, eunoia,* and *philitimia* towards the city", and adds a

---

of the patron's *fides*, "demonstrating his valuable character and virtue and promoting his image in public life".

124 Cf. Hand, *Charities*, D52 (*IG* 2.1187); D3 (*SEG* 1.366); D53 (*SEG* 1.368); D64 (*I. Cret.* 4.168); D66 (Dittenberger, 620). Cf. Harrison, *Paul's Language of Grace*, 30-31 (*I. Délos* 4.1519); 42 (*I. Délos* 4.1519); 51 (*SEG* 11.948); 52 (*SEG* 2.564); 58 (*I. Priene* 112-14).

125 Hand, *Charities*, D13 (*IG* 5.2).

126 Cf. Hand, *Charities*, D3 (*SEG* 1.366); D10 (*IG* 7.190); D56 (Dittenberger, 714); D62 (Dittenberger, 714); D64 (*I. Cret.* 4.168); D66 (Dittenberger, 620); D68 (*IG* 5.1145); D69 (*IG* 12.9, 236); Harrison, *Paul's Language of Grace*, 42 (*SEG* 24.100); Welles, *Royal Correspondence*, §11, lines 12-14; §15, lines 6, 16, 32; §71, lines 1-8. See also Seaford, "Introduction," 2; Van Wees, "The Law of Gratitude," 25.

127 Cf. Hand, *Charities*, D14 (*IGRP* 3.493), D25 (Dittenberger, 850), D39 (*TAM* 3.4), D47 (Dittenberger, 578), D48 (Dittenberger, 577), D52 (*IG* 2.1187), D55 (4x; *OGIS* 339), D56 (Dittenberger, 714), D57 (*IG* 12.9, 235), D62 (Dittenberger, 335), D66 (Dittenberger, 620), D67 (*IG* 12.1032), D68 (*IG* 5.1145); Harrison, *Paul's Language of Grace*, 30-31 (*I. Délos* 4.1519); 51 (*SEG* 11.948); 58 (*I. Priene* 112-14). See also Versnel, "Religious Mentality in Ancient Prayer," 51 and Paul Veyne, *Le Pain Et Le Cirque: Sociologie Historique D'un Pluralisme Politique* (Paris: Seuil, 1976).

128 Hand, *Charities*, 437. Plutarch, however, in *Crass.* 27.4 does not herald φιλοτιμία as a virtue, at least in excess (Plutarch couples it with ἀβουλία). Crassus's ambition drove him to not be satisfied with being great among many but to be the greatest of all. Crassus's "love of honor" drove him to engage in a disastrous campaign against the Parthians in which he lost his son because he coveted the trophies and triumphs of Caesar (cf. 14.4). Cf. S. Swain, "Plutarchan *Synkrisis*," *Eranos* 90 (1992): 101-11.

fourth quality, "for *eusebeia* towards the gods".[129] This language of honorific inscriptions is ubiquitous and represents the fulfillment of the ideal character and motives of the benefactor-beneficiary relationship in the Greco-Roman culture.[130]

INTRINSIC TO THE BENEFACTOR/BENEFICIARY

So we have seen in the reciprocity systems, especially that of benefaction—both secular and religious—careful consideration was given to the character of each party and the success of the relationship was attributed to the moral excellence and noble motives of each. But was the capability of that character and those motives understood to be intrinsic to human nature? The common motif, "worthy of grace/gratitude (χάρις)", points to the belief that the benefactor's and beneficiary's character and motives were attributable to themselves.[131] Writing of friendship, Aristotle states, "People who give affection to one another according to each other's merit (κατ' ἀξίαν) are lasting friends" (*Eth. nic.* 1159 A35-36).[132] For Seneca, a benefactor should "help the deserving man" (*Ben.* 3.11.1 [Basore, LCL]), and "we should give...to the most worthy" (*Ben.* 4.3.1 [Basore, LCL]). In fact, according to Seneca, one of the reasons why ingratitude is so common is that "[w]e do not pick those worthy of receiving gifts" (*Ben.* 1.1.2 [Basore, LCL]). Cicero echoes the same sentiments:

> [Benefactions] shall be proportioned to the worthiness of the recipient. (*Off.* 1.42 [Miller, LCL])

> [W]e should weigh with discrimination the worthiness of the object of our benevolence. (*Off.* 1.45 [Miller, LCL])

---

129 Hand, *Charities*, D23 (*IG* 12.389).
130 Chryssoula Veligianni-Terzi examines honorific decrees from the fifth century to the end of the classical period in Athens (*Wertbegriffe in den attischen Ehrendekreten der Klassischen Zeit* [Heidelberger althistorische Beiträge und epigraphische Studien 25; Stuttgart: Franz Steiner Verlag, 1997]). In part 2 chapter 1 she identifies the typical vocabulary or "*Formulierung*"of these decrees: φίλος; χρήσιμος; καλῶς; ἀδωροδοκήτως; ἐπιμελεῖσθαι; εὐποιεῖν; ἀνὴρ ἀγαθός ἐστι; ἀνδραγαθία; ἀρετή ; δικαιοσύνη; ἐπιμέλεια; εὔνοια; εὐσέβεια; φιλοτιμία. See also Versnel, "Religious Mentality in Ancient Prayer," 47.
131 Cf. Dieter Zeller, *Charis bie Philon und Paulus* (Stuttgarter Biblestudien 142; Stuttgart: Weralg Katholisches Bibelwerk, 1990), 21, who states that the Greek ethical conception was grace for the worthy. Cf. Parker, "Pleasing Thighs," 113 n. 28: from *SIG*³ 708.25 (Istros, late Hellenistic), "Those who conduct themselves admirably and with piety earn a certain χάρις both from gods and those they benefit."
132 Konstan ("Reciprocity and Friendship," 288) observes that the character of a person becomes central in selecting friends.

[T]he more a man is endowed with these finer virtues—temperance, self-control... the more he deserves to be favored. (*Off.* 1.46 [Miller, LCL])

Plutarch relates that both a beneficiary's gratitude (χάρις) and praise (ἔπαινος) will usher in deserved good will (εὐνοίας δικαίας) from the virtuous (ἀρετῆς) benefactor (καλοκαγαθός; cf. Mor. 786F). Likewise, Dio affirms that those who have honored their benefactors "all men regard as worthy (ἀξίους) of their favour (χάριτος)" (*Or.* 31.7 [Cohoon and Crosby, LCL]).[133] Conversely, Dio asserts, "Those who have insulted their benefactors will by nobody be esteemed to deserve a favour (χάριτος ἀξίους)" (*Or.* 31.65 [Cohoon and Crosby, LCL]). The honorific inscriptions also witness to the worthiness of the beneficiary. An inscribed letter (109 BCE) from King Antiochus declares that because of the loyalty of the people of Seleucia in Pieria, "We have therefore furthered their interests generously [as they deserve (ἀξίως)]....Now, being [anxious to reward (καταξιῶσαι σπουδάζοντες)] them fittingly with the first [and greatest] benefaction, [we have decided that they are] for all time free."[134] In the inscribe letter from Attalus III to Cyzicus, he commends Athenaeus for the priesthood writing, "Because of his goodwill and faith (εὔνοιγ και πίστιγ) toward us, we thought him worthy (ἠξιώσομεν) of the priesthood of Dionysius Cathegemon."[135] Moreover, the beneficiaries thought themselves to repay "worthy gratitude/favor" in the honors they bestowed on their benefactors. Again, the previously cited inscription from Chalkis reads, "In order, therefore, that the People may manifestly return the appropriate favours (τὰς καταξίας ἀποδιδοὺς χάριτας)."[136] The inscription from Olymni (first century BCE/CE) attests that the people by "remembering fine and good men, manifestly distributes appropriate gratitude (τῆς καταξίαν χάριτα) and honour to all".[137] Κατάζιος and ἄξιος regularly appear with χάρις in the manifesto clause of honorific inscriptions.[138] So not only did the beneficiaries of these honorary inscriptions believe they were worthy of the favors they had received but believed that they showed worthy gratitude deserving of future favors.

The inscriptions also attest the worthiness of the benefactor.[139] An

---

133 Again, see Julian, *Or.* 4.154, where he argues that he deserves further recompense and favor from Helios because of his zeal in expressing his praise for Helios.
134 Welles, *Royal Correspondence*, §65, lines 1-8.
135 Welles, *Royal Correspondence*, §66, lines 10-12. See also §65, line 5; §45, lines 7-8.
136 Translation follows Harrison, *Paul's Language of Grace*, 42 (*IG* 12.9, 899).
137 Translation follows Harrison, *Paul's Language of Grace*, 51 (*SEG* 2.564). See also Welles, *Royal Correspondence*, §15, line 34.
138 Harrison, "Augustan Age of Grace," 91.
139 Nicols ("Pliny and Patronage," 369) conjectures that "inscriptions protest (perhaps

inscription from Gortyn reads, "It seemed to us to commend Hermias [a doctor] for his merits and goodwill towards the city...a worthy man."[140] Again, in the rhetoric from Lysias's forensic speeches previously discussed, the wealthy citizen pleads, "In return (ἀνθ' ὧν) I ask from you the grace that I deserve (τὴν χάριν καὶ ἀξιῶ)" (21.24 [Lamb, LCL]), and "those who bestowed some benefit on the people as worthy recipients of their favours (χάριτος παρ' αὐτῶν ἠξίουν)" (24.13 [Lamb, LCL]).[141]

In sum, the ethos demonstrated in the writings of various philosophers, orators, and historians and in the inscriptional evidence reveals a predominantly optimistic anthropology. Benefactors and beneficiaries were ideally chosen on the basis of their character while moral excellence and noble motives were attributed to them in successful reciprocal relationships. Further, such character seems to be intrinsic to the capabilities of humanity (and divinity) since both parties were thought to be—both by themselves and the other—worthy of favor for their displays of virtue.

Additional Proof: Giving Produces Gratitude

The other predominant way the sources for the various reciprocity systems in the Greco-Roman world expressed their optimistic anthropological assumption was in the belief that giving benefits or doing a kindness could generate the dispositions of gratitude and goodwill in the beneficiary. Aristotle commends the example of Tarentum's wealthy who use "their property with the poor and thereby secure the goodwill (*eunoun*) of the masses" (*Pol.* 1320 B10).[142] Thucydides relates the Athenians' confidence in their liberality, which secures amicable relationships with other cities. In Book 2 of Thucydides's *History of the Peloponnesian War*, Pericles is the spokesperson for this confidence:

---

  too much) that the honor had been won by merit, but it was probably an all too frequent occurrence that communities bestowed the honor as an incentive in the hope that it would be eventually well deserved".

140 Hand, *Charities*, D64 (*I. Cret. 4.168*); see also D53, D66, D67.
141 DeSilva ("Patronage and Reciprocity," 61) argues, "'[G]race' is never earned in the ancient world.... Once favor has been shown and gifts conferred, however, the result must invariably be that the recipient will show gratitude, will answer grace with grace....The indicative and imperative are held together by this circle of grace." DeSilva has overstated his case that grace is not earned. Clearly from the above evidence, beneficiaries felt themselves as worthy of the grace they received as benefactors did of the gratitude and honor shown them. Furthermore, in the dance of reciprocity, though the initial grace may not be earned, subsequent grace is.
142 Hand, *Charities*, D1.

Again, in nobility of spirit (ἀρετὴν), we [Athenians] stand in sharp contrast to most men; for it is not by receiving kindness, *but by conferring it, that we acquire our friends.* Now he who confers the favour (χάριν) is a firmer friend, in that he is disposed, by continued goodwill (εὐνοίας) toward the recipient, to keep the feeling of obligation alive in him; but he who owes it is more listless in his friendship, knowing that when he repays the kindness it will count, not as a favour bestowed, but as debt repaid. And, finally, we alone confer our benefits without fear of consequences, not upon a calculation of the advantage we shall gain, *but with confidence in the spirit of liberality* (τῆς ἐλευθερίας τῷ πιστῷ) which actuates us. (40.4-5 [Smith, LCL], emphasis mine)

Cicero also reflects this point of view when he writes, "Men aim to be kind for the sake of winning good-will" (*Off.* 2.54 [Miller, LCL]). Diodorus implies a similar perspective when he recounts that Osiris went out to teach humanity to cultivate the earth *"for he supposed* that if he made men give up their savagery [cannibalism] and adopt a gentle manner of life he would receive immortal honours because of the magnitude of his benefactions" (1.17.1-2 [Oldfather, LCL], emphasis mine). From the previously cited inscribed letter of Ptolemy II to Miletus, the belief that giving benefits secures goodwill is implied for Ptolemy seeks ongoing friendship, alliance, and goodwill (εὐνοίας) with Miletus (lines 8-10), and then implies that their ongoing benefactions toward the city will continue to secure the goodwill of the citizens: "We shall try to requite you with benefactions, and we summon (παρακαλῶμεν) you for the future to maintain the same policy of friendship towards us so that in view of your faithfulness we may exercise even more our care for the city" (lines 11-12).[143] Likewise, Seneca explicitly affirms that "[t]he giving of benefits is a social act, it wins the goodwill of someone, it lays someone under obligation" (*Ben.* 5.11.5 [Basore, LCL]).[144]

Moreover, Seneca believes that through persistently doing kindness or giving benefits, a person can eventually cultivate goodwill and gratitude in his or her beneficiary:

> Still persist in conferring them [benefits] on others; this will be better even if they fall into the hands of the ungrateful, for it may be that either shame or opportunity or example will some day make these grateful. (*Ben.* 1.2.4)

> That man will waste his benefits who is quick to believe that he has

---

143 Welles, *Royal Correspondence*, §14.
144 Concerning the benefit exchange in the sacred realm, Price writes, "Gifts to the gods were not a way of buying the gods, but of creating goodwill from which humans hope to benefit in the future" (*Religions of the Ancient Greeks*, 38).

wasted them; but he who presses on, and heaps new benefits upon the old, draws forth gratitude even from a heart that is hard and unmindful. (*Ben.* 1.3.1)

If you wish to have gratitude from those whom you lay under obligation, you must not merely give, but love your benefits. (*Ben.* 2.11.5)

Your aim is to bear with an ungrateful man so long that he will in the end become grateful. Nor will your method deceive you; vices will yield to virtue if you do not hasten too quickly to hate them. (*Ben.* 5.1.4)

Some accounts have been made good by a long-suffering and wise creditor who has kept alive and nursed them by waiting. We ought to do the same; let us strengthen a weak sense of good faith [*fidem*]....Persistent goodness wins over bad men. (*Ben.* 7.29.2–7.31.1 [Basore, LCL])

But I do not despair of a hardened sinner. There is nothing that will not surrender to persistent treatment; to concentrated and careful attention. (*Ep.* 50.5-6 [Gummere, LCL])

Pliny in a correspondence indicates that gratitude and honor are maintained among one's clientele through persistent benefactions: "I thought it fit to maintain the merit (*meritum*) of my former services, by rendering a fresh one. For such is the disposition of mankind, you cancel all former benefits (*beneficia*), unless you add to them a heap of subsequent favours" (*Ep.* 3.4 [Melmoth, LCL]). In his *Life of Dion*, Plutarch echoes a similar sentiment. In reference to Dion having mercy upon Heracleides who had opposed Dion's rule in Syracruse, Plutarch extrapolates from this incident that "baseness in a man, even though it be a grievous thing, was not so altogether savage and obstinate that it could not be conquered by frequent benefactions and altered by a sense of gratitude" (47.4). Harrison states, "Plutarch seems to refer to giving and receiving as an example of a much larger program of ethical change."[145] Furthermore, according to Seneca, "No creature is so savage that it will not be softened by kindness and made to love the hand that gives it" (*Ben.* 1.2.5 [Basore, LCL]), and the hearts of "bad men" who remember benefits may someday express gratitude urged to it by shame, a momentary impulse toward what is honorable, or a favorable opportunity (cf. *Ben.* 3.1.4). Human nature is not so irrecoverably corrupt that giving benefits or doing favors will not eventually bring forth gratitude and goodwill from the recipient. All these examples are sufficient to show that there was a general belief that giving could bring forth the noble dispositions of indebted gratitude and goodwill and that persistent giving

---

145 Harrison, *Paul's Language of Grace*, 179.

could soften the hearts of even the ungrateful to be gratefully obligated. This belief assumes an optimistic anthropology, namely that humans have the intrinsic ability to do or be what they should do or be.

Additional Proof: Optimistic Anthropology Made Explicit in Aristotle and Seneca

In bringing this section to a close, we should discuss the philosophical moral anthropology of Aristotle and Seneca since this served as the basis of their ethical instruction on the reciprocity systems of friendship/benefaction. What we will see is that they hold to an optimistic anthropology that leads them to have confidence in the dynamic of reciprocity to secure and sustain amicable long-term relationships. Aristotle at the beginning of *Ethica nichomachea* lays out his moral anthropology. First, virtuousness and morality are predicated upon the acquisition of knowledge. "Now every wicked man is in a state of ignorance [of the major premise of a syllogism] as to what he ought to do and what he should refrain from doing, and it is due to this kind of error that men become unjust and, in general immoral" (1110 B27-29). Furthermore, Aristotle cites Socrates as arguing that for a person to become morally weak is impossible if he or she posses knowledge (1145 B25). Second, humans have the innate ability to acquire virtue, even though virtue is only actually acquired by doing virtuous actions:

> Moral virtue...is formed by habit[146]...none of the moral virtues is implanted in us by nature, for nothing which exists by nature can be changed by habit....Thus the virtues are implanted in us neither by nature nor contrary to nature: we are equipped by nature with the ability to receive them, and habit brings this ability to completion and fulfillment. (1103 A17-26; cf. 1103 A30-B1)

Again, Aristotle asserts that "our character is determined by choosing good or evil" (1112 A2). Moreover, "[C]hoice seems to be concerned with the things that are within our power" (1111 B30; cf. 1113 A10-11). "Consequently, virtue or excellence depends on ourselves, and so does vice" (1113 B6-7). Clearly, concerning Aristotle, we are dealing with an optimistic anthropology. Humans have the intrinsic ability to become virtuous (or vicious). Aristotle, however, has a tempered optimism for once one gets in an orientation by the choices and habits he or she forms it is virtually impossible to extract himself or herself from it: an unjust person

---

[146] For Aristotle habit means that a person after "being often moved in a certain way under guidance which is not innate, is now active in that way" (*Eth. eud.* 1220 A39; see note on p. 74 of Oswald's translation).

"has acquired these traits voluntarily; but once he has acquired them it is no longer possible for him not to be what he is" (1114 A20-23), and "We control only the beginning of our characteristics" (1114 B33). Thus, for Aristotle, the habits one forms in childhood are of no small significance (1103 B21-25).

Seneca's moral anthropology stems from his Stoic philosophical leanings. Commenting on Stoic moral anthropology, Ludwig Edelstein asserts, "The originally good nature of man—no concept is more characteristic of the basic optimism of the Stoa....Left to his own devices, that is following his own nature, he will always act in the right way....Evil comes from without....Wrong opinions and civilization subvert the human being."[147] Stoics believed, including Seneca, that all of creation was possessed of the *divine reason*. For Seneca, every human is by nature possessed of the divine spark rendering them intrinsically capable of virtue. In *Epistulae Morales* 41, Seneca writes "On the God Within Us", arguing:

> You are persisting in your effort to obtain sound understanding; it is foolish to pray for this when you can acquire it from yourself. We do not need to lift up our hands toward heaven...as if in this way our prayers were more likely to be heard. God is near you, he is with you, he is within you. (1-2 [Gummere, LCL])

Elsewhere he writes, "In fact reason is common to gods and men, perfected in them, perfectible in us" (*Ep.* 92.27), and "There is no presumption in climbing up to the point from which one has descended, and why should we not believe that there is some element of the divine in one who is a part of God" (*Ep.* 92.30).[148]

Therefore, Seneca shares Aristotle's basic optimism that humans are born intrinsically capable of virtue. Like Aristotle as well, humans only acquire virtue through the acquisition of knowledge and continual practice. This belief is plainly set forth in Seneca's moral epistles:

> It is easy to rouse a listener so the he will crave righteousness, for Nature has laid the foundations and planted the seeds of virtue in us all. And we

---

147 Edelstein, *The Meaning of Stoicism*, 54-55. The evidence from Seneca supports this general assessment when he writes, "The easiest thing in the world, to live in accordance with his own nature. But his has turned into a hard task by the general madness of mankind; we push one another into vice. And how can a man be recalled to salvation when he has not to restrain him" (*Ep.* 41.7-9 [Gummere, LCL]).

148 Translation from Seneca, *Seventeen Letters* (trans. C. D. N. Costa; Wiltshire: Aris and Phillips Ltd., 1988). Cf. Anna Lydia Motto, *Seneca* (New York: Twayne Publishers, Inc., 1973), 66.

are all born to these general privileges; hence, when the stimulus is added, the good spirit is stirred as if it were freed from bonds. (*Ep.* 108.8)

The soul carries within itself the seed of everything that is honourable, and this seed is stirred to growth by advice, as a spark that is fanned by a gentle breeze develops its natural fire. (*Ep.* 94.29)

No man is good by chance. Virtue is something which must be learned. (*Ep.* 123.16 [Gummere, LCL])[149]

For nature does not give virtue; to become a good man is a practical art. (*Ep.* 90.44)[150]

Furthermore, for Seneca, reformation is possible through learning. "It is the evil mind that gets first hold on all of us. Learning virtue means unlearning vice" (*Ep.* 50.7 [Gummere, LCL]). Seneca goes on to say that though beginning is difficult in cultivating virtue it is easy to maintain (cf. *Ep.* 50.8-9). Therefore, Motto concludes about Seneca's anthropological optimism:

> Seneca is committed to the belief in the possibility of the moral progress in men. He does not despair even of the man who has plunged into the worst habits....Believing each individual to have the divine seed of virtue in him, he is hopeful that advice, guidance, and cultivation will stir it into growth....He is therefore eager to present men with the tools and principles that will serve him as a rule of life.[151]

Unlike Aristotle, Seneca is more hopeful that a person is able to extract themselves from a previously acquired, bad orientation. Reformation/recovery is possible.

These sentiments are also expressed in Seneca's discussion of benefaction. First, Seneca is writing not to the "ideal wiseman who rules his own spirit" but to the "man with all his imperfections desires to follow the perfect path, yet has passions that are often reluctant to obey" (*Ben.* 2.18.4 [Basore, LCL]). Seneca depicts his audience as those who are on the way to perfection and have the intrinsic ability to achieve the ideals of reciprocity

---

149 The instruction of a philosopher is what the mind needs to give birth to virtue. Wise men are the reformers of vice. Cf. *Ira* 2.10.7; *Vit. beat.* 26.5. This belief appears to be typical. See Arnold, *Roman Stoicism*, 285; Thomas Schmeller, "Stoics, Stoicism," *ABD* 6:211; Kiempe Algra, "Stoic Theology," *The Cambridge Companion to the Stoics* (ed. Brad Inwood; Cambridge: Cambridge University Press, 2003), 171.
150 Translation from Seneca, *Seventeen Letters* (trans. C. D. N. Costa).
151 Motto, *Seneca*, 51. Cf. Arnold, *Roman Stoicism*, 355.

since "[t]he mind is its own master and is free and unshackled" (*Ben.* 3.20.1), and "[t]hat inner part cannot be delivered into bondage" (3.20.2 [Basore, LCL]). Hence, no one is irrecoverable from an evil disposition. Humans always retain the intrinsic ability to obtain virtue.[152]

> Few men follow reason as their best guide, next best are those who return to the right path when they are admonished...the eyes, even when they are closed, still have the power of sight, but do not use it; but the light of the day, when it has been admitted to them, summons their power of sight into service....Our minds all the while posses the virtuous desire, but it lies torpid....Virtuous desire needs some reminder to call it to the repayment of gratitude. (*Ben.* 5.25.5-6 [Basore, LCL]).

Thus, "[e]ven a bad man must necessarily retain some traces of good; virtue is never so wholly extinguished as not to leave upon the mind indelible imprints that no change can ever erase"[153] (*Ben.* 7.19.5 [Basore, LCL]). Consequently, Seneca believes his instructions will not be in vain but can awaken and recover the virtuous dispositions of goodwill and indebted gratitude in his audience (cf. *Ben.* 4.17.4; 4.22.2).[154] I would add that Seneca, similar to Aristotle, has a tempered optimism. Seneca freely acknowledges the deplorable moral condition of humanity,[155] but this does not negate his belief that human nature possesses all the resources and capability for virtue; though in many, virtuous dispositions lie dormant.

Conclusion

In conclusion, reciprocity in the Greco-Roman world was characterized as a relational bond that is voluntary, long-term, cooperative, filled with risk, and the success of which was predicated upon an optimistic anthropology. This optimistic anthropology was further demonstrated through the ancient sources' emphasis upon the worthy character of each partner in a successful reciprocity relationship and through the belief that giving benefits can produce virtuous character or dispositions. Also, for Aristotle and Seneca, the optimistic anthropology that undergirds their ethical instruction on

---

152 Cicero believed that external tokens of favor (wealth, honor, security) were an indication of divine beneficence while the acquisition of virtue was entirely the individual's own achievement. See *Nat. d.* 3.36.87-88.

153 Plutarch writes, "Yet somehow there inheres, in even the more disreputable and humble creatures, some portion of grace or faculty (δυνάμεως) of natural aptitude for some good things" (*Mor.* 485A [Babbitt, LCL]).

154 See also Cicero, "Let us speak of kindness [*beneficentia*] and generosity. Nothing appeals more to the best in human nature than this" (*Off.* 1.42 [Miller, LCL]).

155 Cf. *Ben.* 1.10.1-3; 5.17.3.

friendship and benefaction is explicit and gives rise to their confidence in reciprocity to produce durable amicable relationships.

In the next chapter we will look at the characterization of the dynamic of reciprocity in the religious heritage of Hebrews, that is, the Jewish subculture of the Greco-Roman world. We will see that the belief in the possibility of reciprocity to secure ongoing fidelity in the divine-human relationship, likewise, rested upon an optimistic anthropological assumption. We will also examine, within this subculture, what consequence a pessimistic anthropological assumption had on the perception for how fidelity was secured in the divine-human relationship.

CHAPTER 3

The Religious Background of Hebrews: Divine-Human Reciprocity Relationships and the Consequences of Their Anthropological Assumptions in the Jewish Milieu

The religious heritage of Hebrews is the Jewish Scriptures and the variegated Jewish lenses by which they were interpreted. In order to better understand how Hebrews relates to the reciprocity systems that in many ways defined the social and, more importantly, religious structures in the ancient Mediterranean world, we should study the divine-human reciprocity relationship in the Jewish subculture of that world. To this end, this chapter is organized into two major sections. The first describes some streams of ancient Jewish and Middle Judaic religious traditions that understood the divine-human relationship in terms of the dynamic of reciprocity.[1] The categories used to describe reciprocity in the Greco-Roman context will prove helpful for describing reciprocity between God and Israel in the Jewish context.[2] The second section will analyze the consequences different Jewish anthropological assumptions had for the perceived success or failure of reciprocity to secure a long-term mutually beneficial relationship between God and Israel. I will argue that the possibility of reciprocity to secure a long-term favorable relationship between God and Israel was undergirded by an optimistic anthropology while those Jewish religious traditions that held to a pessimistic anthropology understood reciprocity to be a failed dynamic for securing fidelity. Consequently, where a pessimistic anthropology was assumed, we will see that the solution to a failed divine-human reciprocity relationship was a new relational dynamic—the dynamic of divine enablement. Additionally,

---

1   These designations are taken from Gabrielle Boccaccini, *Middle Judaism: Jewish Thought 300 BCE to 200 CE* (Minneapolis: Fortress Press, 1991), 20. According to Boccaccini, Israelite religion belongs to the time period prior to the sixth century BCE, ancient Judaism from the sixth to the fifth centuries BCE, and Middle Judaism from 300 BCE to 200 CE Boccaccini defines Middle Judaism as a family of monotheistic systems that sprang from the same Middle Eastern roots in which several competing ideological approaches existed.
2   I am using the term Israel as a religious designation for God's chosen people.

gratitude functions differently in a context of divine enablement. It does not secure loyalty but becomes that disposition that honors God and combats self-exaltation and merit.

Divine-Human Reciprocity Relationships in the Jewish Milieu

In this section, we will examine a stream of Judaism from the sixth/fifth century BCE through the second century CE that defined the divine-human relationship in terms of reciprocity. Three examples will serve as the chief representatives of this stream of Judaism. The first and earliest example is the Mosaic covenant in the tetrateuchal narrative and the Deuteronomistic History. These narratives represent the Mosaic covenant in the form of ancient suzerainty-vassal treaties. The relationship between the suzerain and vassal was governed by the dynamic of reciprocity. The next example is Josephus's *Antiquitates judaicae* which casts the relationship between God and Israel in the mold of Greco-Roman patronage/benefaction. Finally, in rabbinic Judaism, which looks back to the traditions of the rabbis from the first and second centuries CE, reciprocity is the governing dynamic for obedience and faithfulness between God and the Jews.

The description of reciprocity in the Mosaic covenant of the Tetrateuch and Deuteronomistic History and in Josephus's *Antiquitates judaicae* will employ the categories from the previous chapter in an effort to demonstrate that the depiction of reciprocity, whether Greco-Roman or Jewish, was typical of the ancient Mediterranean world. We should not be surprised that we find a convergence in the depiction of reciprocity in such sources as the Tetrateuch, the Deuteronomistic History, Josephus, and the Greco-Roman sources from the previous chapter. There was already by the fourth and fifth centuries BCE a "Greco-Egyptian-Asiatic" culture. According to Martin Hengel, "It is therefore necessary for the Old Testament scholar to know the Greek literature between Homer and Hesiod and Polybius, as well as the Egyptian and Akkadian ancient Near Eastern text."[3] This cultural overlap leads to shared expectations in reciprocity relationships.

The Mosaic Covenant and the Suzerainty-vassal Treaty

The research of a past generation has demonstrated the congruence between the Mosaic covenant in the narratives of Exodus and the Deuteronomistic History[4] and Hittite suzerainty-vassal treaties.[5] The relationship between

---

3   Martin Hengel, "Judaism and Hellenism Revisited," *Hellenism in the Land of Israel* (ed. John J. Collins and Gregory E. Sterling; Christianity and Judaism in Antiquity Series 13; Notre Dame: University of Notre Dame Press, 2001), 12.
4   I follow Martin Noth (*The Deuteronomistic History* [JSOTSup 15; Sheffield: JSOT Press, 1981], 13-14) who argues that Deut 1:1–4:43 serves as the introduction and

suzerain and vassal was sustained by the dynamic of reciprocity.[6] By adopting or retaining this genre for the Mosaic covenant, the author of Exodus and the Deuteronomist depict the relationship between God and Israel in terms of reciprocity. Therefore, the Mosaic covenant attempts to

---

beginning of the Deuteronomistic History. I also understand the present form of the Deuteronomistic History to be written from an exilic point of view. Thus, I read the final form of the Deuteronomistic History as Noth has suggested, i.e., as a self-contained unity written by one exilic author (10, 99). Let me add a proviso. I do not have to accept Noth's notion of the historic authorship of this history in order to read the history in the way he suggests. I only need to affirm that I read it *as though* it was written by one exilic author. In narrative critical terms this exilic author is the implied author who is constructed from the narrative and distinct from the real author of the Deuternomisitic History. By so reading the Deuteronimistic History, I am affirming its essential unity and coherence. I am not concerned with the diachronic reading of the text or with speculation of its redactional layers but with the interpretation of its final canonical form. For a survey of the issues concerning authorship and the diachronic reading of the Deuteronomistic History see Steven L. McKenzie, "Deuteronomistic History," *ABD* 2:162-66.

5   The seminal work that correlated the Hittite treaty form with the Mosaic covenant was done by George Mendenhall, "Covenant Forms in Israelite Tradition," *BA* 17 (1954): 50-76. Mendenhall was followed by Delbert R. Hillers, *Treaty-curses and the Old Testament Prophets* (Biblica et Orientalia; Rome: Pontifical Biblical Institute, 1964); idem, *Covenant: The History of a Biblical Idea* (Seminars in the History of Ideas; Baltimore: John Hopkins Press, 1969); and Dennis J. McCarthy, *Treaty and Covenant: A Study in Form in the Ancient Oriental Documents and in the Old Testament* (AnBib 21a; Rome: Pontifical Biblical Institute, 1981). Earnest W. Nicholson provides a survey of the research done on the treaty-covenant correlation. Nicholson (*God and His People: Covenant and Theology in the Old Testament* [Oxford: Clarendon Press, 1986], 56-82) offers a critique of this position, but his critique is built on a speculative redaction-critical history of the text. Nicholson acknowledges, however, that in the final form of the text the Mosaic covenant resembles what one finds in these treaties (77). The debate among scholars of the Hebrew Scriptures revolves around the dating of the Mosaic covenant. Was it an early construct or something later fabricated by the prophets? Nicholson wants to revive the old Wellhausen thesis that proposed the covenant was a later construct, in which case, the Hittite treaty correlation is a major obstacle to such a thesis (192). This debate is not my concern. The final form of the text will be my focus where there is a powerfully persuasive convergence of form and language between the depiction of the Mosaic covenant and suzerainty-vassal treaties (cf. Hiller, *Covenant*, 150-51; McCarthy, *Treaty and Covenant*, 186). For a recent defense of the covenant-treaty correlation see, Noel Weeks, *Admonition and Curse: The Ancient Near Eastern Treaty/Covenant Form as a Problem in Inter-Cultural Relationships* (JSOTSup 407; London: T & T Clark, 2004). Weeks has argued anew for the close correlation between the Mosaic covenant and Hittite suzerainty treaties (134-73, esp. 172-73).

6   George Mendenhall, "Covenant," *ABD* 1:1181, cf. 1192.

secure a long-term relational bond by the feeling of indebted gratitude. That bond was also characterized by cooperation based upon mutual dependence between both parties. To the fleshing out of this characterization we now turn.

A RELATIONAL BOND

The language of the Mosaic covenant is the language of a durable personal relationship. The covenant was a symbol of the bond between God and Israel.[7] The core affirmation was "I will be your God, and you will be my people".[8] The bond was a noncommercial, nonlegislated bond.[9] (1) As a noncommercial bond, the focus was not on the transaction of benefits for the sake of benefits (whether blessings or honor) but on each party choosing the other for a mutually beneficial relationship. Israel out of all the nations would be God's "treasured possession" (Exod 19:5), and Israel was not to seek benefits or blessings elsewhere.[10] The worship of other gods or loyalty to another suzerain in order to obtain benefits was strictly forbidden (cf. Exod 20:3; Deut 6:13; 13:1-18). (2) Moreover, this bond was not forged by third party legislation, but was voluntary. Hillers comments that these suzerainty-vassal treaties were implemented because there was no recourse to any independent law to enforce the loyal behavior of the vassal.[11] According to Mendenhall, suzerainty-vassal treaties were an attempt to place the bond out of coercive forces and under voluntary acceptance of a mutually beneficial relationship.[12] Therefore, many of the ancient treaties were sealed by oaths.[13] This oath-taking symbolized the voluntary,

---

7   See also Weeks, *Admonition and Curse*, 153 (151-56), who sees ancient treaties as devices primarily for securing "certain forms of personal relationship".
8   Cf. Exod 6:7; 19:5; 29:45-46; Lev 26:12-13; Deut 7:6; 29:13.
9   Noel Weeks (*Admonition and Curse*, 182), in her survey of ancient Near Eastern treaty traditions, has observed there was no interpenetration between treaties and commercial contracts. Moreover, contracts fell under the purview of the ordinary courts so that they were not "regularly strengthened by oaths, god lists and curses".
10 Nelson Glueck (*Hesed in the Bible* [trans. Alfred Gottschalk; Cincinnati: Hebrew Union College Press, 1967], 92) makes the interesting point that central to the longing for deliverance in the Hebrew Scriptures was the assurance of being in covenantal relationship with God. Ideally, the relational bond was of chief importance.
11 Hillers, *Covenant*, 28.
12 Mendenhall, "Covenant," 1:1181.
13 Cf. McCarthy, *Treaty and Covenant*, 184, who points out that sometimes the suzerain took an oath. Oath-taking was an important ritual in some Hellenistic households, see Stanley K. Stowers, "A Cult from Philadelphia: Oikos Religion or Cultic Association?" in *The Early Church in Its Context: Essays in Honor of Everett Ferguson* (ed. Abraham J. Malherbe, Frederick Norris, and James W. Thompson; NovTSup 90; Leiden: Brill, 1998), 298. S. N. Eisenstadt and L. Roniger

nonlegislated nature of the relationship, as well as the good faith of the vassal and suzerain.[14] Oath-taking was also central to the symbolization of the voluntary nature of the relationship between Israel and Yahweh (cf. Exod 19:8; 24:3; Josh 24:16-18, 24).

These Hittite treaties, however, often appealed to the gods to enforce the agreement through blessings for faithfulness to the stipulations and curses for unfaithfulness.[15] This was a measure, however, that the vassal voluntarily accepted and was a secondary motivation to induce faithfulness to the relationship. The appeal was always primarily to the goodwill of the vassal and only then to the gods. To appeal to the gods to enforce voluntarily accepted, mutually beneficial relationships was not uncommon in the ancient world. In Homer the gods are the chief guardians of reciprocity relationships among humans and executed vengeance on those who violated the convention. Zeus is the "god of hospitality (ξεινίου)" (*Il.* 13.625); "from Zeus is all strangers (ξεῖνοί) and beggars (πτωχοί)" (*Od.* 6.208-209); Zeus "walks in the footsteps of reverend suppliants" (*Od.* 7.165, 181); and "Zeus is the avenger of suppliants and strangers—Zeus, the stranger's (ξείνοις) god" (*Od.* 9.269-71). Because of this, imprecatory prayers are uttered in the *Iliad* and *Odyssey* when the relational bond has been violated:

> Zeus, Lord, grant that I may get revenge...so that many a man, even those yet to be, may shudder to do harm to the host who shows him friendship. (*Il.* 3.351-54)

> May Zeus, the suppliant's god, requite them, who watches over all men, and punishes him who transgresses. (*Od.* 13.213-14)

The gods in Homer also defended and enforced reciprocal relations by bestowing blessing for faithfulness to the relationship. One could call upon the gods to bestow appropriate requital. Beggar-Odysseus, after receiving a charitable donation of food from Telemachus, prays, "King Zeus, grant, I pray thee, that Telemachus may be blest among men, and may have all that his heart desires" (*Od.* 17.354-55). Beggar-Odysseus had prayed earlier on behalf of Eumaeus, "Stranger, may Zeus and the other immortal gods grant you what most you desire, since you with a ready heart have given me welcome" (*Od.* 14.53-54). In the *Iliad*, after Nestor receives a gift from

---

(*Patrons, Clients, and Friends: Interpersonal Relations and the Structure of Trust in Society* [Themes in the Social Sciences; New York: Cambridge University Press, 1984], 58) observe that oaths of allegiance to a Roman general were the institutionalized equivalent in a military context to the morning *salutation* to one's patron.

14 Hillers, *Covenant*, 28-29.
15 Mendenhall, "Covenant," 1:1181-92; Hillers, *Treaty-curses*, passim.

Achilles, Nestor prays, "And to you may the gods in return for these things grant favor (τῶν δ'ἀντὶ χάριν) to satisfy your heart" (23.650). In the case of the covenant-treaty Yahweh makes with Israel, there is no appeal to the gods to enforce the relational bond forged, since Yahweh is both Israel's suzerain and exclusive God. He is the enforcer—the bestower of blessings and curses—in this relationship.

The relational bond forged in these ancient suzerainty-vassal treaties was meant to be enduring.[16] The relationship was not violated lightly. More so than in the Greco-Roman sources, a premium was placed on exclusive fidelity to the relationship. Other reciprocity relationships that brought loyalties into conflict were expressly forbidden. Furthermore, this exclusive fidelity to the suzerain in the ancient Hittite treaties was grounded upon indebted gratitude, the centerpiece of the reciprocity rationale.

FIDELITY: INDEBTED GRATITUDE

This section will highlight three major points: (1) the relational bond symbolized by the Mosaic covenant demanded exclusive loyalty, (2) exclusive loyalty was grounded on the feeling of indebted gratitude, and (3) a primary concept for expressing this indebted gratitude, that is, fidelity to the relationship, was חסד. First, the suzerainty-vassal treaties called for exclusive loyalty even threatening the vassal with the penalty of death for violating the suzerain's trust.[17] The suzerain, Mursilis, warns, "Do not turn your eyes to anyone else", and in another treaty the suzerain cautions, "Henceforth however recognize no other lord".[18] In Exodus, the demand for exclusive fidelity is one of the first stipulations of the covenant: "You shall have no other gods before me", declares Yahweh (20:3; cf. Exod 20:23, 23:24-25, 32-33). The extremity of the covenant curses recounted for disobedience in Deut 28:15-68 is a reminder of the grave value that was placed on singular devotion to Yahweh, Israel's king. In fact, McCarthy makes fidelity the central theme to Moses' farewell speech in Deuteronomy. McCarthy organizes Moses' speech around the call to fidelity: (1) Deut 5–11, an exhortation to fidelity, (2) Deut 12–26, a definition of fidelity, and (3) Deut 28, the consequences of fidelity.[19] Based on the demand for exclusive loyalty, the Deuteronomist justifies the annihilation of the Canaanites from the promised land, since intermingling with the native population would compromise Israel's loyalty to Yahweh:[20]

---

16 Cf. Hillers, *Covenant*, 32.
17 Mendenhall, "Covenant," 1:1180.
18 Examples are cited in Jon D. Levenson, *Sinai and Zion: An Entry into the Jewish Bible* (New Voices in Biblical Studies; New York: Winston Press, 1985), 28-29.
19 McCarthy, *Treaty and Covenant*, 185.
20 According to Hillers (*Covenant*, 33), the chief test of loyalty for the vassal was when the suzerain called upon the services of the vassal in time of war. The

When the LORD you God brings you into the land that you are about to enter and occupy, and he clears away many nations before you...and when the LORD your God gives them over to you and you defeat them, then you must utterly destroy them. Make no covenant with them and show them no mercy. Do no intermarry with them, giving your daughters to their sons or taking their daughters for your sons, for that would turn away your children from following me, to serve other gods. Then the anger of the LORD would be kindled against you and he would destroy you quickly. But this is how you must deal with them: break down their altars, smash their pillars, hew down their sacred poles, and burn their idols with fire. For you are a people holy to the LORD your God; the LORD your God has chosen you out of all the peoples of the earth to be his people, his treasured possession.[21] (Deut 7:1-6; cf. Deut 4:15-20; 12; 29:16-18; Josh 24:14-15)

In the covenant-treaty with Yahweh there were to be no other gods and no other suzerains to compete for the affections and loyalty of Israel.

Second, what was the foundational dynamic that secured this singular fidelity between the suzerain (Yahweh) and vassal (Israel)? The relational bond forged was sustained by the feeling of indebted gratitude. The feeling of indebted gratitude was expressed in two primary ways: (1) through the juxtaposition of the history of Yahweh's benefits with the obligations of Israel and (2) through the exhortations to remember and not forget Yahweh's benefits. First, in the Hittite suzerainty-vassal treaties the historical prologue recounted the history of the relationship between the suzerain and vassal by describing the benefits the suzerain had bestowed on the vassal. The historical prologue is then followed by the stipulations of the treaty, that is, the suzerain's demands on the vassal.[22] The juxtaposition of these two elements in the treaties implies that the foundation for the vassal's obedience and fidelity to the suzerain is based upon the vassal's gratitude for all the benefits the suzerain has bestowed. McCarthy writes:

They [the treaties] also emphasize the bounty of the Hittite king, his

---

Deuteronomist portrays Yahweh as waging war against the inhabitants of Canaan because of their wickedness. They are Yahweh's enemies and Yahweh calls upon Israel to join in this battle (cf. Deut 9:4). This was a test of their fidelity, as demonstrated by the episode of Israel's original failure to enter the promised land and wage war against its inhabitants (cf. Num 13–14).

21 All quotes taken from the Hebrew Scriptures and Old Testament Apocrypha, unless otherwise specified, follow the NRSV in the *New Oxford Annotated Bible with Apocrypha* (3d ed.; New York: Oxford University Press, 2001).

22 Mendenhall, "Covenant," 1:1180; Hillers, *Covenant*, 29. Hillers lists the six parts that were typical of the Hittite treaty: (1) preamble, (2) historical prologue, (3) stipulations, (4) provisions for the deposit of the text and public reading, (5) list of divine witnesses, and (6) blessing and curses.

generosity and his readiness to forgive. Often enough they bring out that the vassal owes his very place to the king. All this is doubtless aimed at producing gratitude as a motive for fidelity.[23]

We find this juxtaposition of a history of benefits and exhortations to fidelity in the description of the Mosaic covenant in Exodus and Deuteronomy. Exodus 19:3-8 relates the initial covenant agreement. Yahweh offers the covenant to Israel in which He[24] recounts how He delivered Israel from slavery in Egypt and promises them further benefits if they will prove loyal to Yahweh (vv. 3-6). In the extended recounting of the enactment of the covenant in Exod 20:1–24:11, Yahweh's deliverance of Israel from Egypt introduces and serves as the foundation for obedience to the Ten Commandments. Yahweh declares, "I am the LORD your God who brought you out of the land of Egypt, out of the house of slavery" (20:1). This is a short concise statement of the history of beneficence of Yahweh toward Israel, which is not typical of suzerainty-vassal treaties. These treaties typically contained a lengthy history of the king's beneficence toward the vassal. What we need to remember is that, by locating the description of the covenant within a narrative context, the author has already related the history of benefits bestowed by Yahweh; therefore, only a short summary statement was needed.[25]

This juxtaposition of benefits and obligation is even more frequent in Deuteronomy. In Deut 4:15-20, the Israelites are said to owe Yahweh exclusive loyalty because "the LORD has taken you and brought you out of the iron-smelter, out of Egypt, to become a people of his very own possession, as you are now" (v. 20). Again, Deut 10:20–11:7 sets forth Yahweh's past benefits as the basis for present loyalty. Moreover, Deut 11:8-17 goes on to promise future benefits for continued fidelity. Thus the dance of reciprocity comes full circle.[26] Finally, in Josh 24:1-24, we have the renewal of the covenant at Shechem, where Joshua first recounts the history of Yahweh's benefits toward Israel (vv. 2-13), then Joshua calls Israel to exclusive fidelity to Yahweh (vv. 14-15), and finally Israel confirms their allegiance to Yahweh with an oath (vv. 16-18, 24).

---

23 McCarthy, *Treaty and Covenant*, 145. Sea also Hillers, *Covenant*, 31, 69, 155; Mendenhall, "Covenant," 1:1180-81, 1192; Weeks, *Admonition and Curse*, 172, 179-80

24 Again, I follow Mary Isaacs's (*Reading Hebrews and James: A Literary and Theological Commentary* [Macon: Smyth & Helwys, 2002], vii) reasoning for using the capitalized pronoun when referring to God, i.e., to indicate "not that the deity is male but that God is above gender".

25 Cf. Weeks, *Admonition and Curse*, 155.

26 Further examples from Deuteronomy are 4:37-40; 6:20-25; 29:2-29. In Deut 4:37-40, the benefit of election is the focus and, one might argue, the foundation for the initial benefit of deliverance and the offer of the covenant with Yahweh.

Since the feeling of indebted gratitude was imperative to maintaining the vassal's loyalty to the suzerain, ingratitude then led to infidelity. We find such a correlation in 2 Kgs 17:7-17. There the Deuteronomist summarizes the reasons for the exiles of the northern and southern kingdoms. The chief reason is because of idolatry, which is tantamount to infidelity toward Yahweh. But more can be said. We find here as well a similar juxtaposition of the history of Yahweh's benefits toward Israel (v. 7) with the account of Israel's disobedience to the covenant (vv. 8-17). Mendenhall states that the "net effect of this juxtaposition [Yahweh's past benefits with Israel's apostasy] was to characterize the Israelites...as *ungrateful* sinners".[27]

The second expression of indebted gratitude is remembering benefits. Remembering benefits is essential to persevering in gratitude. If the benefit is forgotten, the bond is broken because the indebted gratitude that was grounded on the reception of that benefit and sustained the bond has vanished. The call to remember Yahweh's benefits is a regular exhortation in Deuteronomy. In Deut 6:12, Moses admonishes the Israelites, "[T]ake care that you do not forget the LORD, who brought you out of the land of Egypt, out of the house of slavery", and then he summons them to obedience and fidelity, "Do not follow other gods" (v. 14). In Deut 8:2-5, Moses exhorts the Israelites to remember Yahweh's benefits recounting how Yahweh had cared for them for forty years in the wilderness, and then he calls Israel to obedience and fidelity (cf. v. 6). Conversely, one also finds the admonition not to forget Yahweh's benefits. In Deut 8:19, forgetfulness is explicitly linked to infidelity. Forgetting the Lord is equivalent to following others gods in order to serve and worship them. So the juxtaposition of benefits with stipulations and the exhortations to remember and not forget Yahweh's benefits constitute expressions of indebted gratitude in Exodus and Deuteronomy. This indebted gratitude was meant to sustain Israel's loyalty to Yahweh.

Finally, one of the key terms for fidelity in the Hebrew Scriptures and in the Tetrateuch and Deuteronomistic History is חסד.[28] חסד functions much like χάρις and its cognates in reciprocity contexts in the sense that a debt of gratitude (χάρις) is owed for a favor (χάρις) done.[29] In the same way,

---

27 Mendenhall, "Covenant," 1:1187.
28 According to Glueck (*Hesed*, 55), the component parts of this concept are reciprocity, mutual assistance, sincerity, friendliness, duty, loyalty, love. Other significant treatments of the term in the Old Testament after Glueck have been Katherine Doob Sakenfeld, *The Meaning of Hesed in the Hebrew Bible: A New Inquiry* (HSM 17; Missoula: Scholars Press, 1978) and Gordon R. Clark, *The Word Hesed in the Hebrew Bible* (JSOTSup 157; Sheffield; Sheffield Academic Press, 1993). For a useful summary of the contributions of each scholar to defining this term see D. A. Baer and R. P. Gordon, "חסד," *NIDOTTE* 2:211-12.
29 What is particularly interesting is that we find חסד describing relationships between relatives, hosts and guests, friends, and subjects and kings (cf. H.-J. Zobel,

to one whom חסד is given חסד is owed.³⁰ We find this notion in the relationships among humans. Rahab's response to the Israelite spies whom she has hidden reads, "Now then, since I have dealt kindly (חסד) with you, swear to me by the LORD that you will in turn deal kindly (חסד) with my family." Upon the Ammonite king's, Hanun, ascension to the throne, David decrees, "I will deal loyally (חסד) with Hanun son of Nahash just as his father dealt loyally (חסד) with me" (2 Sam 10:2). In Judg 1:24, the spies inquire of a man about the way into Bethel. They appeal to the man to "show us the way into the city and we will deal kindly (חסד) with you". In 1 Sam 15:6, Saul spares the Kenites because they showed חסד "to all the people of Israel when they came out of Egypt". Likewise, we find this dynamic operative in the relationship with Yahweh. Yahweh shows חסד in the form of blessing and deliverance to those who show Him חסד in the form of enduring obedience and loyalty. In Exod 20:6, after Yahweh commands Israel not to make for themselves idols, Yahweh declares that He shows חסד "to the thousandth generation of those who love me and keep my commandments".³¹ In 1 Kngs 3:6, Solomon says to God, "You have shown great and steadfast love (חסד) to your servant my father David, because he walked before you in faithfulness and in uprightness toward you; and you have kept for him this great and steadfast love (חסד), and have given him a son to sit on his throne today." Because inhabitants of Jabesh-gilead showed loyalty to Saul by retrieving his body and the body of his sons from the Philistines (cf. 1 Sam 3:11-13), David prays, "May the Lord show steadfast love and faithfulness (חסד) to you!" (2 Sam 2:6). D. A. Bauer and R. P. Gordon write, "Though the prior commitment is usually on the part of God toward humankind, there is an expected reciprocity and mutuality that demands service, fear, and even a corresponding exercise of *hesed* in return."³²

We also find the failure to show חסד paralleled to the admonition of forgetting benefits, which is a common expression for ingratitude and infidelity. Judges 8:35 reads that the Israelites "did not exhibit loyalty (חסד) to the house of Jerubbaal (that is, Gideon) in return for all the good that he had done to Israel". This statement is linked to v. 34 that says the

---

"חֶסֶד," *TDOT* 5: 46-47). These were the primary reciprocity relationships in the ancient Mediterranean world.

30 Zobel, *TDOT* 5:47. Zobel goes on to note that חסד is the virtue that binds society together (52-53) much like what was affirmed about the function of indebted gratitude in the context of reciprocity in the previous chapter. Glueck (*Hesed*, 52) cites E. Reuss who even translated חסד as gratitude in Gen 40:14.

31 We find the same declaration in Deut 5:10 and 7:9-10.

32 Baer and Gordon, *NIDOTTE* 2:213. There are also contexts where the divine חסד is emphasized to the exclusion of human merit or loyalty (e.g., Exod 34:6-7; Num 14:19). Consequently, חסד is not always tied to notions of reciprocity.

Israelites did not remember the benefits of the Lord and there is an ellipsis that the auditor is to fill in, namely that they did not remember the benefits of Gideon either. Thus, failure to show חסד is rooted in forgetting benefits, i.e., ingratitude.

The long-term, bilateral nature of the Mosaic covenant called for cooperation characterized by mutual dependence. I will discuss these final two characteristics in turn.

COOPERATION

Fidelity in the Mosaic covenant was defined by specific obligations each party undertook in the relationship. Like the reciprocity systems of patronage and benefaction, Yahweh's obligation was to bestow benefits, and Israel's obligation was to honor Yahweh exclusively. First, I will outline Yahweh's obligations. In general, Yahweh promises to keep Israel as His "treasured possession" (Exod 19:5). He also promises them a land, Canaan (Exod 23:20-33; Josh 1:3-8). Deuteronomy 28:1-14 lays out the most extensive list of benefits Yahweh will bestow upon Israel. They will have fruitful wombs, an abundance of food, victory in battle, and superiority over their neighboring nations.

Israel's obligation can be generally described as honoring Yahweh.[33] We saw that this was typical of asymmetrical reciprocity relationships in the Greco-Roman context. Benefits were given by the superior party in return for honor, sometimes in the form of subservience from the inferior. We also described several forms honor took in that context: obedience, sacrifice, votive offerings, hymns, and inscriptions. In the Mosaic covenant, the principle way Yahweh was honored was not by sacrifice or votive gifts but by obedience to the stipulations of the covenant. Furthermore, Yahweh demanded exclusive honor from Israel. In the light of this demand, Yahweh identifies Himself as a jealous God who will not give the honor He is due to any other (Exod 20:5; 34:14; Deut 4:24; 6:15; 32:21).

Thus the dance of reciprocity was maintained between Yahweh and Israel. Yahweh bestowed benefits on Israel who in return honored Yahweh by obeying His stipulations that elicited further benefits from Yahweh. The very structure of the Hittite suzerainty-vassal treaties and, by association, the Mosaic covenant emphasizes this dance. The suzerain (Yahweh) has bestowed benefits upon the vassal (Israel) who then acquiesces to the stipulations of the suzerain who then calls upon the gods to bestow further blessings upon his loyal vassal (but in the case of Israel that is Yahweh,

---

33 Saul M. Olyan ("Honor, Shame, and Covenant Relations in Ancient Israel and Its Environment," *JBL* 115 [1996]: 217) states that the covenant was characterized by reciprocity and that honor was the public means of demonstrating fidelity. In fact, like חסד, honor is reciprocal. Yahweh honors those who honor Him (205; cf. 2 Sam 2:30).

their suzerain).³⁴ The possession of the promised land—a key feature of the Mosaic covenant—also highlights this threefold movement of the dance of reciprocity. Yahweh bestows the land upon Israel who lives in it gratefully honoring Yahweh who then continues to bless the land and Israel in it. With this rational, Moses exhorts the Israelites, "Do what is right and good in the sight of LORD, so that it may go well with you, and so that you may go in and occupy the good land that the LORD swore to your ancestors to give to you" (Deut 6:18; cf. Deut 8:6-20; Josh 1:6-9). As long as each remained faithful to the relationship, Israel would experience unparalleled blessing and Yahweh would be glorified and honored among Israel and before the nations.³⁵

Characteristic of this cooperation—more narrowly defined than what we observed in many of the Greco-Roman reciprocity systems—was the mutual dependence it entailed. Each party, Yahweh and Israel, had to rely on the fidelity of the other to ensure the continuance of the relationship.

MUTUAL DEPENDENCE

In this last section of our characterization of reciprocity in the Mosaic covenant of the Tetrateuch and Deteronomistic History, we will examine how mutual dependence was expressed, measures taken to assure the other partner of his or her commitment to the relationship, and the voluntary nature of the bond that required such assurances. Let me preface this section by saying that this feature is somewhat muted in the Mosaic covenant as compared to suzerainty-vassal treaties and many Greco-Roman reciprocity contexts. This muteness arises from the theological conviction that Yahweh is the ruler of history and knows the future.³⁶ Therefore, the risk that is apparent in relationships of mutual dependence is not evident for Yahweh. With that said, there are clear indications that suzerainty-vassal treaties and the Mosaic covenant were characterized by mutual dependence.

First, how was the notion of mutual dependence expressed? With the Mosaic covenant we are dealing with an obligatory covenant, that is, a

---

34 Cf. Exod 19:3-8; 20:1-24:11; Deut 29:1-9.
35 Deuteronomy 4:5-8 affirms that Israel's obedience to Yahweh was meant to have international implications. It reads: "I now teach you statues and ordinances for you to observe in the land that you are about to enter and occupy. You must observe them diligently, for this will show your wisdom and discernment to the peoples, who, when they hear all these statutes, will say, 'Surely this great nation is a wise and discerning people!' For what other great nation has a god so near to it as the LORD our God is whenever we call on him? And what other great nation has statutes and ordinances just as this entire law that I am setting before you today?"
36 One way this theological conviction is expressed in the narrative of the Tetrateuch and Deuteronomistic History is by the prophecy-fulfillment schema, e.g., Gen 15:13-16; Exod 7:3-6; 1 Kngs 11:9-13, 31-39. The passages cited are all prophecies that are subsequently fulfilled in the narrative.

covenant relationship that relies upon each party fulfilling his or her obligations to the other. This is expressed by the language of condition in the covenant. Exodus 19:5 reads, "Now therefore, *if* you obey my voice and keep my commandment, you shall be my treasure possession out of all the peoples" (emphasis mine). The Hebrew introduces this conditional statement with the conditional conjunction אִם while the translators of the LXX employed a third class conditional clause (ἐὰν + subjunctive [ἀκούσητε] + future [ἔσεσθέ]), which in Hellenistic Greek can carry a range of meanings from likely to occur in the future, to what can possibly occur, to what is only hypothetical.[37] There is, therefore, contingency in this reciprocity relationship. *If* Israel obeys *then* Yahweh will bless them. We also find this contingency in Deuteronomy. Moses declares to Israel, "There will, however, be no one in need among you, because the LORD is sure to bless you in the land that the LORD your God is giving you as a possession, *if only* you will obey the LORD your God by diligently observing this entire commandment that I command you today" (Deut 15:4-5, emphasis mine).[38] Further, the blessings in Deut 28 are conditioned upon Israel's obedience, "If you will only obey the LORD your God, by diligently observing all his commandments...all these blessing shall come upon you and overtake you, if you obey the LORD your God" (vv.1-2). Conversely, the curses are predicated upon the condition of disobedience (cf. v. 15). The conditional nature of the blessing and curses was one measure taken to attempt to assure the suzerain of the vassal's loyalty. By making blessings contingent upon the vassal's loyalty to the suzerain, the vassal had motivation to carefully keep suzerain's treaty.

This last observation leads to our second point—what other measures were taken by each partner to assure each of his or her commitment to the relationship. Relationships of mutual dependence typically require some type of affirmation, proof, or collateral as a way of alleviating the contingency that arises when one must rely upon another. Yahweh seeks to assure Israel of His faithfulness and reliability be recounting the history of His beneficence toward them. This is another function of the historical prologue in the suzerainty-vassal treaties. Joshua 24:2-13 is one of the most extensive histories of benefits of Yahweh toward the people of Israel. The history relates Yahweh's faithfulness stretching all the way back to His promise to give Abraham the land of Canaan to Israel's possession of that land in the time of Joshua. Levenson writes, "In sum, the historical prologue provides the data from which the nature of YHWH the reliable

---

37 Daniel B. Wallace, *Greek Grammar Beyond the Basics: An Exegetical Syntax of the New Testament* (Grand Rapids: Zondervan, 1996), 696.
38 This is the same syntactical structure we observed in Exod 19:5. In Hebrew, the conditional clause is introduced by אִם, and in the Greek, the protasis contains ἐὰν + the subjunctive (εἰσακούσητε) while the apodosis contains a future verb (ἔσται).

suzerain can be known."³⁹

In the case of Israel, Israel seeks to "assure" Yahweh of their commitment to the relationship by taking an oath. Exodus 19:8 concludes with Israel swearing, "Everything that the LORD has spoken we will do". This oath is made even more serious in the ceremony that concludes the giving of the covenant in Exod 24:3-8. There Moses sacrifices an oxen whose blood he dashes upon the altar as symbol of Yahweh's presence and then sprinkles it upon the people who say, "All that the LORD has spoken we will do, and we will be obedient" (v. 7). The covenant sacrifice likely has the sobering significance of declaring, "as we have done to this animal so may it be done to us if we violate the covenant" (cf. Jer 34:18-20; *Il.* 3.264-301). Though Israel is primarily the one who symbolizes their intention to be faithful with oaths, Yahweh occasionally makes oath-like declarations to Israel. In Deut 26, mutual declarations or oaths that are taken by both Israel and Yahweh seal the covenant:

> You have today declared the LORD to be your God, and that you would walk in his ways and keep his statutes, his commandments and his ordinances, and listen to his voice. And the LORD has today declared you to be his people, a treasured possession, as he promised you, and that you should keep all his commandments; and that he shall set you high above all nations which he has made, for praise, fame, and honor; and that you shall be a consecrated people to the LORD your God, as he has spoken. (vv. 17-19 NAS)

Third, the voluntary nature of the covenant-treaty reciprocity bond introduces this need for assurance. Hillers argues that the mutuality of the covenant-treaty depicts two distinct parties with a certain freedom and initiative in concluding the agreement.⁴⁰ Israel is free to take Yahweh as their God/suzerain and swear fealty to Him while Yahweh is free to choose Israel as His people/vassal and bless them. This freedom or mutuality introduces the element of contingency, even uncertainty, in the suzerainty-vassal treaties as well as the Mosaic covenant—keeping in mind the proviso at the beginning of this section.⁴¹

---

39 Levenson, *Sinai and Zion*, 42.
40 Hillers, *Covenant*, 52.
41 James R. Harrison in his book, *Paul's Language of Grace in Its Graeco-Roman Context* (WUNT 2.172; Tübingen: Mohr Siebeck, 2003), attempts to shield the Mosaic covenant from reciprocity (cf. 114 n. 80, 130, 137, 140, 146). Rightly so, Harrison emphasizes the initiative of the divine grace in choosing Israel, but Harrison fails to reckon with the genre of the Mosaic covenant and any of the data discussed above. Harrison is even forced into inconsistency at times when he acknowledges that God participates in reciprocal honor and then, as to diminish the reciprocity implied by this statement, says, "God's grace imposes obligation upon

This stream of understanding the relationship between God and Israel as a reciprocity relationship continued into the first century CE with Josephus. We now take up the characterization of reciprocity in his biblical paraphrase, *Antiquitates judaicae*.

Josephus and Greco-Roman Patronage/Benefaction

Josephus wrote his works in the latter part of the first century CE.[42] Just as the Mosaic covenant in the Tetrateuch and Deuteronomistic History employed the reciprocity relationship between the suzerain and vassal to depict the divine-human relationship, Josephus adapts the relationship between God and Israel to the reciprocity relationships of Greco-Roman patronage and benefaction.[43] Josephus was no stranger to patronage and benefaction. He received patronage from Nero's consort, Poppaea (*Vita* 16), he was recognized by towns in Galilee as "benefactor and savior" (*Vita* 244, 259), and he was a client of the Flavian house (*Vita* 419-29).[44] As in the previous section, we will characterize Jospehus's depiction of divine-human reciprocity using the categories already implemented: a relational bond, fidelity as indebted gratitude, cooperation, and mutual dependence.

A RELATIONAL BOND

For Josephus, the bond between Israel and God was not one that was automatic due to one's birth into a specific people. The bond was defined by personal commitment to God. For instance, after Israel's first failure to enter into and take the promised land, God through Moses prohibits them from subsequently attempting to go up and take the land. Josephus relates

---

His beneficiaries, it also extends to them the promise of recompense" (114 n. 80). Harrison's latter statement actually fits well into the reciprocity system of the Mosaic covenant discussed above. Let me add that I believe Harrison's instincts are right concerning the unilateral nature of the divine grace in the Pauline context that even overturns the ethos of reciprocity (see 18, 343). See also my "Enabling Χάρις: The Transformation of the Convention of Reciprocity by Philo and in Ephesians," *PRSt* 30 (2003): 346-57.

42 The order of Josephus's writings are likely *Bellum judaicum*, *Antiquitates judaicae*, and *Vita* with *Contra Apionom*, see Louis H. Feldman, "Josephus," *ABD* 3:982.
43 Paul Spilsbury, "God and Israel in Josephus–A Patron-client Relationship," in *Understanding Josephus: Seven Perspectives* (JSPSup 32; ed. Steve Mason; Sheffield: Sheffield Academic Press, 1998), 172-91. Spilsbury has done the seminal work in drawing attention to this aspect of Josephus's thought. This section will be an expansion and adaptation of the foundation he has already laid. Cf. H. W. Attridge, *The Interpretation of Biblical History in the* Antiquitates Judaicae *of Flavius Josephus* (HDR 7; Missoula: Scholars Press, 1979) 79-91, esp. 79.
44 See Spilsbury, "God and Israel in Josephus," 175-81, for a more detailed description.

in *A.J.* 4.1-8 that the Israelites were, however, so weary of living in the desert that they ignored God's prohibition via Moses and went up to take the land. Josephus, in an expansion of the biblical narrative, records their reasoning in the following way:

> They were accordingly bent on war with the Canaanites, declaring that it was from no favour for Moses that God succoured them, but because in general He had a care for their race out of regard for the ancestors who He had taken under His protection. It was thanks to them and to their own valour that He had in the past given them their liberty, and now, would they but exert themselves, He would be ever at their side as their ally.[45] (4.2)

Of course, as the story unfolds, the Israelites were summarily defeated by the Canaanites. According to Spilsbury, "we can conclude that [for Josephus] membership in a group is not simply a matter of physical descent from illustrious and meritorious forebears" but of personal obedience to God whose will is made known through the lawgiver, Moses.[46] Attridge argues that, according to Josephus, the ongoing benefits the Israelites derived from God were not based on an inherited, privileged status with God but on personal conformity to the will of God in the law of Moses.[47] Josephus makes this point clear from the outset of his work:

> [T]he main lesson to be learnt from this history by any who care to peruse it is that men who conform to the will of God, and do no venture to transgress laws that have been excellently laid down, prosper in all things

---

45 Unless specified, the translation and Greek text of Josephus depends upon the LCL edition of Josephus's *Antiquitates judaicae* translated and edited by Thackeray, Marcus, Wikgren, and Feldman.

46 Paul Spilsbury, "Josephus," in *Justification and Variegated Nomism: The Complexities of Second Temple Judaism* (ed. D. A. Carson, Peter T. O'Brien, and Mark Seifrid; vol. 1; WUNT 2.140; Tübingen/Grand Rapids: Mohr Siebeck/Baker Academics, 2001), 250.

47 Attridge, *The Interpretation of Biblical History*, 86-87. This statement needs to be qualified. Attridge does acknowledge that Josephus believed God had a special concern for Israel primarily due to the special virtue of the people's leaders (83). Spilsbury acknowledges also that Josephus understood God to have a special relationship with Israel. Josephus cites the Balaam episode as evidence for this assertion (cf. *A.J.* 4.122). Spilsbury ("Josephus," 250-51) argues, however, that, according to Josephus, the chief benefit Israel receives from their special relationship with God is the law of Moses. Therefore, "God's dealings with Israel are predicated on the Law of Moses" (255). These laws define the reciprocal obligations of the patron-client relationship between God and Israel. Though favored, Israel's relationship is not automatic but contingent upon their observance of the law of Moses.

beyond belief, and for their reward are offered by God felicity; whereas, in proportion as they depart from strict observance of these laws, things (else) practicable become impracticable, and whatever imaginary good thing they strive to do ends in irretrievable disasters. (*A.J.* 1.14; cf. 1.20)

Consequently, fidelity was vital to maintaining an enduring, favorable relationship with God. Fidelity for Josephus was secured by indebted gratitude, which is a typical fixture we have come to expect in the dynamic of ancient reciprocity.

FIDELITY: INDEBTED GRATITUDE

How does Josephus express this motif of indebted gratitude that provides the foundation for fidelity to God, the cornerstone of reciprocity relationships? Josephus does this in three primary ways. Josephus juxtaposes exhortations to faithfulness with the benefits God bestowed and will bestow upon Israel; he uses the typical expression for grateful loyalty of remembering and not forgetting benefits; and finally, he understands ingratitude to be equivalent to infidelity. First, Josephus juxtaposes God's benefits with exhortations to obedience and faithfulness. We have already witnessed this juxtaposition in the Mosaic covenant of the Tetrateuch and Deuteronomistic History. A prime example of this juxtaposition is when Josephus recounts God's command to Abraham to sacrifice Isaac. Josephus relates the demand in the following manner, "[A]fter numerating all the benefits that He [God] had bestowed upon him [Abraham]...He required him to offer up that son by his own hand as a sacrifice" (*A.J.* 1.223).[48] In a similar way, Josephus relates that, at Sinai, Moses entreats the Israelites to accept and obey the laws that God is giving them because of all the benefits God has bestowed on them and will bestow on them if they are obedient (cf. *A.J.* 3.86-88).[49] Spilsbury observes that for Josephus gratitude for God's benefactions is appropriately expressed by obedience or faithfulness to the law.[50] I would only slightly modify this observation in light of the above evidence. Enduring obedience is grounded upon and sustained by the feeling of indebted gratitude not merely the expression of gratitude. To what extent were the people of God expected to be faithful to God's

---

48 This is a very different motivation from what we find in Heb 11:17-19. There the author recounts Abraham offered up Isaac believing God would resurrect Isaac since the fulfillment of God's promises to Abraham was to come through Isaac.

49 In the Joseph narrative, Joseph exemplifies the connection between the giving of benefits and securing loyalty. As Joseph manages the resources of Egypt during the famine, Josephus, in an expansion of the biblical narrative, recounts that Joseph returned to the people the land that they had ceded to him in the famine. Such an action was said to have inspired loyalty/goodwill (εὔνοιαν) toward the pharaoh (*A.J.* 2.192-93).

50 Spilsbury, "Josephus," 250.

ordinances? Abraham was expected to sacrifice his promised and beloved son, Isaac. Jews were to remain obedient to the ordinances of God even under the pain of death (cf. *C. Ap.* 2.218-19, 233).[51]

Second, Josephus employs the typical expression for grateful loyalty of remembering and/or not forgetting benefits. Josephus writes about Joshua's farewell speech to the Israelites that Joshua "recalled (ἀνεμίμησκεν) to them all the benefactions (εὐεργεσίας) of God...and exhorted them to keep God's goodwill unchanged towards them, for by showing him every honour and that piety (εὐσεβείᾳ) alone could they retain the friendship (φίλον) of the Diety" (*A.J.* 5.115-16). Josephus even describes God's fidelity to the relationship in terms of God remembering the people's piety. After Amaram supplicated God for the deliverance of his unborn son, Moses, from imminent death and for the Hebrews from Egyptian bondage, Josephus writes that God "had their piety (εὐσέβιαν) in remembrance (διὰ μνήμης) and would ever give the recompense (ἀμοιβὴν)" (*A.J.* 2.212). On the other hand, Josephus describes the infidelity of the Sodomites as impious arrogance (ὑβρισταὶ) "to the Divinity, insomuch that they no longer remembered (μηκέτι μεμνῆσθαι) the benefits that they had received from Him" (*A.J.* 1.194).

Third, Josephus relates infidelity to ingratitude toward God. When the Israelites fail to go and take the land of Canaan the first time, God is described as castigating Israel for their ingratitude: "God had recalled to him [Moses] how, after all that He had done for them after all those benefits (εὐεργεσιῶν) received, they proved ungrateful (ἀχάριστοι) to Him" (*A.J.* 3.312). Further, Josephus describes the rebellious actions of Abiram and Datham against Moses by joining Korah's insurrection as ingratitude (ἀχαριστίαν; *A.J.* 4.41). Josephus has Moses set forth the benefits that he had bestowed on Israel along with the benefits of God in order to highlight the vicious nature of the ingratitude or infidelity that Korah's rebellion typified (cf. 4.42-45).[52] All these passages indicate that Josephus conceived of the relational dynamic between God and Israel as one of reciprocity, when he implemented the relational system of patronage/benefaction to describe the relationship between God and Israel. Thus, fidelity was secured by indebted gratitude for benefits bestowed. Spilsbury aptly writes:

---

51 Cf. Spilsbury, "Josephus," 257-58.
52 In *A.J.* 2.56, Potiphar's wife falsely accuses Joseph of ingratitude (ἀχάριστος), that is infidelity, towards Potiphar by attempting to rape her. Joseph, then, is portrayed as violating the trust in which Potiphar had placed the care of his household and the benefits that went along with such management. For a listing of passages in the works of Josephus that highlight the dangers of ingratitude, see Harrison, *Paul's Language of Grace*, 143 n. 253. Spilsbury ("God and Israel in Josephus," 190) notes that infidelity for Josephus dissolves the relationship between God and the individual.

Josephus' depiction of the relationship between God and Israel may best be understood in terms of the patron-client system of relations prevalent in Roman society at the time. In Josephus' grand scheme it is the Law of Moses that is presented as God's most important benefaction. Gratitude for this gift is expressed primarily in due obedience of the Law itself....This wonderful gift, which enables them to live a life superior to any other people on earth, calls forth gratitude of the people. This gratitude is expressed primarily in obedience to the Law. This obedience then secures God's continued favor.[53]

This statement by Spilsbury also highlights the cooperative dance that is characteristic of asymmetrical reciprocity relationships—benefits result in a grateful return of honor that leads to further benefits.

COOPERATION

As in most asymmetrical reciprocity relationships, cooperation was exemplified by the ongoing obligations undertaken by each party. Benefits by the superior were exchanged in expectation of honor from the inferior. As honor was returned for benefits bestowed, further benefits were given, and thus, the circular dance of reciprocity continued unbroken. Nowhere is this threefold cooperative dance more succinctly stated by Josephus than in the rationale for the thrice yearly pilgrimage to Jerusalem. The Israelites are to journey to Jerusalem "in order to render thanks (εὐχαριστῶσι) to God for benefits received" and "to intercede for future mercies" (*A.J.* 4.203). Elsewhere the Israelites are instructed to pray twice each day acknowledging "before God the bounties which He has bestowed on them". Josephus goes on to explain, "Thanksgiving is a natural duty, and is rendered alike in gratitude for past mercies and to incline the giver to others yet to come" (*A.J.* 4.212). The first two steps of the dance—benefits for honor—are also represented in a statement of Abraham to Isaac. Even as Abraham is preparing to sacrifice Isaac, Abraham declares that God "claims from us this homage (τιμῆς) in return for gracious favor (ἀνθ᾽ ὧν εὐμενὴς) He has shown me as my supporter (παραστάτης) and ally (σύμμαχος)" (*A.J.* 1.229).[54] With a similar rational, the Israelites are exhorted to "hold God, who is ever our helper (βοηθὸς) and ally (σύμμαχος), in lasting honor (διὰ τιμῆς ἔχομεν)" (*A.J.* 3.302). The dance is completed by God when Josephus records that, in light of the honor Abraham showed God in being willing to sacrifice his beloved son, "God never failed to regard with tenderest care both him and his race" (*A.J.* 1.234). Benefits are bestowed, honor gratefully returned, leading to further

---

53 Spilsbury, "Josephus," 251.
54 Cf. Zeba A. Crook, *Reconceptualizing Conversion: Patronage Loyalty, and Conversion in the Religions of the Ancient Mediterranean* (BZNW 130; New York: Walter de Gruyter, 2004), 85.

benefits given. The same cooperative dance is found in the lives of Jacob and Moses. Jacob's piety (εὐσεβείᾳ) toward God received the recompense (ἀμοιβῆς) that his righteousness (δίκαιον) deserved (cf. *A.J.* 2.196). Josephus makes clear in the previous narrative that God had already been Jacob's protector (παραστάτην) and helper (βοηθὸν) to whom Jacob owed his allegiance (*A.J.* 2.172). Moses also serves as a paradigm of this harmonious cooperation between God and those faithful to Him. In *A.J.* 4.315-19, Josephus narrates Moses' final speech to the Israelites. Moses sets forth himself as the appropriate example of the obligations a beneficiary fulfills in the dance of reciprocity. He says that he renders "thanks (χάριν) to Him" for His benefits and that he renders "this return that is His due (ὀφειλυμένην ἀμοιβὴν ἀποδιδοὺς)...leaving in [the Israelites'] memory the thought that it behooves [them] to revere and honour Him and to observe His laws". The implication is that as the Israelites continue to gratefully honor God for His past benefits, God will continue to bless the Israelites for their unswerving obedience to His commands, and so the dance comes full circle again.[55]

Josephus also narrates the three major forms of honor that a beneficiary often gave his or her benefactor, especially his or her divine benefactor: obedience, sacrifice, and hymns of praise. (1) In many of the examples just cited, Josephus put the primary emphasis upon obedience to God's laws as the way to honor God. (2) Though obedience is the primary form for honoring God, Josephus also depicts the Israelites offering sacrifices of thanksgiving as a form of honor for God's beneficial deliverances (cf. *A.J.* 2.269). For example, the Israelites "offered sacrifices in return for (ἠμείβοντο) God's care for their welfare" by providing them water in the desert (*A.J.* 3.38). Joshua "offered sacrifices of thanksgiving (χαριστηρίους) to God for these mercies" (*A.J.* 5.114). (3) Finally, Josephus mentions hymns being sung to God "as the author and dispenser of [the Israelites'] salvation and their liberty" from bondage in Egypt (*A.J.* 3.64).

A final point needs to be made about Josephus's portrayal of the cooperation characteristic of reciprocity. Josephus negates the element of need from God's side of the equation that the cooperation of reciprocity might imply. In Solomon's prayer at the dedication of the temple, Josephus has Solomon confess, "Not by deeds is it possible for men to return thanks to God (ἀποδοῦναι...χάριν) for the benefits they have received, for Deity stands in need of nothing and is above any such recompense (ἀμοιβῆς)."[56]

---

55 Spilsbury ("Josephus," 248) states that for Josephus piety is linked with observance of the law and leads to divine favor. See also Spilsbury, "God and Israel in Josephus," 187.

56 "In need of nothing (ἀπροσδεὶς)" is a Stoic attribute of the deity (see n. d with this passage in the LCL edition by Thackeray).

This passage, however, does not suggest that whatever one does in honor of God is vain. Such an argument finds no place in Josephus's theology or the relational bond Josephus depicts between God and Israel. Such an argument would undercut the very relationship sustained by reciprocity. On the other hand, Josephus would seem to make a mutually beneficial relationship beneficial to one party only. If one cannot repay one's benefactor then it seems as though the dance of reciprocity is aborted. Though God has no needs for which humans may provide, that does not argue that God does not value the relationship itself and what their offerings and actions symbolize in His beneficiaries. Ideally, *what* is exchanged in ancient reciprocity relationships is penultimate to *who* exchanges. Though God has no needs, that does not undo the possibility of a relationship with Him or the fact that there are obligations that are appropriate to that relationship. The obligations of a reciprocity relationship have already been discussed. Despite whether there is need in the partner or not, to fail to uphold one's obligations in that relationship is effectively to dissolve that relationship. Josephus, therefore, does not end Solomon's prayer in the above manner but has Solomon continue, "But with that (gift of speech), O Lord, through which we have been made by Thee superior to other creatures, we cannot but praise Thy greatness and give thanks for Thy kindness to our house and the Hebrew people, for with what other thing is it fitting to appease Thee when wrathful, and when ill disposed, to make Thee gracious than with our voice" (*A.J.* 8.111). The praise and honor that come from God's people is what is valuable and effective with God. Need might strengthen the bond established by means of reciprocity, but it is not a necessary feature of such a relationship. If we hold that, for Josephus, God values the relationship, then God will be interested in how that relationship is carried out without suggesting that God needs what humans can repay Him.

Finally, the cooperative nature of the reciprocity bond brings to light the contingency of relationship. Each party relies upon the other to fulfill his or her obligations. We will briefly look at how Josephus portrays the mutual dependence that is between God and Israel.

MUTUAL DEPENDENCE

Josephus at times expresses the mutual dependence of the reciprocity relationship between God and Israel by the "testing" motif.[57] In the "binding of Isaac" episode, after God has stopped Abraham from sacrificing Isaac, Josephus writes that God "wished but to test [Abraham's] soul and see whether even such orders would find him obedient" (*A.J.* 1.233). Josephus here uses a fourth class conditional protasis (εἰ + the optative [ὑποκούοι]) that highlights the contingency in the test that was

---

57 In this regard, Josephus appear to follow closely the biblical narrative and language of testing, cf. Gen 22:1, 12; Exod 20:20; Deut 8:2, 16.

given to Abraham. This syntactical construct gives the semblance of risk that arises from the voluntary nature of mutual dependence. We also find the testing motif in a wilderness episode when the Israelites are in need of water but cannot find a sufficient source to provide for them. They rise up against Moses who admonishes them that "it was probably to test their manhood (ἀρετὴν), to see what fortitude they possessed, what memory of past services, and whether their thoughts would not revert to those services because of the troubles now in their path, that He was exercising them with the trails of the moment" (*A.J.* 3.15). Again, we have another fourth class conditional statement regarding the actions Israel might have taken in the face of the test. Moreover, this episode highlights the mutual dependence between both God and Israel. Would God prove reliable to provide for Israel and would Israel prove faithful to remember God's past faithfulness and so remain steadfast in their commitment to God?

CONCLUSION

Josephus serves as a significant representative in Middle Judaism who conceptualizes the relationship between God and Israel as a reciprocity relationship. We have seen all the characteristic elements of reciprocity present in Josephus's paraphrase of the biblical material that we found in the Greco-Roman context and in the tetrateuchal narrative and Deuteronomistic History. In the following section, I will demonstrate in a limited way that Josephus was not the sole representative of this conception of the divine-human relationship in Middle Judaism. This stream ebbs and flows in the Middle Judaic literature preceding Josephus. Several examples suffice.

Reciprocity and Other Streams of Middle Judaism

We find the language of repayment for honor shown God in Sirach 35:12-13:

> Give to the Most High as he has given to you...
> For the Lord is the one who repays (ἀνταποδιδούς)
>   and he will repay you sevenfold.[58]

In the Wisdom of Solomon, we see the reciprocity motifs of forgetting benefits and ingratitude used to characterize infidelity. In Wis 14:26, forgetfulness of God's favors (χάριτος ἀμνηστία) leads to idolatry. Likewise, there is no hope for the ungrateful (ἀχαρίστου) who do not

---

58 The Greek text of Sirach also uses the typical expressions and understanding of reciprocity in the ancient Mediterranean world to portray relationships among humans, cf. 3:31 and 20:16.

acknowledge God's blessings (Wis 16:29). On the other hand, benefits are bestowed on those who remain faithful to God. For the eunuch who obeys the Lord, "special favor (χάρις) will be shown to him for his faithfulness (πίστεως)" (Wis 3:14). Further, Wis 16:24 says, "Creations relaxes as a benefit (εἰς εὐεργεσίαν) for those who trust God."

Fourth Ezra also employs a reciprocity motif of forgetting benefits as infidelity. In 4 Ezra 9:10-11, the ungodly are described as those who did not acknowledge God while they lived even though they had received God's benefits (*beneficia*).[59] The judgment in 4 Ezra 8:59-60 is that "those who were created have defiled the name of him who made them, and have been ungrateful to him who prepared life for them now".

Likewise, 4 Maccabees utilizes the reciprocity motifs, remembering benefits for fidelity and ingratitude for infidelity. In 4 Macc 16:8-19, the mother exhorts her son who is facing martyrdom, "Remember that it is through God you have had a share in this world and enjoyed life, and therefore, you ought to endure any suffering for the sake of God." Later, the mother's seventh son reprimands Antiochus by accusing Antiochus of heinous ingratitude towards God by killing God's servants. The son exclaims, "You profane tyrant, most impious of all the wicked, since you have received good things and also you kingdom from God, were you not ashamed to murder his servants" (12:11). In fact, Antiochus enters into a reciprocity contest for the loyalty of the seven Jewish brothers he has taken captive. Antiochus offers benefits to the sons who will avoid extreme torture if they would only take his offer and become loyal to him. He attempts to persuade them saying, "I can be a benefactor (ἐρεργετεῖν) to those who obey me" (8:6). But as each son chooses fidelity to God over Antiochus's generosity, Antiochus is described as becoming infuriated over the sons' ingratitude (ἀχαρίστων; 9:10).

First through Third Maccabees are full of the language of benefaction and reciprocity, especially and almost exclusively at the political level. In 1 Maccabees, the Jewish political leaders are routinely referred to as the "friends (φίλος)" of the Seleucid rulers or Roman ally.[60] Friendship was the euphemistic way of referring to a patron-client or benefactor-beneficiary relationship. The Jews honor Simon in the typical way a benefactor would be honored. They dedicate an honorific inscription to him that is publicly displayed and outlines the honors the people bestow upon him for his leadership, heroics, and benefits (14:4-46).[61] The high priest, Onias, in 2 Macc 4:2 is referred to as the benefactor (εὐεργέτην) of

---

59 See G. H. Box, *The Ezra-Apocalypse* (London: Sir Isaac Pitman & Sons, 1912), 204 n. c.
60 Cf. 1 Macc 2:18; 8:1, 12; 10:18-20
61 Cf. Edgar Krentz, "The Honorary Decree for Simon the Maccabee," in *Hellenism in the Land of Israel*, 146-53.

Jerusalem. In 2 Macc 5:16, there might be an implicit approbation of God as the divine benefactor and the reciprocity that often went along with such affirmation. The author tells us that Antiochus took votive offerings (ἀνατοθέντα) from the temple which were given by kings and made to enhance the glory and honor of the place. Votive offerings in temples were a typical expression of gratitude for benefits received by a suppliant in the ancient world, and these offerings were often dedicated to ensure future benefits. Finally, 3 Maccabees portrays the infidelity of the falsely accused Jews toward the ruler Ptolemy as ingratitude in light of Ptolemy's beneficence toward the Jews (cf. 3:15-24).[62]

The Apostle Paul provides us with our final example from the Middle Judaic milieu.[63] In Rom 1:18-23, he conceptualizes the relationship between the creator and humanity in terms of the reciprocity that sustained the benefactor-beneficiary bond. In this short passage, Paul draws upon the reciprocity relationship of the benefactor-beneficiary in three primary ways. First, Paul sets forth God (θεός)[64] as the creator, who has made all things and, by implication, who gives all that is necessary for the sustaining and enjoyment of His creation (v. 20). Thus, God is the benefactor of all creation.[65] The gods were commonly acknowledged in the ancient

---

62 In light of this literature, Zeba Crook's (*Reconceptualizing Conversion*, 79) bold generalization is erroneous: "It can be stated categorically from the outset that pre-common era Palestine did not have a patron-client or benefactor-client social structure." E. S. Gruen's (*Heritage and Hellenism: The Reinvention of Jewish Tradition* [Berkeley: University of California Press, 1998], 1-40) description of the Hasmonaean period in Jewish history demonstrates that the Hasmonaean-Seleucid, interstate relationship was conducted along the lines of a benefactor-beneficiary relationship. Furthermore, precommon era Palestine was not a culturally isolated phenomenon. Hellenism had made significant inroads into Palestine. The classic defense of the aforementioned assertion is still Martin Hengel, *Judaism and Hellenism* (2 vols.; Philadelphia: Fortress Press 1974).

63 First-century Christian messianists like Paul are included in the Middle Judaic milieu. Christianity was a competing Jewish sect that was multinational with its own interpretation of the Jewish scriptures. See Boccaccini, *Middle Judaism*, 20-21, 23-24. In Acts, Christianity is routinely understood as a sect of Judaism by the early Christians (see Acts 3), by Paul (see Acts 21-22; 24:10-20; 26:1-8), by other Jewish sects (see Acts 24:1-9; 28:17-22), by Roman officials (see 18:12-17; 25:18-19), and by the narrator himself (Acts 15:1-5). Furthermore, the Pauline mission is the narrowest sphere of the religious heritage for Hebrews if one accepts that Hebrews, though not written by Paul himself, comes out of the Pauline circle (cf. William L. Lane, *Hebrews 1-8* [WBC 47a; Nashville: Thomas Nelson Publishers, 1991], xlix).

64 Philo uses the term θεός as synonymous with εὐεργέτης in his writings, cf. *Sobr.* 55; *Leg.* 1.95-96.

65 Klaus Haacker, *Der Brief de Paulus an die Römer* (THKNT 6; Leipzig: Evangelische Verlagsanstalt, 1999), 50. See also Harrison, *Paul's Language of Grace*, 212-19.

Mediterranean world as the chief benefactors because of their superior power and gifts.⁶⁶ Second, Paul uses the typical expressions and responses the beneficiary owes his or her benefactor in verse 21. Humanity is to honor (ἐδόξασαν)⁶⁷ and thank (ηὐχαρίστησαν) God as their divine benefactor. As we have already come to expect from ancient asymmetrical reciprocity relationships, benefits were given by the superior in exchange for honor from the inferior. Moreover, the fidelity sought through giving benefits was sustained by the feeling of indebted gratitude. Thus, Paul portrays human infidelity as ingratitude to their divine benefactor. In verse 21, Paul asserts, "They did not honor or thank God as God" and goes on to say that they gave the honor that belonged to God to their idols (vv. 22-23). Third, as a consequence of ingratitude, dishonor of the superior by the inferior in asymmetrical reciprocity relationships often precipitated the indignation and wrath of the superior.⁶⁸ Thus, Paul opens this section of his letter with a declaration of God's wrath and indignation against humanity's ingratitude and dishonor (v. 18). In Rom 1:18-23, Paul is addressing his Gentile Christian auditors in a manner that would have resonated with them—God the divine benefactor has been dishonored by human ingratitude and disloyalty.⁶⁹

Finally, we will take up one last significant example that understands

---

66 Cf. Seneca, *Ben.* 2.29.5-30.2; 7.31.2; Philo, *Spec.* 1.152; *Legat.* 118; *Ebr.* 117-19; *Congr.* 96.

67 We find δόξα alongside τιμή in some honorific inscriptions. For example, see C. Bradford Welles, *Royal Correspondence in the Hellenistic Period: A Study in Greek Epigraphy* (Chicago: Ares Publishers, Inc., 1974), §52, line 37 (εἰς τιμὴν καὶ δόξαν [cf §44, lines 19-20]). See also, Harrison, *Paul's Language of Grace*, 215-17.

68 We have already observed in the previous chapter such responses of indignation towards ingratitude in ancient reciprocity relationships. In the *Iliad*, Agamemnon's ingratitude towards Achilles which dishonors Achilles results in Achilles's wrath against Agamemnon. Achilles will not be satisfied until his honor is restored. Odysseus slays the suitors who are plundering his property because of their ingratitude toward him who was their beneficent ruler in Ithaca. In Pindars's ode, the gods punish Ixion for his arrogant ingratitude. In Polybius's *History*, the Romans are quick to execute retribution on those who prove ungrateful and disloyal. See also Aristotle, *Rhet.* 2.2.8; Plutarch, *Mor.* 548-68; Aulus Gellius, *Noctes atticae* 7.14.2-4; and Philo, *Opif.* 169, who declares humanity would be fittingly destroyed because of their ingratitude towards God, their benefactor. See also Harrison, *Paul's Language of Grace*, 53, 56.

69 C. E. B. Cranfield, *A Critical and Exegetical Commentary on The Epistle to the Romans* (ICC; Edinburgh: T. & T. Clark, 1975; repr., 1998), 1:117, demonstrates how easily the language of reciprocity lends itself to an exegesis of this passage: "They ought to have recognized their *indebtedness* to His goodness and *generosity*, to have recognized him as the source of all good things enjoyed, and so to have been *grateful* to Him for His *benefits*," (emphasis mine).

reciprocity to be the divine-human dynamic for securing faithfulness. Rabbinic Judaism shows how reciprocity continued beyond Middle Judaism as a way of conceptualizing the divine-human relationship.

Rabbinic Judaism and Reciprocity

Among the teachings of the rabbis, the *Mekhilta* of R. Ishmael provides an excellent illustration of reciprocity as the foundational dynamic of the relationship between God and Israel.[70] In Bahodesh 5, the opening question concerns why the "Ten Commandments were not stated at the very beginning of the Torah" but followed the introductory statement, "[And God spoke all these words, saying,] 'I am the Lord your God, [who brought you out of the land of Egypt, out of the house of bondage.]'"[71] The following illustration and explanation is supplied:

> The matter may be compared to the case of king who came into a city. He said to the people, "May I rule over you?"
> They said to him, "Have you done us any good, that you should rule over us?"
> What did he then do? He built a wall for them, brought water for them, fought their battles.
> The he said to them, "May I rule over you?"
> They said to him, "Yes, indeed."
> So the Omnipresent brought the Israelites out of Egypt, divided the sea for them, brought manna down for them, brought up the well for them, provided quail for them, made war for them against Amalek.
> Then he said to them, "May I rule over you?"
> They said to him, "Yes, indeed?"

In this passage all the previously delineated characteristics of reciprocity are present. God's benefits towards the Israelites secured their grateful fidelity to Him as their king.[72] We might also speculate that God was also understood to be gratefully loyal to Israel since they chose God as their king, for later in the Bahodesh 5, we are told that all other nations rejected God's offer to rule over them except Israel.[73] We also see in this brief

---

70 Rabbi Ishmael allegedly headed one of the two great rabbinic schools in the second century CE. See Robert Goldenberg, "Ishmael, Rabbi," *ABD* 3:513.
71 All quotations from the *Mekhilta* are from Jacob Neusner, *Mekhilta according to Rabbi Ishmael: An Analytical Translation* (vol. 2; BJS 154; Atlanta: Scholars Press, 1988).
72 Cf. E. P. Sanders, *Paul and Palestinian Judaism: A Comparison of Patterns of Religion* (Philadelphia: Fortress Press, 1977), 86.
73 Other reasons cited in the rabbinic literature for God's election of Israel are the merit of the patriarchs, the merit of the Exodus generation, or the anticipation of future obedience. Sometimes election is based upon God's own will and for the

passage the element of cooperation characteristic of reciprocity. The Israelites receive God's benefits and care while God is given the honor of their obedience. Further, the element of mutual dependence is exemplified in the portrayal of God asking for permission to rule over the Israelites, having first demonstrated that He will care for them as their ruler. Mutual dependence also required Israel to trust God. E. P. Sanders notes that the rabbinic concern for Israel to obey the laws God issued reflects reliance upon God's fidelity to the covenant.[74] We also witness mutual dependence in the oath-taking between God and Israel. When the Israelites received the Torah, they were said to have been "unanimous in receiving the dominion of God with a whole heart. And not only so, but they exacted pledges from one another". This statement appears to affirm that both God and Israel swore oaths to one another to formally confirm their commitment and fidelity toward one another—a procedure, as we have seen, that is meant to alleviate the feeling of risk involved in such mutual reliance and alliance.

Now, having traced a stream of Judaism that conceptualizes the divine-human relational dynamic in terms of reciprocity, we next will examine what consequences optimistic and pessimistic anthropological assumptions had upon the perceived success of the ability of reciprocity to secure fidelity to God.

Consequences of Anthropological Assumptions in the Jewish Milieu

The success of reciprocity to secure fidelity to God has two opposite, perceived consequences in the Jewish context depending on what anthropology is assumed, whether optimistic or pessimistic. This section, therefore, will be organized under two major headings: (1) the consequence of an optimistic anthropology and (2) the consequence of a pessimistic anthropology.

Consequence of an Optimistic Anthropological Assumption

First, an optimistic anthropology undergirds the belief that reciprocity is able to secure the possibility of fidelity in the divine-human relationship. Humans, in general, are able to be gratefully indebted and thus persevere in honoring God through obedience to the covenant stipulations. Such an assumption, as we will see, is found in both Josephus and rabbinic Judaism. Further, each represents the realization of fidelity via reciprocity in key individuals and generations of Jewish history.

---

sake of His name, cf. Sanders, *Palestinian Judaism*, 87-88.
74 Sanders, *Palestinian Judaism*, 235.

POSSIBILITY OF SUCCESS

Josephus principally indicates his optimistic anthropological orientation through the affirmation that God's benefits are secured by the worthy. Worthiness is based on a person's virtue. A second expression of this optimism regards virtue as a person's own achievement, since God has granted humanity free-will. First, Josephus uses the typical concept of "grace for the worthy" that we observed in Greco-Roman reciprocity contexts. "Grace for the worthy" is prevalent among the key personalities in the opening narrative of *Antiquitates judaicae*. In *A.J.* 1.75, God is said to have loved Noah "for his righteousness". Later, in 1.96-100, Noah entreats God on the basis of his righteousness not to destroy the world again.[75] Likewise, the worthy virtue of the patriarchs is portrayed as securing God's favor. Abraham is commended by God for his virtue (ἀρετήν) and given the gift (χάρις) of a son because of Abraham's worthy (ἄξιόν) deed in rescuing Lot (cf. *A.J.* 1.183). Josephus characterizes Abraham as "a man in every virtue (ἀρετήν) supreme, who received from God the due (ἀξίως) meed of honor for his zeal (σπουδῆς) in His service" (*A.J.* 1.256). Josephus also describes Isaac as "a man beloved of God and was deemed worthy (ἠξιωμένος) of His special providence" (*A.J.* 1.346). Finally, Jacob is described as "coming behind none of his forefathers in piety (εὐσέβιαν) towards God" and was therefore given the recompense (ἀμοιβῆς) of old age and happiness that "such virtue deserves" (*A.J.* 2.196). Moses is especially rendered as the supreme bearer of virtue and worthy of God's favor not only for himself but for Israel as well. In *A.J.* 3.63-65, the Israelites are blessed by God because of the virtue (ἀρετήν) of Moses. Further, Moses is eulogized along with God with hymns and encomiums. In fact, unashamedly, Josephus recounts that Moses thought himself to be worthy of the honor (τῆς τιμῆς ἄξιον) of becoming the high priest because he labored for the salvation of the Hebrews (cf. *A.J.* 3.190). The worthiness of Noah, the patriarchs, or Moses was not unique to them alone, for the Israelites are told, in a statement of gnomic quality, that God "alone has power to give these good things to those who merit them (τοὺς ἀξίοις)" (*A.J.* 4.180).

Such statements of "worthiness" because of the attainment of virtue and the demonstration of piety assumes that humans are capable of such achievements, and this "worthiness" renders them praiseworthy before others and God. This leads to the second point. Josephus contains some explicit, though limited, statements concerning his affirmation of the inherent ability of humans to be virtuous. In *A.J.* 1.154-57, Abraham comes

---

75 This is an interpretive expansion of the biblical text. Josephus may have assumed that the pleasing odor of the sacrifice was due to Noah's righteousness, but nowhere in the text is Noah said to plead with God to secure God's promise not to destroy the world again.

to his knowledge of the one God through his own contemplation of creation and his superior reasoning. Moses was said to be directly translated to God "because of his inherent virtue (διὰ τὴν προσοῦσαν ἀρετήν)" (*A.J.* 3.97). In *A.J.* 3.102, The Hebrews, when they provided provisions for constructing the tabernacle, "failed not to show all the zeal of which they were capable (τῆς κατὰ δύναμιν αὐτῶν σπουδῆς)". One of the most explicit statements Josephus makes about inherent human ability comes in his description of the three major sects or philosophies of Judaism concerning their views on divine sovereignty and human freedom. The description of the Pharisaic position is agreeable to the synergism of reciprocity and the optimistic anthropology such synergism requires. In one place Josephus writes:

> Now at the time there were three schools of thought among the Jews, which held different opinions concerning human affairs....As for the Pharisees, they say that certain events are the work of Fate, but not all; as to other events, it depends upon ourselves whether they shall take place or not. The sect of the Essenes, however, declares that Fate is a mistress of all things, and that nothing befalls men unless it be in accordance with her decree. But the Sadducees do away with Fate, holding that there is no such thing and that human actions are not achieved in accordance with her decree, but that all things lie within our own power.[76] (*A.J.* 13.171-73)

Elsewhere we read,

> The Pharisees...though they postulate that everything is brought about by Fate, still they do not deprive human will of the pursuit of what is in man's powers, since it was God's good pleasure that there should be a fusion and that the will of man with his virtue and vice should be admitted to the council-chamber of Fate....The doctrine of the Essenes is wont to leave everything in the hands of God. (*A.J.* 18.11-13, 18)

Josephus, even though he speaks approvingly of the Essenes (because of their manner of living, not their theology), is sympathetic to the Pharisee position. There are two pieces of evidence for such an assertion. His biblical paraphrase seems to affirm as much. For instance, God delivers Israel from bondage, but that deliverance does not neglect the piety of the Hebrews towards Him (cf. *A.J.* 2.212). Thus, virtue is "admitted to the council-chamber of Fate". Also, in *Vita* 12, Josephus identifies himself with the sect of the Pharisees over other Jewish sects. We may, therefore,

---

76 Cf. Gerhard Maier, *Mensch und freier Wille: Nach den jüdischen Religionsparteien zwischen Ben Sira und Paulus* (WUNT 12; Tübingen: Mohr-Siebeck, 1971), who attempts to validate the veracity of Josephus's description of the theology of these three Jewish sects.

assume that Josephus's uncritical description of this Pharisaic theology in his works is also indicative of his own position. Therefore, for the Pharisees according to Josephus and for Josephus himself, there is free-will for humans—a free-will that bequeaths to humans the inalienable ability to choose between virtue and vice and thus influence the divine will. Such an optimistic anthropology befits the cooperative, mutual dependence characteristic of ancient reciprocity. It enables the belief in the possibility for reciprocity to procure faithfulness to the relationship.

Again, Josephus is not alone in the Middle Judaic milieu that precedes him in affirming reciprocity as the divine-human dynamic along with the optimistic anthropology such a dynamic requires for its success. Several examples suffice. Sirach 15:14-17 resembles Josephus's description of the Pharisaic position:

> It was he who created humankind in the beginning,
>   and he left them in the power of their own free choice
> If you choose, you can keep the commandments,
>   and to act faithfully is a matter of your own choice.

Fourth Ezra would seem to have a pessimistic anthropology since so few are believed to be finally saved (cf. 7:45-48, 140; 8:3). Fourth Ezra may be more accurately described as having a tempered optimism. According to the definition of what constitutes an optimistic anthropology in the previous chapter, the author of 4 Ezra believes that human beings have the capability to do what they ought. The righteous themselves overcome their native evil inclination and so achieve final salvation. For instance, seven orders of rest await those who have kept the law. The first order belongs to those who "have striven with great effort to overcome the evil thought that was formed with them, so that it might not lead them astray from life into death" (7:92). On the other hand, those who perish "when they had the opportunity to choose, they despised the Most High....For the Most High did not intend that anyone should be destroyed for those themselves have defiled the name of him who made them and have been ungrateful to him who prepared life for them now" (8:56-60). Finally, 4 Maccabees has an explicit optimistic anthropology. Fourth Maccabees is a philosophical treatise written to demonstrate that "devout reason is over the emotions" (1:1). The author goes on to affirm that duty implies ability. Citing the condemnation of anger in Scripture, "[C]ursed be their anger", the author says, "[F]or if reason could not control anger, he would not have spoken thus" (2:19-20). Furthermore, all humans have this ability since all were created with reason to rule the passions (cf. 2:21-23; 7:18). The optimistic anthropology of 4 Maccabees is also implicitly expressed in the two encomiums composed for two Jewish martyrs, Eleazar and the mother of her seven martyred sons (cf. 7:6-15; 17:2-10). They and not God are praised for their faithfulness in the face of torture and death because they are examples of reason ruling the passions in the most extreme context.

Rabbinic Judaism will provide the final example, this one from a later period, that grounds the possibility of successful reciprocity relationships upon an optimistic anthropological assumption.

Rabbinic Judaism evidences its optimism in human ability to honor God for His benefits in three primary ways: (1) it employs the common reciprocity motif of "grace for the worthy", (2) it holds that humanity is given free-will creating the possibility and ability to choose good or evil equally, and (3) it lacks a doctrine of original sin. In regards to "grace for the worthy", in *Mek.* Bahodesh 5, Israel demonstrates its worthiness because, though every other nation rejected God and the Torah, Israel chose God for their king and the Torah as their rule of life. In this way, Israel becomes praiseworthy before God and the nations. In *Sifre Deut* 311, God chooses Israel because God foresaw that Israel would be worthy on account of their future obedience.[77]

Secondly, the rabbinic literature affirms free-will for humanity. Free-will, here, does not simply mean that a persons feels that he or she makes his or her own choices, but as Timo Laato states, "On the basis of free will man has not only the capacity always to *choose* good instead of evil. He has also the power always to *do* good."[78] Rabbi Hanina is quoted in *b. Ber.* 33b as saying, "Everything is in the hands of heaven except the fear of heaven. For its is said, 'And now, Israel, what does the Lord, your God, require of you but to fear.'"[79] Such a statement implies that what humans *should* do they also *can* do. God requires humans to fear Him which humans are intrinsically able to do and thus fulfill the commandment. George Foot Moore has argued that this anthropological viewpoint is characteristic of early rabbinic thought as a whole. He locates early rabbinic Judaism in the stream of Sirach, *Psalms of Solomon*, and 4 Ezra that hold to the belief in human religious and moral self-determination.[80] Moore concludes that for early rabbinic Judaism, God determines all that befalls humans but not whether they will be pious or impious, and concerning this moral self-determination within rabbinic Judaism, "there is [sic] no dissentient

---

77 This conclusion contradicts what we find in the Deut 31-32 where God foretells through Moses to Israel their future apostasy from the covenant.
78 Timo Laato, *Paul and Judaism: An Anthropological Approach* (trans. T. McElwain; South Florida Studies in the History of Judaism 115; Atlanta: Scholars Press, 1995), 73.
79 See also *b. Meg.* 25a.; *m. Avot* 3:15.
80 George Foot Moore, *Judaism in the First Centuries of the Christian Era: The Age of the Tannaim* (Cambridge: Harvard Univesity Press, 1927; repr. Peabody: Hendrickson, 1997), 455-56. Cf. George Foot Moore, "Fate and Free Will in the Jewish Philosophies according to Josephus," *HTR* 22 (1929): 381-82.

voices".[81] This intrinsic moral capability of humans is further supported by the rabbinic teaching of the two impulses that God placed within humans. Moore describes the impulses as "native" to humans. He points to the teaching of Rabbi Simeon ben Lakish who teaches that the evil impulse is overcome by persons stirring up within themselves their good impulse.[82] In sum, the rabbinic understanding of free-will gives expression to its optimistic anthropological assumption. Humans have the intrinsic capability to do what they ought. Human nature has not been impaired to render people incapable of enduring, grateful piety toward God. This leads to our final proof, namely the the lack of any notion of original sin in early rabbinic Judaism attests to its optimistic anthropology.

Tannaitic rabbinic Judaism had no doctrine of original sin. What I mean here by original sin is not the full-blown doctrine that one finds in such places as the *Westminster Confession* or even Augustine's statement on the topic. What is meant here is that the moral ability of human nature was somehow inalterably corrupted and made impotent by the sin of Adam and Eve or, in some streams of Judaism, the Watchers. Sanders categorically states that the rabbis had no such doctrine of original sin: "Yet it is important to note that the Rabbis did not have a doctrine of original sin or of the essential sinfulness of each man in the Christian sense."[83] Concordantly, Moore writes, "[T]here is no notion [in early rabbinic Judaism] that the original constitution of Adam underwent any change in consequence of the fall, so that he transmitted to his descendents a vitiated nature in which...the will to do good was enfeebled or wholly impotent."[84] The lack of such doctrine follows from the affirmation of human free-will and the capability of remaining faithful to God. To introduce a notion of human depravity would introduce a pessimistic anthropology and endanger the whole rabbinic conception of the divine-human dynamic. Fidelity could no longer be secured through cooperative, mutual dependence and the persistent feeling of indebted gratitude that is characteristic of ancient reciprocity relationships and the rabbinic divine-human relationship in particular.

REALIZATION OF FIDELITY

In each of the examples cited above from the Middle Judaic milieu and

---

81 Moore, *Judaism*, 456. This rabbinic teaching sounds similar to the late Stoic position described in the previous chapter. Humans have no control over what Fortune allots to them. The only thing that is under human control is their control over their inward dispositions.
82 Moore, *Judaism*, 490-91. See pp. 480-93 for a full discussion of the teaching of the two impulses in early rabbinic Judaism.
83 Sanders, *Paul and Palestinian Judaism*, 114.
84 Moore, *Judaism*, 479.

beyond, an optimistic anthropology undergirds the potential of the dynamic of reciprocity to secure fidelity in the divine-human relationship. Not only does their optimistic anthropology indicate the potential of success, but also they see the realization of that success in their recounting of the history of God's people. We have already cited from Josephus's biblical paraphrase that Noah, the patriarchs, and supremely Moses were all commended for their fidelity to God, their benefactor. They all persevered in gratitude toward God. They realized the ideals of reciprocity in the divine-human relationship and provided good hope to future generations of achieving such success. Spilsbury observes that another benefit for Josephus of translating the covenant into patron-client terms "was the opportunity to praise both the contemporary Jews and their forebears for being of such caliber as to secure the protection of the most powerful patron in the universe".[85] In 4 Ezra, Ezra represents one who is among the "saved" because of his faithfulness. He is repeatedly told not to count or compare himself to the unrighteous by his angelic interpreter (cf. 7:77; 8:47). In fact, even when he does confess wrongly his human frailty and unrighteousness, he is commended for exhibiting the praiseworthy virtue of humility (cf. 8:48-49). And finally, 4 Maccabees sets forth the Jewish martyrs of the Antiochene persecution as the ultimate realization of fidelity to God via reciprocity. Eleazar, the seven brothers, and their mother are all brutally tortured but remain faithful to God through unimaginable bodily agony.

In conclusion, we find the same optimistic anthropological assumption undergirding the belief in the potential of reciprocity to secure fidelity in the Jewish milieu that we found in the Greco-Roman context. We do find, however, another stream in the Jewish milieu which held a pessimistic anthropological assumption. We now will consider the consequence such an assumption had upon the belief in reciprocity's potential to secure fidelity to God.

Consequence of a Pessimistic Anthropological Assumption

In short, a pessimistic anthropology accompanied the belief that Israel had failed to gratefully honor God or, in other words, failed to keep the covenant because they were unable to do so. Further, they would continue to fail as long as reciprocity is the foundational dynamic of the relationship. Such a perspective is found among some exilic and postexilic documents. In this section we will explore this perspective in the Tetrateuch and Deuteronomic History, Jeremiah, Ezekiel, and the Dead Sea Scrolls of the Qumran community. We will also examine this perspective in Paul's letter to the Romans as it relates to humanity's reciprocity relationship with God, the creator. We will also find that a common solution to this problem is set

---

85 Spilsbury, "Josephus," 252.

forth among these documents. Instead of reciprocity, divine enablement and inward transformation will be the relational dynamic that secures the fidelity of God's people. God's power will transform the corrupted human nature so that Israel may honor and obey God from their heart. Furthermore, gratitude functions differently in a context of divine enablement and human transformation than in a reciprocity context. Gratitude, instead of securing fidelity through the feeling of indebtedness, honors God and combats self-exaltation by expressing the appropriate humility for a humanity that is frail and corrupted.

FAILURE OF THE RELATIONSHIP

The tetrateuchal narrative points to a pessimistic anthropological assumption in two primary ways. First, it represents Israel as incorrigibly rebellious against Yahweh in the wilderness. Second, the very beginning of the narrative, after the fall of Adam and Eve, points to the indomitable corruption of the human nature. In Exodus and Numbers of the tetrateuchal narrative, we find the repeated portrayal of Israel's failure to keep the covenant in spite of their miraculous deliverance by God from Egyptian bondage and the repeated benefits God bestowed upon them in their wilderness wanderings. In fact, Israel's fidelity was shortlived. Forty days had not even lapsed after Israel swore fealty to Yahweh at Sinai and Israel's request of Aaron to make for them gods to worship (cf. Exod 32:1-6). Israel's rebellions are such a central feature of the tetrateuchal narrative in Exodus and Numbers that the narrative can be organized as a chiasm around the various rebellions in the desert:[86]

  A Idolatry: the Golden Calf (Exod 32:1-35)[87]
     B Murmuring (Num 11:1-3)
        C Desire for meat (Num 11:4-35)
           D Miriam and Aaron (Num 12:1-15)
               E Failure to enter Canaan (Num 13-14)

---

[86] Philip J. Budd observes a chiastic pattern in the rebellions in the wilderness, *Numbers* (WBC 5; Waco: Word Books, 1983), 162. My organization is a modification of his observation.

[87] To begin characterizing the episodes of rebellion after the covenant at Sinai is fitting because in the narrative plot that spans from Exodus to Numbers the people can be said to rebel against Yahweh only after they have ratified the covenant with the Lord and pledged loyalty and obedience to Him. This observation is confirmed by the fact that in Exod 15-17, prior to the ratification of the covenant, the murmurings of Israel come to positive conclusions. This observation is also further evidence of the bilateral, cooperative nature of the Sinai covenant. Cf. W. H. Bellinger, Jr., *Leviticus and Numbers* (NIBCOT; Peabody: Hendrickson, 2001), 220 and Francis Watson, *Paul and the Hermeneutics of Faith* (New York: T & T Clark, 2004), 366, 368.

D´ Korah (Num 16:1-50)
C´ Quarrel about water (Num 20:1-13)
B´ Murmuring (Num 21:4-9)
A´ Idolatry: Baal-Peor (Num 25:1-9)

Such a narrative portrayal argues for a pessimistic anthropological assumption.[88] The bestowing of repeated benefits upon the Israelites was not enough to sustain their feeling of indebted gratitude and thus their loyalty.

Such an assumption is further corroborated if we go back to the beginning of the tetrateuchal narrative. There we find that, after the sin of Adam and Eve and their expulsion from the garden, wickedness and rebellion against the creator dominates the human condition (cf. Gen 3–11). Gordon J. Wenhem states that the fall narrative is more than just a paradigmatic story of "everyperson". The sin of Adam and Eve irrevocably altered the human condition from that point forward. Wenhem states, that at least according to the final form of the text, Gen 2 belongs to the retelling of history. Consequently, Adam and Eve are more than just symbols but flesh-and-blood people in the narrative. Their expulsion from the garden was irreversible for all later generations.[89] I would also add that the ground was not only cursed for Adam nor pain in child birth only for Eve. The promise of deliverance from the effects of the serpent's deceit made at the end of the judgments against the serpent had in view Adam's and Eve's progeny. The genealogy of Gen 5 repeatedly asserts that each person died— the penalty for Adam's and Eve's sin in the garden. Finally, there is the "avalanche of sin", as Wenhem puts it, that overtakes humanity in the subsequent narrative. We are told before the flood that "the LORD saw that the wickedness of humankind was great in the earth, and that every inclination of their hearts was only evil continually" (Gen 6:5). God still gives the same assessment of the human condition after the flood (cf. Gen 8:21). Even those who are "righteous" in a qualified sense are significantly flawed. Noah gets drunk after departing from the ark. Abraham lies, Lot commits incest, Jacob deceives, Judah solicits a prostitute, Jacob's sons attempt to kill their brother but end up selling him into slavery, even Moses is forbidden to enter the promised land because of his disobedience. The

---

88 Francis Watson in his book, *Paul and the Hermeneutics of Faith*, argues that Paul reads the tetrateuchal narrative in this manner. He writes, "In moving from Leviticus to Numbers, then, we find that the Law's conditional promise of life is overtaken by the reality of death" (355). Elsewhere, Watson writes that the narrative in Numbers manifests Israel's latent resistance to God (368) and that the "catastrophe" in the wilderness is "paradigmatic of life under the Law" (374).

89 Gordon J. Wenhem, *Genesis 1-15* (WBC 1; Waco: Word Book Publishers, 1987), 90. Cf. Bernard W. Anderson, *From Creation to New Creation: Old Testament Perspectives* (OBT; Minneapolis: Fortress Press, 1994), 92, 128.

tetrateuchal narrative would then seem to point to a corruption of human nature that is not extinguishable even in the few who are righteous.

In the Deuteronomistic History, we find the same pessimistic anthropological assumption expressed in the portrayal of the total history of Israel. In this narrative, the whole history of Israel is characterized as one of rebellion and failure to keep the covenant. In Deut 9:7, Moses declares that Israel has been "rebellious against the LORD from the day [they] came out of the land of Egypt until [they] came to this place [on the verge of taking the promised land]". Moses then goes through a recounting of their rebellions and concludes by saying, "You have been rebellious against the LORD as long as he has known you" (v. 24). In fact, Moses makes clear that God is not giving Israel the promised land because of their righteousness (v. 6). Furthermore, Deuteronomy concludes with a prophetic song that Yahweh teaches Moses as a witness against Israel. This song foretells of Israel's continued infidelity to the covenant once they enter the promised land (cf. Deut 31:14–32:43). Later, when Joshua renews the covenant and Israel declares their intention to obey and honor God, Joshua declares, "You cannot serve the LORD, for his is a holy God. He is a jealous God; he will not forgive your transgressions or your sins. If you forsake the Lord and serve foreign gods, then he will turn and do you harm, and consume you, after having done you good" (Josh 24:19-20). Joshua seems to foretell the inevitability of the curses Israel has called down on themselves seeing that they will not keep the covenant.[90] When we get to the book of Judges, Israel is locked into a pattern of constant infidelity to God who delivers them only for them to rebel again. Even the judges grow more deplorable. Eli's sons, the penultimate judges of Israel, are characterized as utterly corrupt (cf. 1 Sam 2:12). By the time we get to 2 Kngs 17, the author can generally characterize the two kingdoms of Israel as wholly unfaithful to Yahweh, forsaking the covenant to worship other gods. This is the ultimate explanation offered as to why the northern kingdom has been destroyed by the Assyrians and why the southern kingdom goes into exile (cf. vv. 7-20).

Another way the Deuteronomistic History communicates its pessimistic assumption is through the characterization given to Israel of being "stiff-necked" (קְשֵׁה־עֹרֶף / σκληροτράχηλος [LXX]; cf. Deut 9:6, 13; 31:27; 2 Kngs 17:14). Israel is "stiff-necked"—a condition of stubborn

---

90 Trent C. Butler (*Joshua* [WBC 7; Waco: Word Books Publishers, 1983], 275) writes that the inability of Israel to keep the law is connected with the nature of God who is holy (i.e., God demands perfection) and jealous (i.e., God will not ignore Israel's infidelity). Butler states that the situation is bleak because humans are incapable of that type of perfection and subsequently will not avoid the intense gaze and attention of the Deity. Butler points out and contends against the opinion of others who view this saying as an insertion into Joshua's speech in light of the exile. Either view, however, points to a pessimistic anthropological assumption.

rebelliousness that will plague Israel for their entire history. Such a historical characterization of the infidelity God's people would seem to assume a pessimistic anthropology. Not just one instance of infidelity is portrayed but hundreds of years of constant rebellion against Yahweh are set forth. No matter how many benefits God bestows, mercies He extends, and deliverances He enacts, God is unable to secure Israel's gratitude and thereby loyalty.

According to the narratives of the Tetrateuch and Deuteronomistic History, the reciprocity dynamic that undergirds the covenant-treaty between Yahweh and Israel is a defunct means of securing fidelity to Yahweh because the people are "stiff-necked". This pessimistic anthropology, which informs the tetrateuchal and deuteronomistic narrative and gives shape to it, is more explicitly stated in the prophecies of Jeremiah.

The book of Jeremiah relates its pessimistic anthropology by declaring the former covenant relationship to be a failure because of the human condition. First, Jeremiah offers the same explanation as the Deuteronomistic History concerning why Jerusalem is destroyed and Judah goes into exile: "Because they abandoned the covenant of the LORD their God, and worshiped other gods and served them" (22:9; cf. 9:13-16; 11:10-11). Israel has abandoned the reciprocity relationship with Yahweh symbolized by the covenant-treaty established at Sinai. Consequently, Israel has fallen under the curses of the covenant (cf. 32:23).[91] Israel's infidelity is even represented as ingratitude. Jeremiah 3:19-20 portrays God believing that He could secure Israel's faithful gratitude by bestowing benefits upon them only to find them ungrateful and unfaithful:

I [Yahweh] thought
    how I would set you among my children,
and give you a pleasant land,
    the most beautiful heritage of all the nations.
And I thought you would call me, My Father,
    and would not turn from following me.
Instead, as a faithless wife leaves her husband,
    so you have been faithless to me, O house of Israel. (cf. 2:7; 5:7)

But why have God's people proven ungratefully unfaithful? What does Jeremiah assert about the human condition? Jeremiah construes, at times, God's people's infidelity as insanity: "The have forsaken me [Yahweh], and dug out cisterns for themselves, cracked cisterns that can hold no water" (2:13). Additionally, they have "stubborn and rebellious hearts"

---

91 Hillers (*Treaty-curses*, passim; *Covenant*, 138-39) has argued that the curses for infidelity in the prophets assumes a covenant relationship between God and Israel along the lines of ancient Near Eastern suzerainty-vassal treaties.

(5:23). The fear of God is not in them (cf. 2:19; 44:8-9). They have always been "stiff-necked" (cf. 7:24-26). They have "uncircumcised hearts" (9:26; cf. 4:4). Moreover, God's people have been incorrigibly faithless. They have been stiff-necked since they came out of Egypt (cf. 7:24-26). They have been irresistibly drawn to idols. Jeremiah portrays Israel as a donkey in heat drawn to her idol-mates declaring, "It is hopeless for I have loved strangers and after them I will go" (2:25). God's people have such a bent toward unfaithfulness and injustice, that they are described as "skilled in doing evil, but do not know how to do good" (4:22). Moreover, to change their condition is beyond their ability, for Jeremiah writes,

Can Ethiopians change their skin
   or leopards their spots?
Then also you can do good
   who are accustomed to do evil. (13:23)

Such statements indicate that the book of Jeremiah represents a pessimistic anthropology. Further such an anthropology leads to the conclusion that the reciprocity covenant God has established with Israel is defunct, not because God is unreliable but because Israel has been unable to keep it—that is, to persevere in gratitude to God—from the very beginning of the relationship. Moreover, reciprocity, because it relies upon the innate capacities of humans, can never secure fidelity, according to Jeremiah. Now, let us consider the anthropological assumption of another exilic prophet, Ezekiel.

As in Jeremiah, Ezekiel represents the covenant between Israel and God as a failure because of Israel's inability to keep it. In Ezekiel, judgment comes upon Israel because they have "despised the oath, breaking the covenant" (16:59). Israel did not prove faithful to their end of the reciprocity covenant-treaty with God. The reciprocity relational dynamic between God and Israel appears to be assumed in Ezekiel. For instance, Israel's infidelity is equated to ingratitude. Israel has proven unfaithful because they "did not remember (οὐκ ἐμνήσθης, LXX) the days of [their] youth" when God delivered them and cared for them (16:22, 43). Furthermore, Ezek 16 relates the imagery of God saving Israel who was like an abandoned baby. God cared for and nurtured them. He adorned them with blessings only for them then to pursue idols and foreign alliances with the very blessings God had bestowed on them. This juxtaposition of blessings with unfaithfulness points to ingratitude as the root of their unfaithfulness (cf. 2 Kngs 17:7-20).

Israel is therefore given the common epithet in Ezekiel of being a "rebellious nation" (מְרִי / παραπικραίνοντα [LXX]; cf. 2:3; 12:1-2;

17:12; 24:3; 44:6).[92] Such an epithet does not argue for just a one time lapse in faith but of a settled disposition to throw off God's yoke. For example, Israel is rebellious from the very beginning, that is, from their deliverance in Egypt to the time of Ezekiel (cf. 20:8, 13, 21; 23). Thus, Israel is aptly described as "stubborn and obstinate" (קְשֵׁי־גֵב, חִזְקֵי־מֵצַח / φιλόνεικος, σκληροκάρδιος [LXX]; 3:7 NAS). Their rebellious tendencies against God are not rooted out easily, not even by gratitude for benefits bestowed. Reciprocity is a deficient dynamic for securing fidelity to God.

Ezekiel, then, appears to have a pessimistic anthropological assumption—Israel *cannot do* what they *should*. This will become more evident when we examine what Ezekiel presents as the solution to Israel's stubborn rebelliousness and ingratitude. Another example from the Jewish milieu that represents Israel's and God's relationship as a failure due to a pessimistic anthropology is the Dead Sea Scrolls of the Qumran community.

As with the other texts discussed above, the Dead Sea Scrolls[93] represent a consistent view that Israel has apostasized from the covenant, and God has left Israel only with a remnant of the faithful.[94] The reason for the apostasy is two-fold—(1) because God has predestined those who are apostate and (2) because the human condition is frail and given to unfaithfulness toward its creator. First, the general belief found in the Qumran texts is that Israel has apostasized from the covenant. In the *Damascus Document* (CD II, 14-III, 12), the history of the human race in general and the history of Israel in particular is portrayed as one of rebellion against God. In the *Rule of the Community* (1QS I, 23-24), at the time of the

---

92 See further Ezek 2:5, 6, 7, 8; 3:9, 26, 27; 12:3, 9, 25, 27.
93 I recognize that much scholarship has been devoted to tracing the development of the theology of the community and the historical background of the documents. First, I accept that these documents are representative of an organic, identifiable community over time. I am not, however, requiring that the community have absolute uniformity of thought or a univocal theology, though there seems to be much in common among the texts from which an identifiable community emerges. The evidence collected is not meant to argue for what all Essenes or members of the Qumran sect believed at all times and everywhere. It is only meant to demonstrate beliefs that existed in and were preserved by a Jewish sect in Middle Judaism. Second, I am concerned with the views expressed in the final form of the texts and how those views add their voice to the Jewish milieu being defined in this chapter.
94 Craig Evans ("Covenant in the Qumran Literature," in *The Concept of Covenant in the Second Temple Period* [ed. Stanley E. Porter and Jacqueline C. R. de Roo; JSJSup 71; Leiden: Brill, 2003], 79) points out some common elements from his survey of the Qumran documents. Among them are the need for renewal of the covenant arose from Israel's apostasy, God has preserved a remnant, and ultimate salvation depends on faithfulness to the covenant.

yearly covenant renewal, the levites were to recite all the sins of the children of Israel "during the dominion of Belial".[95] Everyone who enters the community is to confess his or her former identification with the apostasy of Israel:

> We have acted sinfully,
> [we have transgressed,
> we have si]nned, we have acted irreverently,
> we and our fathers before us,
> inasmuch as we walk
> [in the opposite direction to the precepts] of truth and justice
> [...] his judgment upon us and upon our fathers. (I, 24-26; cf. 1QH^a XII, 34-35)

Second, why has Israel become so rebellious and why is there only a remnant of the faithful among Israel?[96] The first answer to these inquiries is because God has ordained the path and outcome of each person's life. This viewpoint is a part of the larger confession that God is sovereign over all the affairs of human history.[97] Therefore, we find the psalmist confessing,

---

95   The translation and edition of the Dead Sea Scrolls consulted here is Florentino García Martínez, *The Dead Sea Scrolls Translated: The Qumran Texts in English* (trans. W. G. E. Watson; 2d ed.; New York: Brill; Grand Rapids: Eerdmans, 1996).

96   The covenant Israel has apostasized from, especially at the time of the writing of these texts, is the Mosaic covenant as it was interpreted by the Teacher of Righteousness (cf. CD I, 6-21). To enter the community, the initiate must return to the covenant of Moses (cf. 1QS I, 3; V, 8; CD XV, 9-10; XVI, 1-7). But this is a renewed Mosaic covenant as it is interpreted by the Teacher of Righteousness. To not heed his teaching is to become subject to destruction (cf. 1QpHab II, 1-2). Most scholars agree that the new covenant of the Qumran community is the Sinai covenant renewed and specially interpreted by the Teacher of Righteousness. Cf. Evans, "Covenant in the Qumran Literature," 55-59; Michael O. Wise, "The Concept of the New Covenant in the Teacher Hymns from Qumran (1QHa X-XVII)," in *The Concept of Covenant*, 115, 126; Martin G. Abegg, "The Covenant of the Qumran Sectarians," in *The Concept of Covenant*, 84, 86; Susanne Lehne, *The New Covenant in Hebrews* (JSNTSup 44; Sheffield: Sheffield Academic Press, 1990), 50-52.

97   Armin Lange (*Weisheit und Prädestination: Weisheitlich Urordnung und Prädestination und den Textfunden von Qumran* [STDJ 18; Leiden: Brill, 1996]) revives Von Rad's thesis of the connection between wisdom and apocalyptic and details that connection in the Qumran literature. He argues that the community's predestinarian theology developed from the postexilic wisdom cosmology and ordering of history. For an earlier study on predestination at Qumran see E. H. Merrill, *Qumran and Predestination: A Theological Study of the Thanksgiving Hymn* (STDJ 8; Leiden: Brill, 1975). Merrill holds the paradoxical tension of divine predestination and human responsibility together in the Qumran community. He states that such a juxtaposition defies logical reconciliation. For the sectarians,

"And with [your approval] everything happens, and without you nothing occurs" (1QH^a IX, 20) and "Without your will nothing happens" (XVIII, 9). The community, as a result, believes that all people's destinies are established by God. The wicked are so by God's predestination and so is the righteous remnant: "For to man (does not belong) his path nor to human beings the steadying of his step....by his knowledge everything shall come into being" (1QS XI, 10-11; cf. 4Q402 4, 13). The psalmist is even more explicit:

> [N]or can the human being establish his steps.
> I know that every spirit is fashioned by your hand. . . .
> You have created the just man.
> For him, from the womb, you determined the period of approval,
> so that he will keep you covenant and walk on all (your paths). . . .
> But the wicked you have created for the time of your wrath,
> from the womb you have predestined them for the day of annihilation. . . .
> You have fashioned the spirit
> and have organized its task.
> From you comes the path of every living being. (1QH^a VII, 17-26)

Thus, the confession in the *War Scroll* reads, "You, [have cre]ated [us] for you, eternal people, and you have made us fall into the lot of the light" (1QM XIII, 9). The faithful remnant are those who are "selected by God for an everlasting covenant" and the "selected ones" for whom God cares (1QS IV, 22; XI, 7, 16; cf. 4Q171 II, 5) and who are preserved and protected by God (cf. 1QM XIV, 8-10; cf. CD I, 4).

The second answer as to why most of Israel has apostatized relates to the community's pessimistic anthropological assumption.[98] Many have failed

---

according to Merrill, predestination is the rationale for why humans choose freely (58). I believe Merrill is essentially correct. Holding this tension together without diminishing either affirmation in favor of the other does more justice to the literature and the theology within the Qumran community. To not allow for any paradox to exist within a deterministic worldview evident in such communities as Qumran ultimately ends up misrepresenting that community's view and experience.

98 Early work that focused on Qumran's anthropology, psychology, and view of sin was done by Jürgen Becker, *Das Heil Gottes: Heils- und Sundenbegriffe in den Qumrantexten und in Neuen Testament* (SUNT 3; Göttingen: Vandenhoeck & Ruprecht, 1964). Becker argued that sin in its singular form in the Qumran texts indicates the sphere in which a person exists and not individual transgressions (144-48). Sanders (*Paul and Palestinian Judaism*, 274-79), however, gives much attention to refuting Becker's position. See also Herbert Braun, "Römer 7, 7-25 und das Selbstverständnis des Qumran-Frommen," *ZTK* 56 (1959): 1-18 and J. Licht, "The Doctrine of the Thanksgiving Scroll," *IEJ* 6 (1956): 1-13, 89-101. Hermann Lichtenberger (*Studien zum Menschenbild in Texten der Qumrangemeinde* [SUNT 15; Göttingen: Vandenhoeck & Ruprecht, 1980], 58-173) devotes his attention to

not only because God has predestined them to fail but also because they are unable to remain faithful, left to their own human resources and capabilities. Two documents will serve as the primary evidence: the *Rule of the Community* (1QS) and the *Thanksgiving Hymns*^{a} (1QH^a). In the *Rule of the Community*, we find a conjoining of God's predestination with a pessimistic anthropology. In *Rule of the Community* II, 14-4.26, we find that in every person is the spirit of truth and deceit/injustice (cf. III, 19; IV, 23).[99] Further, God has divided humanity and given them to the Prince of Lights or the Angel of Darkness, according to God's predestinating will (III, 15-19, 25-26; IV, 15-17, 22-26). Arthur Sekki writes that the "main point in 3:15-19a is that a man's inner spirituality does not have its origin in his own autonomy or free will but in God's power of predetermination and creation". Later Sekki argues that the "innermost religious life [of those outside the community]...has its primary source in a great cosmic Well of Darkness (3:19) which totally and unchangeably defines who they are spiritually according to the predetermining and creative act of God".[100] Here, we are dealing with a pessimistic view of the human condition and its capabilities toward God and fellow humans. We also find a pessimistic anthropological assumption in the *Thanksgiving Hymns*^{a}. The psalmist confessed that in the "depravity of [his] heart" he "wallowed in impurity" and "[separated (himself)] from the foundation of [truth]" (IV, 19). He declares about the frailty and depravity of all humanity:

He is a structure of dust shaped with water,
his base is the guilt of sin,
vile unseemliness, source of impurity,
over which a spirit of degeneracy rules. (V, 21)

---

    defining the multiform anthropology of the community. He argues that the acknowledgement of human inability to be faithful to God apart from God's help arises from the confessions of creaturely baseness and poverty (*Niedrigkeitdoxologie / Elendbetrachtung*; 207-12, esp. 211). Lichtenberger writes earlier, however, that the warnings (*Mahnreden*) against apostasy point to the conflicting belief in human freedom and ability to choose (154). I acknowledge there is logical inconsistency in the affirmations of absolute dependence and affirmation of responsibility. But I believe that this paradox was held in tension with the community's notion of predestination without attempting to fully reconcile the paradox, cf. William Hugh Brownlee, "Anthropology and Soteriology in the Dead Sea Scrolls and the New Testament," in *The Use of the Old Testament in the New and Other Essays: Studies in Honor of William Franklin Stinespring* (ed. James M. Efrid; Durham: Duke University Press, 1972), 221.

99 This passage has been notoriously difficult to interpret among scholars. See Arthur Everett Sekki, *The Meaning of Ruah at Qumran* (SBLDS 110; Atlanta: Scholars Press, 1989), 193-219. Sekki traces the history of scholarship on this passage while presenting his own exegetical arguments.

100 Sekki, *The Meaning of Ruah*, 198, 202.

He later confesses of himself:

> [A]lthough I am a creature of clay, fashioned with water,
> foundation of shame, source of impurity,
> oven of iniquity, building of sin,
> spirit of mistake, astray, without knowledge. (IX, 21-22)

Moreover, humans are dominated by such moral frailty over the whole course of their lives (cf. XII, 29).[101] We also find a similar view point in the hymn in the *Rule of the Community*. There the community acknowledges:

> However, I belong to evil humankind
> to the assembly of wicked flesh;
> my failings, my transgressions my sins, {...}
> with the depravities of my heart,
> belong to the assembly of worms
> and of those who walk in darkness.
> For to man (does not belong) his path,
> nor to the human being the steadying of his step. (1QS XI, 9-10)

There is no strength in humans to determine their own lives; moreover, there is within humans no strength to be faithful to God and walk in the ways of the covenant.[102]

---

101 Cf. Helmer Ringgren, *The Faith of Qumran: The Theology of the Dead Sea Scrolls* (ed. James H. Charlesworth; trans. Emilie T. Sander; exp. ed.; New York: Crossroads, 1995), 94-104.

102 Cf. Markus Bockmuehl, "1QS and Salvation at Qumran," in *Variegated Nomism*, 1.398. See also Merrill, *Qumran and Predestination*, 37-38. On the other hand, Sanders (*Paul and Palestinian Judaism*, 272-84) believes the Qumran community held to an optimistic anthropology, though he states that "the sectarian theologians reached a profound and pessimistic view of human ability" (284). He calls it avoidable disobedience (273). According to Sanders, entrance into the community was within the range of human achievement. Sander's discussion of the Qumran literature is inconsistent and confusing. First, Sanders does not appear willing to hold the tension between the logical paradox of God's sovereignty and human responsibility—a paradox the Qumran community seemed to hold. Sanders writes, "In short, a man's destiny was really in his own hands," thus making God's will subservient to human will (267). Second, Sanders reduces all talk about sin in the texts to acts of sin and the willfulness that accompanies it (273). While this may by the case, there is clearly an assumption the community holds in regard to why people willfully transgress God's commands. Sanders even states that, according to the Qumran texts, humanity on its own is not capable of righteous acts "and *this is always the case*" (278). Such an acknowledgement would appear to point, contrary to Sanders's argument, to a pessimistic anthropological *assumption* for such a state of affairs to result. For what a person *should* do they *cannot do* left to his or her own resources.

Finally, Paul shares the pessimistic anthropology characteristic of the Qumran community and exilic documents surveyed above. In Romans, Paul relates this pessimism to the divine-human reciprocity relationship between the creator and humanity. Paul's conclusion is that humans have been ungrateful beneficiaries of God's benefits through creation. This ingratitude is grounded in the overall human condition which is depraved and impotent and, thereby, rendered incapable of fidelity through the cooperative dependence that is characteristic of the dance of reciprocity.

Paul's pessimistic anthropology comes into view in his letter to the Romans in two primary ways: (1) all humanity is under the power of sin (Rom 1:18–3:20) and (2) this enslavement to sin is characteristic of the human condition because of Adam's sin (Rom 5:12-21).[103] First, in Rom 1:18–3:20, Paul is arguing for the conclusion that "both Jews and Gentiles are all under sin" (3:9). To be "under sin" signifies that Jews and Gentiles are not only both guilty of rebellion against God but also dominated by an orientation of rebelliousness toward God (3:10-18).[104] Hence, in Rom 1:18-23, Paul telescopes the entire human response to their creator as one of ingratitude and, thus, infidelity. As discussed above, the relational dynamic between God, the creator, and humanity is portrayed as one of reciprocity in Rom 1:18-23. In light of the pessimistic view of the human condition, reciprocity emerges a failed dynamic for securing fidelity to God. Despite the benefits God has bestowed on humans through creation and the innate revelation God has given of Himself, humanity has failed to gratefully honor God. Second, according to Paul, the human condition is this way because of the sin of Adam, the corporate head of the present created order. Adam's sin provides the historic explanation for Paul's pessimistic

---

One wonders if Sanders is pressing too hard to form the Qumran documents into his mold of covenantal nomism. Sanders's covenantal nomism is synergistic (see Timo Eskola, *Theodicy and Predestination in Pauline Soteriology* [WUNT 2.100; Tübingen: Mohr Siebeck, 1998], 57), a synergism that requires an anthropological optimism (see Laato, *Paul and Judaism*, 167). Sanders, however, never clearly states his anthropological viewpoint but assumes an answer to it (see Laato, *Paul and Judaism*, 51). The answer he assumes appears to be an optimistic anthropology. Thus, he has difficulty in forcing the Qumran literature, which represents a pessimistic assumption, into his "pattern of religion".

103 Charles Talbert (*Romans* [Smyth and Helwys Bible Commentary; Macon: Smyth and Helwys, 2002], 145) has noted that Paul's first major argument spans from Rom 1:18–5:11. The second major argument spans from Rom 5:12–8:39. In each of these sections, Paul begins with a description of the human condition.

104 Thomas R. Schreiner, *Romans* (Baker Exegetical Commentary on the New Testament; Grand Rapids: Baker Books, 1998), 165-66. Cf. Haacker, *Der Brief de Paulus*, 81, who emphasizes that the use of sin in the singular means "Sünde also einer *Machte*." Haacker previously stated that 1:18-23 dealt with the guilt determination (*Schuldfeststellung*) of the Gentiles (48).

anthropology.[105] In Rom 5:12, Paul asserts that through the sin of Adam a state of death and alienation from God now reigns over humanity.[106] This is a condition into which all the posterity of Adam, as the head of the human race, are born and an orientation to which they are committed from birth. Accordingly, Laato concludes from his exposition on Rom 5:12, "Human sinfulness ultimately goes back to Adam."[107] In sum, Charles Talbert provides a fitting conclusion to Paul's pessimistic representation of the human condition in Romans:

> For Paul, sin is more than an act I commit. It is also an orientation to life. Indeed sin involves my being before it involves my doing. Furthermore, sin is more than that for which I am responsible. I am born into a world of sin before I contribute my share to it. There is an accumulated web of sin involving all human life that has grown...through the centuries. This accumulation affects the corporate life of humans and the history of humans. Historical and corporate falleness then affect individuals born in this web. No one born into such falleness stands in a neutral position with the possibility of deciding whether to choose to sin or not to sin. One stands in a sinful place and chooses to participate in it. It is not necessary, but it is inevitable![108]

What then is the solution? How can frail, ungrateful, and incorrigible humans become faithful to God? If we examined the picture as a whole from all the texts surveyed that hold to a pessimistic anthropology, we find that the solution is not for God to persist in giving benefits in the hope that such giving overcomes stubborn and ungrateful hearts. God's people cannot persevere in indebted gratitude generated by the dynamic of reciprocity. The constant solution we will find among this literature is that God's people are divinely enabled to be faithful. Though set in the context of victory in battle, the *War Scroll* contains a fitting transition to our next section:

> And it is from you that power comes,

---

105 See Talbert, *Romans*, 155

106 See Laato, *Paul and Judaism*, 102-104, for a brief discussion on the fuller meaning of death in Paul and the Hebrew Scriptures. Cf. Talbert, *Romans*, 149-50.

107 Laato, *Paul and Judaism*, 105. See pp. 96-109 for his complete argument. See also Talbert (*Romans*, 148) who succinctly lists the interpretive options for ἐφ' ᾧ in Rom 5:12. The interpretation of Rom 5:12 here resembles more closely what Talbert (*Romans*, 148) has called the Orthodox reading and is defended by Schreiner, *Romans*, 275-76. No matter what nuanced interpretation one takes of ἐφ' ᾧ in Rom 5:12, those exegetes who see Adam as the head and beginning of human history recognize that, for Paul, sin/rebellion characterize the human condition because of Adam's sin. This is a condition that each individual after Adam has not chosen for himself or herself but a condition into which one is born.

108 Talbert, *Romans*, 156.

and not from our own being.
It is not our might
nor the power of our own hand
which performs these marvels,
except by your great strength
and your mighty deeds. (1QM XI, 4-5; cf. XIV, 6)

Where a pessimistic anthropology is assumed in the Jewish context, God's power must transform the human condition. The persistent infidelity of God's people is thereby transformed into steadfast faithfulness.

SOLUTION TO INFIDELITY

A pessimistic anthropology must look for a solution to human infidelity outside the human condition and capabilities. In this section we will explore from the previously cited literature how the common solution of divine enablement was expressed, transforming the human condition from unfaithfulness to faithfulness. We also will look at the function gratitude has in the context of divine enablement. In short, gratitude promotes God's honor and combats pride and self-exultation in the individual.

The transformation of the human condition[109] by means of divine enablement is variously expressed in the texts of Deuteronomy, Jeremiah, Ezekiel, the Dead Sea Scrolls, and Paul's letter to the Romans. We will examine the enablement/transformation motifs in each of these texts. First, in Deuteronomy the solution is to have Israel's hearts circumcised. Moses, early in his speech to Israel, exhorts them to "[c]ircumcise, then, the foreskin of your heart, and do not be stubborn any longer" (10:16). Circumcision of the heart is then the solution to stubborn rebellion. Israel, however, was unable to do what was needed to secure their fidelity to God, as the Deuteronomistic History bears out. We later find in Deut. 30:6-8 that Yahweh will perform this circumcision of the heart when He restores Israel from exile:

> Moreover, the LORD your God will circumcise your heart and the heart of your descendents, so that you will love the LORD your God with all your heart and with all your soul, in order that you may live....Then you shall again obey the LORD, observing all his commandments that I am commanding you today.[110]

---

109 What I mean by "human transformation" is that there is something endemic to the human condition that requires correction. That correction is outside human ability to achieve and so requires divine intervention, power, infusion, and change to bring about the correction.

110 Cf. H. W. Wolff, "Das Kerygma des deuteronomischen Geischichtswerk," *ZAW* 73 (1961): 171-86. Wolff attempts to argue that the cyclical pattern one finds in Judges

Israel will, upon being restored from exile, become faithful to God because God will enable their faithfulness by circumcising their hearts.

Jeremiah utilizes the metaphors of circumcision of the heart, Yahweh giving the people another heart, Yahweh putting the fear of Him in the people, and Yahweh making a new covenant as the solution to Israel's infidelity. As in Deuteronomy, Israel is exhorted to circumcise themselves to Yahweh (cf. 4:4), but Israel remains rebellious and "uncircumcised in heart" (9:26). Thus, Yahweh declares that He will restore the relationship Israel has broken and will guarantee their faithfulness by enabling them. Yahweh "will give [Israel] a heart to know that I am the LORD; and they shall be my people and I will be their God, for they shall turn to me with their whole heart" (24:7). Elsewhere, Yahweh declares, "I will put the fear of me in their hearts, so that they may not turn from me" (32:40b; cf. 32:39-41). Jeremiah's most famous solution to the problem of Israel's infidelity is found in the prophecy in 31:31-34. Yahweh, when He restores Israel, will make a new covenant with Israel. Further, this covenant will not be like the one Yahweh made through Moses at Sinai. The primary difference between the covenants is elaborated in verse 33. In the new covenant, Yahweh "will put [his] law within them and [he] will write it on their hearts." As opposed to the first covenant, which was characterized by cooperation and mutual dependence, Yahweh will enable Israel to keep the covenant. The *newness* of the covenant lies in this transformation and divine enablement. Finally, Mendenhall observes that the new covenant in Jeremiah lacks, among other things, the feature of a historical prologue characteristic of ancient treaties and the Mosaic covenant.[111] Indebted gratitude will no longer be the foundation for securing fidelity to the relationship. Reciprocity will no longer define the dynamic of the relationship between God and Israel. God will guarantee the relationship. He will ensure Israel's faithfulness, not by forced submission through a display of superior power, but through a transformation of the human affections engendering enduring love and holy fear.

Ezekiel represents God's enablement of the fidelity of Israel through such expressions as God giving Israel a new heart and new spirit, removing Israel's heart of stone, and giving Israel His spirit. In Ezek 11:19-20, God foretells of the restoration of Israel from exile. Characteristic of that

---

(apostasy, punishment, repentance, and deliverance) is determinative for understanding the Deuteronomistic History as a whole. Wolff, therefore, concludes that the Deuteronomist wrote his history to point out to the exiles that they were in the phase of punishment and so needed to repent and return to the Yahweh to experience deliverance. This argument would seem to presuppose an optimistic anthropology for the Deuteronomistic History. Furthermore, it does not reckon with Deut 30:6-8 in the scheme or theology of the Deuteronomistic History.

111 Mendenhall, "Covenant," 1:1192-93.

restoration is that God "will give them one heart, and put a new spirit within them; [he] will remove the heart of stone from their flesh and give them a heart of flesh, so that they may follow [his] statutes and keep [his] ordinances and obey them. Then they shall be [his] people, and [he] will be their God." In another prophecy of restoration, God declares,

> A new heart I will give you, and a new spirit I will put within you; and I will remove from your body the heart of stone and give you a heart of flesh. I will put my spirit within you, and make you follow my statutes and be careful to observe my ordinances. Then you shall live in the land that I gave your ancestors; and you shall be my people, and I will be your God. (36:26-28)

This echoes the previous prophecy quoted but also introduces a new wrinkle. God will enable Israel's fidelity not only by removing the heart of stone and giving Israel a new heart and new spirit but also by putting His spirit within them (cf. 37:14; 39:29). For Ezekiel, God transforms the human condition by removing hearts of stone and giving new hearts and spirits. God also imparts something of Himself to engender the affections and love of Israel that secure their fidelity.

In the Qumran texts we find many of the same enablement motifs just explored plus a variety of others. We will find that the *Thanksgiving Hymns*^{a} is especially rich with enablement motifs. First, among the Qumran texts, the motif of circumcision of the heart is employed as a metaphor for divine enablement and transformation. In the *Words of Luminaries*, we find the petition for God to "[c]ircumcise the foreskin of [our heart...]", which is explained in the following statement, "Strengthen our heart...to walk in your paths" (4Q504 4, 11-12; cf. 4Q402 1 I, 4). Second, among the fragments of the same text, we also find the language similar to what is found in the new covenant in Jeremiah:

> [...]...to plant your law in our hearts, [so that we do not stray] either to the right or to the left. For, you will heal us of madness, blindness and confusion [of heart...] For our faults were we sold, but in spite of our failing you did call us [...] and you will free us from sinning against you. (4Q504 1-2 II, 13-16)

Likewise, we find in the *Thanksgiving Hymn* the following confession:

> [You, Lord, prevent] your servant
> from sinning against you ...
> Engrave your com[mandments in him]
> so that he can hold himself up against [fiendish] spirits
> so that he can walk in all that you love
> and loathe all that you hate,
> [so he can do] what is good in your eyes. (1QH^a IV, 23-24; cf. XII, 10)

Third, we find expressions of divine enablement similar to Ezekiel's language. The psalmist thanks God "for the spirits you have placed in me" (1QH^a IV, 17) and for "putting wisdom in the heart of your servant" (1QH^a VI, 8). God also spreads His holy spirit over His servant so as to preserve him from stumbling (1QH^a XV, 7). Fourth, we find other expressions of divine enablement. We find expressions of God strengthening and upholding the heart of the elect so that they remain faithful. The psalmist declares, "[A]nd at their taunts you have not let me lose heart so as to desert serving you" (1QH^a X, 35-36; cf. X, 28).[112] Elsewhere, the psalmist expresses the same sentiment in a rhetorical question:

[How] will my steps stay secure
[if you do not] strengthen [me] with strength? (1QH^a XX, 35)

In a fragment of a text, we find an analogous affirmation:

You govern my heart and you sharpen my kidneys so that I do not forget your laws. [...] your law, and you will open my kidneys and you will strengthen me so that I will follow your paths [...]...You have strengthened my feet...you have removed from me [the evil inclination],[113] and in its place you will put a pure heart. (4Q436 1, 5-10)

Fifth, human transformation resulting in perfected fidelity will only be realized at the end of the age when God "will purify for himself the configuration of man, ripping out the spirit of deceit from the innermost part of his flesh, and cleansing him with the spirit of holiness from every irreverent deed....and to [those selected by God] shall belong all the glory of Adam" (1QS IV, 20-23). Finally, as we have already had a chance to observe, human fidelity to God is because of God's predestination and sovereign determination over the course of a person's life: "From the womb, you determined the period of approval, so that he will keep your covenant and walk in all (your paths)" (1QH^a VII, 19; cf. 1QH^a IV, 21-22; 1QS III, 15-19). The implicit connection between this last observation and the foregoing ones is that God's predestination leads to the enabling and transforming of the elect so that they remain faithful.[114]

---

112 In 1QM XIV, 6, God strengthens Israel for battle so that they do not lose heart.
113 The text is incomplete. This is my own conjecture based upon the words that follow at the end of this statement.
114 To these motifs of divine enablement and human transformation just surveyed I could add the perspective of Isa 65:17-20. Already at the beginning of this chapter, Yahweh accuses Israel of being incorrigibly rebellious (v. 2). In vv. 17-20, however, Yahweh foretells a new creation/a new order where in this new creation/new order Yahweh will (re-)create Israel to be a joy (v. 18). Here is the theme of transformation of the human situation by God in the context of the transformation and recreation of the entire corrupted created order. This insight

Finally, in Paul's letter to the Romans, we find the solution to the human impotency put in terms of God's justification of the sinner. Talbert has argued based on an examination of the δικαι- word group in the Septuagint that God's justification of the sinner in Romans involves three aspects: forgiveness of sin (Rom 4:3-8), freedom from the bondage/dominion of sin (Rom 6:7), and divine enablement to live with the same faithfulness of Jesus (Rom 5:19; cf. Gal 2:20).[115] So in Paul's argument in Romans, both the failed reciprocity relationship of Gentiles with God and the Jews' failure under the law have been rectified and transformed through God justification of the sinner in the death and resurrection of Jesus.

Paul also employs other enablement motifs. He speaks of God "working in [the Christian] to will and to do God's good pleasure" (Phil 3:12). Elsewhere, Paul speaks about divine enablement and human transformation in terms of being inwardly renewed day by day (2 Cor 3:17), being transformed as part of a new creation (2 Cor 5:17; cf. 2 Cor 4:6), being indwelt by the living Christ to live with his faithfulness (Gal 2:20), being indwelt and taught by the Spirit of God (1 Cor 2:6-16), and being raised to live a new life unto God (Rom 6:4).

Paul also draws upon in 2 Cor 2:14–4:6 the enablement motifs of the new covenant from Jeremiah and the metaphor from Ezekiel where hearts of stone are replaced with hearts of flesh.[116] Here, Paul is providing an apology for his ministry (cf. 2:14–3:1). He points to the transforming presence of the Spirit among the Corinthian church as Christ's living letter of recommendation of Paul's apostolic ministry (cf. 3:2-3). Paul, therefore, asserts that he is a minister of Jeremiah's eschatological new covenant. His is a ministry, empowered by God, that transforms the fallen human. Through Paul's apostolic ministry, God removes the "veil" that blinds people from seeing the glory of Christ and causes the light of the divine glory that is manifest in Jesus Christ to shine within the hearts of the Corinthian Christians (cf. 3:4–4:6).[117] Furthermore, this divinely enabled beholding of the glory of Christ is transformative. The Christian is transformed into the image of Christ (cf. 3:18). In all these ways, Paul can be located in the stream of exilic and Middle Judaism that understood divine enablement and human transformation to be the solution to its pessimistic anthropology—an anthropology that informed its perceived

---

from the text of Isaiah was graciously passed on to me by Dr. James Kennedy at Baylor University.

115 Talbert, *Romans*, 35-41.

116 See Richard B. Hays, *Echoes of Scripture in the Letters of Paul* (New Haven: Yale University Press, 1989), 128. Cf. Frank Theilman, *Paul and the Law: A Contextual Approach* (Downers Grove: IVP, 1994), 109-10.

117 This reading of 2 Cor 2:14–4:6 is informed by Hays's (*Echoes of Scripture*, 122-53) interpretation of this passage.

failure of the divine-human reciprocity relationship.

THE FUNCTION OF GRATITUDE

A corollary rises from this discussion of divine enablement and human transformation from the Jewish context, namely, the function that gratitude has when the dynamic of the relationship between God and Israel is one of divine enablement. The indebted gratitude of reciprocity is no longer required to secure the fidelity of the recipients of benefits from their divine benefactor. On the other hand, in the *Thanksgiving Hymns*^{a} of the Qumran texts, we find abundant expressions of enablement and strong affirmations of predestination alongside jubilant declarations of gratitude. How then does gratitude function in the context of divine enablement? An answer may be found in Jean LaPorte's study on εὐχάριστια in the works of Philo of Alexandria.[118] Before we look at Laporte's synthesis and conclusions, let us examine Philo's view of the divine-human relational dynamic. First, for Philo, the immortal life, which is the life of virtue, is only possible through God's enabling.[119] For example, in *Her.* 58-60, Philo explains the allegorical significance of the name Eliezar, "God is my Helper",

> For this mass of clay and blood...holds together and is quickened by the providence of God...The spirit called Pharaoh, whose tyranny rife with lawlessness and cruelty it is impossible to escape, unless Eliezer be born in the soul and looks with hope to the help which God the only Saviour can give.[120]

Thus, the very nature of the human condition requires God's help.

---

118 Jean LaPorte, *Eucharistia in Philo* (Studies in the Bible and Early Christianity 3; New York: Edwin Mellen Press, 1983). Philo is difficult to analyze in regards to harmonizing his thought on what humans are actually capable of doing in the attainment of virtue, on divine sovereignty, and on reciprocity in the divine-human relationship. To give an answer to such topics would require its own extensive study. I would be confident in placing Philo among those representatives of Middle Judaism who place a singular emphasis on divine enablement (though possibly not human transformation). I am also confident that the evidence presented in this section and the assertions that will be derived from it reflect Philo's primary concerns.

119 The soul's attainment of virtue and thereby immortality is solely the initiative of God. Philo emphasizes this point throughout *De Cherubim*. For a concise discussion of this point in *De Cherubim* see Fred W. Burnett, "Philo on Immortality: A Thematic Study of Philo's Concept of παλιγγενεσία," *CBQ* 46 (1984): 450-53.

120 Cf. Dieter Zeller, *Charis bei Philon und Paulus* (Stuttgarter Bibelstudien 142; Stuttgart: Weralg Katholisches Bibelwerk, 1990), 74-75. The Greek text and quotes from the Philonic corpus follow the edition of Philo's works in the LCL by Colson and Whitaker.

Furthermore, even fidelity and perseverance is from God. Speaking about Isaac's wife Rebecca whose name means "constancy", Philo says,

> For he [Isaac] has ready beside him in their fullness the gifts of God, conveyed by the breath of God's higher graces (χάρισι), but he wishes and prays that these may remain with him constantly. And therefore I think his Benefactor, willing that His graces once received should stay for ever with him, gives him Constancy for his spouse. (*Congr.* 38)

In *Plant.* 90, Philo writes, "He shall do away with fear we feel before Him as Master, and implant in the soul the loyalty and affection (φιλίαν καὶ εὔνοιαν) that goes out to Him as Benefactor." Therefore, for Philo the chief danger on the soul's spiritual journey in attaining virtue is pride.[121] Philo writes,

> There are others who...have clung to self-assertion (φιλαυτίαν) rather than piety and regarded themselves as the source of their achievements. All these are to be condemned. He alone is worthy of approval who sets his hope on God both as the source to which his coming into existence itself is due and as the sole power which can keep him free from harm and destruction. (*Praem.* 12-13)

The danger of such "self-assertion" is explicated in *Agr.* 171: "For there is no fall so grievous as to slip and fall away from rendering honour to God, through ascribing victory to oneself instead of to Him....For he that fails to honour That which Is slays his own soul, so that the edifice of instruction ceases to be of use to him." Even thankfulness comes from God's work in the soul:

> But as long as the mind supposes itself to be the author of anything, it is far away from making room for God and from confessing or making acknowledgment to Him. For one must note that the very confession of praise itself is the work not of the soul but of God who gives it thankfulness (εὐχάριστον). (*Leg.* 1.82)

In *Leg.* 3.136-37, Philo is more emphatic:

> The soul should not ascribe to itself the toil of virtue, but it should take it away from itself and refer it to God, confessing that not its own strength and power acquired nobility, but He who freely bestowed also the love of it [virtue]...For only then does the soul begin to be saved, when...toil has

---

[121] The pilgrimage of the soul towards perfection is the primary concern of Philo's allegorical interpretation of the biblical text. Cf. David M. Hay, "Philo of Alexandria," in *Justification and Variegated Nomism*, 1:364-65.

come to create in it not self-satisfaction, but a readiness to yield the honour to God, the Bestower (εὐεργέτῃ) of the boon.[122]

In light of these observations, how does thanksgiving/gratitude function for Philo? Laporte argues that "To take pleasure in one's good deeds, or to consider oneself as their only author without further distinction, is to deny the necessity of God and to introduce impiety at the summit of spiritual life, at the moment when perfection seems close at hand....As a remedy to this perversion, Philo offers thanksgiving, since it is the antidote to self-love."[123] Such appears to be the function of gratitude in the Qumran *Thanksgiving Hymn*[a]: "[I give you thanks, Lord,] for the spirits you have placed in me" (IV, 17), "[I give you thanks,] Lord, for putting wisdom in the heart of your servant" (VI, 8), and "I give you thanks, Lord, because you have sustained me with your strength, you have spread your holy spirit over me so that I will not stumble" (XV, 6-7).[124] Gratitude, as in reciprocity relationships, retains the function of honoring God for His benefits. Unlike reciprocity relationships, gratitude does not secure loyalty (it cannot where a pessimistic anthropology is assumed); instead, gratitude is an expression of the humility and acknowledgment of the spiritual poverty in an individual who depends wholly on God's power to live unto God.[125]

Such also appears to be the function of thanksgiving in the letters of

---

122 Cf. *Leg.* 2.46; 3.32; 3.78; *Mut.* 28; *Ebr.* 118-19.
123 Laporte, Eucharistia, 5. See also his more extensive discussion on pp. 172-78. Cf. Emile Bréhier, *Les idées philosophiques et religieuses de Philon d'Alexandrie* (Etudes de philosophie médiévale 8; Paris: Librairie philosophique J. Vrin, 1925), 298; David Winston, "Philo's Ethical Theory," *ANRW* 21.1:376-77.
124 Cf. 1QH[a] IV, 17-26; VI, 23-27; VII, 16b-29; XV, 6-25; XV, 26-32; XV, 33-36; XIX, 3-14.
125 A secondary motif one finds in the Jewish literature surveyed that held to a pessimistic anthropology is an emphasis upon the motive for which God acts in a salvific manner. This motive serves as the foundation for God's faithfulness to the relationship. The motif we find is that God does or will act for His name sake, without regard to Israel's infidelity (cf. Exod 32:11-12; Num 14:13-23; Deut 9:26-28; Ezek 20:9, 14, 22, 44; 36:21-23; Bar 1:18; 2:14, 19; 1QH[a] VII, 24; IX, 10; XII, 28; XIV, 10; 1QM XI, 14-15). Though we find that benefactors in reciprocity relationships acted for their own honor, their actions were often predicated upon the beneficiary's worthy character. The foundation for God's salvific acts is solely grounded in the pursuit of His glory. There is nothing in the beneficiary to make him or her worthy of God's benefits or to make God grateful. In fact the opposite is the case. The beneficiary has provoked God and has brought all the curses of his or her infidelity down upon himself or herself. God, however, is faithful to the relationship *because* God will not have His glory profaned or honor impugned by anyone. Moreover, by enabling the fidelity of Israel, God guarantees the preservation of His honor among Israel.

Paul.¹²⁶ Here, I will focus on the thanksgiving periods with which Paul opens many of his letters.¹²⁷ In 1 Cor 1:4-9, Paul thanks (εὐχαριστῶ) God for the χάρις which is given the Corinthian church in Jesus. He goes on to delineate these divinely wrought benefits: the Corinthians have been enriched with every spiritual gift by God and they are preserved blameless by God until Jesus Christ's parousia. Part of Paul's thanksgiving (εὐχαριστῶ) in Phil 1:3-6, is that God will bring to completion the redemptive work He had begun in the Philippian Christians. In Col 1:3-4 Paul gives thanks (εὐχαριστοῦμεν) to God for the Colossian Christians' faith in Jesus and their love for all the saints. In verses 12-14, Paul goes on to give thanks (εὐχαριστοῦντες) to God for strengthening the Colossians to share in the inheritance of the saints, for saving them from the dominion of darkness and transferring them to the kingdom of Jesus Christ, and for forgiving their sins. In 1 Thess 2:13, Paul thanks (εὐχαριστοῦμεν) God that the Thessalonian Christians received the gospel as God's word. Paul thanks (εὐχαριστεῖν) God in 2 Thess 1:3 for the Thessalonians' increasing faith toward Jesus and love for all the saints. In Phlm 4-5, Paul thanks (εὐχαριστῶ) God for Philemon's love and faith toward Jesus Christ and all the saints. In all these instances, thanksgiving in Paul is not an expression of indebted gratitude that secures loyalty but an expression of spiritual poverty and conversely praise to God who is the giver and sustainer of the life of the church. Paul regularly affirms in his opening thanksgivings that the Christian's life of faith, love, and perseverance comes from God. We could even add here the prayer formulas that are often a part of these opening periods. Here again, Paul is acknowledging that the Christian life is only made possible by God's enabling power. Even the very Christian's "worthy manner of living" is from God. One example will suffice. In 2 Thess 1:11, Paul prays that the Thessalonian Christians be empowered by God to live worthy of their calling (ἀξιώσῃ τῆς κλήσεως). God does not give grace to the worthy. God Himself makes them "worthy" by enabling them. To conclude, in the writings of Philo, Qumran, and Paul, thanksgiving or gratitude shares a common theological function. It exalts God while it also combats pride, promotes humility, and acknowledges

---

126 Harrison (*Paul's Language of Grace*, 272) states in his examination of 2 Cor 9 that thanksgiving expresses dependence upon God and the interdependence of the universal body of Christ. He further comments that thanksgiving in the writings of Paul avoids, even opposes, the merit thinking (ἀξία) that arises from the reciprocity rationale in Greco-Roman benefaction (270-71).

127 For some key studies on introductory periods in letters of Paul and the New Testament see P. Schubert, *Form and Function of the Pauline Thanksgivings* (BZNW 20; Berlin: Topelmann, 1939); Peter T. O'Brien, *Introductory Thanksgivings in the Letters of Paul* (Leiden: Brill, 1977); and Fred O. Francis, "The Form and Function of the Opening and Closing Paragraphs of James and 1 John," *ZNW* 61 (1970): 110-26.

joyfully one's own spiritual poverty in the light of God's enabling and transformative work. It does not secure fidelity since fidelity is from God, and it does not indebt God for future favors since all is from God, even the thankfulness. Gratitude, therefore, remains a vital part of the life of piety, but it has been freed from its synergistic moorings in reciprocity.

Conclusion

In sum, this section has characterized the presence of divine-human reciprocity relationships in the Jewish milieu. The treaty-genre of the Mosaic covenant assumes this to be the case. Josephus's translation of the Mosaic covenant in terms of Greco-Roman benefaction/patronage imports as well this foundational dynamic into the divine-human relationship. Finally, rabbinic Judaism picks up on this thread and employs it to explain the foundational dynamic of the covenant between God and Israel. There are also two strands of tradition in the Jewish context based upon their anthropological assumption that had differing views of the success of reciprocity to secure fidelity to the relationship. An optimistic assumption believed in the potential success of such a relational dynamic to secure fidelity. On the other hand, a pessimistic assumption viewed such a relational dynamic as a failure. A new dynamic was then sought and hoped for, namely divine enablement of fidelity, thereby transforming the human condition. Finally, within the context of divine enablement, gratitude takes on a different function. While gratitude honors God, it also promotes the recognition of spiritual poverty, cultivates humility, and combats pride. Gratitude no longer repays God nor secures the feeling of indebtedness and thus loyalty to the relationship.

We have characterized reciprocity in the Greco-Roman and Jewish contexts. We have examined the consequences of differing anthropological assumptions in both contexts regarding the belief in reciprocity to successfully secure fidelity to the divine-human relationship. We have now laid an appropriate foundation for reading Hebrews with the authorial audience who lived in a world marked by the rationale of reciprocity and yet inherited a religious tradition that, at least in part, looked to divine enablement, not reciprocity, as the means of fidelity.

CHAPTER 4

Fidelity in Hebrews: Its Message in Light of an Understanding of Reciprocity

In this chapter we will attempt to listen to "the word of exhortation" in Hebrews in light of our analysis of reciprocity in the ancient Mediterranean world. More specifically, we will determine whether fidelity in Hebrews is secured through indebted gratitude, that is, the dance of reciprocity, or whether fidelity is the result of an ongoing divine enablement that is necessitated by a pessimistic anthropology. The argument in this chapter will seek to demonstrate the latter. To this end, we will begin by examining those elements in Hebrews that echo the immensely widespread reciprocity system of benefaction or patronage. This, however, does not automatically suggest that reciprocity is the dynamic of the divine-human relationship in Hebrews. So, we will next examine how the benefactor-beneficiary metaphor for the divine-human relationship was variously applied by representative first-century Hellenistic Jews and Christians. Josephus represents one example of how that metaphor was applied while Paul represents yet another way. I will, then, offer a preliminary critique of David deSilva's work which, in a manner similar to Josephus, makes the reciprocity of Greco-Roman patronage or benefaction the controlling metaphor for understanding how fidelity to God is secured in Hebrews. We will then turn our attention to how Hebrews understands the fulfillment of the new covenant in Jeremiah. We will examine how the author of Hebrews interprets the new covenant's emphasis on divine enablement that transforms the human condition. The understanding of the fulfillment of the new covenant in Hebrews will locate Hebrews in that stream of Judaism that held to a pessimistic anthropology and looked not to reciprocity but to a transformation and ongoing divine enabling that secure fidelity to God. Finally, we will see that the dual emphasis in Hebrews on divine enablement and human responsibility, acutely felt in the warning passages, constitutes a paradox in the theology and experience of the author.

Hebrews and Its Milieu: Echoes of Benefaction in Hebrews

Greco-Roman patronage or benefaction was a key part of the social and political culture at the time Hebrews was written in the first-century CE. We could hardly expect that "word of exhortation" to have escaped the influence of such a widespread and ingrained social system. Moreover, that the first auditors of this sermon would not have heard some intersecting elements with Greco-Roman benefaction in the sermon is unlikely. There are both conceptual and lexical echoes in Hebrews that could have called to mind the benefactor-beneficiary relationship.

Conceptual Echoes

First, let us examine the conceptual echoes. The divine-human relationship in Hebrews is clearly an asymmetrical one where a superior party benefits an inferior one.[1] For instance, God through Jesus Christ frees Christians from the fear of death (2:14-15), atones for their sins (2:17), perfects them (10:14), forgives their sins (10:17-18), and cleanses their consciences (9:14). God promises extraordinary benefits to believers in the future: they will share in Christ's glory (2:10), enter God's rest (4:1, 3), inhabit an abiding heavenly city (11:16; 12:22; 13:13), and inherit a kingdom that cannot be shaken (12:28). Hebrews, however, never refers to God as benefactor (εὐεργέτης). In fact, the whole canon of the New Testament only contains four instances of the εὐεργε- word group (Luke 22:25; Acts 4:9; Acts 10:38; 1 Tim 6:2) and in none of those instances is God ever designated εὐεργέτης, though Jesus is depicted as bestowing benefits in Acts 10:38. Nonetheless, the basic structure of the divine-human relationship brings to mind the notion that God through Jesus is the divine benefactor of Christians.

Another conceptual echo involves the centrality of honor in many of the warnings of Hebrews.[2] The first warning (2:1-4) is predicated on the superior honor of Jesus over angels that is established in the syncrisis of chapter 1: "For if the word which was spoken by angels was binding and every transgression and disobedience received just punishment, how will we escape if we ignore such a great salvation which was first spoken by the Lord and was confirmed to us by those who heard him."[3] One of the most

---

1   See also the discussion of these conceptual parallels by David deSilva, *Perseverance in Gratitude: A Socio-Rhetorical Commentary on the Epistle to the Hebrews* (Grand Rapids: Eerdmans, 2000), 62.
2   David deSilva, in his published dissertation, *Despising Shame: Honor Discourse and Community Maintenance in the Epistle to the Hebrews* (SBLDS 152; Atlanta: Scholars Press, 1995), has given particular emphasis to the aspects of honor and shame in Hebrews.
3   Syncrisis was a progymnasmatic exercise that was typical in the beginning of stages of rhetorical training. Syncrisis, generally defined, is evaluative comparisons in the form of double encomiums, double invectives, or encomium-invective that can be employed for deliberative purposes. Cf. *Progymnasmata: Greek Text Books of Prose Composition and Rhetoric* (trans. George A. Kennedy; Atlanta: Society of

sobering warnings comes in 6:4-6, where the apostate is said to publicly shame Jesus (παραδειγματίζοντες) by falling away and therefore will not be admitted again into God's favor (cf. 12:16-17).[4] Filtering this passage through the lens of Greco-Roman benefaction, deSilva writes, "Not making a fair return to one's benefactor was unjust; to act so as to inflict dishonor upon one who had been a benefactor was an even more egregious act of injustice."[5] Likewise, the warning in 10:26 declares that the one who tramples the Son of God underfoot, treats as a profane thing the blood of the covenant, and insults the Spirit of grace is worthy of punishment (ἀξιωθήσεται τιμωρίας). Τιμωρία was a term used to refer to the punishment of an offense, especially an offense that necessitated the restoration of the honor of the one who had been offended. We find such an understanding of this terminology in the writings of Aulus Gellius (second century CE). Writing on the reasons for punishment, he states,

> It has been taught that there are three reasons for punishing crimes. One of these . . . is the infliction of punishment for the purpose of correction and reformation, . . . The second (τιμωρία). . . exists when the dignity and prestige of one who is sinned against must be maintained, lest the omission of punishment bring him into contempt and diminish the esteem in which he is held; and therefore they think that was given a name derived from the preservation of honor (τιμή). (*Attic Nights* 7.14.2-4 [Rolfe, LCL])[6]

These last two examples from Hebrews also fit well within the matrix of decrying the evil of ingratitude. Clearly, for the author of Hebrews, God's honor has a central place in his thinking, and we know that honor was the chief commodity sought by both human and divine benefactors in the Greco-Roman world. Honor was also a central value of God in the Old Testament. Isaiah 42:8 states, "I [Yahweh] will not give my glory to another or my praise to idols." Later in Isa 48:11 God declares, "For my own sake, I do it [restore Israel]. . . . How can I let myself be defamed? I

    Biblical Literature, 2003), 52-55, 83-84, 113-5, 162-64. For an excellent discussion of syncrisis see Michael Martin, "Philo's Use of Syncrisis: An Examination of Philonic Composition in the Light of the Progymnasmata," *PRSt* 30 (2003): 272-81. For the explicit mention of the use of syncrisis for deliberative ends see Nicolaus (60; Kennedy 126).

4   On the meaning of "repentance" and the failure to be renewed again to it see deSilva, *Perseverance in Gratitude*, 227 n. 39.

5   DeSilva, *Perseverance in Gratitude*, 238.

6   Also cited by DeSilva, *Perseverance in Gratitude*, 350. Aristotle writes concerning the anger of a slighted benefactor: "Men are angry at slights from those by whom they think they have a right to expect to be well treated; such are those on whom they have conferred or are conferring benefits, . . . and all those whom they desire, or did desire, to benefit" (*Rh.* 2.2.8 [Freese, LCL]).

will not yield my glory to another." Likewise, Ezekiel declares that God will not act salvifically for the sake of Israel but for "the sake of my holy name" (Ezek 36:22). The Old Testament ubiquitously affirms that God is a jealous God (Exod 20:5; Deut 4:24; 6:15; 32:21; Josh 24:19; Ezek 26:38; Nah 1:2; Zeph 3:8); in fact His name is Jealous (Exod 34:14). Furthermore, God's jealousy for His name is almost always associated with His demand to be worshipped alone.[7] The emphasis upon honoring God, Christ, and the Spirit and the honor God seeks from His people in Hebrews intersects with one of the chief values in Greco-Roman benefaction. We have not yet determined in Hebrews how this honor is secured through the fidelity of God's people.

Another potential echo of benefaction (and possibly reciprocity) can be found in Heb 6:10. In this verse the author assures his audience that "God is not unjust to overlook your works and the love you have shown his name by serving the saints and continuing to serve them". If we were to filter this through the lens of Greco-Roman benefaction, then we might hear that God is not an ungrateful deity but gratefully repays those who honor Him.[8] If, on the other hand, we filter this verse through the lens of a Jewish and Christian eschatology that expected a final reckoning by God, then God, in this verse, is declared to be a just judge who judges every person

---

7 Jonathan Edwards's treatise on *The End for which God Created the World* is an enriching and mature theological argument for God's disposition to glorify Himself through the communication of Himself in creation and salvation. Though written in the 1750s, I have not read a better treatment of this important subject anywhere else.

8 The author states that God is not unjust (ἄδικος) instead of not ungrateful (ἀχάριστος). Aristotle, however, when he discusses just and unjust actions (τῶς δικαίων καὶ τῶν ἀδίκων), states that "to be grateful to a benefactor, to render good for good" belongs to the unwritten laws of just actions (*Rh.* 1.13.11-12 [Freese, LCL]). Also ἐπιλανθάνομαι is employed in the LXX in various contexts such as not forgetting what God has done (Deut 4:9; 25:19; Ps 77:7); not forgetting God (Deut 6:12; 8:11, 14, 19); not forgetting God's law (Deut 4:23; 1 Macc 1:49; 2 Macc 2:2; Ps 118:93); not forgetting Jerusalem (Ps 136:5); not forgetting the kindness of a guarantor (Sir 29:15) or a friend (Sir 37:6) or God's benefits (Ps 103:2). Also to forget God is to be unfaithful to God (Pss 9:18; 49:22; Job 8:13; Jer 23:27: Isa 65:11). When the term is used with reference to God in the LXX, it usually refers to God's faithfulness to the covenant relationship with Israel or His gracious deliverance of the poor, oppressed, and afflicted (Pss 9:19, 33; 43:25; 73:19, 23; Isa 44:21; 49:15; Jer 14:9). In Phil 3:13, Paul uses the term to talk about forgetting the things that are behind him and pressing forward to his heavenly calling in Jesus Christ. The verb is used two more times in Hebrews (13:2, 16) where the audience is reminded to heed certain injunctions, i.e., hospitality and sharing with others. So while the term can be employed in a manner suggesting reciprocity (not forgetting benefits and forgetting being equated with infidelity), the context determines the specific nuance of this term.

impartially (i.e., he is not ἄδικος) according to his or her deeds.⁹ With the emphasis Hebrews places upon God as judge (cf. 6:2; 9:27; 12:23), the latter interpretation is likely. Consequently, this echo, though possible, is not probable.

Certain relational expectations described and prescribed by the author of Hebrews echo expectations characteristic of the benefactor-beneficiary relationship. In Heb 13:15, the author exhorts the believers to offer to God the sacrifice of praise (θυσίαν αἰνέσεως). DeSilva describes this statement as the response of gratitude expressed in cultic terms.¹⁰ We have already seen that praising one's divine benefactors was one way to honor them. While the terminology of this verse is drawn from Ps 49:14 and Hos14:3 (cf. *Pss. Sol.* 15:2-3) in the LXX, William Lane writes, "The writer has drawn upon a biblical and Jewish tradition of the song of praise that is offered to God in response to his grace."¹¹ This "tradition" also resembles the expectations typical of benefactor-beneficiary relationship. Another expectation typical of benefaction is the expression of gratitude by the beneficiary. The author exhorts his audience to show gratitude (ἔχωμεν χάριν) to God because they are receiving an unshakeable kingdom. Atypically, this is gratitude that is based upon a benefit not yet received, but we will have more opportunity to discuss this verse below. Nevertheless, the response is the commonly expected one from a beneficiary.¹²

The key relational expectation that is the central concern in Hebrews (and was the central concern among benefactors and beneficiaries) is fidelity. The purpose of this sermon was to exhort a group of Christians to remain faithful to God in the face of persecution (10:36; 12:3-4). For our author, without fidelity there is no hope for inheriting God's promise but only fearful expectation of judgment.¹³ The author uses the adjective πιστός to describe Jesus' and Moses' faithfulness to God (3:2-6). Their

---

9   In Zeph 3:5 and 1 Esd 4:36, God is said not to be or to do ἄδικος. In 1 Esd 4:39 and Rom 3:5, God's judgment is specifically declared not to be ἄδικος. For other references in the New Testament to God's impartial eschatological judgment that examines what a person does see Matt 25:31-46; Rom 2:2, 5-11; 1 Cor 3:13-15; 4:5; Gal 6:4-8; 1 Pet 1:17; Rev 20:11-15; 22:12. Cf. Harold Attridge, *The Epistle to the Hebrews* (Hermeneia; Philadelphia: Fortress Press, 1989), 174, who also locates 6:10 within the context of God's just judgment.
10 DeSilva, *Perseverance in Gratitude*, 504.
11 William Lane, *Hebrews 9-13* (WBC 47B; Nashville: Thomas Nelson Publishers, 1991), 551. See pp. 548-52 for a thorough examination of this verse.
12 The expression ἔχωμεν χάριν is also used by Josephus, *A.J.* 2.162, 2.339, 8.112, meaning to render or show gratitude. The expression appears to be typical when describing beneficiaries' responses to a benefactor. Aristotle uses the phrase, τό χάριν ἔχειν, to refer to being grateful to a benefactor (*Rh.* 1.13.12 [Freese, LCL]).
13 See Heb 2:13; 3:6; 3:12-14; 4:1, 6; 6:4-8; 6:11-12; 10:26-31; 10:35-39; 12:16-17; 12:25.

faithfulness is in contradistinction to the unbelief (ἀπιστία) that led to the unfaithfulness of the wilderness generation who failed to enter God's rest. The author of Hebrews, also, chooses to use other terminology to convey the idea of fidelity that the Christians are to show toward God: not drifting away (2:1); holding on to the hope one boasts (3:6); to show the same earnestness to the end (6:11); to exhibit faith and patience (πίστεως καὶ μακροθυμίας, 6:12)[14]; holding on to one's confession of hope (10:23); not throwing away their confidence but enduring (10:35-36); not to shrink back (10:39); to endure shame for the joy that lays before them (12:2); and to endure discipline as beloved children (12:7). Just as fidelity was a central quality in the beneficiary, it was equally as essential in the benefactor. Thus, in Hebrews, God is said to be faithful (πιστός) to His promises (10:23; 11:11). Such an affirmation is necessary for believers who are being asked to put their trust in God to be able and willing to provide for them and to ensure their future.[15] These responses of praise, gratitude, and fidelity all intersect expectations belonging to the benefactor-beneficiary relationship in the ancient Mediterranean world and very well may have called such relationships to mind among the first auditors of this sermonic letter.

Lexical Echoes

Also, Hebrews shares some lexical terminology that we find used with reference to benefaction and patronage. In Heb 2:18, Jesus is able to help (βοηθῆσαι) those who are being tempted; in Heb 4:16, the author encourages the believers to come to God's throne of grace and mercy to find timely help (βοήθειαν); and in Heb 13:6, the author quotes Ps 117:6 (LXX) which declares, "The Lord is my helper (Βοηθός)". Aristotle recommends helping (βοηθητικὸν) one's friends in the context of discussing just actions such as being grateful to a benefactor and repaying good for good (*Rh.* 1.13.12 [Freese, LCL]). Plutarch relates how the Sicilian Greeks sought aid (βοήθειαν) from the Corinthians because the Corinthians had benefited (εὐεργέτηντο) them previously (*Tim.* 2.1 [Perrin, LCL]). Elsewhere, Plutarch writes that as Pelopidas and his companions were brought before the assembly, they were calling upon the citizens "to come to the aid (βοηθεῖν) of their country and their gods". As a result the assembly cheered and proclaimed Pelopidas and his companions benefactors and saviors (εὐεργέτας καὶ σωτῆρας; *Pel.* 12.4 [Perrin, LCL]). Xenophon in discussing the advantages of being physically fit

---

14 Lane (*Hebrews 1-8* [WBC 47A; Nashville: Thomas Nelson Publishers, 1991], 145) writes that "faith is seen as the steadfast persistence that pursues the divine promise".

15 DeSilva, *Perseverance in Gratitude*, 62.

writes, "Many help friends and do good to their country (βοηθοῦσι καὶ . . . ἐρεργετοῦσι) and for this case earn gratitude (χαρίτος τε ἀξιοῦνται); get glory (δόξαν) and gain very high honors (τιμῶν)" (*Mem.* 3.12.4 [Marchant, LCL]).[16] Aid (βοήθεια) was a benefit given to those who had a pressing need, and it is what God provides through Christ to God's sojourning people.

There are other corresponding terms. In Heb 5:9, Jesus is called the believer's source of eternal salvation (αἴτιος σωτηρίας αἰωνίου). DeSilva cites *Or.* 31.75 where Dio refers to benefactors as sources of greater goods (μειζόνων ἀγαθῶν αἰτίους).[17] We find another term of commonality in the exempla list of Heb 11. In this chapter the author employs the term μαρτυρεῖσθαι (vv. 2, 4, 5, 39). Among the inscriptional evidence, the term is used with reference to a candidate concerning whom authorities approve to be worthy to receive honor for his or her beneficence.[18] This contextual designation may not be the primary one in Hebrews. Within Hebrews the term specifically refers to the approving testimony of Scripture (cf. 7:8, 17; 10:15). Lane refers to this list of personages in chapter 11 as a *"list of attested examples"* and μαρτυρεῖν in the passive is a technical term that "refers to the reception of attestation from God, discovered on the pages of Scripture, which validates the exemplary function of the persons listed for the edification of the audience".[19] Thus, in Hebrews, if this term called to mind benefaction among the auditors, the impression was secondary since none of the exempla listed in Heb 11 are honored for their beneficence to the community but for their faith by which they lived and died. The fact that this term is used within the context of benefaction does not mean that such a context is the primary reference every time the term is used. In the case of Heb 11, the overlap in terminology seems more incidental than actual.

Of all the lexical intersections in Hebrews with Greco-Roman benefaction, χάρις is the key one. Χάρις was a leitmotif in the language of

---

16 See also Diogenes Laertius, *Vita Philosophorum* 3.96. While there are numerous βοηθ- cognates in the LXX, there are only eight uses of any of these cognates in the New Testament with three of the eight occurring in Hebrews.
17 DeSilva, *Perseverance in Gratitude*, 194.
18 Frederick Danker, *Benefactor: Epigraphic Study of Graeco-Roman and New Testament Semantic Fields* (St. Louis: Clayton Publishing House, 1982), 442-43. Also cited in deSilva, *Perseverance in Gratitude*, 385.
19 Lane, *Hebrews 9-13*, 317 (cf. 330). For other such lists cited by Lane (317) see Sir 44:1-49:16; 1 Macc 2:51-61; 1 *Clem.* 7:5-7; 10:1–12:8; Philo, *Virt.* 198-255. For a fuller discussion of exempla lists and its function in Heb 11 see Michael R. Cosby, *The Rhetorical Function of Hebrews 11: In Light of Example Lists in Antiquity* (Macon: Mercer, 1988) and Pamela Michelle Eisenbaum, *The Jewish Heroes of Christian History: Hebrews 11 in Literary Context* (SBLDS 156; Atlanta: Scholars Press, 1997).

benefaction in the ancient Mediterranean world.[20] Its dual definition embodies the reciprocity characteristic of benefaction, meaning both the favor or benefit given and the gratitude shown for a favor.[21] Hebrews employs χάρις eight times. Seven of those eight instances (2:9; 4:16x2; 10:29; 12:15; 13:9; 13:25) are references to God's favor or benefits through Jesus Christ. Only in one instance is the term employed to characterize the gratitude of the recipients for a future benefit for which they hoped (12:18). At this point, however, we have yet to determine whether the author of Hebrews understands this to be indebted gratitude that secures fidelity to the relationship or whether this gratitude exalts God for His beneficence and faithfulness while simultaneously being an expression of poverty of spirit and humility. We will examine this issue later in the discussion below.

At this point, all that I wish to have demonstrated is that Hebrews communicated its message in a cultural setting where benefaction and patronage were part of the warp and woof of everyday life in the ancient Mediterranean world. Hebrews at points contains both conceptual and lexical echoes of this relationship in its message. This observation, however, does not necessarily imply that reciprocity was understood to be the foundation of the divine-human relationship in Hebrews. There were, in fact, two very different ways that the conceptual and lexical framework of Greco-Roman reciprocity was appropriated among first-century CE Jews and Christians. To this issue we will now briefly turn.

The Religious Appropriation of Benefaction-Patronage: Two Models

In the previous chapter we examined the influence that the reciprocity systems of antiquity had on the Middle Judaic milieu. Within that milieu, we observed two different models of appropriation from two key first-century representatives—Josephus and Paul.

---

20 James Harrison (*Paul's Language of Grace in Its Graeco-Roman Context* [WUNT 2.172; Tübingen: Mohr Siebeck, 2003]) has marshaled a plentitude of evidence from the inscriptions, philosophers, and Jewish corpus that demonstrate this point.

21 Cf. Harrison, *Paul's Language of Grace*, 48, who writes: "χάρις, therefore, captures the attitudinal aspects behind the reciprocity system, spotlighting not only the conventional return of favor but also the importance of a genuine and commensurate gratitude on the part of the beneficiary." Elsewhere, Harrison rightly cautions: "But the dominant use of the word was subsumed under the ethos of reciprocity—whether human or divine. In this respect, as a semantic starting point for the New Testament understanding of grace, χάρις—unless carefully defined—carried as many dangers as advantages" (63).

Josephus

Josephus demonstrates what happens when the biblical narrative of God's ongoing relationship with Israel is depicted in terms of the ideals of Greco-Roman benefaction and patronage. For Josephus, that includes reciprocity as the foundational dynamic of that relationship. God's people respond with worthy gratitude demonstrated primarily through obedience to God thus meriting further favor. This indebted gratitude is the motivation for fidelity to God, and is undergirded by an optimistic anthropological assumption. I have already laid the foundation for these generalizations in the previous chapter. Spilsbury aptly summarizes the divine-human relationship in Josephus, writing, "[G]ratitude is expressed primarily in obedience to the Law. This obedience then secures God's continued favor."[22] Josephus not only uses some of the language of Greco-Roman benefaction to describe the divine-human relationship, but he also carries over the rationale of reciprocity as the dynamic that ideally sustained the relationship between the benefactor and beneficiary in the ancient Mediterranean world.

Paul

On the other hand, Paul represents a different appropriation of Greco-Roman benefaction. In the previous chapter, I examined how Paul is critical of the dynamic of reciprocity to secure fidelity in the divine-human relationship. That criticism arises out of his pessimistic anthropology. Paul sets himself against synergism in any form, including reciprocity, and emphasizes God's initiative and enabling that establishes human fidelity to the relationship.

This last assertion has been painstakingly argued by a few scholars recently but in a different context. This context has been defined by E. P. Sanders's monumental work, *Paul and Palestinian Judaism*, which seeks to correct, in Sanders's opinion, the caricature of ancient Judaism as a legalistic religion—a caricature that developed from the Protestant Reformers' interpretation of Paul's polemic against the "works of the Law". Sanders's analysis of Palestinian Judaism led him to coin a new term. He described Palestinian Judaism of the first century CE as covenantal nomism. By covenantal nomism Sanders means:

> (1) God has chosen Israel and (2) given the law. The law implies both (3) God's promise to maintain the election and (4) the requirement to obey. (5) God rewards obedience and punishes transgression. (6) The law provides for means of atonement, and atonement results in (7)

---

22 Paul Spilsbury, "God and Israel in Josephus–A Patron-client Relationship," in *Understanding Josephus: Seven Perspectives* (ed. Steve Mason; JSPSup 32; Sheffield: Sheffield Academic Press, 1998), 251.

maintenance or re-establishment of the covenantal relationship. (8) All those who are maintained in the covenant by obedience, atonement and God's mercy belong to the group which will be saved.[23]

Further, *"[O]bedience maintains one's position in the covenant, but it does not earn God's grace as such."*[24] Sanders's description of covenantal nomism is shaped by the questions "how getting in and staying in are understood" in the religious life of a community.[25] While Sanders's discussion is not tied to a discussion of benefaction and patronage, his description of covenantal nomism appears to be grounded on the dynamic of reciprocity. Obedience in a covenantal nomistic relationship arises out of gratitude for election by God and the bestowal of benefits.[26] Further, those benefits are retained and continued as a result of the elect individual's ongoing faithfulness.

Though Sanders believed Paul's pattern of religion was different ("participatory eschatology"), James Dunn has argued that Paul's pattern of religion is covenantal nomistic.[27] Moreover, Paul's polemic is not against legalism (or synergism) but particularism. Significant critiques, however, of Sanders's covenantal nomism and Paul's relationship to this construct have recently come from two Scandinavian scholars. Timo Eskola believes Sanders has overstated his case about the gracious character of covenantal nomism. According to Eskola, if one places covenantal nomism in an eschatological context, then "staying in" by keeping the law results in "getting in" the age-to-come. Thus covenantal nomism becomes legalistic nomism.[28] Eskola concludes, *"In the theory of covenantal nomism Sanders defines a synergistic nomism."*[29] The other Scandinavian scholar, Timo

---

23   E. P. Sanders, *Paul and Palestinian Judaism: A Comparison of Patterns of Religion* (Philadelphia: Fortress Press, 1977), 422, cf. 75.
24   Sanders, *Paul and Palestinian Judaism*, 420.
25   Sanders, *Paul and Palestinian Judaism*, 17.
26   Sanders even entitles a section of his discussion of covenantal nomism in rabbinic Judaism, "The Theme of Gratuity" (*Paul and Palestinian Judaism*, 85-87).
27   Cf. James D. G. Dunn, The *Theology of Paul the Apostle* (Grand Rapids: Eerdmans, 1998), 632 n. 29. See also idem., "The New Perspective on Paul," *BJRL* 65 (1982-83): 95-122; idem., *Jesus, Paul and the Law: Studies in Mark and Galatians* (Louisville: Westminster/John Knox, 1990); idem., *The Parting of Ways Between Christianity and Judaism and Their Significance for the Character of Christianity* (London: SCM Press/Philadelphia: Trinity Press, 1992); idem., "Yet Once More—'The Works of the Law': A Response," *JSNT* 46 (1992): 99-117.
28   Timo Eskola, *Theodicy and Predestination in Pauline Soteriology* (WUNT 2.100; Tübingen: Mohr Siebeck, 1998), 56. See also Timo Laato, *Paul and Judaism: An Anthropological Approach* (tran. T. McElwain; South Florida Studies in the History of Judaism 115; Atlanta: Scholars Press, 1995), 156-57.
29   Eskola, *Theodicy and Predestination*, 57.

Laato, has pointed out that Sanders's covenantal nomism requires an optimistic anthropology. He argues that this Jewish pattern of religion is synergistic due to this optimism whereas Paul's pattern of religion is monergistic arising out of a pessimistic assumption.[30] Consequently, in the realm of salvation from conversion to consummation, Paul opposes synergistic cooperation between God and humanity—a synergism that is characteristic of ancient reciprocity. Laato references 2 Cor 4:6 and writes that "[God's] creative action excludes human cooperation totally".[31] Paul emphasizes divine enabling and human transformation. Charles Talbert points to Gal 2:20 among others passages as a primary way Paul understands the divine enabling of God in the believer. Here, Paul speaks about being indwelt by Christ and being empowered to live out his transient life with the faithfulness of the Son of God.[32] Also, on the basis of this verse, Laato affirms that *"Christ does the good works of the Christians"*.[33]

In sum, Paul opposed the synergism characteristic of ancient reciprocity, but he still drew upon terminology and ideological facets from the reciprocity system of benefaction to communicate the message of the gospel in his Greco-Roman context. For instance, we have had opportunity to point out that James Harrison has conclusively demonstrated that χάρις was a leitmotif of Greco-Roman benefaction. Moreover, we must hear and understand Paul's use of that term against that context—a term that gains central significance in Paul's theology. Harrison also notes, "Paul endorsed traditional conventions of clientage (Rom 15:24, 16:1-2), employed reciprocity terminology (2 Cor 6:13; Phil 4:15; 1 Tim 5:4), and argued for the social expression of reciprocity within his churches (Rom 13:8-10; 15:27; 2 Cor 8:13-15; Phil 4:10-20; Phlm)."[34] On the other hand, Harrison asks:

> How far did Paul's understanding of grace differentiate itself from traditional Graeco-Roman reciprocity ideology? Was Paul—whether implicitly or explicitly—critiquing the prominent social convention, in the hope of transforming the ethos of commensurability that was axiomatic in the world-view and social practice of his converts?[35]

Harrison draws attention to the "ethos of reciprocity" that surrounded Greek euergetism and Roman patronage and demonstrates how Paul both draws his language from these reciprocity systems while at the same time

---

30 Laato, *Paul and Judaism*, 167. See also Charles Talbert, "Paul, Judaism, and the Revisionists," *CBQ* 63 (2001): 1-22.
31 Laato, *Paul and Judaism*, 150.
32 Charles Talbert, *Romans* (Macon: Smyth & Helwys; 2002), 101.
33 Laato, *Paul and Judaism*, 162. Cf. Phil 2:12-13.
34 Harrison, *Paul's Language of Grace*, 21.
35 Harrison, *Paul's Language of Grace*, 20.

redefining the reciprocity rationale in light of the gospel of Jesus Christ. For Paul, according to Harrison, God's overflowing grace undermines the obligation of reciprocity and love subverts the dynamic of Greco-Roman reciprocity systems.[36]

In conclusion, to define benefaction or patronage in the larger Greco-Roman context does not automatically translate into an understanding of how Paul depicts the dynamic of the divine-human relationship. To understand Paul one has to listen both for resonance and dissonance in his message within his context. Paul serves as a first-century Christian model of how some of the language and concepts of benefaction can be used to characterize the divine-human relationship without importing reciprocity as the dynamic of that relationship as the foundation of fidelity. Our question then is whether Hebrews follows the model of Josephus or that of Paul. One scholar, David deSilva, has attempted to translate the message of Hebrews in terms of Greco-Roman benefaction or patronage in a manner characteristic of Josephus. This necessitates our examining his thesis and offering some initial critiques before turning to the major argument for understanding the message of Hebrews according to the Pauline model.

Interpreting Fidelity in Hebrews:
A Critique of DeSilva's Reciprocity Model

In order to understand David deSilva's interpretation of Hebrews, I will briefly describe his methodology and then examine his appropriation of ancient reciprocity as the means of securing fidelity in Hebrews. I will next offer some preliminary critiques of deSilva's appropriation of ancient reciprocity in his interpretation of Hebrews.

DeSilva's Methodology

In regards to methodology, DeSilva follows, what he calls, a socio-rhetorical method in his efforts to interpret Hebrews.[37] First, his approach uses the ancient guidelines for rhetorical training to understand what topics and methods a person would have employed to persuade his or her audience. Second, deSilva attempts to define the social, cultural, and ideological values in antiquity that would have shaped and influenced an author's rhetorical strategy. For deSilva, the controlling social metaphor for understanding the overall rhetorical strategy of Hebrews is Greco-Roman benefaction or patronage.

---

36 Harrison, *Paul's Language of Grace*, 349.
37 While my generalizations come from my impression of reading deSilva's work as a whole one can find his summary discussion of his method in his commentary, *Perseverance in Gratitude*, 58.

DeSilva's Appropriation of Ancient Reciprocity

This social metaphor and its values, according to deSilva, are the primary way to understand how the author of Hebrews seeks to persuade his audience to remain faithful to God, their divine benefactor, in the face of persecution. This interpretive strategy is made clear by the title of deSilva's commentary on Hebrews, *Perseverance in Gratitude*. My focus here is not on all the ways deSilva translates the message of Hebrews into terms of the benefactor-beneficiary relationship, but more specifically, how he carries over the reciprocity dynamic for securing fidelity in Greco-Roman benefaction into his interpretation of Hebrews. I will examine both deSilva's explicit affirmation of reciprocity in his interpretation of Hebrews and the characteristics of reciprocity that carry over into his interpretation. Then, I will focus on deSilva's affirmation of indebted gratitude (= the sense of owing or having to repay a favor done on one's behalf) as the principle of faithfulness.[38]

First, deSilva explicitly affirms reciprocity as the foundational dynamic between God and the believer in Hebrews. He writes, "The author of Hebrews makes extensive use of the social code of reciprocity, the mutual expectations and obligations of patrons and clients, in his sermon."[39] DeSilva also quotes approvingly Seneca's allegory of the Graces that depicts the dance of reciprocity.[40] DeSilva affirms, "Hebrews provides us with an understanding of 'grace' that is informed by the social system that gave that term meaning for the first hearers. 'Grace' is a relationship with mutual obligations and expectations into we which we are welcomed. Accepting God's gifts means accepting an obligation to the Giver."[41]

As a result, deSilva interprets the divine-human relationship in Hebrews as a synergistic one characterized by the cooperation and mutual dependence typical of reciprocity. For instance, commenting on Heb 6:9-12, deSilva writes that by remaining faithful "the hearers would preserve God's recognition of their worthy receptions of his benefits and thus stimulate him to continue to benefit them".[42] Moreover, this cooperation implies mutual dependence. While, the believer's dependence on God through Jesus is not in dispute, deSilva, in an interesting twist of interpretation of Heb 2:13a, attempts to show that Jesus is dependent on the believer to fulfill his or her obligations to the relationship. Hebrews 2:13a contains a quote from Isa 8:17, "I will put my trust in him". Here, the author has put this quote from Isaiah in the mouth of Jesus. This is not in

---

38 The sense of owing is what creates and maintains the bond where reciprocity is involved.
39 DeSilva, *Perseverance in Gratitude*, 59, cf. 62, 438.
40 DeSilva, *Perseverance in Gratitude*, 223, 474 n. 72.
41 DeSilva, *Perseverance in Gratitude*, 77.
42 DeSilva, *Perseverance in Gratitude*, 247, cf. 505 n. 60.

dispute. The issue arises over to whom "him" refers. The "him" in Isa 8:17 is a reference to God and most commentators maintain that this remains the referent in Hebrews.[43] DeSilva, however, in light ancient reciprocity, asserts that the referent is the believer. Therefore, the believer and not God is the object of Jesus' declared trust. In a manner characteristic of relationships of mutual dependence, deSilva notes that there is uncertainty in Jesus' alignment with believers since they might prove unfaithful in the end.[44]

Expectedly, deSilva carries over not only the cooperative mutual dependence of reciprocity but also its optimistic anthropological assumption. DeSilva gives no explicit discussion of his anthropological assumption or what anthropological assumption he believes Hebrews represents. Such comments on Heb 2:11b (Christ "is not ashamed to call them brothers"), however, point to such an optimistic assumption. DeSilva writes about Heb 2:11b:

> This indicates that Jesus' beneficence toward the hearers is accompanied by Jesus' estimation of them as people of worth, judging them to be suitable beneficiaries and reliable clients who will not disappoint or bring shame upon him.[45]

What is the basis for such worthiness or reliability? DeSilva does not answer this question but such language points to an optimistic assumption. This is the language of synergism that requires an optimistic anthropological assumption in order to be viable. This statement is reminiscent of previous statements from Seneca and Cicero among others, namely, that grace was given to the worthy. DeSilva tries to deny that this

---

43 Cf. Lane, *Hebrew 1-8*, 60; Paul Ellingworth, *The Epistle to the Hebrews: A Commentary on the Greek Text* (NIGTC: Grand Rapids: Eerdmans; Carlisle: Paternoster Press, 1993), 169; Attridge, *Hebrews*, 90-91; James Moffatt, *A Critical and Exegetical Commentary on the Epistle to the Hebrews* (ICC; Edinburgh: T&T Clark, 1986), 33; Craig R. Koester, *Hebrews: A New Translation with Introduction and Commentary* (AB 36; New York: Doubleday, 2001), 238-39; Mary Isaacs, *Reading Hebrews and James: A Literary and Theological Commentary* (Macon: Smyth & Helwys, 2002), 43; F. F. Bruce, *The Epistle to the Hebrews* (NICNT; rev. ed.; Grand Rapids: Eerdmans, 1990), 84; Hans-Friedrich Weiss, *Der Brief an die Hebräer* (KEK 15; Göttingen: Vandenhoack & Ruprecht, 1991), 216; Ceslaus Spicq, *L'Épître aux Hébreux* (2 vols.; Paris: Gabalda, 1953), 2:42. The context of this quotation deals with Jesus' solidarity with God's people. Therefore, during his earthly sojourn like the present Christian pilgrims, he had to put his unwavering trust in God. In Heb 5:7-8, we see that trust in action as the author depicts Jesus intensely crying out to God who can deliver him from death and thus submitting to God's will.
44 DeSilva, *Perseverance in Gratitude*, 116.
45 DeSilva, *Perseverance in Gratitude*, 115.

means that believers are deserving of God's favor because of their faithfulness, but what else could such a statement mean when deSilva affirms that Jesus' benefits are based upon his estimation of the believer's worth and reliability to make an equitable return for benefits received. DeSilva even cites *Ben.* 4.29.5 as support of his statement, and the moral worthiness of the beneficiary is clearly what Seneca has in view. Though such an optimism about the essential human condition is typical of ancient reciprocity systems, deSilva has not shown that Hebrews shares such an optimism.

Second, deSilva is repetitively insistent that fidelity to God in Hebrews is motivated by and arises out of indebted gratitude. DeSilva contends that Heb 12:28 ("Let us be thankful because we are receiving an unshakeable kingdom and so worship God acceptably with reverence and awe.") is the overarching exhortation for the entire sermon. In fact, he follows his comments on this verse with an excursus on gratitude and how it functions within ancient reciprocity systems, which, for deSilva, is also the way it functions in Hebrews.[46] There are numerous places where deSilva reads this understanding of gratitude back into the sermon. (1) Gratitude is the primary motive for obedience. DeSilva states that the author focuses on the Son's "unparalleled benefits in order to motivate gratitude".[47] Again, the warnings and exhortations in Hebrews are primarily employed to encourage obedience and loyalty that come "from a grateful heart".[48] Supposedly, contemplation of the Son's benefits throughout the sermon serves to stimulate gratitude and motivate appropriate responses.[49] (2) Gratitude is a debt owed or to be repaid.[50] Commenting on Heb 1:2, Christ as creator is "thus owed a debt of gratitude".[51] Concerning 1:3, deSilva writes about Christ's purification of the believer from sin, "This recalls for the hearers the debt that they particularly owe the Son."[52] In an amplification of Heb 2:9, deSilva claims that the focus on the costliness of

---

46 DeSilva, *Perseverance in Gratitude*, 474-76, cf. 61. I find interesting the fact that only in Heb 12:28 is χάρις clearly used to refer to the believer's gratitude. In fact, this is the only place where the author explicitly mentions gratitude as the appropriate Christian response. DeSilva's commentary, however, is filled with hundreds of uses of the term gratitude. This is obviously disproportionate and gives the impression that Hebrews is being forced into a mold of Greco-Roman benefaction.
47 DeSilva, *Perseverance in Gratitude*, 63.
48 DeSilva, *Perseverance in Gratitude*, 63-64.
49 DeSilva, *Perseverance in Gratitude*, 111.
50 Another way the debt of gratitude was brought to bear on a person was through the reminding of benefits. DeSilva also points to this as part of Hebrews's rhetorical strategy, see *Perseverance in Gratitude*, 121.
51 DeSilva, *Perseverance in Gratitude*, 87.
52 DeSilva, *Perseverance in Gratitude*, 89.

Jesus' gifts should intensify the feeling of obligation in his beneficiaries. DeSilva goes on to say that the author of Hebrews maintains the commitment of his auditors by arousing their sense of debt and gratitude.[53] Commenting on Heb 12:2, deSilva believes that focusing on Jesus' sufferings for his beneficiaries will enhance their "awareness of debt".[54] Referring to the exhortation in Heb 13:16, deSilva states that believers "repay" God's generosity indirectly by extending generosity to one another.[55] (3) Perseverance manifests gratitude. This is deSilva's conclusion about what motivates the believer to finish the race in Heb 12:1-3.[56] (4) Infidelity is expressed as forgetting God's benefits. This is deSilva's understanding of the warning in Heb 2:1-4. He states that the "drifter" or the one who neglects such a great salvation has forgotten God's past benefits and future promises and so fails to live out of gratitude, that is, remain loyal to God the benefactor. DeSilva is emphatic: "This is the dynamic behind the author's response."[57] In all these cases, the language of indebtedness, owing, repaying, even gratitude, though well-suited to Greco-Roman benefaction, is not found in Hebrews (except in 12:28). Like Josephus, deSilva translates the message of Hebrews in a way that mirrors the values, expectations, and reciprocity of Greco-Roman benefaction or patronage.

A Preliminary Critique of DeSilva's Interpretation

There are, however, some initial problems with what deSilva has done. First, there are methodological problems. I have already mentioned deSilva's transformation of the rhetoric of Hebrews into that of ancient reciprocity, although the language of reciprocity is not used in Hebrews, except in two possible instances.[58] Methodologically, deSilva does not just describe the context in which Hebrews emerges, but embeds those contextual values in Hebrews. Moreover, Seneca provides the key for understanding reciprocity in Greco-Roman benefaction and thereby the key to the divine-human relationship in Hebrews. Such a method does not allow for the author's or audience's experience of salvation in Jesus Christ to

---

53 DeSilva, *Perseverance in Gratitude*, 111-12.
54 DeSilva, *Perseverance in Gratitude*, 433. Also see deSilva's amplification of Heb 13:13 (501).
55 DeSilva, *Perseverance in Gratitude*, 506.
56 DeSilva, *Perseverance in Gratitude*, 427.
57 DeSilva, *Perseverance in Gratitude*, 105-106.
58 Here I mean specifically the language of reciprocity not benefaction in general. Hebrews 6:10 was a possible echo of reciprocity, but the context of eschatological judgment, and not reciprocity, was determined to be more suitable there. Also Heb 12:28 was another possible echo but we have yet to determine if that is the appropriate context for this statement.

shape and transform the cultural values and language of the world in which they lived. Related to this issue is the fact that deSilva subsumes other metaphors in Hebrews under benefaction. For instance, his discussion of Hebrews 12:1-4 is laced with commentary on benefaction and reciprocity, yet in this passage the athletic metaphor is primary and does not easily lend itself to a benefaction or patronage interpretation.

Another significant problem has to do with the primary motivation for faithfulness to God in Hebrews. While the author does mention past benefits that believers have received from Christ, his primary strategy for fidelity is to encourage their faith in the future that God has promised to those who hold onto their confidence.[59] Believers are on a pilgrimage, and they are looking to enter God's rest (4:1); they see Jesus who has gone before them as a representative of the glory they will inherit in the world-to-come (2:5-10); and they are looking to an abiding heavenly city God has prepared for them (11:16; 12:22; 13:13). God has promised and confirmed all of this in Jesus Christ, but the promised inheritance is still not possessed by the Christian pilgrims. DeSilva rightly observes that for the author of Hebrews "salvation" is the deliverance that awaits the faithful pilgrim at the return of Christ (9:28).[60] Lane aptly writes, "The pattern in Hebrews is promise, reaffirmed with intensity, and fulfillment yet in the future. . . . The faith the writer commends to his audience is a confident reliance upon the future, which make possible responsible action in the present in the light of that confidence."[61] Fidelity motivated by faith in a promised future is not the same as indebted gratitude that arises out of past benefits given. Even Heb 12:28 ("Because we are receiving an unshakeable kingdom, let us be thankful.") grounds gratitude on the certainty of faith in the promised future. Gratitude is the proleptic response to the affirmation of one's hope. Faith is primary; gratitude is secondary. Further, in Heb 12:2, Jesus, who is the prime example of enduring faithfulness, despised the shame of the cross "for the joy set before him" and not because he was gratefully indebted to God.[62] All the heroes of Heb 11 "were commended for their faith and yet did not receive the promise" but died waiting for the fulfillment of the

---

59 For another key Jewish text that employs the same strategy see the *Testament of Job*. In fact, similar to the motif in Hebrews 11:13-16 and 13:13-14, Job depicts himself on a voyage to the resplendent city of God (*T.Job* 18:1-15). Therefore, he endures whatever difficulties and sacrifices whatever he presently possesses in order to reach God's promised glorious city.
60 DeSilva, *Perseverance in Gratitude*, 221.
61 Lane, *Hebrews 1-8*, cxlviii-cxlix, cf. 394..
62 See Clayton Croy, *Endurance in Suffering: Hebrews 12:1-13 in Its Rhetorical, Religious, and Philosophical Contexts* (SNTSMS 98; Cambridge: Cambridge University Press, 1998) esp. 66-67, 177-85, for the convincing proof and argument that ἀντὶ τῆς προκειμένης αὐτῷ χαρᾶς should be understood as "for the joy set before him" and not "instead of the joy set before him".

promise because "faith is the essence of things hoped for and the firm conviction of things unseen" (11:1). This is not a fidelity motivated by gratitude but one that is sustained by the certainty of the future promised because the Christian pilgrim is convinced that God who promised this future is faithful (10:23). Elsewhere, in a manner uncharacteristic of the dynamic of reciprocity, the author of Hebrews exhorts his auditors to find ongoing strength for faithfulness by going to God's throne of grace where he or she receives the necessary grace and mercy (4:16). The author does not try to call to mind all that God has done for them or try to exhort them to repay their debt to God so that God will then continue to be gracious to them. Additionally, the memory of past benefits can function in such a way as not to promote the feeling of indebted gratitude but to bolster faith in the benefactor. Plutarch in his *Life of Timoleon* writes,

> [T]he Sicilian Greeks, in their fright, wished to send an embassy to Greece and ask for assistance (βοήθειαν) from the Corinthians, not only because they trusted (πιστεύοντες) them on account of their kinship and in consequence of the many benefits they had already received (εὐεργέτηντο) from them. (2.1 [Perrin, LCL])

Here is a case where past benefits stimulated trust and the boldness to ask for continued assistance. We can, likewise, understand the author's of Hebrews encouragement to approach God and seek further grace. God's past benefits or assurances through Jesus Christ to the Christian pilgrim encourage that pilgrim's ongoing faith and confidence in God to seek continuing aid from God therein proving that God is the rewarder of those who seek Him (11:6). DeSilva recognizes that the author attempts to "stimulate a forward-looking attitude" and seeks "perseverance in faith",[63] but he does not grasp the discord such statements have with his primary emphasis on faithfulness that springs from indebted gratitude, which is a backward-looking attitude.

If fidelity springs from faith in the promised future, then the author of Hebrews understands infidelity springing from unbelief. The wilderness generation, the primary example of infidelity, is not castigated for their ingratitude (though clearly they could be charged with this) but for their failure to trust God and believe His promises (3:19; 4:2). Even here, we possibly find that the author understood that God's deliverance of Israel from Egypt and continued care during Israel's desert wandering was meant to stimulate trust in God, for the author describes the wilderness generation as "all who came out Egypt through Moses" and still rebelled (3:16). Unbelief also stems from an improper valuation of the promised future. Esau can be blamed for selling his birth right because he did not apprehend

---

63 DeSilva, *Perseverance in Gratitude*, 316, 385.

Fidelity in Hebrews 145

the value of his future inheritance in comparison to his present "godless" desires (12:16-17). Esau showed reckless disregard for his future inheritance. Lastly, since unbelief leads to infidelity for the author of Hebrews, the Christian pilgrims are exhorted to see that no one among them has an unbelieving (ἀπιστίας) evil heart that turns away from the living God.[64]

Finally, our major concern for the remainder of this chapter is that deSilva gives no discussion of what he, or Hebrews for that matter, believes to be the capacity of human beings to engage in a relationship of reciprocity with God. We have already seen that deSilva assumes the necessary optimistic anthropology characteristic of ancient reciprocity. There are other emphases of deSilva that lend themselves to an optimistic anthropology. DeSilva's emphasis on rhetorical strategy implies an optimistic anthropology. To lay considerable significance on the means and strategy of persuasion suggests that all humans require is instruction and convincing arguments in order to take the necessary action. The strategy of persuasion needs theological underpinning. What does the author assume about the capacity of his hearers to receive the instruction he gives?[65] Also, deSilva's emphases on honor and shame imply an optimistic assumption. DeSilva states, "Honor and shame are the primary tools of social control in the ancient world." Moreover, humans construct "courts of reputation" from which they seek approval.[66] But from where does the desire to please one "court" over another come? What gives the believer the desire to seek God's honor and to feel ashamed when he or she dishonors God? Why convert and forsake the majority culture for a despised minority one? Moreover, deSilva's emphasis upon honor and shame strategies suggests that behavior is controlled heteronomously (from without) whereas Hebrews's emphasis on the conscience and internality of the new covenant would suggest a behavior that is controlled from within.[67] In fact, when

---

64 Related to this passage in Hebrews, deSilva (*Perseverance in Gratitude*, 144) provides a helpful summary of how the πιστ- word group was understood in reciprocity relationships, but context determines whether this is the relational dynamic suggested by the use of this word group. For Paul, a Christian's faithfulness (πίστις) is the work of the indwelling Christ, not reciprocity. In Hebrews, as we will see, infidelity is rooted in something deeper than ingratitude or unbelief. It is rooted in the defiled human condition.

65 For Paul, such a capacity was the provenance of the Spirit (cf. 1 Cor 2:14-16).

66 DeSilva, *Perseverance in Gratitude*, 64-65.

67 Zeba Crook (*Reconceptualizing Conversion: Patronage Loyalty, and Conversion in the Religions of the Ancient Mediterranean* [BZNW 130; New York: Walter de Gruyter, 2004], 184-86) explicitly confirms my observation. She accepts that the ancient Mediterranean world was an honor-shame culture. Therefore, she concludes that it was less important what one believed or internally preferred than that one showed the appropriate behavior, i.e., loyalty to one's benefactor. At least one Jesus

deSilva speaks about the internality of the new covenant in Hebrews, he seems to believe that knowledge of what pleases God is the extent of what is given to the believer.[68] Furthermore, for deSilva, the use of rhetorical strategies by the author of Hebrews is what shapes and energizes this knowledge to produce the desired effect.

What I will argue from this point on is that the extent of the new covenant blessings in Hebrews involves abiding transformation and the ongoing divine enabling of the Christian pilgrim, which are the necessary bases for his or her fidelity to God. Further, this understanding suggests a pessimistic anthropological assumption for the author of Hebrews. In so doing, the theology of Hebrews will be seen to belong to that Middle Judaic stream that was implicitly critical of reciprocity as the foundation for fidelity to God, and Hebrews will be seen to follow the Pauline model in its limited use of the language and concepts of benefaction .

Interpreting Fidelity in Hebrews:
Divine Enablement and Anthropological Assumption in Hebrews

If we desire to understand the divine-human relational dynamic in Hebrews then we must look first to its interpretation of the new covenant for our clue. The new covenant is the primary metaphor for the divine-human relationship in Hebrews. There are some key supports for this assertion. First, the Jeremiah prophecy is the most extensive Old Testament quote in Hebrews. Second, the quotation of the Jeremiah prophecy (8:8-12) is found in the central section (8:1–9:28) of the central exposition in Hebrews (7:1–10:18).[69] Hebrews 8:1 begins by declaring that the author is about to explain what the "chief point" (κεφάλαιον) of the central exposition is. Lane's comment is typical: "Its [8:1–9:28] place at the center indicates the importance that the writer gave to this facet of the message."[70] Third, Susanne Lehne has rightly noticed that, through the cultic reinterpretation of the covenant, the author of Hebrews makes the covenant motif the organizing principle of his sermon.[71] I would also add that the main

---

    tradition was explicitly critical of this perspective. The Matthean Jesus (Matt 15:8-9a) castigates the religious leaders for this superficial "loyalty", quoting the prophet Isaiah, "These people honor me with their lips but their hearts are far from me. They worship me in vain."

68 DeSilva, *Perseverance in Gratitude*, 326-27.
69 Albert Vanhoye (*La Structure litteraire de l'Épître aux Hébreux* [Paris: Cerf, 1977], 42-60) has argued that Heb 5:9-10 prepares the auditor for the central exposition in 7:1–10:18. Hebrews 7:1-28 focuses on Jesus as "a high priest like Melchizedek", 8:1–9:29 on Jesus who "was made perfect", and 10:1-18 on Jesus as "the source of eternal salvation".
70 Lane, *Hebrews 1-8*, 202, cf. 126. Lane follows Vanhoye, *La Structure*, 44, 134-35.
71 Susanne Lehne, *The New Covenant in Hebrews* (JSNTSup 44; Sheffield: Sheffield

rhetorical feature, syncrisis, further supports Lehne's observation and arguments. Underlying the various syncrises in Hebrews is a comparison of the old covenant and new covenant. The progymnasmatic instruction about syncrisis states that a syncrisis of two subjects (in Hebrews the old and new covenants) is not between the "whole" subjects but between their analogous parts.[72] Hebrews's syncrises are arranged by moving from one analogous part to another—from the mediators of the covenants, to each covenant's representative servants, to their priests, to the cultic ministry and sacrifices associated with each covenant.[73] Concerning the new covenant relationship, Hebrews emphasizes two aspects of the Jeremiah prophecy: that God will write His law upon the heart and God will forgive the people's sins (10:16-17). Our primary concern will be with examining how Hebrews represents the fulfillment of these two promises.

First, the benediction of Hebrews (13:20-21) is predicated upon the fulfillment of these new covenant promises. Thus, the author prays in the benediction that God would equip his audience with all that they need to serve God *and* work in them what pleases Him. The benediction clearly picks up on the divine inner working predicted in the new covenant. The author previously states that the believer's ongoing worship of God is a total response of the whole person to God (cf. 13:15-16), yet here in the benediction, the believers' service to God comes from God.[74] They are divinely enabled to worship God without duplicity and with unfailing single-hearted devotion. But we might ask, how then does the preceding exposition of the high priestly ministry of Jesus Christ, which is the singular focus of Hebrews (esp. 7:1–10:18), provide the foundation for this concluding prayer? This foundation is assumed in the opening verse of the benediction—"May the God of peace who raised the great shepherd of the sheep by the blood of the eternal covenant, our Lord Jesus, equip you . . . and work in us" (13:20). In other words, how does the author represent the fulfillment of the new covenant inaugurated by the Melchizedekian high priest, Jesus—a covenant that promises the forgiveness of sins and the inscribing of the law on the people's hearts? In short, what we will see, through the cultic reinterpretation of the new covenant, is that God chooses

---

Academic Press, 1990), 103.

72 Cf. the progymnasmatic instruction regarding syncrisis by Apthonius ([43]; Kennedy 114) and Nicolaus ([59]; Kennedy 162)

73 DeSilva has described this movement as a "chain of revelation" from the angels to the mediator to the priests (*Perseverance in Gratitude*, 138).

74 Here we also find a modified intersection with benefaction/patronage. God through Jesus receives glory for His ongoing enabling presence in the Christian pilgrim ("[May God] equip you with everything good so that you may do his will and work in you what is pleasing before him through Jesus Christ, to whom is glory forever, amen."). God receives glory as a benefactor but not through indebted gratitude but through being the sole source of the pilgrim's life of faithfulness.

the believers and purifies their consciences through Jesus Christ. This purification then transforms their defiled condition and empowers their approach to God out of which comes the grace and mercy necessary for ongoing fidelity to God. Thus Hebrews (1) affirms a Christian's fidelity arises from God's election and enablement (2) which is necessitated by a pessimistic anthropological assumption. We will examine these assertions in turn.

Election and Enablement

ELECTION MOTIFS

The covenant metaphor central to Hebrews implies a durable personal relationship. The questions we are seeking to answer are: according to Hebrews, how does such a relationship begin and how is it sustained? First, how does a person enter the new covenant relationship with God? For whom is Christ's high priestly ministry meant? The short answer to these questions is those whom God has chosen or called.

Hebrews is rich with election themes. These themes are especially prevalent in Heb 2. In 2:11, the author refers to the many sons who are led to glory as "those who are sanctified" (οἱ ἁγιαζόμενοι). In the same verse, Jesus is referred to as the one who sanctifies (ὁ ἁγιάζων).[75] In the Old Testament, ὁ ἁγιάζων was a reference to God. The specific sense of this terminology is that God has set apart Israel from the other nations to worship Him. This setting apart for service is a way to talk about God's choosing or election. We find such a meaning in Lev 22:31-33 (LXX):

> Keep my commands and follow them. I am the LORD. Do not profane my holy name. I must be acknowledged as holy by the Israelites. I am the LORD who sanctifies you (ὁ ἁγιάζων ὑμᾶς) and who brought you out of Egypt to be your God. I am the LORD.

Here God's sanctifying of Israel is associated with His deliverance of Israel out of Egypt to be His people and to worship Him.[76] In Ezek 20:12 (LXX), God declares that He sanctified Israel (ὁ ἁγιάζων αὐτούς). Again, God's sanctifying of Israel is set in the context of His bringing Israel out of Egypt before the eyes of the nations in order to worship Him. Elsewhere, in Ezek 37:28 (LXX), God declares, "Then the nations will know that I the Lord sanctify Israel (ὁ ἁγιάζων αὐτούς), when my sanctuary is among them forever." In all these instances, for Israel to be sanctified by God means for God to choose Israel from among all the nations to be His people and to

---

75 Lane, *Hebrews 1-8*, 58. Cf. Attridge, *Hebrews*, 88 n. 107; Ellingworth, *Hebrews*, 163.
76 Cf. Exod 31:13 (LXX).

serve Him. "Sanctifying" (ἁγιάζων) is a reference to that choice being enacted in time by God so that God's choice of Israel is now apparent to all the nations. Likewise, Hebrews now applies this terminology to the church as those who have been consecrated by Jesus Christ or chosen by him in order to serve God (cf. 9:14). David Peterson, likewise, states that οἱ ἁγιαζόμενοι is a general designation for believers ("the sanctified") not a reference to an ongoing process.[77]

We encounter yet another more explicit election motif in Heb 2:13. The verse is a citation of Isa 8:18 put on the lips of the exalted Jesus. Jesus upon his entrance into his glory declares, "Here am I and the children God has given to me." In Isa 8:18, the children that God gives to the prophet are the remnant of Israel that awaits God's deliverance. In the context in Hebrews, this statement is a proleptic picture of the Christian pilgrim's hope. Jesus who has already entered into the glory of the world-to-come (2:5-9) leads the many "sons", who are presently awaiting their final deliverance, to this glory. Upon his entrance and the completion of the Christian pilgrim's sojourn, Jesus unashamedly declares that these are the children God has given him. Lane comments that here we are pointed to "the gracious determination of God to bring his children to their destiny through the redemptive mission of the Son".[78]

We are given another proleptic picture and election theme in Heb 12:23, where the Christian pilgrim has come "to the assembly of the firstborn inscribed permanently (ἀπογεγραμμένων) in heaven".[79] Peterson states that this description is an eschatological encounter of the *"ultimate complete company of the people of God"*.[80] A heavenly registry was

---

77 David Peterson, *Hebrews and Perfection: An Examination of the Concept of Perfection in the 'Epistle to the Hebrews'* (Cambridge: Cambridge University Press, 1982), 150. Peterson notes that sanctification is something that is already effected by Christ (10:10, 29; 13:12).
78 Lane, *Hebrews 1-8*, 58.
79 My translation follows Lane (*Hebrews, 9-13*, 467-68) in order to bring out the meaning of the perfect participle. Moffatt (*Hebrews*, 217) states that the whole phrase emphasize God's election.
80 Peterson, *Hebrews and Perfection*, 162. The phrase ἐκκλησίᾳ πρωτοτόκων may be and has been taken by some (Käsemann, Spicq, Montefiore) with the previous verse as a reference to the myriad of angels. The description, "permanently ascribed in heaven", however, is never used of angels. Further, ἐκκλησία and πρωτότοκος are "rooted in the description of Israel in the Pentateuch". Also, πρωτότοκος in the plural was "an apocalyptic title applied to the redeemed community". See Lane, *Hebrews 9-13*, 468-69, for this discussion and the evidence presented in favor of the latter assertions.
  I understand that Heb 12:23 refers to the ultimate complete company of God's people across the ages and not merely to the faithful dead (i.e., "the spirits of the perfected righteous") because the author includes the living faithful to be among

common in apocalyptic thought. There was a registry where the names of the redeemed were recorded. Daniel 12:1 states that all whose names are written in the book will be delivered from times of distress. Revelation 13:8 refers to the redeemed as those whose names have been inscribed in the book of life from the creation of the world.[81] In these passages, the inscription is a reference to both election and divine protection. Craig Koester notes that the passive voice (ἀπογεγραμμένων) is used here to suggest that people are registered by God's initiative.[82] Such an initiative implies the divine election of those inscribed in the heavenly registry.

Other election terminology is found in Heb 2:16 where we are told that Jesus "takes hold of Abraham's seed". The immediate allusion of this phrase is to Isa 41:8-10. In verse 8, Yahweh describes Abraham's seed as those "whom I have chosen". Paul Ellingworth has shown through key lexical overlap between the text of Hebrews and passage in Isaiah that the cumulative allusion in Hebrews is to this whole passage from Isaiah.[83] Just the phrase "Abraham's seed" is replete with notions of election. Abraham was chosen by God. Abraham's progeny of promise, Isaac, was the line of Abraham chosen by God through whom He would bless all nations. The early Christians began to identify themselves as belonging to Abraham's chosen line, as his children of promise through Jesus Christ. They were the true heirs of the promise (cf. Gal 3:29).[84] If Hebrews is addressed to a congregation of both Jews and Gentiles, then it clearly shares in this theological tradition of early Christianity.[85]

In Heb 2:17, we come across another term that carries with it connotations of election. Here the author tells us that Jesus propitiates the

---

that joyful assembly ("for you have come", 12:22).
81   See also Exod 32:32-33; Ps 69:28; *1 En.* 104:1; *Apoc. Zeph.* 3:7; Luke 10:20; Phil 4:3.
82   Koester, *Hebrews*, 545.
83   Ellingworth, *Hebrews*, 176.
84   Attridge, *Hebrews*, 94 n. 179.
85   First Peter is an excellent example of how the terminology associated with Israel in the Old Testament can be reapplied without any polemic to a predominantly Gentile Christian context. Whether this term in Hebrews is seen as a racial designation over a theological one often depends upon what one believes to be the make-up of Hebrews's audience. DeSilva has cogently argued that there is nothing in the text of Hebrews that would not have served the religious and ideological needs of Gentile Christians (*Perseverance in Gratitude*, 2-7). Ellingworth notes that even among Jewish Christians, "seed of Abraham" would not have been heard as an exclusive designation for Jews (*Hebrews*, 178). Mary Isaacs, who believes the audience of Hebrews is Jewish Christians, still invests the term with theological meaning stating that the "seed of Abraham" indicates that Abraham is the father of the elect of Israel (*Reading Hebrews*, 46).

sins of the people (τοῦ λαοῦ).[86] Likewise, we read in Heb 13:12 that Jesus sanctifies the people (τὸν λαόν) through his own blood. In Hebrews, "the people" designates the new covenant community (cf. 4:9; 8:10; 10:30).[87] This designation corresponds to the previous designation of referring to the community as the "seed of Abraham". Ὁ λαός (τοῦ θεοῦ) was a technical term in the LXX for Israel as a nation chosen by God. Strathmann describes the theological significance of this term in the LXX when it serves as a designation for Israel:

> Because Yahweh has separated Israel to Himself as a peculiar possession, they are a holy people. They do not have to become a holy people by cultic or moral sanctification: they are this in virtue of the divine distinction. . . . This relation of possession is by the free act of Yahweh. He chose Israel, Dt. 4:37; 7:6; 14:2; ψ 134:4.[88]

As with the "seed of Abraham", this term as well became a religious designation used by the early Christians (cf. Acts 15:14; Acts 18:10; Rom 9:23-25; 1 Pet 2:9).[89]

We encounter a final election motif in Heb 9:15. Here we are told that Jesus' death redeems from the sins committed under the first covenant so that those who are called (οἱ κεκλημένοι) might receive the eternal inheritance. Again, the designation, οἱ κεκλημένοι, is a perfect passive pointing to the enduring nature of this call and the divine initiative of God who calls. Both aspects refer to the divine election of the one who receives the eternal inheritance.[90] For instance, in Isa 41:9 (LXX), to which the author of Hebrews has previously alluded in 2:16-18, to be called is equated with being chosen.[91] Commenting on Roman 8:29, Charles Talbert writes, "'[C]alling' focuses on the divine choice."[92] In Heb 5:4, the high priest does not take the honor of this office by his own initiative but must be called (καλούμενος) by God, which is another way of saying that he must be chosen by God. Additionally, Heb 9:15 heads the discussion of Jesus' sacrificial death as a covenant sacrifice that inaugurates the new covenant (9:15-20). The author uses Exod 24:3, 6-8 to explain the significance of Jesus' vicarious death as a covenant sacrifice. There God initiates a covenant relation with Israel whom He has chosen who then is sprinkled with the blood of the covenant. Thus, the scope of the covenant sacrifice is limited to those God has chosen or, in the language of Hebrews, to those

---

86 This statement is reminiscent of Heb 9:28 where Jesus "bore the sins of the many".
87 Attridge, *Hebrews*, 398.
88 Strathmann, "λαός," *TDNT* 4:35.
89 See the discussion of Strathmann, *TDNT* 4:54-56.
90 Cf. Attridge, *Hebrews*, 255 n. 19.
91 See n. 86 above.
92 Talbert, *Romans*, 225.

God "has called".

All of these election motifs in Hebrews affirm that the foundation of the benefits the Christian pilgrims receive through Jesus Christ reside in the elective will of God. His choice is necessary for any to experience the benefits of Jesus' high priestly ministry. But does God's grace of election only stand at the beginning of the Christian's sojourn? Is then the Christian's ongoing fidelity to God predicated upon his or her gratitude to God for that choice? For Hebrews, God's election stands not only at the beginning of the Christian's pilgrimage but extends to the Christian's ongoing faithfulness. Therefore, we must discuss Hebrews's representation of human transformation and ongoing divine enablement.

ENABLEMENT

How is this new covenant relationship sustained according to Hebrews? From where does fidelity come? I have already stated my initial answer to this question: fidelity comes from human transformation and ongoing divine enablement through the purification of the believer's conscience by Jesus' high priestly ministry and the resulting approach to God.[93] To unpack this central motif of human transformation and ongoing divine enablement in Hebrews first requires that we understand the cultic reinterpretation of the new covenant in Hebrews. Though the prophecy in Jeremiah or its surrounding context does not mention the cult or sacrifice, Hebrews filters its interpretation of the new covenant through the cult of the old covenant. For Hebrews, a new covenant implies a new cult. Thus, the author of Hebrews, as we will see, uses such language as the purification of the conscience and approaching God to express his notions of human transformation and enablement that fulfill the new covenant blessings—blessings that ensure the people's fidelity to God.

I will first summarize the central exposition of Hebrews (7:1–10:18) in order to understand the significance and extent of Jesus' high priestly ministry on behalf of the people. What we will see is that Jesus perfects the people of God. A foundational component of that perfection involves the cleansing of the Christian's conscience. That cleansing then empowers the

---

93 There is another interesting enablement motif in Heb 9:14. There we read that Christ "offered himself blameless to God through the eternal Spirit". Peterson notes that "the voluntary and rational nature of [Jesus'] sacrifice, 'without blemish' because it was the *culmination of a lifelong obedience to God,* implies a power upholding and maintaining him in his office" (*Hebrews and Perfection,* 138). Lane concurs and sees as well an allusion to the Isaianic servant theme where the servant of the Lord is "qualified for his task by the Spirit of God" (cf. Isa 42:1; *Hebrews 9-13,* 240). This allusion is strengthened if, according to Lane et al, there is an allusion to the servant of the Lord passage in Isa 53:12 in Heb 9:27-28 (250). Thus, (in the spirit of Hebrews) how much more is it necessary for God's people to be sustained by God's enabling presence in order to complete their pilgrimage.

believer's approach to God out of which the believer receives God's ongoing enablement for continuing fidelity. In order better to grasp the meaning and significance of this cultic imagery as a metaphor for human transformation and divine enablement, I will examine the Old Testament background that informs this cultic metaphor. Let me add here that I do not understand purification that empowers approach that then empowers fidelity as a chronological sequence of events. The sequence represents logical connections within a comprehensive whole, that is, the believer's total experience of God's enabling power. The purified conscience that leads to the believer's approach to God which results in his or her ongoing fidelity to God is one lifelong movement initiated (election) and sustained (enablement) by God.

This "movement" is grounded upon Jesus' high priestly ministry that is the focus of the central exposition of Hebrews found in 7:1–10:18. Hebrews 7:1–10:18 is organized in three logical movements. Hebrew 7:1-28 details the appointment of Jesus as a high priest in the order of Melchizedek. Hebrews 8:1–9:28 describes the heavenly ministry Jesus has undertaken as the newly appointed high priest. That ministry has two basic components: (1) the offering of a sacrifice for the sins of the people and the purification of the heavenly tabernacle (9:1-14; 23-26) and (2) the sacrificial ratification of the new covenant (9:15-21). The author fuses these two separate sacrificial functions (Lev 16 and Exod 24) in the death of Jesus Christ. Hebrews 10:1-18 then goes on to discuss the self-oblation that Jesus offered as the high priest on behalf of the people. In this central exposition, then we move from priest, to priestly ministry, to the sacrifice offered. Within this exposition the author focuses on the fruits of Jesus' high priestly ministry for the Christian pilgrim. Our focus will be on the perfection of God's people, which entails the purification of the conscience that transforms the believer and empowers his or her approach to God. For our author, the purification of the conscience is an essential aspect of the superiority of the new covenant inaugurated by Jesus over the old covenant. This purification enables the approach that then results in divine enablement of the believer's fidelity. First, we will define the meaning of perfection of the believer in Hebrews, drawing upon David Peterson's seminal work. Second, we will examine how purification of the conscience and the resulting approach to God serve as a metaphor for divine enablement.

The all-encompassing benefit that Jesus' high priestly ministry provides for God's people is perfection.[94] In Hebrews, the perfection of the believer occurs when the promises of the new covenant blessings are realized in the believer's experience (cf. 10:14-18).[95] While this understanding of

---

94 For a very helpful, succinct discussion of the multifarious aspects of perfection in Hebrews see deSilva, *Perseverance in Gratitude*, 194-204.
95 Peterson, *Hebrews and Perfection*, 155.

perfection is the concluding affirmation of the central exposition of Hebrews, the perfection of the believer is introduced at the beginning of the central exposition as the summary goal of the cult. Thus the new covenant promises are given a cultic foundation and reinterpretation. Hebrews 7:11 explicitly declares that the goal of the Levitical cult and the old covenant that was based upon it was the perfection (τελείωσις) of the worshipper. But because the Levitical priestly ministry was not able to provide perfection (10:1), a new priesthood from a different order was chosen. Hebrews 7:19, then, reads, "For the Law perfected (ἐτελείωσεν) nothing—but a better hope is introduced by which we draw near to God." Though drawing near to God and perfection are not to be equated, the approach to God is the consummate result of perfection.[96]

This approach to God (προσέρχεσθαι) is a key theme in Hebrews (cf. 4:16; 7:25; 10:1, 22; 11:6, 12:18, 22).[97] Only the one who has been perfected is able to approach God in the present and in the future. Peterson has shown that perfection of the believer is a reference to the totality of Christ's work for the believer that brings him or her into God's presence.[98] Thus, the believers, who have been perfected by Jesus' high priestly ministry, are exhorted presently to draw near to God (cf. 10:14, 22) while they also await their perfection with all the faithful that had preceded them looking to that joyful assembly that awaits them at the resurrection (cf. 11:40; 12:22). Peterson likewise notes that in Hebrews there is the experience of some benefits now, but the believer must wait until the resurrection to experience the fullness of the benefits of perfection. Peterson goes on to equate this dual aspect of perfection to the "pledge of the Spirit" in Paul. The present enjoyment of perfection is the foretaste of what is to come.[99] The result in both cases is a present approach to God (cf. 4:16; 10:22) as well as a future consummated joy in the very presence of God (cf. 6:19-20; 12:22-24).

Through this present approach to God, that is, the encounter of the divine presence, the believer receives God's divine enabling to remain faithful even in the midst of trial and temptation: "Let us, therefore, approach (προσερχώμεθα) the throne of grace with confidence so that we may receive grace and mercy and we might find timely help" (4:16).[100] Προσέρχεσθαι is a worship term in Hebrews. Hebrews 10:1 uses the

---

96 Peterson, *Hebrews and Perfection*, 128.
97 Cf. LXX Exod 19:6; 34:32; Lev 9:5; 22:3; Deut 4:11; 5:23 where προσέρχεσθαι is used to refer to the people's coming into God's presence.
98 Peterson, *Hebrews and Perfection*, 126. Cf. Paul Johannes Du Plessis, *TELEIOS: The Idea of Perfection in the New Testament* (Kampen: J. H. Kok, 1959).
99 Peterson, *Hebrews and Perfection*, 157-58, 166.
100 Hebrews 13:9 might represent a similar notion where the author exhorts the audience that it is good for their hearts to be established or strengthened by grace.

substantive plural participle as a synonym for the worshipper and the context of the verb form used in 12:22 is a picture of the anticipated eschatological worship of God.[101] This approach to God through the high priest, Jesus Christ, sustains the Christian pilgrim in his or her sojourn to the heavenly city. Moreover, this timely grace and help is precisely what the Christian pilgrim needs because it comes from the pilgrim's merciful high priest who has been tested in all ways that the pilgrim experiences (cf. 2:18). This approach that enables the believer's fidelity is grounded upon more than just the fact that he or she has a sympathetic high priest. The high priestly ministry of Jesus effects a more fundamental transformation that empowers this confident approach to God. Put another way, we might ask: how can those who have been defiled by sin approach God to serve Him (cf. 9:14a) and experience His enabling presence?

An aspect of the perfection achieved by Christ's ministry that allows and empowers the believer to approach God and experience His ongoing enabling presence is the purification of the conscience, which is a central focus of the exposition and following exhortation in Heb 8:1–10:25 (cf. 9:9, 13-14, 22; 10:1-2, 14-17, 22). The author of Hebrews has already introduced this theme of his discourse in the opening (cf. 1:3) and with respect to what Jesus' ministry accomplished with God. Christ's sacrifice is able to cleanse the believer's conscience because it propitiates the people's sins with God (cf. 2:17; 10:17-18).[102] But in 7:1–10:25, the author focuses on the effect Jesus' high priestly ministry has for those who have been called—a primary benefit being the cleansing of the conscience. Peterson states that cleansing of the conscience is the most significant element of the perfection of the believer.[103] Concerning the old covenant, the Levitical priesthood and the sacrifices offered through it "were not able to perfect (τελειῶσαι) the worshipper with reference to the conscience (κατὰ συνείδησιν)" (9:9). The author of Hebrews again details the ineffectiveness of the old covenant cult in 10:1-2. There the argument states that the sacrifices that were continually offered by the Levitical priests were not able to perfect (τελειῶσαι) those who were approaching (τοὺς προσερχομένους) God, that is, the worshipper. If they could have perfected the worshipper, then they would have ceased to be offered

---

101 Cf. Attridge, *Hebrews*, 141; Lane, *Hebrew 1-8*, 115. In 2 Pet 2:4-5 the approach (προσερχόμενοι) to Christ the living stone results in the transformation of the one approaching into the living stones of the temple of God's people and into a holy priesthood.
102 Scott W. Hahn's ("A Broken Covenant and the Curse of Death: A Study of Hebrews 9:15-22," *CBQ* 66 [220]): 416-36) arguments have shown that Jesus' propitiation should not merely be equated with expiation. Jesus' atonement absorbs the curses of the first covenant out of which comes forgiveness.
103 Peterson, *Hebrews and Perfection*, 136.

because the conscience of the worshipper would have been cleansed (κεκαθαρισμένους).

On the other hand, Christ's high priestly ministry, which includes his once-and-for-all vicarious sacrifice, has perfected forever the sanctified (10:14). This perfection includes the present effect of Christ's ministry that "cleanses our conscience (καθαριεῖ τὴν συνείδησιν) from dead works so that we can serve (λατρεύειν) the living God" (9:14b). This inward cleansing transforms the defiled state of the believer (cf. 9:14a) and empowers the believer to approach God out of which he or she receives all he or she needs for ongoing fidelity to God. This logical connection is made explicit in 9:14. The believer is cleansed *so that* he or she may serve God.[104] The author elsewhere makes this logical connection when he exhorts his audience to approach (προσερχώμεθα) God *because* they have been given a "sincere heart (ἀληθινῆς καρδίας)" and a "heart sprinkled from an evil conscience" (ῥεραντισμένοι τὰς καρδίας ἐν συνειδήσεως πονηρᾶς)" (10:22). Again, through this language of a cleansed conscience or a true heart that empowers one to approach God so that he or she may receive necessary grace and mercy, we can see the fulfillment of the new covenant promises. These promises conclude the exposition of Jesus' high priestly ministry (cf. 10:15-18) and serve as the foundation for the benediction (cf. 13:20-21).[105] Hebrews reinterprets the promises of inscribing the law on the hearts of the people, of knowing God, and the experience of the forgiveness of sin in the new covenant through this cultic metaphor of purification of the conscience that transforms and empowers the worshipper's approach to God. Whereas the old covenant cult only provided an *outward* purification of the "flesh" (9:13), Jesus' high priestly ministry and the new covenant based upon it bring about *inward* transformation through the cleansing of the "conscience" (9:14).

Without this purification there is no ability to "serve the living the God" or "to approach" Him in a way that sustains the worshipper's fidelity. For this reason, Hebrews gives focused attention to this aspect of Christ's high priestly ministry. In Heb 9:14, purification of the conscience is depicted as deliverance from "dead works". James Moffatt notes that "dead works" are

---

104 "To serve" is the Greek term λατρεύειν. This term carries cultic and worship connotations in the LXX (Num 16:9; Deut 10:12; 11:13, 28; 28:14; 29:17; Josh 22:5; 1 Macc 2:19, 22). In Heb 9:9, the substantive participle, τὸν λατρεύοντα, practically means "worshipper" (cf. 9:1).

105 Cf. Lane, *Hebrews 9-13*, 286. Again, deSilva (*Perseverance in Gratitude*, 326-27) seems to suggest that the extent of the internalization of God's law in the new covenant is the provision of knowledge to know what pleases God. The new covenant in Jeremiah, however, connects this internalization with the divine enabling of the people's faithfulness, and in Hebrews, this internalization involves transformation through the cleansing of the conscience that results in faithfulness.

those moral offenses from which a person had to break in order to become a Christian at all and which have "no principle of life in them".[106] They are representative of the former idolatrous worship and defiled state of the believer.[107] Peterson aptly argues that in Hebrews Christian service is lifelong and pleasing to God (cf. 13:16). If there is to be such a response by the believer to God, then the conscience must be cleansed "to empower" the believer to serve and worship God. "The cleansing of the conscience leads to a decisive change in a person's heart with respect to God and enables the person to serve God as he requires."[108] Moreover, this is the initiative of God through Christ for those who have been called: "the blood of Christ . . . cleanses our conscience" (9:14) and "We have been sanctified through the offering of the body of Jesus Christ once and for all" (10:10). Christ's sacrifice consecrates the believer for an abiding relationship with God—a consecration predicated upon cleansing as the beginning of its fulfillment.[109] Thus, this cleansing stands at the beginning of the Christian pilgrim's experience of perfection through Christ, transforms the human condition, and empowers the Christian's approach to God.

Moreover, Christ's cleansing of the conscience does not only stand at the beginning of the Christian's pilgrimage but is the basis of the empowering that the pilgrim experiences to approach God throughout the pilgrimage to the heavenly Jerusalem. We can think of an initial decisive cleansing experienced at the beginning of the journey that transforms the human condition. But Hebrews also represents this transformation as abiding and the experience of an empowered approach to God as ongoing.[110] First, Hebrews 9:14 states that Jesus "cleanses (καθαριεῖ) our conscience". By putting καθαριεῖ in the future tense (but with present force for the audience of Hebrews), the cleansing of Jesus is not relegated to a past action but is represented as a present experience.[111] Second, Hebrews 10:2 represents both aspects. There we read that if the sacrifices offered under the old cultus were effective, then they would have ceased because they would have cleansed once and for all (ἅπαξ κεκαθαρισμένους) the conscience of the worshipper. Of course, the argument follows that Jesus' sacrifice

---

106 Moffatt, *The Epistle to the Hebrews*, 74. He is followed by Peterson, *Hebrews and Perfection*, 139.
107 DeSilva (*Perseverance in Gratitude*, 216-17) draws a parallel with Wis 15:17 and suggests that "dead works" is a reference to idolatry.
108 Peterson, *Hebrews and Perfection*, 140.
109 Peterson, *Hebrews and Perfection*, 149. Cf. E. Riggenbach, *Der Brief an die Hebräer* (Leipzig: Deichert, 1922), 307; Spicq, *L'Épître aux Hébreux*, 2:282.
110 Cf. Barnabas Lindars, "The Rhetorical Structure of Hebrews," *NTS* 35 (1989): 385.
111 Ellingworth (*Hebrews*, 456) describes καθαριεῖ as a gnomic future and parallels the present tense verb ἁγιάζει in v. 13. Καθαριεῖ, appears as a future tense due to the representation of the sanctifying effects of the old covenant sacrifices in the present tense.

accomplishes what the old cultus could not (cf. 10:5-18, esp. v. 10). The use of the perfect tense (κεκαθαρισμένους) with ἅπαξ conveys that the cleansing the old cultus could not effect but that Jesus did was a past completed act with continuing effect. Third, in Heb 10:14, Christ perfects forever the sanctified. The use of the perfect tense (τετελείωκεν) in this verse indicates the permanent abiding nature of the believer's perfection through Christ. The abiding quality of what Jesus has done for the believer is made even more emphatic by the adverbial phrase εἰς τὸ διηνεκὲς. Hebrews 7:28 has already used a similar statement and syntax with reference to Christ. Christ "has been perfected forever (εἰς τὸν αἰῶνα τετελειωμένον)". This phrase refers to Jesus' exaltation to the unshakable, abiding realm where he performs his permanent priestly ministry.[112] Thus, the high priestly ministry of Christ also has permanent results for the Christian pilgrim.[113] Since cleansing was an element of perfection of the believer in Hebrews, we may deduce that cleansing has decisive and ongoing validity for the believer's fidelity.[114] Fourth, in Heb 10:22, we read that Christ "has sprinkled (ῥερατισμένοι) the heart from an evil conscience". Again, the perfect tense participle, ῥερατισμένοι, not only indicates a past, completed, decisive cleansing of the believer's conscience

---

112 DeSilva, *Perseverance in Gratitude*, 278. Hebrews opens with the declaration of the Son's enthronement in the world-to-come and thus the guarantee of God's promise (cf. 1:6). Kenneth L. Schenck, "A Celebration of the Enthroned Son: The Catena of Hebrews 1," *JBL* 120 (2001): 469-85, esp. 477-79; DeSilva, *Perseverance in Gratitude*, 96-98, 278; Lane, *Hebrews 1-8*, 27; A. Vanhoye, "L'οὐκομ́νη dans l'Épître aux Hébreux," *Bib* 45 (1964): 248-53. Spicq (*L'Épître aux Hébreux*, 2:17), Moffatt (*Hebrews*, 10-11), and Attridge (*Hebrews*, 55-56) among others believe the Son's entrance into the world in 1:6 is a reference to the incarnation. See Attride, *Hebrews*, 55 ns. 61-63, for a fuller list of the various scholarly representatives of the interpretive options for this verse. To see 1:6 as reference to the incarnation was also a popular interpretation among the early Christians (cf. Erik M. Heen and Philip D. W. Krey, eds., *Hebrews* [ACCS NT10; Downers Grove: IVP, 2005], 22-23). The interpretation of οἰκομένη in 1:6 hinges on whether one equates it with its use in 2:5 and finds Christ's exaltation after his incarnation (when he was made a little lower than the angels) in 2:5-9 determinative for what the author describes in 1:6. I have chosen to side with those commentators who have advocated this position. Schenk's arguments are convincing for understanding the whole catena of Heb 1:5-14 as praise of the resurrected, ascended, and exalted Son. Moreover, he demonstrates how this view of Jesus Christ sets the stage for the entire discourse. Also when the author of Hebrews refers to the present "shakable" created order, he uses the term κόσμος (4:3; 9:26; 10:15; 11:7; 11:38; cf. 9:1 [κοσμικόν]).
113 Peterson, *Hebrews and Perfection*, 148-49.
114 In Hebrews, a believer's perfection encompasses his or her purification (cf. 9:9, 13-14), sanctification (cf. 10:10; 13:12), and finally glorification (cf. 7:28; 11:40; 12:23) to the world-to-come and enjoyment of God's presence.

but also that cleansing has an ongoing abiding effect in the believer's present experience.[115] As a result, the believers are presently exhorted to approach God with confidence (cf. 10:19-22), an approach that that leads to enablement for fidelity to God (cf. 4:16). Lastly, we encounter the abiding validity of Christ's high priestly ministry in the eschatological vision of the future consummation of all God has promised those He has chosen in Heb 12:22-23. I have already noted that this picture is of the *"ultimate complete company of the people of God"* across history who have joined the myriads of angels in joyous celebration.[116] I have noted, as well, that the reference to God as judge of all suggests that this is a post-judgment picture and the assembled multitude has passed through the judgment with positive results since they are celebrating (πανηγύρει).[117] The assembly of the firstborn whose names have been enrolled (ἀπογεγραμμένων) in heaven is made up of the righteous who have been perfected (τετελειωμένων; v. 23), that is, have reached the goal of their pilgrimage (cf. 2:10; 11:40).[118] These perfect passive participles point to the decisive and enduring initiative of God to bring those He has chosen to their final appointed end. Again, those whom

---

115 The use of the perfect tense should not be overlooked in the interpretation of Hebrews, though the nuances of the perfect will vary according to the context. The author has shaped his discourse with great skill. Commonplace among commentators on Hebrews is to note the precision and skill with which the discourse was written, so attention should be given to the choice of verbal tense among other things (e.g., deSilva, *Perseverance in Gratitude*, 35, 155 and Lane, *Hebrews 1-8*, 1). For instance, we see very deliberate, subtle, and theologically significant choices between verbal tenses (perfect and aorist) in Heb 2:14 (cf. Bruce, *Hebrews*, 78 n. 55). For a discussion and definition of the perfect tense see Daniel B. Wallace, *Greek Grammar Beyond the Basics: An Exegetical Syntax of the New Testament* (Grand Rapids: Zondervan, 1996), 572-82. Wallace also discusses an interesting use of the perfect, the "perfect of allegory" (581-82, esp. n. 28). He states that this perfect is used in the New Testament to relate an event from the Old Testament in a way that conveyed its abiding significance for the present. Though rare in the New Testament, Wallace especially notes that Hebrews is fond of this usage of the perfect (e.g., Heb 7:6; 11:17; 12:3). This usage lends further support to the sophistication of syntax and style present in Hebrews. See also F. Blass and A. Debrunner, *A Greek Grammar of the New Testament and Other Early Christian Literature: A Translation and Revision of the Ninth-tenth German Edition Incorporating Supplementary Notes of A. Debrunner by Robert W. Funk* (Chicago: University of Chicago Press, 1961), §342.5.
116 Peterson, *Hebrews and Perfection*, 162-64.
117 Cf. Lane, *Hebrews 9-13*, 471.
118 Many current commentators identify the assembly of the firstborn with the spirits of the perfected righteous. Cf. Peterson, *Hebrews and Perfection*, 164-65; Lane, *Hebrews 9-13*, 471-72; DeSilva, *Perseverance in Gratitude*, 467; Attridge, *Hebrews*, 375-76; Koester, *Hebrews*, 548; Weiss, *Der Brief an die Hebräer*, 680-81.

God has elected (i.e., those who have been enrolled in heaven) are also those who inherit the world-to-come (i.e., those who have been perfected).[119] Weiss recognizes the paradox evident here. He observes that those who are presently on their way to the heavenly Jerusalem already have their names enrolled there.[120]

From the discussion to this point, what we have seen is that Christ's high priestly ministry which inaugurates the new covenant relationship is initiated by God's election, provides forgiveness of sins, cleanses the conscience that enables one's worship, empowers one's fidelity, and effects lasting transformation.[121] Christ's high priestly ministry, which cleanses the conscience and provides fidelity-sustaining mercy and grace, is thus the foundation of the Christian's life and faithfulness from beginning to end.[122] Therefore, our author prays with confidence that God will equip his auditors with everything good for doing His will and work in them what is pleasing to Him through Jesus Christ, to His Own glory.

Our author has precedents from the Scriptures of Israel for understanding purification as transformation of the human condition that enables service and fidelity to God. First, in the implementation of the cult, the tools used in cult had to be cleansed and thus sanctified or set apart. Leviticus 8:15 (LXX) relates that Moses cleansed the altar with blood, which was then sanctified so that atonement could be made upon it: "He cleansed (ἐκαθάρισεν) the altar . . . He sanctified (ἡγίασεν) it so that atonement can be made upon it." On the Day of Atonement, atonement is made for the sanctuary and Most Holy Place because of the uncleanness (ἀπὸ τῶν ἀκαθαρσιῶν) of the people that results from their sins and transgressions (Lev 16:16 [LXX]). Again, we read on the Day of the Atonement that the high priest "sprinkles upon the altar the blood [of the sacrifice] with his finger seven times and cleanses (καθαριεῖ) it and consecrates (ἁγιάσει) it from the uncleanness (τῶν ἀκαθαρσιῶν) of the children of Israel" (Lev 16:19 [LXX]). In 2 Macc 2:18, Judas Maccabeus rededicates the temple which has been defiled. In order for the temple to once again be employed in the worship of God, it had to be cleansed (ἐκαθάρισεν; cf. v. 19).

The ceremonial cleansing of both the objects employed in worship and the worshipper as well was necessitated by the dangerous holiness of God. In Lev 22:3 (LXX), we read that the one who approaches God unclean (ἀκαθαρσία) will be destroyed (ἐξολεθρευθήσεται). Further, the failure to

---

119 Cf. 7:28; 11:40. See deSilva, *Perseverance in Gratitude*, 96-98, 278, 425; Peterson, *Hebrews and Perfection*, 158.
120 Weiss, *Der Brief an die Hebräer*, 680.
121 Peterson, *Hebrews and Perfection*, 158. Paul uses perfection to refer to final redemption or glorification in 1 Cor 10:13 (τέλειον) and Phil 3:12 (τετελείωμαι).
122 Peterson (*Hebrews and Perfection*, 151) notes that the Christian is thereby called to "exhibit" his or her consecration by living a life of holiness (ἁγιασμόν; 12:14).

regard God as holy precipitated God's wrath. Fire from God's presence consumed Aaron's sons, Nadab and Abihu, because they offered this enigmatic unauthorized fire. God, however, makes clear that their death was a result of the failure to honor Him and regard Him as holy (cf. Lev 10:3). God was ready to destroy all the Israelites for their idolatry when they worshipped the golden calf at Sinai (cf. Exod 32:9-10). God's wrath broke out against the Israelites who engaged in sexual immorality with the Moabite women. God's wrath was stayed only when Phinehas in his zeal slew an Israelite man and his Midianite woman (cf. Lev 25). The holiness of God which consumes and destroys unclean, sinful humans makes the approach to God dangerous. The author of Hebrews appears to pick up on this line of thinking when he admonishes his audience that those who deliberately continue to sin are left with the fearful expectation of judgment and raging fire that will consume God's adversaries (cf. 10:26-27). Moreover, to fall into the hands of the living God is a fearful prospect (10:31). Thus, we understand the importance of cleansing and the need of assurance that one will be accepted with God. Only once one is empowered to come into the divine presence can he or she receive God's enabling presence that sustains fidelity to Him.

Second, the ceremonial cleansing of the cult also became a metaphor for the inward spiritual cleansing the worshipper required in order to approach God and serve Him. In Ps 23:3-4 (LXX), the psalmist asks "Who shall ascend to the hill of the LORD? And who shall stand in his holy place?" The psalmist replies that the one who has "clean hands and a clean heart (καθαρὸς τῇ καρδίᾳ)" may ascend to the holy place. Conversely, in Ps 50 (LXX), the psalmist confronts the guilt of his sin before God. He pleads with God to cleanse (κυθάρισόν) him from his sin (v. 4; cf. v. 9). Only God can do this. He seeks for God to "create in [him] a clean heart (καρδίαν καθαρὰν κτίσον) and to renew a right spirit (πνεῦμα εὐθὲς ἐγκαίνισον) within in [his] inward parts" (v. 12). Marvin Tate writes, "The divine activity results in a new order of existence, a new arrangement, or a new emergence shaped by the divine power and will."[123] If the Lord does not grant these things then the psalmist will be forever cast from God's presence and will not have the experience of God's sustaining holy spirit (cf. v. 13). Out of this experience of the divine presence comes a willing spirit to sustain him (πνεύματι ἡγεμονικῷ στήρισόν με; v. 14). Only when God has granted the psalmist's request for a clean heart will he then be able "to teach transgressors [God's] ways" (v. 15). Here we see that the individual who is defiled by sin can neither come into God's presence nor serve Him. God must cleanse the person from his or her sin and create in him or her a clean heart, which is equated with being renewed with a right spirit. Moreover, the purified individual is sustained by God's presence in

---

123 Marvin E. Tate, *Psalms 51-100* (WBC 20; Dallas: Word Books, 1990), 23.

order to remain faithful to Him. Only then can he or she serve God.

We find a similar movement in Isa 6:1-8 (LXX). Isaiah is confronted with the vision of Yahweh seated upon His throne in the heavenly temple. Yahweh is surrounded by seraphim who declare Yahweh's holiness before Isaiah (cf. vv. 1-4). Isaiah, then, curses himself because he is a man of unclean (ἀκάθαρτα) lips in the presence of a holy God (v. 5).[124] In his defiled state, he cannot serve Yahweh or enjoy His presence. The seraph, however, takes a burning ember from the altar which cleanses (περικαθαριεῖ) Isaiah from his sins (v. 7). Only then, is Isaiah able to serve Yahweh and deliver Yahweh's message to Israel (cf. v. 8). Again, we have the movement from defilement from sin, to an inward cleansing, to the ability to serve God. This spiritual inward purification transforms the defiled human condition so that those called by God may enjoy Him and faithfully serve Him.

We discover analogous notions among the prophetic books of Jeremiah and Ezekiel. Jeremiah 40:8 (LXX) relates God's promise to restore Israel: "I will cleanse (καθαριῶ) them from all the guilt of their sin against me, and I will not remember their sins concerning which they sinned against me and rebelled from me." The result of God's cleansing is that Jerusalem "shall be to me a name of joy, a praise and glory before all the nations of the earth who hear of all the good that I do for them" (v. 9). Implicit in this prophecy is that once God cleanses the people they will faithfully and joyfully serve and honor Him thus becoming "a name of joy" and "a praise and glory before all nations". Jeremiah 32:29 (LXX), however, relates what happens when God "will not certainly cleanse with cleansing (καθάρσει οὐ μὴ καθαρισθῆτε)" Israel. Israel will not go unpunished but will bear the stroke of the sword that God summons against all the inhabitants of the earth who fail to honor Him.

What is implicit in the prophecy of Jer 40:8 is explicit in Ezek 36:24-33. Ezekiel 36:24-33 (LXX) is another prophecy of God's restoration of Israel. Here, God will cleanse the people from all their uncleanness and idolatry (καθαρισθήσεσθε ἀπὸ πασῶν τῶν ἀκαθαρσιῶν ὑμῶν καὶ ἀπὸ πάντων τῶν εἰδώλων ὑμῶν; v. 25). The nature of this cleansing is then elaborated in the next verse. God will give a "new heart" and a "new spirit" to His people and will remove their rebellious unfaithful "heart of stone". The result of this transformation is that God "will cause [Israel] to follow [his] statutes and be careful to observe [his] judgments" (v. 27). Again, this restoration of Israel to a faithful, enduring relationship with God is summarily declared to take place on the day God cleanses the people (ἐν ἡμέρᾳ ᾗ καθαριῶ ὑμᾶς; v. 33). Elsewhere, Ezek 37:23 (LXX), states that

---

[124] In Matt 5:11, the Matthean Jesus associates uncleanness with what comes out of a person's mouth. In v. 18, the mouth and the heart are related. The mouth gives vent to what is in the heart.

God will save Israel from their apostasy when he cleanses them (καθαριῶ αὐτούς). At that time Israel will belong to God in an enduring personal relationship because God has cleansed them from their idolatry thus enabling their faithfulness to Him. The cleansing is so complete that the land will never become defiled again. Thus the cleansing has an abiding transformative benefit. In both Jeremiah and Ezekiel, Israel's restoration from their defiled, rebellious condition is dependant upon God's cleansing them. This cleansing, moreover, enables faithfulness to the renewed relationship with God.

In both the cultic setting and the spiritual inward application of the cultic imagery of cleansing, the Scriptures of the author of Hebrews state that cleansing is the necessary transformative act that consecrates a person or object for service to God. In the Ps 50 (LXX) and the prophetic books of Isaiah, Jeremiah, and Ezekiel, God's cleansing of the people takes on broader notions than the mere forgiveness of sin. While cleansing includes this, it also denotes the transformation of the human heart or spirit which leads both to the ability to serve and to enjoy God as well as to ongoing faithfulness to the relationship. Again, the author of Hebrews draws upon this stream of thought when he declares that the blood of Christ cleanses the worshipper's conscience so that he or she can serve the living God, that the believer has been given a sincere heart, or that his or her heart has been sprinkled from an evil conscience (9:14; 10:22). The Christian pilgrim's approach to God is thereby continuously empowered, results in mercy and favor that enables the pilgrim's fidelity even in the face of approaching or present persecution (cf. 4:16), and is filled with joyful anticipation (cf. 12:22-23).

In short, we have seen that ongoing divine enablement is the source of the believer's faithfulness in Hebrews. It is grounded in Jesus' high priestly ministry, which effects abiding transformation through the purification of the conscience. This purification empowers the believer's approach to God out of which he or she receives ongoing enablement for fidelity to the relationship—an empowering that is sufficient for any trial or temptation. This cleansing of the conscience and approach to God directly relates to the cultic reinterpretation of the new covenant, which is the organizing principle of Hebrews. In this way, Hebrews voices the fulfillment of the new covenant promises inaugurated by Jesus' vicarious death—promises which include a durable personal relationship with God in which He enables the people's faithfulness.

Anthropological Assumption

This emphasis on divine enablement of human faithfulness to God suggests that the author of Hebrews holds a pessimistic anthropological assumption. Unlike Paul who gives extensive exposition of his pessimistic anthropology, the author of Hebrews does not give explicit attention in his discourse to this aspect of his beliefs. The reason likely is due to the occasional nature of his discourse and the needs of his audience. The primary focus was a summons to a community of Christians to faithfulness in the face of the pressures of the dominant culture that was forcing conformity to its values and beliefs. There are, however, some indications in the discourse that demonstrate the author's pessimistic anthropological assumption.

UNIVERSAL NEED FOR PURIFICATION

First, the emphasis the author places on the need for a person's conscience to be cleansed and sins forgiven by God already suggests that all humanity starts from a place of defilement, exclusion from God's presence, and subjection to God's judgment. The movement in Hebrews is from a state of defilement, to being cleansed, to then being able to approach God. The old covenant cult was only able to cleanse those who were ceremonially defiled (τοὺς κεκοινωμένους), but Jesus' vicarious sacrifice is able to remove that defilement that results from "dead works" (cf. 9:13-14). This movement is due to the divine initiative. God consecrates through Jesus (cf. 10:10). Moreover, as we have already seen, there is no approach to God, no serving Him, no ongoing faithfulness to Him apart from Jesus cleansing a person's conscience.

SUBJECTION OF HUMANITY TO DEATH

Second, in Heb 2:14-15, the author refers to people's subjection to the fear of death and to the devil who holds the power of death. Lane writes, "The identification of the tyrant as the devil exposes the depth of the human plight. The devil did not possess control over death inherently but gained his power when he seduced humankind to rebel against God. . . . Hopeless subjection to death characterizes earthly existence apart from the intervention of God."[125] Only Christ is able to destroy the power of the devil over humanity and thereby free God's children from the fear of death. Moreover, this enslavement does not only belong to old age but is lifelong

---

125 Lane, *Hebrews 1-8*, 61. See notes 153-56 in Attridge, *Hebrews*, 92, for a list of primary ancient sources that relate the apocalyptic imagery of the Messiah's victory over demonic forces, the appropriation of this imagery in the Christian tradition, and the traditional association of the devil and death in the Jewish and Christian traditions. See also Koester, *Hebrews*, 231-32, 239-40. See especially, Lane, *Hebrews 1-8*, 61-63, who argues that Jesus as the champion (ἀρχηγός) of God's children calls to mind the exploits of Hercules's victory over death, the divine warrior motif from the Old Testament, and the gospel tradition of the "strong man" (cf. Luke 11:21-22).

(διὰ παντὸς τοῦ ζῆν).[126] According to Hebrews, after death, there awaits the judgment of God (cf. 9:27), which is a fearful prospect for those who are defiled by their sins or "dead works" that have alienated them from God.[127]

THE HISTORY OF ISRAEL

Finally, there is the succinct statement in Heb 8:8 that precedes the extensive quote from Jer 38:31-34 (LXX). The author writes that "if the first covenant was blameless, no occasion would have been sought for a second" (v. 7). He goes on to say, however, that fault was found with the covenant and the people (v. 8).[128] We have already learned that the old covenant perfected nothing in Heb 7:19. Moreover, God's people under this covenant were generally characterized by infidelity.[129] The quoted prophecy from Jer 38 (LXX) implicates Israel as "not remaining in [God's] covenant" and so God "disregarded them" (cf. Heb 8:9). The old covenant could not solve the radical infidelity of Israel because the cultic ordinances associated with it were only able to cleanse the flesh and not the heart or

---

126 Moffatt, *Hebrews*, 35; P. E. Hughes, *A Commentary on the Epistle to the Hebrews* (Grand Rapids: Eerdmans, 1977), 114.

127 Cf. Patrick Gray, *Godly Fear: The Epistle of Hebrews and Greco-Roman Critiques of Superstition* (Academia Biblica 16; Atlanta: SBL, 2003), 113-14, 118, 120, 124, 151.

128 This statement is in agreement with the text critical decision adopted by Lane, *Hebrews 1-8*, 202 n. s.

129 Obviously, according to the exempla in Heb 11, the Scriptures attest to some who were faithful to God. We should not think of those individuals as the people of the old covenant. The author takes some pains not to associate them with the old covenant. For one, he clearly focuses on individuals that preceded the giving of the covenant (Abel, Noah, Enoch, Abraham, Isaac, Jacob, the early life of Moses). We should think of these as *the called* whose faithfulness and communion with God was predicated on the future and retroactive ministry of Jesus Christ (cf. 9:15). In fact, these heroes have been "Christianized" in the discourse of Hebrews. For instance, In Heb 3:2, 6, Moses serves in God's "house" to which the faithful Christian pilgrim also belongs. "House" then is a designation for the new covenant people of God that includes the faithful ones from the past, such as Moses. Mary R. D'Angelo (*Moses in the Letter to the Hebrews* [SBLDS 42; Missoula: Scholars Press, 1979], 187-99, cf. 64 n. 122) asks the interesting question how Moses became a Christian in Hebrews. She points out that Moses became a Christian because he was a visionary and saw Christ. Moses was a seer, believer, and witness (cf. 8:5; 11:26-27). Eisenbaum (*The Jewish Heroes of Christian History*, 178) observes that the heroes of Heb 11 are portrayed "standing outside the nation of Israel", thereby avoiding tying them to any national identity. Moreover, Moses is not depicted as a leader of the exodus (183). Eisenbaum concludes that the author is attempting to produce a biblical ancestry for Christians apart from the nation of Israel and the old covenant (187-88).

conscience (cf. 9:13), only served as an annual reminder of sins (cf. 10:3), and were not able to take away the sins of the people (cf. 10:4, 11). This succinct statement in Heb 8:8 along with the subsequent quote of the Jeremiah prophecy regarding the need for a new covenant appears to telescope the entire history of Israel under the old covenant as one of infidelity. This radical infidelity suggests a defunct human condition that can only be transformed through the action of God who must enable the faithfulness of the people.[130]

To sum up, Hebrews belongs to that exilic perspective and Middle Judaic stream that held a pessimistic anthropological assumption. This assumption necessitated a divine intervention to transform the human condition and enable the required fidelity to the divine-human relationship. Furthermore, Hebrews falls in line with the Pauline model that draws upon benefaction and beneficiary terminology and notions without importing reciprocity as the foundational dynamic of the divine-human relationship. Instead, God through Christ enables the Christian pilgrims' fidelity by cleansing their conscience that empowers their approach to God where they receive ongoing grace and mercy for fidelity. Gratitude, while a response that magnifies God's gifts (12:28), does not secure the Christian's fidelity. Moreover, the cooperative mutual dependence characteristic of reciprocity finds no place in the theology of the author of Hebrews. The Christian pilgrim's entire life with God is from God through Christ. The "getting in" and the "staying in" are due to the divine initiative. With this said, we lastly need to discuss how we should understand the acute emphasis placed on human responsibility in the extensive warnings against infidelity throughout the discourse of Hebrews.

The Paradox of Divine Enablement and Human Responsibility

The Paradox in Hebrews

Clearly such an argument that has been presented above creates dissonance with Hebrews's severe warnings against apostasy (cf. 6:4-8; 10:26-31; 12:16-17). The whole discourse is a summons to faithfulness addressed to a group of Christians who are feeling the pressures of the majority culture to abandon their first convictions. Possibly, some have already succumbed to these pressures and abandoned the Christian fellowship (cf. 10:25). The severest judgment awaits those who have initially identified with God's

---

130 A similar perspective on Israel's history is depicted in Stephen's speech in Acts 7:2-53. See also Joachim Jeska, *Die Geschichte Israels in der Sicht des Lukas: Apg 7,2b-53 und 3,17-25 im Kontext antic-jüdischer Summarian der Geschischte Israels* (FRLANT 195; Göttingen: Vandenhoeck & Ruprecht, 2001), for an extensive discussion of summaries of Israel's history in ancient and Middle Judaism, including Acts.

new covenant community and have experienced in some measure the realities of the age-to-come in that community.[131] Moreover, faith is a necessary response of an individual in order to share in God's Sabbath rest (cf. 4:2-3). The one approaching (προσερχόμενον) God must (δεῖ) have it (cf. 11:6). In light of these considerations, one might argue that the divine initiative is necessary in Hebrews and stands at the beginning of the Christian pilgrim's sojourn but then the outcome of that sojourn depends upon the pilgrim's initiative, thus, the warnings against falling away.[132]

The dual emphasis, however, on divine enablement and human responsibility is not the synergism typical of reciprocity or covenantal nomism but a paradox in the experience and theology of the author of Hebrews. The paradox is evident in that God's salvific action in Christ is necessary for *ongoing* human fidelity to the relationship while at the same time the author existentially feels the real possibilities of falling away or living in a manner pleasing to God. To attempt a rigidly logical reconciliation between these two aspects distorts the author's theology and experience. The only way to resolve this paradox is to go back to the complex relational experience between the worshipper and God that generated it. The author and his auditors simultaneously experienced God's enabling presence that sustained them as well as acutely felt their responsibility before God for the way they lived their lives before Him.

Therefore, we should not think of Hebrews's strong warning against apostasy as disingenuous.[133] They arise out of this complex relational reality with the living God. For instance, our author emphasizes both those aspects about the character of God that on the one hand draw and woo the believer and on the other hand humble, alarm, and make sober that very same believer.[134] On the one hand, God is unflinchingly faithful (cf. 6:13-18); He has given believers a sympathetic high priest (cf. 2:17-18); and He is the rewarder of those who earnestly seek Him (cf. 11:6). At the same time, our author knows that God is a righteous judge (cf. 12:23; 4:13); He does not suffer dishonor lightly, consuming all His enemies in a raging fire

---

131 For a similar castigation of those who had extraordinary experiences and knowledge but fell away or continued unrepentant see *Acts John* 69, 84, 107; *Acts Pet.* 7; *Acts Thom.* 35; *Acts Andrew*.

132 This position is held by Lehne who uses Sanders's categories of "getting in" and "staying in" (*The New Covenant in Hebrews*, 107). She states, without any elaboration, that "getting in" is a result of election and perfection but that the warnings apply to "staying in".

133 Cf. Brent Nongbri, "A Touch of Condemnation in a Word of Exhortation: Apocalyptic Language and Graeco-Roman Rhetoric in Hebrews 6:4-12," *NovT* 45 (2003): 265-79.

134 Jonathan Edwards in his *Thought on the Revival* emphasized both the usefulness and necessity of such a seemingly paradoxical view of God for genuine conversion and religious affections.

(cf. 10:26-31); and while His word sustains life, it also pierces to one's innermost thoughts (cf. 4:12-13). Just as the certainty of God's promised future for those whom He has called is meant to motivate ongoing faithfulness, the fearful prospect of God's judgment against those who dishonor Him is meant to encourage faithfulness, make the believers humbly grateful so that they worship God with reverence and awe, and instill a sober joy in the "fearsome" God who has dealt mercifully with them.

Other Representatives of This Paradox

We find a similar paradoxical notion in Paul. In Rom 9–11, Paul deals with God's hardening of Israel that has lead to their apostasy as part of His plan to bring salvation to the Gentiles. Moreover, this salvation is for those whom God has predestined, delivered from the bondage of sin, enabled for faithfulness, and called to glory (cf. 8:29-30). Yet Paul severely warns his Gentile Christian auditors not to be arrogant but to be afraid (in the terms of Hebrews, to worship God with reverence and awe) "for if God did not spare the natural branches (the apostate among Israel), he will not spare you (the Gentile converts) either. Consider therefore the severity and kindness of God: severity to those who fell, but kindness to you provided that you continue in his kindness. Otherwise, you also will be cut off" (Rom 11:20-22). Again, we see the paradox in the convergence of God's predestinating will, divine enabling, and human responsibility—a responsibility demonstrated through severe warnings of divine disfavor.[135]

Hebrews and Paul are not unique within Middle Judaism in maintaining this paradox of God's necessary enabling alongside the affirmation of human responsibility often reflected in strong warnings against infidelity.[136]

---

135 Paul in his letter to the Galatians can speak about fidelity that arises from the indwelling Christ (cf. 2:20), of those who belong to Christ as those who have crucified their flesh with its passions and desires (cf. 5:24), and of extraordinary experiences of the Spirit in the reception of the gospel (cf. 3:2). In the same letter he can also warn his audience against falling from grace (cf. 5:4), being under a curse (cf. 3:10), and reaping destruction if they sow to please the flesh (6:7-8). In 2 Corinthians, Paul can talk about the creative act of God in causing the light of the gospel of the glory of Christ to shine in the believer's heart while leaving unbelievers to perish in their blindness and subjection to "the god of this age" (cf. 4:4, 6). At the same time he can speak about the sobering reality of facing the judgment of Christ (cf. 5:10) and so declare that "knowing the fear of the Lord, we persuade people" (5:11). Yet Paul can subsequently say in the following verses that Christ's love "compels us" (5:14).

136 This paradox is evident in the scriptures of Israel themselves. In Gen 20:6, God keeps Abimelech from sinning against him; Pharaoh's unrepentance is due to God's hardening of Pharaoh's heart in Exod 7:3-4; in 1 Kngs 22:21-23, God puts a lying

The Qumran community reflects this paradox. We have already seen that the *Thanksgiving Hymn* (1QH^a) is filled with enablement motifs. For instance, the psalmist acknowledges that God's spreads His Spirit over the psalmist so as to preserve him and keep him from stumbling (cf. XV, 7). Yet he also confesses the guilt of his sins before God, acknowledging his responsibility to live in a manner pleasing to God (cf. XII, 34-35). He points to the necessity of fidelity for salvation (IV, 13-14). He even decries the apostasy in his own community (cf. XII, 18-20; XIII, 22-25; XIV, 14, 19-21, 32). In the *Damascus Document*, apostates are acknowledged as those whom God has not chosen (CD-A II, 7, 13), yet they are also culpable for their apostasy and will be subjected to the punishment of the wicked (CD-B XIX, 5-6, 13-14). Thus, the severe punishment of the apostate serves as an exhortation to faithfulness among the community (cf. CD-A II, 13). In the *Rule of the Community* (1QS) those who enter the covenant of the community have been selected by God (IV, 22; XI, 7, 16). Yet, they are also the ones who submit freely or volunteer to join the covenant community (I, 7, 11; V, 1). Moreover, apostates are cursed for their duplicity (II, 11-17). At the same time, the "sons of deceit" are predestined by God (III, 15-16), and they are under the dominion of the Angel of Darkness (III, 20-21). Eugene Merrill's statement from his examination of the Qumran thanksgiving hymns is once more apt:

> The very fact that a man joined the Community proved that he was one of the predestined. He did not do so to become one of the Elect; he did so because he was one of the Elect. Predestination did not contradict free will; it provided the rationale as to why men chose "freely" as they did.[137]

Svend Holm-Nielsen also recognizes that in the Qumran theology responsibility and predestination are not played off against each other. Predestination explains theologically the existing state of affairs while human responsibility was demonstrated by practical experience.[138]

---

spirit in the prophets' mouths so that Ahab will be deceived; in Isa 63:17, the writer complains that God has hardened the people's hearts so that they do not revere Him (cf. Isa 64:7). Yet these texts also affirm human responsibility before God. For instance, Pharaoh is castigated by God for "refusing to humble [himself] before [God]" (Exod 10:3). Cf. Madeleine Boucher, *The Mysterious Parable: A Literary Study* (CBQMS 6; Washington D.C.: Catholic Biblical Association of America, 1977), 60-61, who also points out these paradoxical elements but ends up collapsing the paradox by opting to reconcile the two poles in the rabbinic manner (62-63).

137 Eugene H. Merrill, *Qumran and Predestination: A Theological Study of the Thanksgiving Hymns* (STDJ 8; Leiden: Brill, 1975), 58.

138 Svend Holm-Nielsen, *Hodayot: Psalms from Qumran* (Aarhus: Universitetsforlaget, 1960), 279-82, esp. n. 16. He tersely concludes about the

We find this paradox in the Apocalypse of John. Revelation opens by addressing seven churches and emphasizing the necessity of fidelity in order to receive God's eschatological blessings (cf. 2:7; 2:10-11; 2:17; 2:26-28; 3:5; 3:11-12). These letters to the churches also include severe warnings against infidelity, that is, apostasy (cf. 2:16; 2:23; 3:3). The Apocalypse, however, is filled with notions of divine enabling and preservation: God seals His servants (7:1-8); He measures the temple (11:1-2); the names of the redeemed are written in the book of life from the foundation of the world (13:8); and the deeds of the redeemed righteous are given to them by God (19:8).[139]

This paradox is evident in the other Johannine literature. In the Fourth Gospel, the Johannine Jesus declares, "All that the Father gives me will come to me and the one who comes to me I will certainly not cast out." (John 6:37).[140] The Johannine Jesus goes on to affirm, "This is the will of the one who sent me that I should lose nothing of all that he has given me, but raise it up on the last day. . . . [E]veryone who sees the son and believes in him has eternal life and I will raise him or her in the last day" (6:39). Yet disciples desert Jesus (cf. 6:60-66), and Judas, the supreme deserter, is declared to be the "son of perdition" (13:12). Likewise, in 1 John, though the author affirms that "anyone born from God does not go on sinning" and "the one who is born from God, God keeps him or her safe and the evil one cannot harm him or her" (5:18). Yet in the preceding statement, the author warns his audience that there is a sin unto death from which no one will be delivered (5:16-17). Here, again, we see affirmations of God's enabling and preserving activity coupled with strong warnings against infidelity, that is, apostasy.

Though we do not typically like living with paradoxes, the paradox of ongoing transformative divine enablement of human faithfulness, on the one hand, and human responsibility to live faithfully, on the other, is central to the experience and theology of the author of Hebrews. To diminish the paradox in any way would be to distort the sermon's message.

---

affirmation of divine sovereignty and human responsibility in the Qumran community, "The problem is insoluble". Acts 3:17-23 is another interesting example of this paradox from the New Testament corpus. Here, Peter castigates the crowd for putting Jesus to death but then declares that it was precisely by means of (οὕτως) their evil intentions that God fulfilled all He had planned. Peter then follows this with an exhortation to repentance and concludes with a strong warning against rejecting God's messenger, i.e., Jesus (v. 23).

139 I am thankful to Dr. Charles H. Talbert for sharing this evidence of God's enabling activity from the Apocalypse with me.

140 Cf. John 6:65 where the Johannine Jesus declares, "[N]o one is able to come to me unless the Father has enabled him."

Conclusion

We now come back to our query. How would the message of Hebrews be heard in light of the reciprocity systems of the ancient Mediterranean World? There is little doubt that the first auditors would have heard elements of the benefactor-beneficiary relationship in the discourse of Hebrews. Though God is not called benefactor (εὐεργέτης), He would be conceptually recognized as such in the discourse. Hebrews, however, follows the Pauline model in that reciprocity characteristic of the benefactor-beneficiary relationship does not define the God-Christian relationship. Hebrews stands in that Middle Judaic stream that offers an implicit critique of this relational dynamic. Faithfulness is not secured by an exchange of gratitude and favors, but through God's election and enabling of human fidelity. God transforms the human plight through the perfection of the believer that Jesus Christ provides by means of his high priestly ministry. That perfection fulfills the new covenant promises. It is grounded upon the purification of the conscience that enables the worshippers' approach to God through which they experience God's enabling presence. Moreover, Hebrews's pessimistic anthropology is incompatible with the optimism characteristic of the synergism of reciprocity. According to the author of Hebrews, God is involved from the beginning to the end of the Christian's pilgrimage to the heavenly city, guaranteeing his or her faithfulness on the journey. The dual emphasis on God's enabling and on human responsibility is a paradox in the theology and experience of the author of Hebrews and should not be mistaken for the synergism typical of ancient reciprocity.

CHAPTER 5

Conclusion

In bringing this study to a close, where do the results of this study lead us? After offering a summary of the results of this monograph, I will examine the location of Hebrews within trajectories of the church's theological tradition, represented by Pelagius and Augustine, suggested by these results. I will also put forward future avenues of exploration that these results might have for pastoral/practical theology, and the questions that the results raise concerning the topic of canon.

Summary

In the ancient Mediterranean world, relationships of reciprocity were an everyday reality in the lives of everyone, from the lowest peasants to those in the highest seats of power. Asymmetrical relationships of reciprocity also defined the religious life and were a primary way the divine and human realms related. There were common characteristics associated with the reciprocity dynamic in the Greco-Roman world. Reciprocity secured fidelity in noncommercial, nonlegislated, voluntary relationships. It was supposed to create stability in amicable relationships. The primary way reciprocity secured fidelity was by means of indebted gratitude. The recipients of favors were bound to their benefactors by a sense of owing or having to repay the kindness that was shown to them. When the beneficiary or benefactor lost this sense of grateful indebtedness, the relationship was dissolved. What is more, reciprocity was defined by a cooperative, mutual dependence. Each party fulfilled certain expectations in the relationship, yet such relationships were marked by risk and uncertainty. Those who advocated that reciprocity could successfully secure ongoing fidelity were sustained in their belief by an optimistic anthropological assumption, that is, human beings are inherently capable of doing what they ought. In other words, human beings can be properly affected and motivated by a kindness done on their behalf. Thus, a grateful recipient who showed gratitude often perceived himself or herself as offering a "worthy" response to his or her benefactor, whether divine or human, thereby indebting the benefactor and earning future favor.

When we examined the Jewish subculture of the ancient Mediterranean world, we found two responses to reciprocity in the divine-human relationship. First, there were those streams of Middle Judaism that appropriated reciprocity as the way to define the bond of the divine-human relationship. The Mosaic Covenant was predicated upon it; Josephus adapts his biblical paraphrase to it; and the rabbinic literature advocates it. Furthermore, the same general characteristics that defined reciprocity in the pagan context were also typical of reciprocity in the Middle Judaic context. There was, however, a stream of Middle Judaism extending back to the exile that was implicitly critical of reciprocity as the way fidelity to God could be secured among God's people. This criticism was engendered by a pessimistic anthropological assumption. Indebted gratitude could not effectively bind God's people to Himself. Human beings were incapable of fidelity to God where cooperative, mutual dependence defined the relationship—a characteristic of the indebted gratitude of reciprocity. What, therefore, was needed was a transformation of the human condition and an ongoing divine enabling of the people's fidelity. God would have to circumcise their hearts, write His law upon their hearts, take away their heart of stone, give them a new heart and spirit, and give them His holy spirit. Gratitude in this context was not a means for securing fidelity but was an expression of humility and poverty of spirit, and yet it still honored one's divine benefactor. We found such a perspective in the Deuteronomistic History, Jeremiah, Ezekiel, the writings of the Qumran community, and in the writings of Paul.

Finally, our examination of the first-century Christian document, Hebrews, was an attempt to listen to this discourse in a milieu that was significantly shaped by the expectations of reciprocity. Chief among the reciprocity systems at that time was benefaction or patronage. The lexical and conceptual framework in Hebrews at points intersected with that of Greco-Roman benefaction. There were, however, two models of appropriation for this social relationship as a way of understanding the divine-human relationship among representative Hellenistic Jews and Christians. Both Josephus and Paul draw significantly upon the lexical and conceptual expectations associated with benefaction. Concerning the divine-human relationship, we saw, however, that Josephus appropriates the relational dynamic of reciprocity whereas Paul is critical of reciprocity and the synergism associated with it. David deSilva has recently attempted an interpretation of Hebrews along the lines of Josephus's model. But when we listened to the discourse of Hebrews, we found a strong emphasis on the ongoing divine enablement of the Christian pilgrim's fidelity that transformed the human condition. This ongoing enablement is primarily expressed in the metaphor of the cleansing of the conscience. Through the cultic reinterpretation of the new covenant, the cultic metaphor of cleansing was the way the author of Hebrews understood the fulfillment of the new covenant promises that God would write His law upon the people's heart, that they would know Him, and that He would forgive their sins. That cleansing provides the foundation for the believer's bold approach to God's throne of grace from which he or she receives necessary strength for continued fidelity to God. The necessity of God's ongoing initiative in the believer's pilgrimage points to a pessimistic anthropological assumption in Hebrews. Yet, this belief in the necessity and sufficiency of the ongoing divine enabling of the Christian pilgrim does not preclude a correspondingly strong emphasis upon human responsibility in Hebrews, demonstrated by its warnings against infidelity. Such a dual emphasis is logically insoluble and represents a paradox in the message of Hebrews.

Thus we found that Hebrews belongs to that exilic and Middle Judaic stream that was implicitly critical of the dynamic of reciprocity to secure fidelity. Hebrews, moreover, follows the Pauline model that appropriates some of the lexical and conceptual expectations associated with the reciprocity system of benefaction without importing reciprocity as the relational dynamic. Instead of a synergistic bond that is held together by a grateful sense of debt or owing, in Hebrews, we have a new covenant bond that enables fidelity and instills a deep need for God's enabling presence, Christ's high priestly ministry, and God's unchanging fidelity to His promises (cf. 4:16; 6:13-20; 9:14-15; 10:1-18). Consequently, faith in God's promised future and liberality, though not the foundation of fidelity, serves as the primary motivation for fidelity in Hebrews—not gratitude (cf. 4:2-3; 11:1–12:3).

One of the immediate implications of this study is the appeal for more sophisticated applications of ancient reciprocity systems to future studies of the divine-human relationship in the New Testament documents.[1] Not all the aspects of the reciprocity systems transfer over into such writings as those of Paul or Hebrews. Reciprocity is a rationale and characterized complex social interactions that carried certain assumptions. The totality of that rationale needs to be considered against the broader aspects of a New Testament text's soteriological pattern and assumption about human ability. James R. Harrison, recently in his study of χάρις in Paul's writings, and this study have attempted to demonstrate some of the complexities of the ancient Mediterranean reciprocity rationale that were not accordant with the broader aspects and emphases of the writings of Paul and, specifically here, Hebrews. Yet, at the same time, the message of the gospel in these writings was tailored in such a way so as to communicate relevantly in a context

---

1 Past application of Greco-Roman patronage to 1 Corithians (John K. Chow, *Patronage and Power: A Study of Social Networks in Corinth* [JSNTSup 75; Sheffield: JSOT Press, 1992]; Andrew D. Clarke, *Secular and Christian Leadership in Corinth: A Socio-historical and Exegetical Study of 1 Corinthians 1-6* [AGJU 18; New York: Brill, 1993]) and the Pastorals (Reggie M. Kidd, *Wealth and Beneficence in the Pastoral Epistles: A "Bourgeois" Form of Early Christianity?* [SBLDS 122; Atlanta: Scholars Press, 1990]) have demonstrated some of the problems the ethos of patronage presented for these early Christian congregations concerning how the members of these communities related to one another.

where benefaction/patronage and the reciprocity rationale often typified daily life.

Hebrews's Place in the Theological Tradition of the Church

Now that we have located Hebrews's message in its own context, where do these above conclusions locate Hebrews in the broader theological issues of the church?[2] If we wish to treat Hebrews as a religious document that still has a role in addressing and shaping the church's theology, then we must seek to relate it to the theological tradition in the church. The theological issue that will be addressed here is the spectrum of soteriological patterns represented in the church's history and theology. Charles Talbert has defined three general soteriological streams in Middle Judaism: legalism, synergism (= covenantal nomism), and new covenant piety.[3] We may define legalism as the claim that everything in a human's relationship with God is traceable to inherent human ability and achievement whereas with synergism some things are traceable to God's favor and saving activity while other things are traceable to inherent human ability. With new covenant piety, the affirmation is that all things in a person's relationship with God are traceable to God's saving activity. For instance, legalism would affirm that a person's entrance into communion with God, perseverance, and glorification are the sole provenance of the individual. Synergism would affirm that a person's entrance into communion with God belongs to God's initiative while perseverance and finally glorification remain in the realm of human achievement (= covenantal nomism), or with regards to perseverance, the ongoing relationship is a cooperative, mutually dependent dance between human gratitude and ongoing divine favor. God's saving activity is necessary but not sufficient for a person's eschatological salvation. New covenant piety would affirm that entrance into communion with God, perseverance, and glorification are ultimately, even if inexplicably, the provenance of God's saving activity. In later church tradition these positions were modified and represented by Pelagianism, semi-Pelagianism, semi-Augustinianism, and Augustinianism.[4]

---

2 There is a brief and helpful recounting of the interpretive history of Hebrews in Craig R. Koester, *Hebrews: A New Translation with Introduction and Commentary* (AB 36; New York: Doubleday, 2001), 19-64.

3 Charles H. Talbert, "Paul, Judaism, and the Revisionists," *CBQ* 63 (2001): 1-2. In his article he does not use the terminology of new covenant piety but *sola gratia*. In conversations I have had with him, he has coined this term new covenant piety as another way to talk about *sola gratia*.

4 These theological positions and their history are succinctly outlined in Robert A. Peterson and Michael D. Williams, *Why I Am Not An Arminian* (Downers Grove: IVP, 2004), 20-41. Semi-Pelagianism and semi-Augustinianism are both synergistic but in different ways. Peterson and Williams distinguish between semi-Pelagianism

Bultmann sees the roots of the Augustinian-Pelagian conflict present at the beginning of the spread of Christianity. Bultmann recognizes that the proclamation of the gospel did not emancipate converts from the claim of God upon them and the retention of the Old Testament by Christians reinforced this claim. Thus the question arises as to how "God's demanding will and the grace of God" in the gospel relate. "Does the forgiving grace of God only supplement the human deed? Or is there no such thing as human doing of the good until God's prevenient grace makes it possible?" Bultmann, therefore, locates the basis of the problem of Pelagianism versus Augustinianism in the early church between the rise of the ecclesiastical institution of penance and Paul's doctrine of justification.[5] In his discussion of this issue, Bultmann cites Heb 6:4-8 as evidence of a Christian trajectory that affirms that God's grace of forgiveness is for sins committed prior to baptism while after baptism a believer must depend on his or her own works.[6] In fact, proof-texts have often been lifted from Hebrews as evidence for each of the respective theological traditions.[7] Some modern scholars believe Hebrews to be irreconcilable with an Augustinian trajectory. According to these scholars, Hebrews is the one canonical document that explicitly opposes the Augustinian stream in the church.[8] In order to offer a fresh understanding of Hebrews's contribution to this theological spectrum, we must look at the larger soteriological pattern represented in Hebrews.

---

and semi-Augustinianism by arguing that those representatives of semi-Pelagiansim (e.g., John Cassian) held that human initiative was prior to God's gracious activity while semi-Augustinians (e.g., Synod of Orange) believed that God's gracious activity was prior to human initiative or movement toward God (39). They maintain that the synergism of semi-Augustinianism arises from its implicit affirmation of universal preceding grace (38). The synergism of reciprocity can operate in either one of these constructs.

5 Rudolph Bultmann, *Theology of the New Testament* (trans. Kendrick Grobel; 2 vols.; New York: Charles Scribner's Sons, 1951), 1:118-21.

6 Bultmann, *Theology of the New Testament*, 1:120.

7 Cf. Augustine's use of Hebrews to affirm his theological generalizations in *NPNF¹* 5:34, cf. 30 and the Pelagians' cited use of Hebrews for their viewpoint in *NPNF¹* 5:60.

8 E.g., Clark Pinnock, "From Augustine to Arminius: A Pilgrimage in Theology," in *The Grace of God, the Will of Man: A Case for Arminianism* (ed. Clark H. Pinnock; Grand Rapids: Zondervan, 1989), 17. In fact, Pinnock attests that the examination of Hebrews facilitated his shift away from "Augustine" to "Arminius". Cf. Grant Osbourne, "Soteriology in the Epistle to the Hebrews," in *Grace Unlimited* (ed. Clark H. Pinnock; Minneapolis: Bethany House, 1975), 159; David deSilva, "Exchanging Favor for Wrath: Apostasy in Hebrews and Patron-Client Relationships," *JBL* 115 (1996): 112-13; Kenneth Schenk, *Understanding the Book of Hebrews: The Story Behind the Sermon* (Louisville: Westminster/John Knox Press, 2003), 65, esp. 118 n. 19.

The soteriological pattern in Hebrews locates Hebrews within these larger theological trajectories without necessarily addressing itself to all the concerns of the later Pelagian-Augustinian debate. With that said, what we have seen in our study of Hebrews is that the soteriological pattern of Hebrews is at home in the Augustinian stream of the church. From our analysis of Hebrews in the previous chapter, the pattern we find is election, perseverance, glorification. God's election is necessary for an individual to enter into the new covenant relationship with God and experience the redemptive benefits of Jesus' high priestly ministry. Moreover, this new covenant relationship secures the fidelity of the chosen people of God through God's ongoing divine enablement. Consequently, the people's final glorification or entrance into the unshakeable realm of the world-to-come is due to God's election and sufficient enabling presence through the new covenant relationship inaugurated by Jesus Christ. Finally, the necessity and extent of the divine initiative in Hebrews is predicated upon a pessimistic anthropological assumption. While Hebrews's affirmation of election does not offer answers to predestination nor does its pessimistic anthropology lend itself to a specific statement of original sin, it nonetheless combats synergistic views of the divine-human relationship as did Paul and later Augustine. Like Paul and Augustine, Hebrews's new covenant piety does not yield to a moral passivity or fatalism. Hebrews calls for responsibility and radical fidelity to God from its audience—a fidelity that is necessary if they are to inherit God's promise. Like Paul (cf. Phil 2:12-13), Hebrews (e.g., 13:20-21) believes both that human fidelity is necessary and that such human fidelity is due to God's enabling.

Avenues of Future Research

The results of this study also suggest future research and raise further questions in the areas of pastoral/practical theology and canon. First, Hebrews is preeminently a pastoral document. Hebrews is a summons to faithfulness against the dominant societal pressures that attempt to lure, wear down, or even forcibly separate a Christian from his or her confidence and confession of Jesus Christ. Hebrews seeks to motivate fidelity by urging the Christian pilgrim to focus on the future that God has promised and confirmed in Jesus Christ (cf. 2:5-8; 6:13-20; 11:1–12:3; 12:22-24, 28). This motivation is grounded upon the prior and abiding transformative purification and enabling worship of the believer. As we have seen, reciprocity is implicitly rejected. Thus, to attempt to motivate fidelity by endeavoring to generate a feeling of indebted gratitude is to give gratitude a function in the Christian's life that it was not meant to perform, at least not in the theology of Hebrews.

One reason for why the motivation of reciprocity was innately rejected in Hebrews might be due to the "dark side" of reciprocity. A modern sociology study by Martin Greenberg and Solomon Shapiro has shown that the psychological state of indebtedness is aversive, and so people are reluctant to accept favors where there is little or no possibility of paying them back.[9] The aversive nature or "dark side" of reciprocity emerges from some of the ancient sources. For example, Aristotle writes:

> Benefactors seem to love those whom they benefit more than those who have received benefits love those who have conferred them; and it is asked why this is so, as it seems to be unreasonable. The view most generally taken is that it is because the one party is in the position of a debtor and the other of a creditor; just as therefore in the case of a loan, whereas the borrower would be glad to have his creditor out of the way, the lender actually watches over his debtor's safety, so it is thought that the conferrer of a benefit wishes the recipient to live in order that he may receive a return, but the recipient is not particularly anxious to make a return. (*Eth. nic.* 9.7.1 [Rackham, LCL])

The speech of Pericles in the *History of the Peloponnesian War* 2.40.4-5 by Thucydides relates a similar notion:

> Now he who confers the favour is a firmer friend, in that his is disposed, by continued goodwill toward the recipient, to keep the feeling of obligation alive in him; but he who owes it is more listless in his friendship, knowing that when he repays the kindness it will count, not as a favour bestowed, but as a debt repaid. (Smith, LCL)

Part of Seneca's aim in writing *De Beneficiis* was to encourage beneficiaries "not to be fearful of benefits, not to faint under them as if we were weighed down by an intolerable burden" (2.35.3 [Basore, LCL]). Victor Matthews observes after studying specific stories in the Hebrew Bible through the lens of reciprocity that when "an unequal exchange is proposed or imposed...a social tension is created that may lead to open hostility or the loss of personal status".[10]

---

9 Martin S. Greenberg and Solomon P. Shapiro, "Indebtedness: An Adverse Aspect of Asking For and Receiving Help," *Sociometry* 34 (1971): 290-301.

10 Victor H. Matthews, "The Unwanted Gift: Implications of Obligatory Gift Giving in Ancient Israel," *Semeia* 87 (1999): 91. Matthews also cites Racine who states that the donor of a gift too large to be reciprocated can represent enmity on the part of the donor (95). Enriquez Valunta ("Ek Pisteōs eis Pistin and the Filipino's Sense of Indebtedness," *SBL Seminar Papers, 1998* [2 vols.; SBLSP 37; Atlanta: Scholar's Press, 1998], 1:33-45) represents a present example of one who attempts to interpret Paul and to advocate a motivation for obedience in line with the reciprocity rationale. He relates a Christian's response to grace according to the Filipino custom of reciprocity, *utang na loob*, about which he concludes, "It is through people who live their lives as debts of gratitude that God's liberating acts are revealed" (37). Evelyn

On the other hand, Hebrews does not invoke the rationale of reciprocity or this type of "debt thinking" to motivate fidelity to God. The picture we get from Hebrews is that God's gifts liberate through His moment by moment enabling presence instead of shackling the believer with a sense of obligatory indebtedness. God does not continually give gifts to people in a hope that the overwhelming volume and costliness of the gifts would eventually melt a person's heart and bind him or her to Himself out of a feeling of grateful indebtedness. God's gifts through Jesus Christ effectively liberate from the fear of death and judgment those He has called so that they might enjoy and serve Him. Conversely, in light of the immensity of God's gifts in Jesus Christ and within a reciprocity rationale, the overwhelming sense of indebtedness and the impossibility of ever repaying could lead to two possibilities among others: (1) either the believer never seeks or at least reluctantly seeks further favor so as not to increase his or her sense of indebtedness or (2) the believer devalues God's gift or assigns greater value to his or her meritorious grateful behavior so as to conceive of the possibility of repayment. Hebrews instinctively resists either rationale. Gratitude, while it has a function in the worshipping life of the community, does not function to sustain or motivate the believer's fidelity if one is to take the theology of Hebrews, as presented here, seriously for pastoral theology.[11] Whether this perspective is evident in the other New Testament documents and early Christian tradition requires further examination.

Finally, there are two issues that relate the topic of canon to this study. First, how many New Testament documents in some way embody this new covenant piety or soteriological pattern that we see in Hebrews? If all of them do or at least lend themselves to this perspective, was this a factor in the documents that distinguished them from other non-canonical documents? Second, there is a dearth of primary benefactor-beneficiary terminology in the whole New Testament corpus: εὐεργέτης, εὐεργεσία, βοήθεια, βοήθη, with the major exception being χάρις and its cognates. As prominent as the social system was in the ancient Mediterranean world why is this language not more prevalent in the New Testament corpus? For instance, why is God never called εὐεργέτης? A first-century Hellenistic Jew like Philo shows no reticence in referring to God as εὐεργέτης. Is it because the experience of salvation in Jesus Christ as it is reflected in Hebrews is counterintuitive to the reciprocity that undergirded this social system?

Meranda-Feliciano (*Filipino Values and Our Christian Faith* [Manila: OMF, 1990], 70-72), however, points out the aversive and oppressive ethos of *utang na loob* in Filipino culture.

11 Cf. James R. Harrison, *Paul's Language of Grace in Its Graeco-Roman Context* (WUNT 2.172; Tübingen: Mohr Siebeck, 2003), 270-72.

Whatever the answers to these questions, the message of Hebrews was conventional, surprising, grave, and liberating in a social milieu that was dominated and shaped by the expectations and relational dynamic of reciprocity. Hebrews exhorts its audience to look to their divine benefactor for continual supplies of grace and mercy, to trust in God's unchanging fidelity, to look to Jesus who confirms all that God has promised, to be humbly thankful for the enduring inheritance God has promised, and to know God's empowerment through the cleansing of Jesus Christ's high priestly ministry—all to the glory of their divine benefactor and for their joy in Him.

APPENDIX

The Soteriology of Hebrews

Hebrews 9:14-15
By so much more the blood of Christ, who through the eternal Spirit offered himself blameless to God, cleanses our conscience from dead works so that we may serve the living God. And for this reason he is a mediator of the New Covenant, since a death has occurred for the redemption of the transgressions committed under the first covenant, so that the called may receive the eternal inheritance.

Hebrews 10:14
By one sacrifice he has perfected forever the sanctified.

Hebrews 4:16
Therefore, let us approach with confidence the throne of grace with boldness so that we might receive mercy and find grace for timely help.

Hebrews 13:20-21
May the God of peace, who led up from the dead the great shepherd of the sheep by the blood of the covenant, our Lord Jesus, equip you with everything good in order to do his will, by working in you what is pleasing before him through Jesus Christ to whom is glory forever. Amen.

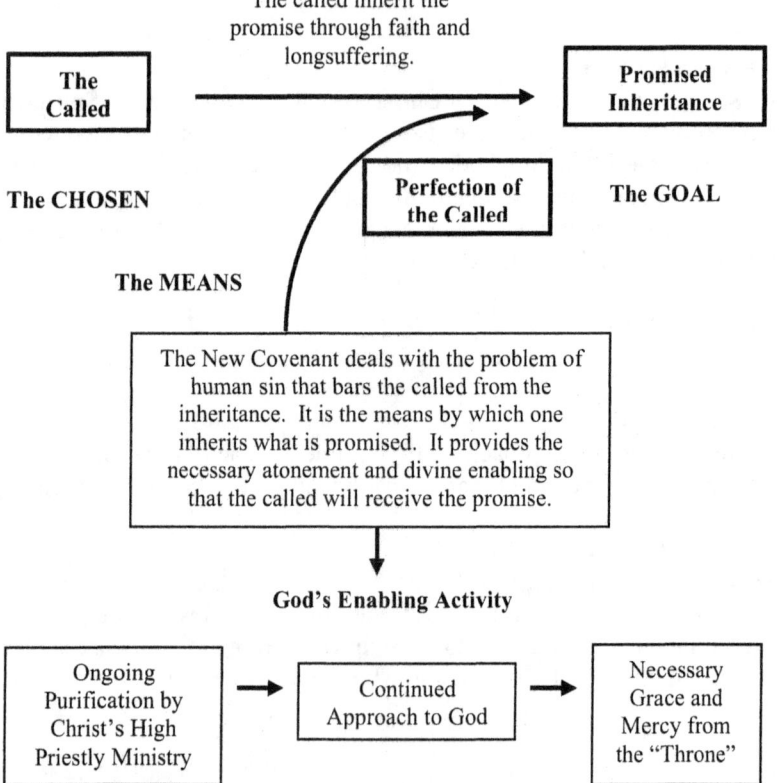

Bibliography

Abegg, Martin G. "The Covenant of the Qumran Sectarians." Pages 81-97 in *The Concept of Covenant in the Second Temple Period*. Edited by Stanley E. Porter and Jacqueline C. R. de Roo. Journal for the Study of Judaism in the Persian, Hellenistic, and Roman Periods: Supplement Series 71. Leiden: Brill, 2003.

Adkins, A. W. *Merit and Responsibility: A Study in Greek Values*. Oxford: Oxford University Press, 1960.

Anderson, Bernard W. *From Creation to New Creation: Old Testament Perspectives*. Overtures to Biblical Theology. Minneapolis: Fortress Press, 1994.

Aristotle. *The "Art" of Rhetoric*. Translated by John Henry Freese. Loeb Classical Library. Cambridge: Harvard University Press, 1959.

— *Nichomachean Ehtics*. Translated by Martin Oswald. New Jersey: Prentice Hall, 1999.

— *Nicomachean Ethics*. Translated by H. Rackham. Vol. 19. Loeb Classical Library. Cambridge: Harvard University Press, 1975.

Arnold, E. Vernon. *Roman Stoicism: Being Lectures on the History of Stoicism with Special Reference to Its Development within the Roman Empire*. Cambridge: Cambridge University Press, 1911. Repr., New York: Humanities Press, 1958.

Attridge, Harold W. *The Interpretation of Biblical History in the* Antiquitates Judaicae *of Flavius Josephus*. Harvard Dissertations in Religion 7. Missoula: Scholars Press, 1979.

Augustus. *Res Gestae Divi Augusti*. Translated by Frederick W. Shipley. Loeb Classical Library. Cambridge: Harvard University Press, 1929.

Barrett, C. K. "The Eschatology of the Epistle to the Hebrews." Pages 363-93 in *The Background of the N.T. and Its Eschatology*. Edited by D. Daube and W. D. Davies. Cambridge: Cambridge University Press, 1956.

Becker, Jürgen. *Das Heil Gottes: Heils- und Sundenbegriffe in den Qumrantexten und in Neuen Testament*. Studien zur Umwelt des Neuen Testaments 3. Göttingen: Vandenhoeck & Ruprecht, 1964.

Bellinger, W. H., Jr. *Leviticus and Numbers*. New International Biblical Commentary on the Old Testament. Peabody: Hendrickson, 2001.

Blass, F. and A. Debrunner. *A Greek Grammar of the New Testament and Other Early Christian Literature: A Translation and Revision of the Ninth-tenth German Edition Incorporating Supplementary Notes of A. Debrunner by Robert W. Funk*. Chicago: University of Chicago Press, 1961.

Boccaccini, Gabrielle. *Middle Judaism: Jewish Thought 300 B.C.E. to 200 C.E.* Minneapolis: Fortress Press, 1991.

Bockmuehl, Markus. "1QS and Salvation at Qumran." Pages 381-414 in *Justification and Variegated Nomism: The Complexities of Second Temple Judaism*. Edited by D. A. Carson, Peter T. O'Brien, and Mark Seifrid. Vol. 1. Wissenschaftliche Untersuchungen zum Neuen Testament 2 Reihe 140. Tübingen: Mohr Seibeck; Grand Rapids: Baker Academics, 2001.

Bodel, Joel, ed. *Epigraphic Evidence: Ancient History from Inscriptions*. Approaching the Ancient World. New York: Routledge, 2001.

Bolkestein, Hendrick. *Wohltätigkeit und Armenpflege im vochristlichen Altertum. Morals and Law in Ancient Greece*. Utrecht: A. Oosthoek, 1939. Repr., New York: Arno Press, 1979.

Botterweck, G. Johannes and Helmer Ringgren, eds. *Theological Dictionary of the Old Testament*. Translator by John T. Willis. 14 vols. Grand Rapids: Eerdmans, 1974.

Boucher, Madeleine. *The Mysterious Parable: A Literary Study*. Catholic Biblical Quarterly Manuscript Series 6. Washington D. C.: Catholic Biblical Association of America, 1977).

Box, G. H. *The Ezra-Apocalypse*. London: Sir Isaac Pitman & Sons, 1912.

Braun, Herbert. "Römer 7, 7-25 und das Selbstverständnis des Qumran-Frommen." *Zeitschrift für Theologie und Kirche* 56 (1959): 1-18.

Bréhier, Emile. *Les idées philosophiques et religieuses de Philon d'Alexandrie*. Etudes de philosophie médiévale 8. Paris: Librairie philosophique J. Vrin, 1925.

Bremer, Jan-Marten. "The Reciprocity of Giving and Thanksgiving in Greek Worship." Pages 127-37 in *Reciprocity in Ancient Greece*. Edited by Christopher Gill, Norman Postelthwaite, and Richard Seaford. Oxford: Oxford University Press, 1998.

Brown, Colin, ed. *New International Dictionary of New Testament Theology*. 4 vols. Grand Rapids: Zondervan, 1975-1985.

Brownlee, William Hugh. "Anthropology and Soteriology in the Dead Sea Scrolls and the New Testament." Pages in *The Use of the Old Testament in the New and Other Essays: Studies in Honor of William Franklin Stinespring*. Edited by James M. Efrid. Durham: Duke University Press, 1972.

Bruce, F. F. *The Epistle to the Hebrews*. New International Commentary of the New Testament. Rev. ed. Grand Rapids: Eerdmans, 1990.

Buchanan, George W. *To the Hebrews*. Anchor Bible. Garden City: Doubleday, 1972.

Budd, Philip J. *Numbers*. Word Biblical Commentary 5. Waco: Word Books, 1983.

Bultmann, Rudolph. *Theology of the New Testament*. Translated by Kendrick Grobel. 2 vols. New York: Charles Scribner's Sons, 1951.

Burnet, John, ed. *The Ethics of Aristotle*. London: Methuen & Co., 1900.

Burnett, Fred W. "Philo on Immortality: A Thematic Study of Philo's Concept of παλιγγενεσία." *Catholic Biblical Quarterly* 46 (1984): 447-70.

Butler, Trent C. *Joshua*. Word Biblical Commentary 7. Waco: Word Books Publishers, 1983.

Calvin, John. *Commentaries on the Epistle to the Hebrews*. Translated by John Owen. Grand Rapids: Eerdmans, 1949.

Charlesworth, James H., ed. *The Old Testament Pseudepigrapha*. 2 vols. Garden City: Doubleday, 1983-1985.

Chatman, Seymour. *Story and Discourse: Narrative Structure in Fiction and Film*. Ithaca: Cornell University Press, 1978).

Chow, John K. *Patronage and Power: A Study of Social Networks in Corinth*. Journal for the Study of the New Testament: Supplement Series 75. Sheffield: JSOT Press, 1992.

Cicero. *De Officiis*. Translated by Walter Miller. Vol. 21. Loeb Classical Library. Cambridge: Harvard University Press, 1975.

Clark, Gordon R. *The Word Hesed in the Hebrew Bible*. Journal for the Study of the Old Testament: Supplement Series 157. Sheffield; Sheffield Academic Press, 1993.

Clarke, Andrew D. *Secular and Christian Leadership in Corinth: A Socio-historical and Exegetical Study of 1 Corinthians 1-6*. Arbeiten zur Geschichte des antiken Judentums and des Urchristentums 18. New York: Brill, 1993.

Collins, John J. and Gregory E. Sterling, eds. *Hellenism in the Land of Israel*. Christianity and Judaism in Antiquity Series 13. Notre Dame: University of Notre Dame Press, 2001.

Cosby, Michael R. *The Rhetorical Function of Hebrews 11: In Light of Example Lists in Antiquity*. Macon: Mercer, 1988.

Craffert, P. F. "More on Models and Muddles in the Social-Scientific Interpretation of the New Testament: The *Sociological Fallacy* Reconsidered." *Neotestamentica* 26 (1992): 123-44.

Cranfield, C. E. B. *A Critical and Exegetical Commentary on The Epistle to the Romans*. The International Critical Commentary. Edinburgh: T. & T. Clark, 1975. Repr., 1998.

Cribiore, Rafaella. *Gymnastics of the Mind: Greek Education in Hellenistic and Roman Egypt*. Princeton: Princeton University Press, 2001.

— *Writing, Teachers, and Students in Graeco-Roman Egypt*. American Studies in Papyrology 36. Atlanta: Scholars Press, 1996.

Crook, Zeba A. "BTB Readers Guide: Loyalty." *Biblical Theological Bulletin* 34 (2004): 167-77.

— *Reconceptualising Conversion: Patronage, Loyalty, and Conversion in the Religions of the Ancient Mediterranean World*. Beihefte zur Zeitschrift für die neutestamentiliche Wissenschaft und die Kunde der älterne Kirche 130. New York: Walter de Gruyter, 2004.

Croy, Clayton. *Endurance in Suffering: Hebrews 12:1-13 in Its Rhetorical, Religious, and Philosophical Contexts*. Society for New Testament Studies Monograph Series 98. Cambridge: Cambridge University Press, 1998.

D'Angelo, Mary R. *Moses in the Letter to the Hebrews*. Society of Biblical Literature Dissertation Series 42. Missoula: Scholars Press, 1979.

Danker, Frederick W. *Benefactor: Epigraphic Study of a Graeco-Roman and New Testament Semantic Field*. St. Louis: Clayton Publishing House, 1982.

— "Reciprocity in the Ancient World and in Acts." Pages 49-58 in *Political Issues in Luke-Acts*. Edited by Richard J. Cassidy and Philip J. Scharper. Maryknoll: Orbis Books, 1983.

Daube, David. *The Exodus Pattern in the Bible*. London: Faber and Faber, 1963.

DeSilva, David A. *Despising Shame: Honor Discourse and Community Maintenance in the Epistle to the Hebrews*. Society of Biblical Literature Dissertation Series 152. Atlanta: Scholars Press, 1995.

— "Exchanging Favor for Wrath: Apostasy in Hebrews and Patron-Client Relationships." *Journal of Biblical Literature* 115 (1996): 91-116.

— *Honor, Patronage, Kinship, and Purity: Unlocking New Testament Culture*. Downers Grove: IVP, 2000.

— "Patronage and Reciprocity: The Context of Grace in the New Testament." *Ashland Theological Journal* 31 (1999): 32-84.

— *Perseverance in Gratitude: A Socio-Rhetorical Commentary on the Epistle "to the Hebrews."* Grand Rapids: Eerdmans, 2000.

Dio Chrysostom. Translated by J. W. Cohoon and Lamar H. Crosby. 5 vols. Loeb Classical Library. Cambridge: Harvard University Press, 1932-1951.

Diodorus of Sicily. Translated by C. H. Oldfather. Vol. 1. Loeb Classical Library. Cambridge: Harvard University Press, 1933.

Doughty, Darrell J. "Priority of ΧΑΡΙΣ: An Investigation of the Theological Language of Paul." *New Testament Studies* 19 (1972-1973): 163-80.

Drummand, Andrew. "Early Roman *Clientes*." Pages 89-115 *Patronage in Ancient Society*. Edited by Andrew Wallace-Hadrill. London: Routledge, 1989.

Du Plessis, Paul Johannes. *TELEIOS: The Idea of Perfection in the New Testament*. Kampen: J. H. Kok, 1959.

Dunn, James D. G. *Jesus, Paul and the Law: Studies in Mark and Galatians*. Louisville: Westminster/John Knox, 1990.

— "The New Perspective on Paul." *Bulletin of the John Rylands University Library of Manchester* 65 (1982-83): 95-122.

— *The Parting of Ways Between Christianity and Judaism and Their Significance for the Character of Christianity*. London: SCM Press/Philadelphia: Trinity Press, 1992.

— *The Theology of Paul the Apostle*. Grand Rapids: Eerdmans, 1998.

— "Yet Once More—'The Works of the Law': A Response." *Journal for the Study of the New Testament* 46 (1992): 99-117.

Edelstein, Ludwig. *The Meaning of Stoicism*. Martin Classic Lectures. Cambridge: Harvard University Press, 1966.

Edlund, I. E. M. "Invisible Bonds: Clients and Patrons through the Eyes of Polybius." *Klio* 59 (1977): 129-136.

Edwards, Jonathan. *The Works of Jonathan Edwards*. 2 vols. Carlisle: Banner of Truth Trust, 1995.

Ehrenberg, Victor and A. H. M. Jones, eds. *Documents Illustrating the Reigns of Augustus and Tiberius*. Oxford: Clarendon Press, 1949.

Ehrman, Bart. *Jesus: Apocalyptic Prophet of the New Millennium*. New York: Oxford University Press, 1999.

Eisenbaum, Pamela Michelle. *The Jewish Heroes of Christian History: Hebrews 11 in Literary Context*. Society of Biblical Literature Dissertation Series 156. Atlanta: Scholars Press, 1997.

Eisenstadt, S. N. and L. Roniger. *Patrons, Clients, and Friends: Interpersonal Relations and the Structure of Trust in Society*. Themes in the Social Sciences. New York: Cambridge University Press, 1984.

Ellingworth, Paul. *The Epistle to the Hebrews: A Commentary on the Greek Text*. New International Greek Testament Commentary. Grand Rapids: Eerdmans; Carlisle: Paternoster Press, 1993.

Elliot, John H. "Patronage and Clientism in Early Christian Society: A Short Reading Guide." *Forum* 3 (1987): 39-48.

— "Social Scientific Criticism of the New Testament: More on Methods and Models." *Semeia* 35 (1986): 1-33.

— *What is Social-Scientific Criticism?* Minneapolis: Fortress Press, 1993.

Eskola, Timo. *Theodicy and Predestination in Pauline Soteriology*. Wissenschaftliche Untersuchungen zum Neuen Testament 2 Reihe 100. Tübingen: Mohr Siebeck, 1998.

Euripedes. *Helen*. Translated by Arthur S. Way. Vol. 1. Loeb Classical Library. Cambridge: Harvard University Press, 1978.

Evans, Craig. "Covenant in the Qumran Literature." Pages 55-80 in *The Concept of Covenant in the Second Temple Period*. Edited by Stanley E. Porter and Jacqueline

C. R. de Roo. Journal for the Study of Judaism in the Persian, Hellenistic, and Roman Periods: Supplement Series 71. Leiden: Brill, 2003.
Feldman, Louis H. "Josephus," Pages 981-98 in vol. 3 of *The Anchor Bible Dictionary*. Edited by David Noel Freedman. 6 vols. New York: Doubleday, 1992.
Festugière, A. J. "'ANΘ'" ΩN. La formle 'en échange de quoi' dans la prière grecque hellénistique." *Revue des sciences philosophiques et théoligiques* 60 (1976): 369-418.
Francis, Fred O. "The Form and Function of the Opening and Closing Paragraphs of James and 1 John." *Zeitschrift für die neutestamentliche Wissenshaft und die Kunde der älteren Kirche* 61 (1970): 110-26.
Garnsey, Peter and Richard Saller. *The Roman Empire: Economy, Society and Culture*. Berkeley: University Press of California, 1987.
Gelardini, Gabriella, ed. *Hebrews: Contemporary Methods—New Insights*. Biblical Interpretation Series 75. Leiden: Brill, 2005.
Gellius, Aulus. *The Attic Nights*. Translated by John C. Rolfe. 3 vols. Loeb Classical Library. Cambridge: Harvard University Press, 1967-1970.
Gill, Christopher. "Altruism and Reciprocity in Greek Ethical Philosophy." Pages 303-28 in *Reciprocity in Ancient Greece*. Edited by Christopher Gill, Norman Postelthwaite, and Richard Seaford. Oxford: Oxford University Press, 1998.
Glueck, Nelson. *Hesed in the Bible*. Translated by Alfred Gottschalk. Cincinnati: Hebrew Union College Press, 1967.
Goldenberg, Robert. "Ishmael, Rabbi." Page 513 in vol. 3 of *The Anchor Bible Dictionary*. Edited by David Noel Freedman. 6 vols. New York: Doubleday, 1992.
Gouldner, Alvin W. "The Norm of Reciprocity: A Preliminary Statement." *American Sociological Review* 25 (1960): 161-178.
The Greek New Testament. 4h ed. United Bible Societies, 1983.
Gray, Patrick. *Godly Fear: The Epistle of Hebrews and Greco-Roman Critiques of Superstition*. Academia Biblica 16. Atlanta: SBL, 2003.
Greenberg, Martin S. and Solomon P. Shapiro. "Indebtedness: An Adverse Aspect of Asking For and Receiving Help." *Suciometry* 34 (1971): 290-301.
Gruen, E. S. "Greek Πιστις and Roman Fides." *Athenaeum* 60 (1982): 50-68.
— *Heritage and Hellinism: The Reinvention of Jewish Tradition*. Berkeley: University of California Press, 1998.
Guthrie, G. H. *The Structure of Hebrews: A Text-linguistic Analysis*. Leiden: Brill, 1994.
Haacker, Klaus. *Der Brief de Paulus an die Römer*. Theologischer Handkommentar zum Neuen Testament 6. Leipzig: Evangelische Verlagsanstalt, 1999.
Hagen, Kenneth. Hebrews Commenting from Erasmus to Bèza 1516-1598. Beiträge zur Geschichte der biblischen Exegese. Tübingen: J. C. B. Mohr (Paul Siebeck), 1981.
Hahn, Scott W. "A Broken Covenant and the Curse of Death: A Study of Hebrews 9:15-22." *Catholic Biblical Quarterly* 66 (220): 416-36.
Hamm, Dennis. "Faith in the Epistle to the Hebrews: The Jesus Factor." *Catholic Biblical Quarterly* 52 (1990): 270-91.
Hand, A. R. *Charities and Social Aid in Greece and Rome*. Ithaca: Cornell University Press, 1968.
Harrison, James R. "Paul, Eschatology and the Augustan Age of Grace." *Tyndale Bulletin* 50 (1999): 79-91.
— *Paul's Language of Grace in Its Graeco-Roman Context*. Wissenschaftliche Untersuchungen zum Neuen Testament 2 Reihe172. Tübingen: Mohr Siebeck, 2003.

Harstine, Stan. *Moses as a Character in the Fourth Gospel: A Study of Ancient Reading Techniques*. Journal for the Study of the New Testament: Supplement Series 229. Sheffield: Sheffield Academic Press, 2002.

Hays, Richard B. *Echoes of Scripture in the Letters of Paul*. New Haven: Yale University Press, 1989.

Heen, Erik M. and Philip D. W. Krey, eds. *Hebrews*. Ancient Christian Commentary Series: New Testament 10. Downers Grove: IVP, 2005.

Hengel, Martin. *Jews, Greeks, and Barbarians: Aspects of the Hellenization of Judaism in the pre-Christian Period*. Translated by John Bowden. Philadelphia: Fortress Press, 1980.

— *Judaism and Hellenism*. 2 vols. Philadelphia: Fortress Press 1974.

— "Judaism and Hellenism Revisited." Pages 6-37 in *Hellenism in the Land of Israel*. Edited by John J. Collins and Gregory E. Sterling. Christianity and Judaism in Antiquity Series 13. Notre Dame: University of Notre Dame Press, 2001.

Hillers, Delbert R. *Covenant: The History of a Biblical Idea*. Seminars in the History of Ideas. Baltimore: John Hopkins Press, 1969.

— *Treaty-curses and the Old Testament Prophets*. Biblica et Orientalia. Rome: Pontifical Biblical Institute, 1964.

Hock, Ronald F. "Homer in Greco-Roman Education." Pages 56-77 in *Mimesis and Intertextuality in Antiquity and Christianity*. Edited by Dennis R. MacDonald. Studies in Antiquity and Christianity. Harrisburg: Trinity Press International, 2001.

Hohenstein, Herbert. "Study of Hebrews 6:4-8: The Passage in the General Setting of the Whole Epistle." *Concordia Theological Monthly* 27 (1956): 433-444, 536-546.

Holmberg, Bengt. *Sociology and the New Testament: An Appraisal*. Minneapolis: Fortress Press, 1990.

Holm-Nielsen, Svend. *Hodayot: Psalms from Qumran*. Aarhus: Universitetsforlaget, 1960.

Homer. *Iliad*. Translated by A. T. Murray. 2 vols. 2d. ed. Loeb Classical Library. Cambridge: Harvard University Press, 1999.

— *Odyssey*. Translated by A. T. Murray. 2 vols. 2d. ed. Loeb Classical Library. Cambridge: Harvard University Press, 1995. Repr., Cambridge: Harvard University Press, 1998.

Horrell, David G., ed. *Social Scientific Approaches to New Testament Interpretation*. Edinburgh: T & T Clark, 1999.

Hughes, P. E. *A Commentary on the Epistle to the Hebrews*. Grand Rapids: Eerdmans, 1977.

— "Hebrews 6:4-6 and the Peril of Apostasy." *Westminster Theological Journal* 35 (1973): 137-55.

Hurst, L. D. *The Epistle to the Hebrews: Its Background of Thought*. Society for New Testament Studies 65. Cambridge: Cambridge University Press, 1990.

Inwood, Briann. *The Cambridge Companion to the Stoics*. Cambridge University Press, 2003.

Isaacs, Mary. *Reading Hebrews and James: A Literary and Theological Commentary*. Macon: Smyth & Helwys, 2002.

Jauss, Hans Robert. "Literary History as a Challenge to Literary Theory." *New Literary History* 2 (1970): 7-37.

Jeska, Joachim. *Die Geschichte Israels in der Sicht des Lukas: Apg 7,2b-53 und 3,17-25 im Kontext antic-jüdischer Summarian der Geschischte Israels*. Forschungen zur

Religion und Literatur des Alten und Neuen Testaments 195. Göttingen: Vandenhoeck & Ruprecht, 2001.
Johnson, Terry and Christopher Dandeker. "Patronage: Relation and System." Pages 219-35 in *Patronage in Ancient Society*. Edited by Andrew Wallace-Hadrill. London: Routledge, 1989.
Josephus. Translated by H. St. J. Thackeray and R. Marcus. 9 vols. Loeb Classical Library. Cambridge: Harvard University Press, 1926-1965.
Joubert, Stephen. "One Form of Social Exchange or Two? 'Euergetism,' Patronage, and Testament Studies." *Biblical Theological Bulletin* 31 (2001):17-25.
— *Paul as Benefactor: Reciprocity, Strategy and Theological Reflection in Paul's Collection*. Wissenschaftliche Untersuchungen zum Neuen Testament 2 Reihe124. Tübingen: Mohr Siebeck, 2000.
— "Religious Reciprocity in 2 Corinthians 9:6-15: Generosity and Gratitude as Legitimate Responses to the χάρις τοῦ θεοῦ." *Neotestimentica* 33 (1999): 79-90.
Julian. *The Works of the Emperor Julian*. Translated by W. C. Wright. 3 vols. Loeb Classical Library. Cambridge: Harvard University Press, 1913-1923
Schenk, Kenneth. *Understanding the Book of Hebrews: The Story Behind the Sermon*. Louisville: Westminster/John Knox Press, 2003.
Kidd, Reggie M. *Wealth and Beneficence in the Pastoral Epistles: A "Bourgeois" Form of Early Christianity?* Society of Biblical Literature Dissertation Series 122. Atlanta: Scholars Press, 1990.
Kittel G., and G. Friedrich, eds. *Theological Dictionary of the New Testament*. Translated by G. W. Bromiley. 10 vols. Grand Rapids: Eerdmans, 1964-1976.
Klauck, Hans-Josef. *The Religious Context of Early Christianity: A Guide to Graeco-Roman Religions*. Translated by Brian McNeil. Minneapolis: Fortress Press, 2003.
Koester, Craig R. *Hebrews: A New Translation with Introduction and Commentary*. Anchor Bible 36. New York: Doubleday, 2001.
Konstan, David. "Reciprocity and Friendship." Pages 279-301 in *Reciprocity in Ancient Greece*. Edited by Christopher Gill, Norman Postelthwaite, and Richard Seaford. Oxford. Oxford University Press, 1998.
Krentz, Edgar. "The Honorary Decree for Simon the Maccabee." Pages 146-53 *Hellenism in the Land of Israel*. Edited by John J. Collins and Gregory E. Sterling. Christianity and Judaism in Antiquity Series 13. Notre Dame: University of Notre Dame Press, 2001.
Laato, Timo. *Paul and Judaism: An Anthropological Approach*. Translated by T. McElwain. South Florida Studies in the History of Judaism 115. Atlanta: Scholars Press, 1995.
Lane, William. *Hebrews 1-8*. Word Biblical Commentary 47A. Nashville: Thomas Nelson Publishers, 1991.
— *Hebrews 9-13*. Word Biblical Commentary 47B. Nashville: Thomas Nelson Publishers, 1991.
Lange, Armin. *Weisheit und Prädestination: Weisheitlich Urordnung und Prädestination und den Textfunden von Qumran*. Studies on the Texts of the Desert of Judah 18. Leiden: Brill, 1996.
LaPorte, Jean. *Eucharistia in Philo*. Studies in the Bible and Early Christianity 3. New York: Edwin Mellen Press, 1983.
Lehne, Susanne. *The New Covenant in Hebrews*. Journal for the Study of the New Testament: Supplement Series 44. Sheffield: Sheffield Academic Press, 1990.

Levenson, Jon D. *Sinai and Zion: An Entry into the Jewish Bible*. New Voices in Biblical Studies. New York: Winston Press, 1985.

Lewis, Thomas. "'And If He Shrinks Back.'" *New Testament Studies* 22 (1975): 88-94.

Licht, J. "The Doctrine of the Thanksgiving Scroll." *Israel Exploration Journal* 6 (1956): 1-13, 89-101.

Lichtenberger, Hermann. *Studien zum Menschenbild in Texten der Qumrangemeinde*. Studien zur Umwelt des Neuen Testaments 15. Göttingen: Vandenhoeck & Ruprecht, 1980.

Lindars, Barnabas. "The Rhetorical Structure of Hebrews." *New Testament Studies* 35 (1989): 382-406.

— *The Theology of the Letter to the Hebrews*. Cambridge: Cambridge University Press, 1991.

Long, Thomas. *Hebrews*. Interpretation. Louisville: Westminster/John Knox, 1997.

Lysias. Translated by W. R. M. Lamb. Loeb Classical Library. Cambridge: Harvard University Press, 1967.

MacLachlan, Bonnie. *The Age of Grace: Charis in Early Greek Poetry*. Princeton: Princeton University Press, 1993.

Maier, Gerhard. *Mensch und freier Wille: Nach den jüdischen Religionsparteien zwischen Ben Sira und Paulus*. Wissenschaftliche Untersuchungen zum Neuen Testament 12. Tübingen: Mohr-Siebeck, 1971.

Malina, Bruce J. *The New Testament World: Insights from Cultural Anthropology*. Rev. ed. Louisville: Westminster/John Knox Press, 1993.

Marshall, Peter. *Enmity in Corinth: Social Conventions in Paul's Relations with the Corinthians*. Wissenschaftliche Untersuchungen zum Neuen Testament 2 Reihe 23. Tübingen: J.C.B. Mohr, 1987.

Martin, Michael. "Philo's Use of Syncrisis: An Examination of Philonic Composition in the Light of the Progymnasmata." *Perspectives in Religious Studies* 30 (2003): 271-97.

Martínez, Florentino García. *The Dead Sea Scrolls Translated: The Qumran Texts in English*. Translated by W. G. E. Watson. 2d ed. Grand Rapids: Eerdmans; New York: Brill, 1996.

Masden, George M. *Jonathan Edwards: A Life*. New Haven: Yale University Press, 2003.

Matthews, Victor H. "The Unwanted Gift: Implications of Obligatory Gift Giving in Ancient Israel." *Semeia* 87 (1999): 91-104.

McCarthy, Dennis J. *Treaty and Covenant: A Study in Form in the Ancient Oriental Documents and in the Old Testament*. Analecta biblica 21a. Rome: Pontifical Biblical Institute, 1981.

McKenzie, Steven L. "Deuteronomistic History." Pages 161-68 in vol. 2 of *The Anchor Bible Dictionary*. Edited by David Noel Freedman. 6 vols. New York: Doubleday, 1992.

Mendenhall, George. "Covenant Forms in Israelite Tradition." *Biblical Archaeologist* 17 (1954): 50-76.

— "Covenant." Pages 1179-1202 in vol. 1 of *The Anchor Bible Dictionary*. Edited by David Noel Freedman. 6 vols. New York: Doubleday, 1992.

Meranda-Feliciano, Evelyn. *Filipino Values and Our Christian Faith*. Manila: OMF, 1990.

Merrill, Eugene H. *Qumran and Predestination: A Theological Study of the Thanksgiving Hymns*. Studies on the Texts of the Desert of Judah 8. Leiden: Brill, 1975.
Michel, Otto. *Der Brief an die Hebräer*. 12h ed. Meyer-Kommentar 13. Göttingen: Vondenhoeck & Ruprecht, 1960.
Mikalson, Jon D. *Ancient Greek Religion*. Blackwell Ancient Religions. Malden: Blackwell Publishing, 2005.
Moffatt, James. *A Critical and Exegetical Commentary on the Epistle to the Hebrews*. The International Critical Commentary. Edinburgh: T&T Clark, 1986.
Montifiore, H. *The Epistle to the Hebrews*. Harper's New Testament Commentaries. New York: Harper & Row, 1964.
Moore, George Foot. "Fate and Free Will in the Jewish Philosophies according to Josephus." *Harvard Theological Review* 22 (1929): 371-89.
— *Judaism in the First Centuries of the Christian Era: The Age of the Tannaim*. Cambridge: Harvard Univesity Press, 1927. Repr., Peabody: Hendrickson, 1997.
Mott, S. C. "The Greek Benefactor and Deliverance from Moral Distress." Ph.D. diss., Harvard University, 1971.
— "The Power of Giving and Receiving: Reciprocity in Hellenistic Benevolence." Pages 60-72 in *Current Issues in Biblical and Patristic Interpretation*. Edited by Gerald F. Hawthorne. Grand Rapids: Eerdmans, 1975.
Motto, Anna Lydia. *Seneca*. New York: Twayne Publishers, Inc., 1973.
Nagle, D. Brendan. *The Ancient World: A Social and Cultural History*. 5h. ed. Upper Saddle River: Prentice Hall, 2002.
Nelson, Richard D. "He Offered Himself." *Interpretation* 57 (2003): 251-65.
Neusner, Jacob. *Mekhilta according to Rabbi Ishmael: An Analytical Translation*. Vol. 2. Brown Judaic Studies 154. Atlanta: Scholars Press, 1988.
Neyrey, Jerome H. *Render unto God: New Testament Understandings of the Divine*. Minneapolis: Fortress Press, 2004.
New Oxford Annotated Bible with Apocrypha. 3d ed. New York: Oxford University Press, 2001.
The Nicene and Post-Nicene Fathers. Series 1. Edited by Philip Schaff. 1886-1889. 14 vols. Repr., Peabody: Hendrickson, 1994.
Nicholson, Earnest W. *God and His People: Covenant and Theology in the Old Testament*. Oxford: Clarendon Press, 1986.
Nicols, John. "Pliny and the Patronage of Community." *Hermes* 108 (1980): 365-385.
Nongbri, Brent. "A Touch of Codemnation in a Word fo Exhortation: Apocalyptic Language and Graeco-Roman Rhetoric in Hebrews 6:4-12." *Novum Testamentum* 45 (2003): 265-79.
Noth, Martin. *The Deuteronomistic History*. Journal for the Study of the Old Testament: Supplement Series 15. Sheffield: JSOT Press, 1981.
O'Brien, Peter T. *Introductory Thanksgivings in the Letters of Paul*. Leiden: Brill, 1977.
Olyan, Saul M. "Honor, Shame, and Covenant Relations in Ancient Israel and Its Environment." *Journal of Biblical Literature* 115 (1996): 201-18.
Oropeza, B. J. *Paul and Apostasy: Eschatology, Perseverance, and Falling Away in the Corinthian Congregation*. Wissenschaftliche Untersuchungen zum Neuen Testament 2 Reihe115. Tübingen: Mohr Siebeck, 2000.
Osbourne, Grant. "Soteriology in the Epistle to the Hebrews." Pages 144-66 in *Grace Unlimited*. Edited by Clark H. Pinnock. Minneapolis: Bethany House, 1975.

Oudersluys, Richard C. "Exodus in the Letter to the Hebrews." Pages 143-52 in *Grace upon Grace: Essays in Honor of Lester J. Kuyper.* Edited by James I. Cook. Grand Rapids: Eerdmans, 1975.

Ovid. *Metamorphoses.* 2 vols. Translated by Frank Justus Miller. Loeb Classical Library. Cambridge: Harvard University Press, 1916.

Parker, Robert. "Pleasing Thighs: Reciprocity and Greek Religion." Pages 103-25 in *Reciprocity in Ancient Greece.* Edited by Christopher Gill, Norman Postelthwaite, and Richard Seaford. Oxford: Oxford University Press, 1998.

Peterman, Gerald W. *Paul's Gift from Philippi: Conventions of Gift-exchange and Christian Giving.* Society for New Testament Studies Monograph Series 92. Cambridge: Cambridge University Press, 1997.

Peterson, David. *Hebrews and Perfection: An Examination of the Concept of Perfection in the 'Epistle to the Hebrews.'* Cambridge: Cambridge University Press, 1982.

Peterson, Robert A. and Michael D. Williams. *Why I Am Not An Arminian.* Downers Grove: IVP, 2004.

Philo. Translated by F. H. Colson and G. H. Whitaker. 10 vols. Loeb Classical Library. Cambridge: Harvard University Press, 1929-1962.

Pindar. *The Odes of Pindar: Including the Principle Fragments.* Translated by Sir John Sandys. Loeb Classical Library. Cambridge: Harvard University Press, 1978.

Pinnock, Clark H. "From Augustine to Arminius: A Pilgrimage in Theology." Pages 15-30 in *The Grace of God, the Will of Man: A Case for Arminianism.* Edited by Clark H. Pinnock. Grand Rapids: Zondervan, 1989.

Plato. *Euthyphro, Apology, Crito, Phaedo, Phaedrus.* Translated by Harold North Fowler. Vol. 1. Loeb Classical Library. Cambridge: Harvard University Press, 1977.

Pliny. *Letters.* Translated by William Melmoth. 2 vols. Loeb Classical Library. Cambridge: Harvard University Press, 1915.

Plutarch. *Plutarch's Lives.* Translated by Bernadotte Perrin. 11 vols. Loeb Classical Library. Cambridge: Harvard University Press, 1967-1975.

— *Plutarch's Moralia.* 15vols. Loeb Classical Library. Cambridge: Harvard University Press, 1968-1976.

Polybius. *The Histories.* Translated by W. R. Paton. 6 vols. Loeb Classical Library. Cambridge: Harvard University Press, 1925-1954.

Price, Simon. *Religions of the Ancient Greeks.* Key Themes in Ancient History. Cambridge: Cambridge University Press, 1999.

Progymnasmata: Greek Textbooks of Prose Composition Introductory to the Study of Rhetoric. Edited and Translated by George A. Kennedy. Fort Collins: Chez l'auteur, 1999.

Rabinowitz, Peter J. "Truth in Fiction: A Reexamination of Audiences." *Critical Inquiry* 4 (1977): 121-41.

— "Whirl without End: Audience Oriented Criticism." Pages 81-100 in *Contemporary Literary Theory.* Edited by G. Douglas Atkins. Amherst: University of Massachusetts Press, 1989.

— *Before Reading: Narrative Conventions and the Politics of Interpretation.* Ithaca: Cornell University Press, 1987.

Rice, George. "Apostasy as a Motif and Its Effect on the Structure of Hebrews." *Andrews University Seminary Studies* 23 (1985): 29-35.

Rich, John. "Patronage and Interstate Relations in the Roman Republic." Pages 117-35 in *Patronage in Ancient Society*. Edited by Andrew Wallace-Hadrill. London: Routledge, 1989.

Riggenbach, E. *Der Brief an die Hebräer*. Leipzig: Deichert, 1922.

Ringgren, Helmer. *The Faith of Qumran: The Theology of the Dead Sea Scrolls*. Edited by James H. Charlesworth. Translated by Emilie T. Sander. Exp. ed. New York: Crossroads, 1995.

Sakenfeld, Katherine Doob. *The Meaning of Hesed in the Hebrew Bible: A New Inquiry*. Harvard Semetic Monographs 17. Missoula: Scholars Press, 1978.

Saller, Richard. "Patronage and Friendship in Early Imperial Rome: Drawing a Distinction." Pages 49-62 in *Patronage in Ancient Society*. Edited by Andrew Wallace-Hadrill. London: Routledge, 1989.

— *Personal Patronage under the Early Empire*. Cambridge: Cambridge University Press, 1982.

Sanders, E. P. *Paul and Palestinian Judaism: A Comparison of Patterns of Religion*. Philadelphia: Fortress Press, 1977.

Schenck, Kenneth L. "A Celebration of the Enthroned Son: The Catena of Hebrews 1." *Journal of Biblical Literature* 120 (2001): 469-85

— *Understanding the Book of Hebrews: The Story Behind the Sermon*. Louisville: Westminster/John Knox Press, 2003.

Schmeller, Thomas. "Stoics, Stoicism." Pages 210-14 in vol 6 of *The Anchor Bible Dictionary*. Edited by David Noel Freedman. 6 vols. New York: Doubleday, 1992.

Schmidt, T. E. "Moral Lethargy and the Epistle to the Hebrews." *Westminster Theological Journal* 54 (1992): 167-73.

Schreiner, Thomas R. *Romans*. Baker Exegetical Commentary on the New Testament. Grand Rapids: Baker Books, 1998.

Schubert, P. *Form and Function of the Pauline Thanksgivings*. Beihefte zur Zeitschrift für die neutestamentliche Wissenschaft 20. Berlin: Topelmann, 1939.

Schulz, Thomas N. *The Meaning of* Charis *in the NewTestament*. Genova: Editrice lanterna, 1971.

Seaford Richard. "Introduction." Pages 1-11 in *Reciprocity in Ancient Greece*. Edited by Christopher Gill, Norman Postelthwaite, and Richard Seaford. Oxford: Oxford University Press, 1998.

— *Reciprocity and Ritual: Homer and Tragedy in the Developing City-State*. Oxford: Clarendon Press, 1994.

Sekki, Arthur Everett. *The Meaning of* Ruah *at Qumran*. Society of Biblical Literature Dissertation Series 110. Atlanta: Scholars Press, 1989.

Seneca. *Ad Lucilium Epistulae Morales*. Translated by Richard M. Gummere. 3 vols. Loeb Classical Library. Cambridge: Harvard University Press, 1917-1925.

— *Moral Essays*. Translated by John W. Basore. Vol. 3. Loeb Classical Library. Cambridge: Harvard University Press, 1935.

— *Seventeen Letters*. Translated by C. D. N. Costa. Wiltshire: Aris and Phillips Ltd., 1988.

Septuaginta. Edited by Alfred Rahlfs. Deutsche Bibelstiftung Stuttgart, 1935.

Sherk, Robert K., ed. and trans. *The Roman Empire: Augustus to Hadrian*. Cambridge: Cambridge University Press, 1988.

Skard, Eiliv. *Zwei religiös-politische Begriffe: Euergetes-Concordia*. Oslo: I kommisjon hos Jacob Dybwad, 1932.

Sophocles. *Ajax*. Translated by F. Storr. Vol. 2. Loeb Classical Library. Cambridge: Harvard University Press, 1924.
— *Oedipus at Clonus*. Translated by F. Storr. Vol. 1. Loeb Classical Library. Cambridge: Harvard University Press, 1927.
Spicq, Ceslaus. *L'Épître aux Hébreux*. 2 vols. Etudes Bibliques. Paris: Gabalda, 1953.
Spilsbury, Paul. "God and Israel in Josephus–A Patron-client Relationship." Pages 172-91 in *Understanding Josephus: Seven Perspectives*. Edited by Steve Mason. Journal for the Study of the Pseudepigrapha: Supplement Series 32. Sheffield: Sheffield Academic Press, 1998.
— "Josephus." Pages 241-60 in *Justification and Variegated Nomism: The Complexities of Second Temple Judaism*. Edited by D. A. Carson, Peter T. O'Brien, and Mark Seifrid. Vol. 1. Wissenschaftliche Untersuchungen zum Neuen Testament 2 Reihe 140. Tübingen: Mohr Seibeck; Grand Rapids: Baker Academics, 2001.
Stegemann, Ekkehard W. and Wolfgang Stegemann. *Urchristliche Socialgeschichte: Die Anfänge in Judentum und die Christusgemeinden in der Mediterranen Welt*. Stuttgart: W. Kohlhammer 1995. English translation, *The Jesus Movement: A Social History of Its First Century*. Translated by O. C. Dean, Jr. Minneapolis: Fortress Press, 1999.
Stowers, Stanley K. "A Cult from Philadelphia: Oikos Religion or Cultic Association?" Pages 287-301 in *The Early Church in Its Context: Essays in Honor of Everett Ferguson*. Edited by Abraham J. Malherbe, Frederick Norris, James W. Thompson. Supplements to Novum Testmentum 90. Leiden: Brill, 1998.
Swain, S. "Plutarchan *Synkrisis*." *Eranos* 90 (1992): 101-11.
Talbert, Charles H. "Paul, Judaism, and the Revisionists." *Catholic Biblical Quarterly* 63 (2001): 1-21.
— *Reading Luke-Acts in its Mediterranean Milieu*. Leiden: Brill, 2003.
— *Romans*. Macon: Smyth & Helwys; 2002.
Theilman, Frank. *Paul and the Law: A Contextual Approach*. Downers Grove: IVP, 1994.
Theognis. *The Elegies of Theognis and Other Elegies Included in the Theognidean Sylloge: A Revised Text Based on a New Collation of the Mutinensis MS. With Introduction, Commentary, and Appendices by T. Hudson-Williams*. London: G. Bell and Sons, Ltd., 1910.
Thucydides. *History of the Peloponnesian War*. Translated by Charles Forster Smith. Vol. 1. Loeb Classical Library. Cambridge: Harvard University Press, 1935.
Valunta, Enriquez. "Ek Pisteōs es Pistin and the Filipino's Sense of Indebtedness." Pages 33-54 in volume 1 of the *SBL Seminar Papers, 1998*. 2 vols. Society of Biblical Literature Seminar Papers 37. Atlanta: Scholar's Press, 1998.
Van Straten, F. T. "Gifts for the Gods." Pages 65-151 in *Faith, Hope, and Worship: Aspects of Religious Mentality in the Ancient World*. Edited by H. S. Versnel. Leiden: Brill, 1981.
Van Wees, Hans. "The Law of Gratitude: Reciprocity in Anthropological Theory." Pages 13-49 in *Reciprocity in Ancient Greece*. Edited by Christopher Gill, Norman Postelthwaite, and Richard Seaford. Oxford: Oxford University Press, 1998.
VanGemeren, Willem, ed. *The New International Dictionary of Old Testament Theology and Exegesis*. 5 vols. Grand Rapids: Zondervan, 1996.
Vanhoye, Albert. "L'οὐκόμνη dans l'Épître aux Hébreux." *Biblica* 45 (1964): 248-53.
— *La Structure litteraire de l'Épître aux Hébreux*. Paris: Cerf, 1977.

— *Le message de l'Épître aux Hébreux.* Paris: Cerf, 1977.
Velignianni-Terzi, Chryssoula. *Wertbegriffe in den attischen Ehrendekreten der Klassischen Zeit.* Heidelberger althistorische Beiträge und epigraphische Studien 25. Stuttgart: Franz Steiner Verlag, 1997.
Versnel, H. S. "Religious Mentality in Ancient Prayer." Pages 1-64 in *Faith, Hope, and Worship: Aspects of Religious Mentality in the Ancient World.* Edited by H. S. Versnel. Leiden: Brill, 1981.
Veyne, Paul. *Le Pain Et Le Cirque: Sociologie Historique D'un Pluralisme Politique.* Paris: Seuil, 1976.
Wallace, Daniel B. *Greek Grammar Beyond the Basics: An Exegetical Syntax of the New Testament.* Grand Rapids: Zondervan, 1996.
Wallace-Hadrill, Andrew. "Introduction." Pages 1-14 in *Patronage in Ancient Society.* Edited by Andrew Wallace-Hadrill. London: Routledge, 1989.
— "Patronage in Roman Society: From the Republic to Empire." Pages 63-87 in *Patronage in Ancient Society.* Edited by Andrew Wallace-Hadrill. London: Routledge, 1989.
Watson, Francis. *Paul and the Hermeneutics of Faith.* New York: T & T Clark, 2004.
Weeks, Noel. *Admonition and Curse: The Ancient Near Eastern Treaty/Covenant Form as a Problem in Inter-Cultural Relationships.* Journal for the Study of the Old Testament: Supplement Series 407. London: T & T Clark, 2004.
Weiss, Hans-Friedrich. *Der Brief an die Hebräer.* Kritisch-exegetischer Kommentar über das Neue Testament (Meyer-Kommentar) 15. Göttingen: Vandenhoack & Ruprecht, 1991.
Welles, C. Bradford. *Royal Correspondence in the Hellenistic Period: A Study in Greek Epigraphy.* Chicago: Ares Publishers, Inc., 1974.
Wenhem, Gordon J. *Genesis 1-15.* Word Biblical Commentary 1. Waco: Word Book Publishers, 1987
Whitlark, Jason. "Enabling Χάρις: Transformation of the Convention of Reciprocity by Philo and in Ephesians." *Perspectives in Religious Studies* 30 (2003): 325-58.
Williamson, Donald. *Philo and the Epistle to the Hebrews.* Leiden: Brill, 1970.
Wilson, Donna F. *Ransom, Revenge, and Heroic Identity in the* Iliad. Cambridge: Cambridge University Press, 2002.
Winston, David. "Philo's Ethical Theory." *ANRW* 21.1:372-416. Part 2, *Principat,* 22.1. Edited by H. Temporini and W. Haase. New York: de Gruyter, 1984.
Winter, Bruce W. *Seek the Welfare of the City: Christians as Benefactors and Citizens.* Grand Rapids: Eerdmans; Carlisle: Paternoster Press, 1994.
Wolff, H. W. "Das Kerygma des deuteronomischen Geschichtswerk." *Zeitschrift für die alttestamentliche Wissenschaft* 73 (1961): 171-86.
Woodhead, A. G. "Competitive Outlay and Community Profit: Φιλοτιμία in Democratic Athens." *Classica et Mediaevalia* 34 (1983): 55-74.
— *The Study of Greek Inscriptions.* London: Cambridge University Press, 1967.
Xenophon. Translated by C. L. Brownson, O. J. Todd, E. C. Marchant, G. W. Bowersock, and Walter Miller. 7 vols. Loeb Classical Library. Cambridge: Harvard University Press, 1968-1980.
Zeller, Dieter. *Charis bie Philon und Paulus.* Stuttgarter Biblestudien 142. Stuttgart: Weralg Katholisches Bibelwerk, 1990.

INDEX OF SUBJECTS

anthropology
   assumption of divine enablement 8, 13, 104, 116-125, 135, 146, 148, 171, 178
   assumptions in Hebrews 1-2, 8, 12, 127, 140-141, 145-146, 148, 163-164, 166, 171, 178
   assumption of reciprocity 1, 5-8, 13, 17, 53-69, 71, 99-100, 102-103, 108, 125, 135, 140-141, 146, 171
   Greco-Roman assumptions 12-13, 17, 53-69, 103, 124, 135, 171
   Jewish assumptions 71, 97-125, 135, 166, 171
   optimistic 1, 8, 12-13, 17, 53-69, 71, 97-103, 113, 125, 135, 137, 140-141, 145, 171
   pessimistic 2, 8, 12-13, 54-55, 69, 71, 97, 100, 102-116, 120-121, 123, 125, 127, 135, 137, 146, 148, 163-164, 166, 171, 178
   Aristotle 17-18, 20, 23, 27, 33-34, 36, 40-41, 44, 47, 49, 55-57, 60, 62, 65 68, 95, 129-132, 179
Augustinianism 14, 102, 173, 176-178
authorial audience criticism 8-12, 14-18, 125, 128

benefaction
   asymmetrical relationships and 2, 5, 24, 34-36, 38, 40-49, 81, 89, 95, 178-179
   benefactor-beneficiary relationship 2-7, 11, 15-24, 28-69, 76-77, 79-85, 87-93, 95, 121, 123, 130-132, 134-135, 139-146, 166, 171, 178-180
   debt and, 22-27, 38, 178-180
   differences from patronage 15-16
   divine b., 4-5, 7, 13, 27, 31-32, 37-38, 43-46, 49-50, 57-58, 68, 76-77, 84-85, 88-97, 103, 114, 121-125, 128-136, 138-142, 144-145, 147, 171, 180-181
   expectations of 3, 6, 29-30, 37, 129, 179
   fidelity and, 6-7, 17, 25-38, 53, 61, 76, 93, 95, 103, 121, 123, 125, 131-132, 134-135, 143-146, 178-179
   friendship and 15-16, 20-26, 33, 35, 37-39, 49, 52-53, 55-57, 60, 63, 65, 69, 75, 88, 93, 179
   indebted gratitude and 2-8, 13, 18-19, 24-30, 32-36, 38, 41-46, 49, 51-52, 54-58, 60-65, 68, 72, 76-80, 87-89, 95, 97, 102-103, 107-109, 115, 121, 123, 130-132, 134-135, 139, 141-144, 178-180
   giving of gifts and 2, 17-19, 21-23, 28, 30, 38-39, 43-46, 60, 62
   giving/receiving of benefits in 21-36, 38-46, 48-50, 53-58, 60, 62-64, 68, 77-84, 87-98, 101, 121, 123, 129-134, 139-144, 178-179
   goodwill and 21-22, 36, 51-65, 68, 179
   grace and 4, 62, 133-134, 137
   Greco-Roman 2-10, 12-13, 15-69, 71-72, 81-82, 85, 92, 98, 103, 124-129, 130, 132-135, 137-142, 144-145, 166, 171, 180
   in Hebrews 2, 6, 10, 125, 127-134, 138-147, 171, 180-181
   honor and 5, 28-29, 32, 34-35, 41-49, 61, 81, 89-90, 95, 123, 123, 129
   Josephus and 72, 85-92, 103, 125, 127, 131, 135, 142
   language of 3, 180
   loyalty and 5-6, 25, 33-36, 48-49, 53, 61, 76, 145-146
   patron-client relationship(s) and 24, 37, 46, 51-52, 58-59, 86, 89, 93, 103, 135, 139
   Pauline studies and 3, 179-180
   reciprocity and 2-7, 5-6, 8-10, 12-

13, 15-69, 71-72, 76-77, 79-85, 87-93, 95, 98, 103, 121, 123-135, 137, 139-146, 166, 171, 178-180
religious appropriation of 5, 137-138
risk of 49-53, 55, 68, 82, 92, 97, 173
social system of 1-3, 5, 9, 11-12, 15-17, 19-25, 33, 37-38, 49, 51-52, 55-56, 60, 62, 65, 71, 81-82, 127-128, 134, 137-38, 141, 171, 180
voluntary nature of 20, 23-25, 40, 50-55, 68, 74-75, 82, 84, 92, 152, 173

benefactor(s) 3, 13, 93, 132
benefactor-beneficiary relationship 2-7, 11, 15-24, 28-69, 76-77, 79-85, 87-93, 95, 121, 123, 130-132, 134-135, 139-146, 166, 171, 178-180
deification of 47-48
dishonor toward 25, 29-31, 95, 123, 129, 145
divine b. 4-5, 7, 13, 27, 31-32, 37-38, 43-46, 49-50, 57-58, 68, 76-77, 84-85, 88-97, 103, 114, 121-125, 128-136, 138-142, 144-145, 147, 171, 180-181
faith in 144
fidelity and 6-7, 17, 25-38, 53, 61, 76, 93, 95, 103, 121, 123, 125, 131-132, 134-135, 143-146, 178-179
giving of gifts and 2, 17-19, 21-23, 28, 30, 38-39, 43-46, 60, 62
giving/receiving benefits and 21-36, 38-46, 48-50, 53-58, 60, 62-64, 68, 77-84, 87-98, 101, 121, 123, 129-134, 139-144, 178-179
the gods as b. 35, 37-38, 43-46, 95
gratitude of 130
gratitude toward 103-104, 107, 109, 116, 121-125, 131-132, 134, 136, 143, 152, 166, 168, 171, 176
honor and 3, 5, 19, 28-29, 32, 34-35, 37-38, 41-49, 61, 63, 81, 89-90, 95, 123, 128-130, 133
indebted gratitude and 2-8, 13, 18-19, 24-30, 32-36, 38, 41-46, 49, 51-52, 54-58, 60-65, 68, 72, 76-80, 87-89, 95, 97, 102-103, 107-109, 115, 121, 123, 130-132, 134-135, 139, 141-144, 178-180
loyalty to, 5-6, 25, 27, 33-38, 48-49, 53, 61, 76-78, 145-146
moral character and 56-62
remembering benefits of 25, 31-33, 39, 41, 61, 64, 77, 79-81, 87-88, 93, 95, 130, 143-144

beneficiaries 3, 36
benefactor-beneficiary relationship 2-7, 11, 15-24, 28-69, 76-77, 79-85, 87-93, 95, 121, 123, 130-132, 134-135, 139-146, 166, 171, 178-180
dishonor and 25, 29-31, 95, 123, 129, 145
fidelity and 6-7, 17, 25-38, 53, 61, 76, 93, 95, 103, 121, 123, 125, 131-132, 134-135, 143-146, 178-179
giving of gifts and 2, 17-19, 21-23, 28, 30, 38-39, 43-46, 60, 62
giving/receiving benefits and 21-36, 38-46, 48-50, 53-58, 60, 62-64, 68, 77-84, 87-98, 101, 121, 123, 129-134, 139-144, 178-179
gratitude of 103-104, 107, 109, 116, 121-125, 131-132, 134, 136, 143, 152, 166, 168, 171, 176
honor and 3, 5, 19, 28-29, 32, 34-35, 37-38, 41-49, 61, 63, 81, 89-90, 95, 123, 128-130, 133
humility of 103-104, 123-125, 134, 174
indebted gratitude and 2-8, 13, 18-19, 24-30, 32-36, 38, 41-46, 49, 51-52, 54-58, 60-65, 68, 72, 76-80, 87-89, 95, 97, 102-103, 107-109, 115, 121, 123, 130-132, 134-135, 139, 141-144, 178-180
loyalty and 5-6, 25, 27, 33-38, 48-49, 53, 61, 76-78, 145-146
moral character and 56-62, 140-141
remembering benefits and 25, 31-33, 39, 41, 61, 64, 77, 79-81, 87-88, 93, 95, 130, 143-144

benefits
friendship and 22, 24-25, 33, 63, 93
giving/receiving of, 21-36, 38-46,

48-50, 53-58, 60, 62-64, 68, 77-84, 87-98, 101, 121, 123, 129-134, 139-144, 178-179
  goodwill and 56, 59, 62-65, 68
  of God, 86-90, 92-98, 101, 104-105, 107, 109, 114-115, 121-125, 128, 130, 132-136, 139, 141-144, 147, 152, 154, 163, 167-168
  of Jesus Christ 5, 7, 128, 133, 140-144, 152-154, 178
  as producing gratitude 62-65, 68, 89-90, 121-123, 135, 152, 180
  remembrance of 25, 31-33, 39, 41, 61, 64, 77, 79-81, 87-88, 93, 95, 130, 143-144
  χάρις as 133-134, 141
bond
  relational b. 19-25, 29, 32-33, 37-38, 49-51, 55-56, 74-82, 84-87, 89, 91, 94
  cooperative b. 37-38, 40-41, 45-46, 49, 55, 68, 100, 102, 117, 139-140, 166
  reciprocal b. 19-25, 29, 32-33, 37-38, 49-51, 55-56, 74-82, 84-87, 94

character (cf. moral character)
Cicero 25, 27, 31, 33, 37, 56-58, 60, 63, 68, 140
client 5, 16, 22-24, 34-35, 37, 46, 51-52, 58, 64, 75, 85-86, 89, 93-94, 103, 135, 137, 139, 140, 177
cooperation 37-38, 40-41, 45-46, 49, 55, 68, 81-82, 85, 89-91, 97, 100, 102, 104, 117, 137, 139-140, 166, 176
covenant 13-14, 72-79, 81-85, 87, 97, 101, 103-104, 106-111, 113-114, 117-120, 125, 127, 129, 130, 135-137, 145-148, 151-157, 160, 163-167, 169, 171, 174-176, 178, 180
covenant-treaty 73, 76-77, 84, 107-108
covenantal nomism 114, 135-137, 176

dance of reciprocity 37-38, 40, 46, 49-50, 62, 78, 81-82, 89-91, 114, 127, 139
Dead Sea Scrolls (cf. also Qumran community) 109-113, 116, 169-170
dedicatory inscriptions 27, 44-45
dependence
  assuaging the risk of 51-53
  in Hebrews 139-140, 166
  goodwill and 51-53, 55
  mutual d. 20, 49-53, 55, 72, 81-85, 91-92, 97, 100, 102, 117, 139-140, 166
depravity 102, 112
DeSilva, David 6-7, 13, 62, 128
  anthropological optimism of 140-141, 145
  critique of 7, 138-146
  divine-human relationships and 139-146
  on fidelity 127, 138-144
  Greco-Roman benefaction and 6-7, 127, 129, 138-143
  on Hebrews 127, 129, 138-146, 150, 153, 156-157, 160, 177
  on honor and shame 145
  on indebted gratitude 139, 141-144
  Josephus and 127, 138, 142
  methodology of 138-142, 145-146
  on reciprocity 7, 127, 138-143, 145
  on rhetorical strategies 145-146
Dio 21, 25-27, 30-31, 33, 35-36, 41-42, 47, 50, 52, 57-58, 61, 133
divine enablement 2, 8, 13, 71, 114
  anthropological assumptions of 8, 13, 104, 116-125, 135, 146, 148, 171, 178
  in the Dead Sea Scrolls/Qumran community 116, 118-119, 169
  in Deuteronomy 116-117
  election and 147-148, 152-153, 159-160, 163, 167, 169, 171, 178
  in Ezekiel 116-120
  fidelity and 13, 104, 116-125, 146-148, 152-153, 155-163, 166-171, 178, 180
  God as divine enabler 104, 116-125, 135, 137, 146-148, 152-157, 160-163, 166-171, 178, 180
  gratitude and 13, 72, 104, 116, 121-125, 135, 166, 171, 180
  in Hebrews 2, 8, 125, 127, 146-148,

152-160, 163, 167-168, 170-171, 178, 180
honor and 104, 116, 123
human responsibility and 127, 166-171, 178
human transformation and 8, 13, 104, 116-122, 125, 127, 137, 146, 148, 152-158, 160-163, 166
humility and 104, 116, 123-125, 168
in Jeremiah 116-117, 120
Jesus Christ and 120, 147-148, 152-158, 160, 163, 166
new covenant and 127, 146-148, 152-154, 156, 158, 160, 178
paradox of 127, 166-171
Philo on 121-123
reciprocity versus 104, 115-117, 120-121, 123, 135, 146, 166, 171, 178, 180
in Romans 116, 120-121
securing fidelity and 116-119, 121, 123, 125, 135, 166, 178
virtue and 121-123
Deuteronomistic history, 73, 116-117
anthropological assumptions in 106-107, 116-117
human condition in 106-107, 116
human corruption in 106
human rebellion in 106-107
Mosaic Covenant and 72-73, 78, 107
reciprocity and 72, 103, 107
Suzerainty-vassal treaties and 72
Tetrateuch and 72, 87, 103, 107
Deuteronomist 73, 76-77, 79, 117
divine-human relationship 1, 4, 11, 16, 43-46, 50, 55, 57, 69-100, 102-103, 114, 116-125, 127-132, 134-135, 137-146, 148-171, 176-178, 180-181
failure of 71, 103-116, 120-121, 125, 132, 144-145
Israel and 71-72, 74-76, 79-92, 96-97, 101, 103-108, 117-118, 121, 123, 125, 135, 144, 148-151, 161-163, 165-166, 168
reciprocity and 1, 4, 11, 13, 16, 43-46, 50, 55, 57, 69-70, 97-103, 107-109, 114, 121, 125, 127, 135, 139-145

enablement, (cf. divine enablement)
euergetism, 15, 137

fidelity 1, 12, 25-49
anthropological optimism and 8, 11, 17, 97, 100, 102-103, 125, 135, 141
anthropological pessimism and 8, 11, 97, 102, 116-117, 123, 125, 135, 146, 148
benefaction and, 6-7, 17, 25-38, 53, 61, 76, 93, 95, 103, 121, 123, 125, 131-132, 134-135, 143-146, 178-179
divine enablement and 13, 104, 116-125, 135, 146-148, 152-153, 155-163, 166-171, 178, 180
extent of 36-37
exhortations to 6, 77-78, 87, 131-132
faith as source of 143-144
to God 11, 13, 76-78, 80, 87-90, 93, 95-97, 102-105, 107, 116-123, 125, 130-132, 135-136, 138-139, 141, 143-148, 152-153, 155-171, 178-180
goodwill as 52-53
gratitude and 116, 121, 123-125, 152, 166, 171, 178
in Hebrews 1, 6, 8, 11, 13, 125, 127, 130-132, 139-141, 143-146, 148, 152-153, 155-156, 158-160, 163-168, 170-171, 178, 180
human transformation and 13, 104, 116-121, 125, 152-153, 155-158, 160-163, 166
indebted gratitude and 26, 35, 49, 97, 102, 105, 124-125, 130-131, 134-135, 141-144, 178, 180
mutual dependence and 102
new covenant and 146-148, 152-153, 158, 160, 165-166
Paul on 120, 135, 138, 145, 168, 178
as πίστις / fides 33-37, 51, 57, 59

Index of Subjects

in rabbinic literature 13, 93, 97,
  100-103, 125
remembering of benefits and 25,
  87-88, 93-98, 130, 144
relationships and 1, 5, 7-8, 11-13,
  17, 19, 25-36, 49, 53, 69, 76-84, 87-
  89, 97, 100, 102-103, 107-109, 121,
  125, 127, 130-132, 135, 139-144,
  146, 171, 178-179
reciprocity and 1, 5, 7-8, 11-13, 19,
  25-36, 49, 53, 69, 76-84, 87-89, 97,
  100, 102-103, 107-109, 121, 125,
  127, 130-132, 135, 139-144, 146,
  178
securing of 8, 11-13, 49, 57, 69, 71,
  102-104, 107-109, 114, 117, 121,
  125, 127, 135, 138-139, 141, 158,
  166, 171, 178-180
securing honor and 130
hesed as 76, 79-81
free-will
  anthropological assumptions
    and, 98-102, 112
  Josephus on 98-100
  Middle Judaism and 100
  Rabbinic Judaism and, 101-102
friendship 15-16, 20-26, 32-35, 37-38,
  49, 52-53, 55-57, 60, 63, 65, 69, 75,
  79, 88, 93, 130, 132-133, 179
  benefaction and 15-16, 20-26, 33,
    35, 37-39, 49, 52-53, 55-57, 60, 63,
    65, 69, 75, 88, 93, 179
  benefits and 22, 24-25, 33, 63, 93
  in Deuteronomy 76-79
  as the goal of reciprocity 21, 33, 53
  goodwill and 22, 36, 52-53, 57, 63
  honor and 93, 133
  moral character and 55-57, 60
  political allegiance and 93-94
  reciprocity and 15-16, 20-26, 33,
    35, 37-39, 49, 52-53, 55-57, 60, 63,
    65, 69, 75, 88, 93, 179

gift(s) 1, 3, 17, 21-23, 27-28, 30-32,
  38-39, 43-45, 48, 50, 57-58, 60, 62-
  63, 75, 81, 89, 91, 95, 98, 122, 124,
  139, 142, 166, 179
God (or Yahweh)

calling of 151-152
cooperation with 89-91, 97, 139-
  140, 176
covenant and 135-137, 146-148,
  151-156, 160, 164-166, 171
covenantal nomism and 135-137,
  167, 176
benefits from 77-84, 86-90, 92-98,
  101, 104-105, 107, 109, 114-115,
  121-125, 128, 130, 132-136, 139,
  141-144, 147, 152, 154, 163, 167-
  168
as bestower of virtue 121-123, 147
blessings of 108, 170
cleansing activity of 160-164, 166,
  171
creation and 93-94, 99, 112, 114,
  119, 130
as creator 94, 97, 114
devotion to 147
dishonor to 95, 103, 114, 122, 145,
  161, 167-168
as divine benefactor 13, 88-89, 92-
  97, 103, 114, 122-125, 128, 130,
  134-136, 138-142, 144-145, 147,
  171, 180-181
as divine enabler 104, 116-125,
  135, 137, 146-148, 152-157, 160-
  163, 166-171, 178, 180
as divine helper 89-90, 121, 132
divine-human relationship and 1, 4,
  11, 16, 43-46, 50, 55, 57, 69-100,
  102-103, 114, 116-125, 127-132,
  134-135, 137-146, 148-171, 176-
  178, 180-181
as divine warrior 77, 164
enabling presence of 154-155, 161,
  167, 171, 178, 180
election and 78, 96, 135-136, 147-
  153, 159-160, 167, 169, 171, 178
faith in 124, 132-133, 143-144, 167
faithfulness of 123, 132, 134, 144,
  167, 181
faithfulness to (or fidelity to) 11,
  13, 76-83, 87-90, 93, 95-97, 102-
  105, 107, 116-123, 125, 130-132,
  135-136, 138-139, 141, 143-148,
  152-153, 155-171, 178-180

fear of 80, 101, 117, 122, 168
fidelity to (or faithfulness to) 11, 13, 76-78, 80, 87-90, 93, 95-97, 102-105, 107, 116-123, 125, 130-132, 135-136, 138-139, 141, 143-148, 152-153, 155-171, 178-180
forgetting 130
forgetting the benefits of 79-81, 92-93, 130, 142
forgiveness of 147, 163-164, 177
generosity of 95, 108, 142
gifts of 139, 166, 180
glory of 129-130, 160
glory to 147
goodwill of 88
grace of 4, 6, 8, 84-85, 98, 101, 122, 124, 131-132, 134, 136, 141, 144, 148, 152, 154-156, 166, 176-177, 181
guilt before 112, 161-162, 169
χάρις of 134
gratitude of 130
gratitude to 5, 7, 13, 72, 79, 87-90, 104, 107, 109, 116, 121-125, 131-132, 134, 136, 143, 152, 166, 168, 171, 176
hesed and 80-81
holiness of 106, 161-162
honor of 129
honor to 81-82, 88-90, 95, 97, 101, 104, 116, 122-123, 130-131, 145, 162, 174
human responsibility before 127, 166-171, 178
human transformation and 120, 127, 137, 146-148, 152-164, 166, 170-171, 181
humility toward 104, 116, 123-125, 134, 168, 174
indebted gratitude to 87-90, 95, 103, 105, 117, 125, 134-135, 141-144, 147, 180
infidelity to 79-80, 92-93, 95, 104, 106-109, 113-114, 116-117, 123, 130, 132, 142, 144-145, 165-166, 168, 170
ingratitude to 79-81, 92-93, 95, 100, 103, 107-109, 114-115, 145

as Israel's king 76, 96, 101
jealousy of 81, 106, 130
judgment of 105, 108, 110, 131, 142, 159, 161-162, 164-169, 180
as just judge 130-131, 159, 167
law of 10, 82, 86-87, 89-90, 97, 100, 105-106, 117-120, 130, 135-136, 147, 154, 156, 174
love of 80, 98, 138
mercy of 132, 136, 144, 148, 154, 156, 163, 166, 168, 181
oaths to 78, 84, 97, 108
obedience to 81, 84, 86-90, 97, 101, 104, 116, 118-119, 135-136, 141, 148
obligations to 77-78, 80-81, 83, 86-91, 95, 97, 138-139, 180
praise to 131
predestination of 109-113, 119, 121, 168-169, 178
prevenient grace and 177
promises of 135, 142-144, 147, 150, 158-159, 162, 168, 178, 181
rebellion against 104-110, 117, 119, 162-164
reciprocal honor and 81-82, 84
remembering the benefits of 79-81, 87-88, 95, 144
sin and, 102, 105-106, 110-115, 118, 120, 124, 128-129, 141, 147, 151-153, 155-156, 160-166, 168-170, 174, 177, 178
salvation and 130, 167-169, 176, 180
as sanctifier 148-149
sovereignty of 99, 110-111, 113, 119, 121, 170
as suzerain lord 76-77, 81, 83-84
suzerainty-vassal treaties and 76-79, 81-83
thanksgiving to 89-91, 119, 122-125, 141
transformation of humanity and 120, 127, 137, 146-148, 152-164, 166, 170-171, 181
trust in 93, 97, 132, 139-140, 144, 166
unbelief and 132, 144-145

Index of Subjects

worship of 130, 141, 147-148, 155-157, 160-163, 168, 178
will of 86, 96, 101, 111-113, 140, 147, 160-161, 168, 170, 177
wrath of 91, 95, 111, 161, 167-168
goodwill 21-22, 36, 51-64, 68, 75, 87-88, 179
   mutual dependence and 51-53, 55
   fidelity as 52-53
   friendship and 22, 36, 52-53, 57, 63
   loyalty as 36, 53, 61
   benefit as 56, 59
   moral character and 57
gratitude 2-3, 35, 44, 56, 97
   balancing power and 2
   divine enablement and 13, 72, 104, 116, 121-125, 135, 166, 171, 180
   beneficiaries and 2-3, 5-7, 41, 43-46, 51, 55-57, 60-65, 87, 121-123, 125, 131-132, 134-135, 143-144, 152, 166, 171, 180
   faith as foundation of 143-144
   fidelity and 116, 121, 123-125, 152, 166, 171, 178
   as generated by benefits 62-65, 68, 89-90, 121-123, 135, 152, 180
   to God 5, 7, 13, 72, 79, 87-90, 104, 107, 109, 116, 121-125, 131-132, 134, 136, 143, 152, 166, 168, 171, 176
   to the gods 43-46, 63
   as honor 32, 41-44, 104, 116, 123
   humility and 104, 116, 123-125, 134, 168, 174
   obedience as 97
   reciprocity *versus* 125, 171, 181
   public expression of g. 46-47, 94
   thanksgiving as 121-125
   votive offerings as 94
Greco-Roman
   anthropological assumptions 12-13, 17, 53-69, 103, 124, 135, 171
   benefaction 2-10, 12-13, 15-69, 71-72, 81-82, 85, 92, 98, 103, 124-129, 130, 132-135, 137-142, 144-145, 166, 171, 180
   cultural context 2, 6, 9-12, 15-69, 71-72, 81-82, 84, 92, 98, 103, 127, 132-135, 137-138, 141-142
   patronage 5-6, 15, 23, 72, 125, 127, 134, 137-138, 142
   reciprocity 2-7, 8-10, 12-13, 15-69, 71-72, 81-82, 85, 92, 98, 103, 124-129, 130, 132-135, 137-142, 144-145, 171, 180

Harrison, James R. 3-7, 10, 19, 26-27, 42, 44, 49, 51, 57-59, 61, 64, 84-85, 88, 94-95, 124, 134, 137-138, 175, 180
Hebrews
   anthropological assumptions in 1-2, 8, 12, 127, 140-141, 145-146, 148, 163-164, 166, 171, 178
   asymmetrical relationships in 128
   Augustinian soteriology and 177-178
   benefaction/patronage in 2, 6, 10, 125, 127-134, 138-147, 171, 180-181
   benefactor-beneficiary relationship in 127-134, 139-145, 147, 166
   calling in 151-152
   canonical implications of 178
   cleansing in 163-166
   conscience purification in 125, 145, 148, 152-153, 155-158, 163-166, 171
   cooperation in 139-140, 166
   covenant relationship in 147-148, 152, 160, 165-166, 178
   cultic reinterpretation of the new covenant in 13-14, 146-147, 152-156, 163, 174
   cultural milieu of 6, 9-10, 12, 15-69, 127-128, 132-135, 138-139, 142, 145, 171, 180-181
   David deSilva's interpretation of 129, 138-146, 150, 153, 156-157, 160, 177
   divine benefaction in 128, 130-133, 139-147, 171, 180-181
   divine enablement in 2, 8, 125, 127, 146-148, 152-160, 163, 167-168, 170-171, 178, 180
   divine-human relationship in 127-

128, 130, 134, 139-160, 163-168, 170-171, 178, 180-181
election in 147-153, 159-160, 163, 167, 171, 178
eschatological hope in 143, 149, 154, 158-160, 163, 178
exhortation(s) in 127-128, 141, 144, 154-156, 159, 167
faith in 132-133, 143-144, 167
fidelity in 1, 6, 8, 11, 13, 125, 127, 130-132, 139-141, 143-146, 148, 152-153, 155-156, 158-160, 163-168, 170-171, 178, 180
giving/receiving of benefits in 128, 130, 139-144, 152
grace in 139, 144, 148, 152, 154-156, 160, 166
gratitude in 134, 141, 143-144, 152, 166, 168, 171, 180
Greco-Roman benefaction and 6, 8-10, 127, 130, 132-134, 138-139, 141-142, 145, 180
Greco-Roman context of 11-12, 15-69, 71, 127, 132, 141-142
God's benefits in 128, 130, 132-134, 139, 142-144, 147, 152, 154, 163, 167, 180
God's judgment in 131, 142, 159, 161, 164-166, 168, 180
God's promises in 143-144, 147, 150, 153-154, 156, 158-159, 163, 168, 178
historical context of 9-12, 15-69
history of Israel in 149, 165-166
honor in 128-130, 145
human condition in 127, 140-141, 145, 148, 157, 160, 164-166, 171
human perfection in 149, 152-160, 167, 171
human responsibility in 127, 166-168, 170-171, 178, ,
human transformation in 127, 146, 148, 152-160, 163-164, 166, 170-171
indebted gratitude and 134, 139, 141-144, 180
infidelity in 142, 144-145, 165-166, 168

ingratitude in 129, 144-145
inheritance in 143-145, 151, 160, 178, 181
Jesus' benefits in 7, 128, 133, 140-144, 152-154, 178
Jesus Christ in 128-130, 132-134, 139-144, 146-160, 163-167, 171, 178, 180-181
Josephus and 138
Middle Judaism and 8, 10, 13, 146, 166, 168, 171
mutual dependence in 139-140, 166
mutual obligations in 139, 142
new covenant in 127, 145-148, 154, 156, 158, 160, 163, 165-167, 171, 178
old covenant in 147, 151-158, 164-166
paradox in 127, 160, 166-168, 170-171, 175
pastoral implications of 178-180
Paul and 138, 145, 154, 163-164, 166, 168, 171, 178
Pauline influence on 94, 138
persecution in 139, 163-164
place in theological tradition 14, 173, 176-178
punishment in 129
religious background of 71-125
religious context of 10-11
religious heritage of 10, 13, 69, 94, 125, 138
reciprocity and 1, 8-11, 13, 125, 127, 130, 134, 138-146, 166-167, 171, 178, 180-181
salvation in 143, 146, 149, 180
sanctification in 148-149, 151-160, 167, 171
soteriology in 2, 13, 146, 149-151, 153, 171, 176-178, 180
theology of 8, 127, 150, 166-167, 170-171, 178, 180-181
transformation in 127, 146, 148, 152-160, 163-164, 166, 170-171
unbelief in 144-145
warnings in 127-129, 142, 161, 166-168
wrath of God in 161, 167-168

Index of Subjects

χάρις in 133-134, 141
Homer 16-18, 22-23, 25-26, 28-29, 31, 35-39, 43-44, 50, 72, 75, 95
honor 3, 5-7, 19, 21, 23, 25, 31-32, 37-38, 41-53, 57-62, 64, 68, 72, 74, 81-82, 84, 89-95, 97-98, 103, 106, 112, 114, 125, 133, 146, 151, 161
   benefactors and 5, 28-29, 32, 34-35, 41-49, 61, 81, 89-90, 95, 123, 128-130
   benefits and 41-46, 81, 89-90, 93, 95, 101, 123, 128-130
   dedicatory inscriptions as 44-45, 81
   divine enablement and 104, 116, 123
   gifts as 43-45
   of God 129
   to God 81-82, 88-90, 95, 97, 101, 104, 116, 122-123, 130-131, 145, 162, 174
   gratitude as 32, 41-44, 104, 116, 123
   in Hebrews 128-130, 145
   humility as 104
   hymnic praise as 45-46, 81, 90, 131-132
   immortal 47-48
   indebted gratitude as 32, 41-46, 61, 89-90
   obedience as 81, 90, 97
   poetry as 46
   reciprocity and 5, 28-29, 32, 34-35, 41-49, 61, 81, 89-90, 95, 123, 129-130
   sacrifice as 43-45, 50, 81, 90
   subservience as 48-49, 81
   votive offerings as 44-45, 81, 94
   warnings and 128-129
honorific inscriptions 19, 42, 47, 49, 53, 58-61, 93, 95
hospitality 15, 20, 23, 38-39, 75, 130
humility 103-104, 116, 123-125, 134, 167-169, 174

indebted gratitude 2-3, 35, 44, 56, 97, 124, 141-142
   aversive nature of 178-179
   balancing power and 2
   beneficiaries and 2-8, 13, 18-19, 24-30, 32-36, 38, 41-46, 49, 51-52, 54-58, 60-65, 68, 72, 76-80, 87-89, 95, 97, 102-103, 107-109, 115, 121, 123, 130-132, 134-135, 139, 141-144, 178-180
   divine enablement *versus* 13, 72, 104, 124-125, 134-135, 147, 178, 180
   fidelity and 26, 35, 49, 97, 102, 105, 124-125, 130-131, 134-135, 141-144, 178, 180
   as generated by benefits 62-65, 68, 89-90, 141-144, 178-180
   to God 5, 7, 13, 72, 87-90, 95, 103, 105, 117, 125, 134-135, 141-144, 147, 180
   g. to the gods 43-46, 63
   as *hesed* 76, 79-81
   honor as 32, 41-46, 61, 89-90
   obedience as 97, 135
   preservation of 49, 51, 62-65, 107-108
   public expression of g. 46-47, 94
   reciprocity and 2-8, 13, 18-19, 24-30, 32-36, 38, 41-46, 49, 52, 54-56, 58, 61, 64, 68, 72, 76-80, 87-89, 95, 97, 102-103, 107-109, 115, 121, 123, 130-132, 134-135, 139, 141-144, 178-180
   as remembrance of benefits 25, 31-33, 39, 41, 61, 64, 77, 79-81, 87-88, 93, 95, 130, 143-144
   securing fidelity and 8, 11-13, 49, 57, 69, 71, 102-104, 107-109, 114, 117, 121, 124-125, 127, 135, 138-139, 141, 158, 166, 171, 178-180
   votive offerings as 94
infidelity 35-36, 79, 88, 123, 165-166
   as forgetting benefits 79-81, 87-88, 92-93, 130, 142
   to God 79-80, 92-93, 95, 104, 106-109, 113-114, 116-117, 123, 130, 132, 142, 144-145, 165-166, 168, 170
   as ingratitude 88, 92-94, 107-108, 114, 130, 142, 144-145
   solution to 116-121, 125

as unbelief 144-145
warnings against 6, 131-132, 166-170
ingratitude 26, 28-33, 35-36, 50, 60, 63-65, 79, 88, 93, 95, 100, 103, 114-115, 129, 144-145
  as infidelity 88, 92-94, 107-108, 114, 130, 142, 144-145
  as forgetting benefits 80-81, 87-88, 92-93, 130, 142
  wrath for 95
Israel 10, 71-93, 96-99, 101, 103-111, 116-119, 121, 123, 125, 129-130, 135, 144, 148-151, 160-163, 165-166, 168, 179
  history of 149, 165-166
  reciprocity between God and 71-72, 74-76, 79-92, 96-97, 101, 103, 107-109, 125, 135
  relationship between God and 71-72, 74-76, 79-92, 96-97, 101, 103-108, 117-118, 121, 123, 125, 135, 144, 148-151, 161-163, 165-166, 168

Jerusalem collection 3-4
Jesus Christ
  benefits of 5, 7, 128, 133, 140-144, 152-154, 178
  as benefactor 128, 133, 140-142
  blessings of 128
  conscience purification by 128, 148, 152-153, 155-158, 163-164, 166
  as creator 141
  dishonor toward 129
  divine enablement and 120, 147-148, 152-158, 160, 163, 166
  as divine enabler 137, 157-158, 160
  exaltation of 158
  indebted gratitude toward 141-142
  indwelling of 120, 137, 168
  faithfulness of 137, 143
  fidelity and 120, 139-141, 143-144, 155-156, 158, 160, 163-164, 166-168
  forgiveness of sins through 147, 151, 155, 160, 164-165
  glory of 120, 143, 149, 168
  heavenly ministry of 153, 158
  in Hebrews 128-130, 132-134, 139-144, 146-160, 163-167, 171, 178, 180-181
  as high priest 146-148, 152-156, 158-160, 163, 167, 171, 175, 178, 181
  honor of 128
  hope in 149
  human perfection and 149, 152-158, 160, 167, 171
  human transformation and 120, 137, 147-148, 152-158, 160, 163-164, 166, 181
  indwelling of 137
  judgment of 168
  obligation toward 142
  redemption through 149, 151, 178
  return of 143
  sacrifice of 151, 153, 155-157, 163-164
  as salvific source 6, 133, 142, 146, 149, 167
  as sanctifier 148-149, 151-158, 160, 163-164, 181
  as servant of the Lord 152
  soteriology and 2, 146, 149-151, 153, 164, 180
  supremacy of 2, 10
  as victor 164
Josephus,
  anthropological assumptions of 97-100, 103, 125, 135
  on benefaction/patronage 72, 85-92, 103, 125, 127, 131, 135, 142
  biblical paraphrase of (*Antiquitates judaicae*) 13, 21, 85-92, 98-99, 103, 125, 131
  on cooperation 85, 89-91
  on divine benefits 87-91, 97-98
  on divine favor 98
  on fidelity 13, 85, 87-88, 97, 103
  on free-will 98-100
  Greco-Roman benefaction and 72, 85, 89, 92, 125, 134-135, 138
  on indebted gratitude 85, 87-90, 97, 103, 131, 135

on infidelity 87-88
on ingratitude 87-88
on the Mosaic Law 86-87, 89-90, 135
on mutual dependence 85, 91-92
on reciprocity 13, 72, 85-92, 97, 99-100, 103, 125, 127, 135
on relational bonds 85-87, 89, 91
on remembrance of benefits 87-88
on obedience 97, 135
on obligations 85-91
on virtue 98-100
on human worthiness 98-99, 135

Judaism
anthropological assumptions of 7-8, 71-72, 97-125, 135, 137, 146, 166, 171
covenantal nomism in 135-137, 176
exilic 7-8, 13, 73, 103, 108, 114, 120, 166, 175
Middle 1-2, 8, 10-11, 13, 71, 92-96, 100-103, 120-121, 125, 134-135, 146, 166, 168, 171, 176
Hebrews and 8, 10, 13, 146, 166, 168, 171
human transformation and 120, 166
Rabbinic 72, 96-97, 101-102, 125, 136
reciprocity and 1-2, 8-9, 11-13, 71-72, 92-97, 100-103, 120-121, 125, 134-135, 146, 171

Laato, Timo 2, 54, 101, 114-115, 136-137
Law, Mosaic (cf. also Mosaic covenant) 10, 82, 86, 87, 89-90, 97, 100, 105-106, 119-120, 130, 135-136, 154
loyalty 5-6, 25, 27, 33-36, 48-49, 53, 61, 76, 145-146
conflicting loyalties 37-38
exclusive l. 76-78
goodwill and 36, 53, 61
reciprocity and 5-6, 25, 33-36, 48-49, 53, 61, 76, 145-146

merit 4-5, 35, 39, 57, 60, 62, 64, 72, 80, 86, 96, 98, 124, 135, 180

Middle Judaism
anthropological assumptions of 97-125, 135, 146, 166, 171
benefaction and 72, 85, 89, 92-93, 125, 134-135, 138
defined 71
divine enablement and 116, 120, 124-125, 135, 137-138, 166, 168, 178
divine-human relationship and 71, 92, 100-103, 121, 135, 146, 166, 171
fidelity and, 13, 85, 87-88, 93, 97, 102-104, 107-109, 114, 116-119, 121-123, 125, 127, 146, 166
free-will and 98, 100-102
Hebrews and 8, 10, 13, 146, 166, 168, 171
human transformation and 120, 166
Paul and 120, 134, 168
reciprocity and 1-2, 8, 11-13, 71, 92-96, 100-103, 120-121, 134-135, 146, 171
religious traditions of 71
soteriological streams in 176
moral character 65-68
benefactors and 56-62
beneficiaries and 56-62, 140-141
fidelity and 57, 100
friendship and 55-57, 60
goodwill and 57
gratitude and 58, 68
humility and 103
Josephus on 98-100
Rabbinic Judaism and 101-102
reciprocity and 55-57, 99-100, 140-141
intrinsic capacity for 101-102
Mosaic Covenant 13, 72-74, 76, 78, 81-82, 84-85, 87, 110, 117, 125, 174
apostasy from 109-110
blessings in 83
conditional character of 83-84
cooperation and 81-82
cooperative nature of 104, 117
curses and 83, 106-107
Deuteronomistic History and 72,

87, 106-107
  divine enablement and 117, 160
  failure to keep the 104, 106-108
  fidelity and 76, 78, 81-83, 97, 107-108, 117, 160
  gratitude and 107
  hesed and 76
  honor and 81-82, 97
  human transformation and 160
  indebted gratitude and 76, 97, 117
  infidelity to 104, 106-108, 113
  mutual dependence and 81-83, 117
  obedience to 86-87, 89-90, 97, 135
  obligations and 81-84
  purification and 160-161
  reciprocity and 72-74, 76-78, 81-85, 92, 97, 107-108, 117, 125
  relational bond and 76, 82, 84
  renewal of 78, 109-110
  Suzerainty-vassal treaties and 72-73, 78, 81-85, 107, 125
  Tetrateuch and 72, 82, 85, 87, 104, 107
  voluntary nature of 82, 84
Mosaic Law (cf. also Mosaic covenant) 10, 82, 86, 87, 89-90, 97, 100, 105-106, 119-120, 130, 135-136, 154
Moses 76, 79, 82-90, 92, 98-99, 101, 103, 105-106, 110, 116-117, 131, 144, 160, 165
mutual dependence 20, 49-53, 55, 72, 81-85, 91-92, 97, 100, 102, 117, 139-140, 166
  assuaging the risk of 51-53
  fidelity and 102
  goodwill and 51-53, 55
  in Hebrews 139-140, 166
  Josephus on 85, 91-92
  in Mosaic covenant 81-83, 117
  reciprocity and 20, 49-53, 55, 72, 81-85, 91-92, 97, 100, 102, 117, 139-140, 166
mutual obligations 1-2, 43,
  in Hebrews 139, 142
  honor as 43-49, 89, 97
  indebted gratitude as 97
  obedience as 97

  Josephus on, 85-91
  in Mosaic covenant 81-84
  reciprocity and 2-3, 17, 20-21, 23-24, 27, 34-35, 38-49, 51-52, 55, 63-64, 77-81, 84, 86-90, 95, 138-139, 179
  voluntary nature of 40
  votive offerings as 44-45, 81, 94

New Covenant 147-148, 151-152, 160
  blessings of 146, 152-153
  community of the 167
  cultic reinterpretation of 13-14, 146-147, 152-156, 163, 174
  divine enablement and 127, 146-148, 152-154, 156, 158, 160, 178
  in Ezekiel 162
  fidelity and 146-148, 152-153, 158, 160, 165-166
  in Hebrews 127, 145-148, 154, 156, 158, 160, 163, 165-167, 171, 178
  internality of, 145-146
  in Jeremiah 116-118, 120, 127, 146-147, 152, 156, 162-163, 165-166
  promises of 147, 153-154, 156, 163, 171
  transformation and 146, 152-154, 156, 158, 160, 163, 166, 171

obligation(s) 2-3, 17, 20-21, 23
  fidelity as 97
  to God 77-78, 80-81, 83, 86-91, 95, 97, 138-139, 180 (not mut. obl.)
  goodwill and 51-53, 63
  honor as 43-49, 89, 97
  indebted gratitude as 97
  obedience as 97
  reciprocity and 2-3, 17, 20-21, 23-24, 27, 34-35, 38-49, 51-52, 55, 63-64, 77-81, 84, 86-90, 95, 138-139, 179
  voluntary nature of 40
  votive offerings as 44-45, 81, 94

paradox 40-41, 55
  in Hebrews 127, 160, 166-168, 170-171, 175

Index of Subjects

of divine enablement 127, 166-171
in Qumran community 110-113
patronage (cf. benefaction)
Paul 3-5, 13, 94-95
  anthropological assumptions of
  114-116, 120-121, 123-125, 135,
  137, 163-164, 166
  as benefactor 3
  as beneficiary 4-6
  on benefactor-beneficiary
  relationship 127, 135, 137-138,
  166, 171
  on Christ 137-138, 145, 168
  conversion of 5-6
  on divine enablement 116, 120,
  124-125, 135, 137-138, 166, 168,
  178
  on divine-human relationship 127,
  135, 137-138, 166, 168, 171, 178
  on fidelity 120, 135, 138, 145, 168,
  178
  on forgiveness 120
  on freedom 120
  on God's benefits 124-125
  on God's grace 138
  on God's wrath 95, 168
  on gratitude 124-125
  Greco-Roman benefaction and 4-6,
  8, 134-135, 137-138, 166
  Hebrews and 138, 145, 154, 163-
  164, 166, 168, 171, 178
  on the human condition 114-115,
  120, 145
  on human cooperation 137
  on human fidelity 120, 135, 138,
  145, 168, 178
  on human infidelity 95, 114, 168
  on human ingratitude 95, 114
  on human rebellion 114
  on human responsibility 168
  on human sin 114-115, 120, 168
  on human transformation 120, 137,
  160
  indebted gratitude and 3-5, 179
  influence on Hebrews 94, 138
  on justification 120, 177
  language of grace 4, 6, 8
  legalism and 135-136
  Middle Judaism and 120, 134, 168
  mission to the Gentiles 3-5
  on original sin 114-115
  paradox in 168
  on predestination 168
  reciprocity and 5-6, 8, 94-95, 114,
  120, 124, 134-135, 137-138, 145,
  166, 171, 179
  on the Spirit 120, 145, 154
  spiritual poverty in 124-125
  thanksgiving and 123-125
  warnings of 168
Pelagianism 14, 176-178
Philo 10, 48, 85, 94-95, 121-124, 129,
  133, 180
Plato 36, 44, 50
Pliny 15, 26-27, 35, 47, 61, 64
Plutarch 26, 40, 48, 50, 52, 57, 59, 61,
  64, 68, 95, 132, 144
predestination 109-113, 119, 121, 168-
  169, 178
purification 119, 125, 128, 145, 148,
  152-153, 155-158, 160-166, 171

Qumran community 13, 103, 109-114,
  116, 118-119, 121, 123-125, 169-
  170, 174

Rabbinic Judaism
  covenantal nomism in 136
  optimistic anthropological
  assumptions of 97, 101-102, 125
  free-will and 101-102
  human worthiness in 101-102,
  reciprocity and 96-97, 101-102, 125
  original sin and 101-102
Rabinowitz, Peter J. 8-9
reciprocal bond(s) 19-25, 29, 32-33,
  37-38, 49-51, 55-56, 74-82, 84-87,
  94
reciprocity
  anthropological assumption of 1, 5-
  8, 12-13, 17, 53-69, 71, 97-103,
  108, 125, 135, 140-141, 145-146,
  171
  assuaging the risk of 51-53
  asymmetrical relationships and 2, 5,
  24, 34-36, 38, 40-49, 81, 89, 95,

178-179
aversive nature of 178-179
benefaction and 2-7, 5-6, 8-10, 12-13, 15-69, 71-72, 76-77, 79-85, 87-93, 95, 98, 103, 121, 123-135, 137, 139-146, 166, 171, 178-180
benefactor-beneficiary 2-7, 11, 15-24, 28-69, 76-77, 79-85, 87-93, 95, 121, 123, 130-132, 134-135, 139-146, 166, 171, 178-180
character and 55-57, 99-100, 140-141
conditional 83
cooperation and 37-38, 40-41, 45-46, 49, 55, 68, 100, 102, 117, 139-140, 166
cultural expectations of 17-69, 72, 137
dance of 37-38, 40, 46, 49-50, 62, 78, 81-82, 89-91, 114, 127, 139
dark side of 178-179
David deSilva on 7, 127, 138-143, 145
debt and 22-27, 38, 178-180
definition of 17-18, 19-20
Deuteronomistic History and 72-73, 82, 85, 92, 103, 107
divine enablement *versus* 104, 115-117, 120-121, 123, 135, 146, 166, 171, 178, 180
divine-human 1, 4, 11, 13, 16, 43-46, 50, 55, 57, 69-70, 97-103, 107-109, 114, 121, 125, 127, 135, 139-145
ethos of 4-5, 19, 62, 85, 134, 137, 175, 180
failure of 103-116, 120-121, 123, 125, 129-130
fidelity and 1, 5, 7-8, 11-13, 19, 25-36, 49, 53, 69, 76-84, 87-89, 97, 100, 102-103, 107-109, 121, 125, 127, 130-132, 135, 139-144, 146, 178
friendship and 15-16, 20-26, 33, 35, 37-39, 49, 52-53, 55-57, 60, 63, 65, 69, 75, 88, 93, 179
forgetting benefits and 130
giving of gifts and 2, 17-19, 21-23, 28, 30, 38-39, 43-46, 60, 62
giving/receiving benefits and 21-36, 38-46, 48-50, 53-58, 60, 62-64, 68, 77-84, 87-98, 101, 121, 123, 129-134, 139-144, 178-179
between God and Israel 71-72, 74-76, 79-92, 96-97, 101, 103, 107-109, 125, 135
goodwill and 21-22, 36, 51-64, 68, 75, 87-88, 179
grace and 4, 6-8, 139, 144
Greco Roman 2-7, 8-10, 12-13, 15-69, 71-72, 81-82, 85, 92, 98, 103, 124-129, 130, 132-135, 137-142, 144-145, 171, 180
guest-friendship and 38-39
Hebrews and 1, 8-11, 13, 125, 127, 130, 134, 138-146, 166-167, 171, 178, 180-181
hesed and 79-81
honor and 5, 28-29, 32, 34-35, 41-49, 61, 81, 89-90, 95, 123, 129
hospitality and, 15, 20, 23, 38-39
indebted gratitude and 2-8, 13, 18-19, 24-30, 32-36, 38, 41-46, 49, 51-52, 54-58, 60-65, 68, 72, 76-80, 87-89, 95, 97, 102-103, 107-109, 115, 121, 123, 130-132, 134-135, 139, 141-144, 178-180
Judaism and 1-2, 8-9, 11-13, 71-72, 92-97, 100-103, 120-121, 125, 134-135, 146, 171
Josephus and 72, 85-92, 97, 99-100, 103, 125, 127, 135
loyalty and 5-6, 25, 33-36, 48-49, 53, 61, 76, 145-146
Middle Judaism and 1-2, 8, 11-13, 71, 92-96, 100-103, 120-121, 134-135, 146, 171
moral character and 55-57, 99-100, 140-141
Mosaic Covenant and 72-74, 76-78, 81-85, 92, 97, 107-108, 117, 125
mutual dependence and 20, 49-53, 55, 72, 81-85, 91-92, 97, 100, 102, 117, 139-140, 166
mutually beneficial 49, 74-75
obligations and 2-3, 17, 20-21, 23-

Index of Subjects

24, 27, 34-35, 38-49, 51-52, 55, 63-64, 77-81, 84, 86-90, 95, 138-139, 179
patronage and 5-7, 15-16, 23, 37, 51-52
Paul and 5-6, 8, 94-95, 114, 120, 124, 134-135, 137-138, 145, 166, 171, 179
protection and 34-35
Rabbinic Judaism and 96-97, 101-102, 125, 136
as relational bond 19-25, 29, 32-33, 37-38, 49-51, 55-56, 74-82, 84-87, 94
remembering benefits and 25, 31-33, 39, 41, 61, 64, 77, 79-81, 87-88, 93, 95, 130, 143-144
risk of 49-53, 55, 68, 82, 92, 97, 173
securing fidelity and 8, 11-13, 49, 57, 69, 71, 102-104, 107-109, 114, 117, 121, 125, 127, 135, 138-139, 141, 158, 166, 171, 178-180
securing gratitude and, 49, 51, 62-65, 107-108
social cohesion and 1, 20-21, 23, 28
the spirit of 51
suzerain-vassal 72-78, 81-84
Suzerainty-vassal treaties and 72-78, 81-84, 125
symmetrical relationships of 38-40
systems of 1-2, 5, 9, 11-12, 15-17, 19-25, 33, 37-38, 49, 51-52, 55-56, 60, 62, 65, 71, 81-82, 134, 137-38, 141, 171, 180
Tetrateuch and 72, 82, 85, 103, 107
virtue and 55-57, 99-100, 140-141
voluntary nature of 20, 23-25, 40, 50-55, 68, 74-75, 82, 84, 92, 152, 173
relationship(s)
asymmetrical 2, 5, 24, 34-36, 38, 40-49, 81, 89, 95, 178-179
benefactor-beneficiary, 2-7, 11, 15-24, 28-69, 76-77, 79-85, 87-93, 95, 121, 123, 130-132, 134-135, 139-146, 166, 171, 178-180
divine-human 1, 4, 11, 16, 43-46, 50, 55, 57, 69-100, 102-103, 114, 116-125, 127-132, 134-135, 137-146, 148-171, 176-178, 180-181
failure of 30, 44, 71, 77, 103-116, 120-121, 125, 144-145
fidelity and 1, 5, 7-8, 11-13, 19, 25-36, 49, 53, 69, 76-84, 87-89, 97, 100, 102-103, 107-109, 121, 125, 127, 130-132, 135, 139-144, 146, 178
between God and Israel 71-72, 74-76, 79-92, 96-97, 101, 103-108, 117-118, 121, 123, 125, 135, 144, 148-151, 161-163, 165-166, 168
mutually beneficial 49, 74-75
mutually dependent 20, 49-53, 55, 72, 81-85, 91-92, 97, 100, 102, 117, 139-140, 166
patron-client 24, 37, 46, 51-52, 58-59, 86, 89, 93, 103, 135, 139
πίστις / fides and 33-37, 51, 57, 59
risk of 49-53, 55, 68, 82, 92, 97, 173
suzerain-vassal 72-78, 81-84, 125
symmetrical 38-40

salvation 1-2, 6, 66, 90, 98, 100, 109, 113, 128, 130, 133, 137, 142-143, 146, 167-169, 176, 180
Seneca 18-27, 31-33, 35-36, 40, 43, 46-49, 51, 55-57, 60, 63-68, 95, 139-142, 179
sin 102, 105-106, 110-115, 118, 120, 124, 128-129, 141, 147, 151-153, 155-156, 160-166, 168-170, 174, 177, 178
soteriology
canon and 180,
church history and 176-177
in Hebrews 2, 13, 146, 149-151, 153, 171, 176-178, 180
Jesus Christ and 2, 6, 133, 142, 146, 149-151, 164, 167, 180
patterns of 13, 176-178, 180
theological traditions and 176-178
Stoicism 22, 66-67, 90, 102
Suzerainty-vassal treaties
appeal to the gods and 75-76

blessings in 75-76, 83
contingent nature of 84
curses in 75-76, 83
Deuteronomistic History and 72
exclusive loyalty and 76-78, 81
fidelity and 76-79
giving/receiving of benefits and 77
goodwill and 75
indebted gratitude and 76-79
infidelity and 79
ingratitude and 79
Mosaic Covenant and 72-73, 78, 107
oaths and 74-75, 78
parts of 77
preservation of fidelity and 75
reciprocity and 72-78, 81-84, 125
Tetrateuch and 72
voluntary nature of 74-75, 84

Tetrateuch 13, 72, 79, 82, 85, 87, 103-105, 107
anthropological assumptions in 104-105, 107
Deuteronomistic History and 72, 87, 103, 107
human condition in 105-106, 107
human corruption in 104
human rebellion in 104-105, 107
Mosaic Covenant and 72, 82, 85, 87, 104, 107
reciprocity and 72, 82, 85, 103, 107
Suzerainty-vassal treaties and 72
transformation
fidelity and 13, 104, 116-121, 125, 152-153, 155-158, 160-163, 166
in Hebrews 127, 146, 148, 152-160, 163-164, 166, 170-171
by God 120, 127, 137, 146-148, 152-164, 166, 170-171, 181
divine enablement and 8, 13, 104, 116-122, 125, 127, 137, 146, 148, 152-158, 160-163, 166
Jesus Christ and 120, 137, 147-148, 152-158, 160, 163-164, 166, 181

Unfaithfulness (cf. also infidelity) 35-36, 75, 106-109, 116, 130, 132, 140, 162

virtue (cf. moral character)
votive offerings 44-45, 57-58, 81, 94

Yahweh (cf. God)

Index of References

Old Testament

Genesis
2 *105*
3-11 *105*
5 *105*
6:5 *105*
8:21 *105*
15:13-16 *82*
20:6 *168*
22:1 *91*
22:12 *91*

Exodus
6:7 *74*
7:3-4 *168*
7:3-6 *82*
10:3 *169*
15-17 *104*
19:3-6 *78*
19:3-8 *78, 82*
19:5 *74, 81, 83*
19:6 *154*
19:8 *75, 84*
20:1 *78*
20:1-24:11 *78, 82*
20:3 *74, 76*
20:5 *81, 130*
20:6 *80*
20:20 *91*
20:23 *76*
23:20-33 *81*
23:24-25 *76*
23:32-33 *76*
24 *153*
24:3 *75, 151*
24:3-8 *84*
24:6-8 *151*
24:7 *84*
29:45-46 *74*
31:13 *148*
32:1-6 *104*
32:1-35 *104*
32:9-10 *161*
32:11-12 *123*
32:32-33 *150*
34:6-7 *80*
34:14 *81, 130*
34:32 *154*

Leviticus
8:15 *160*
9:5 *154*
10:3 *161*
16 *153*
16:16 *160*
16:19 *160*
22:3 *154, 160*
22:31-33 *148*
25 *161*
26:12-13 *74*

Numbers
11:1-3 *104*
11:4-35 *104*
12:1-15 *104*
13-14 *77, 104*
14:13-23 *123*
14:19 *80*
16:1-50 *105*
16:9 *156*
20:1-13 *105*
21:4-9 *105*
25:1-9 *105*

Deuteronomy
1:1-4:43 *72*
4:5-8 *82*
4:9 *130*
4:11 *154*
4:15-20 *77, 78*
4:20 *78*
4:23 *130*
4:24 *81, 130*
4:37-40 *78*
5-11 *76*
5:10 *80*
5:23 *154*
6:12 *79, 130*
6:13 *74*
6:14 *79*
6:15 *81, 130*
6:18 *82*
6:20-25 *78*
7:1-6 *77*
7:6 *74*
7:9-10 *80*
8:2 *91*
8:2-5 *79*
8:6 *79*
8:6-20 *82*
8:11 *130*
8:14 *130*
8:16 *91*
8:19 *79, 130*
9:4 *77*
9:6 *106*
9:7 *106*
9:13 *106*
9:24 *106*
9:26-28 *123*
10:12 *156*
10:16 *116*
10:20-11:7 *78*
11:8-17 *78*
11:13 *156*
11:28 *156*
12 *77*
12-26 *76*
13:1-18 *74*
15:4-5 *83*
25:19 *130*
26 *84*
26:17-19 *84*
28 *76, 83*
28:1-2 *83*

28:1-14 *81*
28:14 *156*
28:15 *83*
28:15-68 *76*
29:1-9 *82*
29:2-29 *78*
29:13 *74*
29:16-18 *77*
29:17 *156*
30:6-8 *116, 117*
31-32 *101*
31:14-32:43 *106*
31:27 *106*
32:21 *81, 130*

Joshua
1:3-8 *81*
1:6-9 *82*
22:5 *156*
24:1-24 *78*
24:2-13 *78, 83*
24:14-15 *77, 78*
24:16-18 *75, 78*
24:19 *130*
24:19-20 *106*
24:24 *75, 78*

Judges
1:24 *80*
8:34 *80*
8:35 *80*

1 Samuel
2:12 *106*
3:11-13 *80*
15:6 *80*

2 Samuel
2:6 *80*
2:30 *81*
10:2 *80*

1 Kings
3:6 *80*
11:9-13 *82*
11:31-39 *82*
22:21-23 *168*

2 Kings
17 *106*
17:7 *79*
17:7-17 *79*
17:7-20 *106, 108*
17:8-17 *79*
17:14 *106*

Job
8:13 *130*

Psalms
9:18 *130*
9:19 *130*
9:33 *130*
23:3-4 *161*
43:25 *130*
49:14 *131*
49:22 *130*
50 *161, 163*
50:4 *161*
50:9 *161*
50:12 *161*
50:13 *161*
50:14 *161*
50:15 *161*
69:28 *150*
73:19 *130*
73:23 *130*
77:7 *130*
103:2 *130*
117:6 *132*
118:93 *130*
136:5 *130*

Isaiah
6:1-4 *162*
6:1-8 *162*
6:5 *162*
6:7 *162*
6:8 *162*
8:17 *139, 140*
8:18 *149*
41:8 *150*
41:8-10 *150*
41:9 *151*
42:1 *152*
42:8 *129*

44:21 *130*
48:11 *129*
49:15 *130*
53:12 *152*
63:17 *169*
64:7 *169*
65:2 *119*
65:11 *130*
65:17-20 *119*
65:18 *119*

Jeremiah
2:7 *107*
2:13 *107*
2:19 *108*
2:25 *108*
3:19-20 *107*
4:4 *108, 117*
4:22 *108*
5:7 *107*
5:23 *108*
7:24-26 *108*
9:13-16 *107*
9:26 *108, 117*
11:10-11 *107*
13:23 *108*
14:9 *130*
22:9 *107*
23:27 *130*
24:7 *117*
30:6-8 *114*
31:31-34 *117*
31:33 *117*
32:23 *107*
32:29 *162*
32:39-41 *117*
32:40b *117*
34:18-20 *84*
38 *165*
38:31-34 *165*
40:8 *162*
40:9 *162*
44:8-9 *108*

Ezekiel
2:3 *108*
2:5 *109*
2:6 *109*

Index of References

2:7 *109*
2:8 *109*
3:7 *109*
3:9 *109*
3:26 *109*
3:27 *109*
11:19-20 *117*
12:1-2 *108*
12:3 *109*
12:9 *109*
12:25 *109*
12:27 *109*
16 *108*
16:22 *108*
16:43 *108*
16:59 *108*
17:12 *109*
20:8 *109*
20:9 *123*
20:12 *148*
20:13 *109*
20:14 *123*
20:21 *109*
20:22 *123*
20:44 *123*
23 *109*
24:3 *109*
26:38 *130*
36:21-23 *123*
36:22 *130*
36:24-33 *162*
36:25 *162*
36:26-28 *118*
36:27 *162*
36:33 *162*
37:14 *118*
37:23 *162*
37:28 *148*
39:29 *118*
44:6 *109*

Daniel
12:1 *150*

Hosea
14:3 *131*

Nahum

1:2 *130*

Zephaniah
3:5 *131*
3:8 *130*

NEW TESTAMENT

Matthew
5:11 *162*
5:18 *162*
15:8-9a *146*
25:31-46 *131*

Luke
10:20 *150*
11:21-22 *164*
22:25 *128*

John
6:37 *170*
6:39 *170*
6:60-66 *170*
6:65 *170*
13:12 *170*

Acts
3 *94*
3:17-23 *170*
3:23 *170*
4:9 *128*
7:2-53 *166*
10:38 *128*
15:1-5 *94*
15:14 *151*
18:10 *151*
18:12-17 *94*
21-22 *94*
24:1-9 *94*
24:10-20 *94*
25:18-19 *94*
26:1-8 *94*
28:17-22 *94*

Romans
1:18 *95*

1:18-23 *94, 95, 114*
1:18-3:20 *114*
1:20 *94*
1:21 *95*
1:22-23 *95*
2:2 *131*
2:5-11 *131*
3:5 *131*
3:9 *114*
3:10-18 *114*
4:3-8 *120*
5:12 *115*
5:12-21 *114*
5:19 *120*
6:4 *120*
6:7 *120*
8:29 *151*
8:29-30 *168*
9:23-25 *151*
9-11 *168*
11:20-22 *168*
13:8-10 *137*
15:24 *137*
15:27 *137*
16:1-2 *137*

1 Corinthians
1:4-9 *124*
2:6-16 *120*
2:14-16 *145*
3:13-15 *131*
4:5 *131*
10:13 *160*

2 Corinthians
2:14-3:1 *120*
2:14-4:6 *120*
3:2-3 *120*
3:4-4:6 *120*
3:17 *120*
3:18 *120*
4:4 *168*
4:6 *120, 137, 168*
5:10 *168*
5:11 *168*
5:14 *168*
5:17 *120*
6:13 *137*

8:13-15 *137*

Galatians
2:20 *120, 137, 168*
3:2 *168*
3:10 *168*
3:29 *150*
5:4 *168*
5:24 *168*
6:4-8 *131*
6:7-8 *168*

Philippians
1:3-6 *124*
2:12-13 137, *178*
3:12 *120, 160*
3:13 *130*
4:3 *150*
4:10-20 *137*
4:15 *137*

Colossians
1:3-4 *124*
1:12-14 *124*

1 Thessalonians
2:13 *124*

2 Thessalonians
1:3 *124*
1:11 *124*

1 Timothy
5:4 *137*
6:2 *128*

Philemon
4-5 *124*

Hebrews
1:2 *141*
1:3 *141, 155*
1:5-14 *158*
1:6 *158*
2 *148*
2:1 *132*
2:1-4 *128, 142*
2:5 *158*

2:5-8 *178*
2:5-9 *149, 158*
2:5-10 *143*
2:9 *134, 141*
2:10 *128, 159*
2:11 *148*
2:11b *140*
2:13 *131, 149*
2:13a *139*
2:14 *159*
2:14-15 *128, 164*
2:16 *150*
2:16-18 *151*
2:17 *128, 150, 155*
2:17-18 *167*
2:18 *132, 155*
3:2 *165*
3:2-6 *131*
3:6 *131, 132, 165*
3:12-14 *131*
3:16 *144*
3:19 *144*
4:1 128, *131, 143*
4:2 *144*
4:2-3 *167, 175*
4:3 128, *158*
4:6 *131*
4:9 *151*
4:12-13 *168*
4:13 *167*
4:16 *132, 134, 144, 154, 159, 163, 175*
5:4 *151*
5:7-8 *140*
5:9 *133*
5:9-10 *146*
6:2 *131*
6:4-6 *129*
6:4-8 *131, 166, 177*
6:9-12 *139*
6:10 *130, 142*
6:11 *132*
6:11-12 *131*
6:12 *132*
6:13-18 *167*
6:13-20 *175, 178*
6:19-20 *154*
7:1-28 *146, 153*

7:1-10:18 *146, 147, 152, 153*
7:1-10:25 *155*
7:6 *159*
7:8 *133*
7:11 *154*
7:17 *133*
7:19 *154, 165*
7:25 *154*
7:28 *158*
8:1 *146*
8:1-9:28 *146, 153*
8:1-9:29 *146*
8:1-10:25 *155*
8:5 *165*
8:7 *165*
8:8 *165, 166*
8:8-12 *146*
8:9 *165*
8:10 *151*
9:1 *156, 158*
9:1-14 *153*
9:9 *155, 156, 158*
9:13 *156, 166*
9:13-14 *155, 158, 164*
9:14 *128, 149, 152, 156, 157, 163*
9:14a *155, 156*
9:14b *156*
9:14-15 *175*
9:15 *151, 165*
9:15-20 *151*
9:15-21 *153*
9:22 *155*
9:23-26 *153*
9:26 *158*
9:27 *131, 165*
9:27-28 *152*
9:28 *143, 151*
10:1 *154*
10:1-2 *155*
10:1-18 *146, 153, 175*
10:2 *157*
10:3 *166*
10:4 *166*
10:5-18 *158*
10:10 *157, 158, 164*
10:11 *166*

10:14 *128, 154, 156, 158*
10:14-17 *155*
10:14-18 *153*
10:15 *133, 158*
10:15-18 *156*
10:16-17 *147*
10:17-18 *128, 155*
10:19-22 *159*
10:22 *154, 155, 156, 158, 163*
10:23 *132, 144*
10:25 *166*
10:26 *129*
10:26-27 *161*
10:26-31 *131, 166, 168*
10:26-31 *164*
10:29 *134*
10:30 *151*
10:31 *161*
10:35-36 *132*
10:35-39 *131*
10:36 *131*
10:39 *132*
11 *133, 143, 165*
11:1 *144*
11:1-12:3 *175, 178*
11:2 *133*
11:4 *133*
11:5 *133*
11:6 *144, 154, 167*
11:7 *158*
11:11 *132*
11:13-16 *143*
11:16 *128, 143*
11:17 *159*
11:17-19 *87*
11:26-27 *165*
11:38 *158*
11:39 *133*
11:40 *154, 158, 159*
12:1-3 *142*
12:1-4 *143*
12:2 *132, 142, 143*
12:3 *159*
12:3-4 *131*
12:7 *132*

12:14 *160*
12:15 *134*
12:16-17 *129, 131, 145, 166*
12:18 *134, 154*
12:22 *128, 143, 150, 154, 155*
12:22-23 *159, 163*
12:22-24 *154, 178*
12:23 *131, 149, 158, 159, 167*
12:25 *131*
12:28 *128, 141, 142, 143, 166, 178*
13:2 *130*
13:6 *132*
13:9 *134, 154*
13:12 *151, 158*
13:13 *128, 142, 143*
13:13-14 *143*
13:15 *131*
13:15-16 *147*
13:16 *130, 142, 157*
13:20 *147*
13:20-21 *147, 156, 178*
13:25 *134*

1 Peter
1:17 *131*
2:9 *151*

2 Peter
2:4-5 *155*

1 John
5:16-17 *170*
5:18 *170*

Revelation
2:7 *170*
2:10-11 *170*
2:16 *170*
2:17 *170*
2:23 *170*
2:26-28 *170*
3:3 *170*
3:5 *170*

3:11-12 *170*
7:1-8 *170*
11:1-2 *170*
13:8 *150, 170*
19:8 *170*
20:11-15 *131*
22:12 *131*

OLD TESTAMENT APOCRYPHA

Baruch
1:18 *123*
2:14 *123*
2:19 *123*

1 Esdras
4:36 *131*
4:39 *131*

1 Maccabees
1:49 *130*
2:18 *93*
2:19 *156*
2:22 *156*
8:1 *93*
8:12 *93*
10:18-20 *93*
14:4-46 *93*

2 Maccabees
2:2 *130*
2:18 *160*
2:19 *160*
4:2 *93*
5:16 *94*

3 Maccabees
3:15-24 *94*

4 Maccabees
1:1 *100*
2:19-20 *100*
2:21-23 *100*
7:6-15 *100*
7:18 *100*
8:6 *93*

9:10 *93*
12:11 *93*
16:8-19 *93*
17:2-10 *100*

Sirach
3:31 *92*
15:14-17 *100*
20:16 *92*
29:15 *130*
35:12-13 *92*
37:6 *130*

Wisdom of Solomon
3:14 *93*
14:26 *92*
16:24 *93*
16:29 *93*

OLD TESTAMENT PSEUDEPIGRAPHA

Apocalypse of Zephaniah
3:7 *150*

1 Enoch
104:1 *150*

4 Ezra
7:45-48 *100*
7:77 *103*
7:92 *100*
7:140 *100*
8:3 *100*
8:47 *103*
8:48-49 *103*
8:56-60 *100*
8:59-60 *93*
9:10-11 *93*

Psalms of Solomon
15:2-3 *131*

Testament of Job
18:1-15 *143*

DEAD SEA SCROLLS

CD
I, 4 *111*
I, 6-21 *110*
II, 14-III, 12 *109*
XV, 9-10 *110*
XVI, 1-7 *110*

CD-A
II, 7 *169*
II, 13 *169*

CD-B
XIX, 5-6 *169*
XIX, 13-14 *169*

1QH^a
IV, 13-14 *169*
IV, 17 *119, 123*
IV, 17-26 *123*
IV, 19 *112*
IV, 21-22 *119*
IV, 23-24 *118*
V, 21 *112*
VI, 8 *119, 123*
VI, 23-27 *123*
VII, 16b-29 *123*
VII, 17-26 *111*
VII, 19 *119*
VII, 24 *123*
IX, 10 *123*
IX, 20 *111*
IX, 21-22 *113*
X, 28 *119*
X, 35-36 *119*
XII, 10 *118*
XII, 18-20 *169*
XII, 28 *123*
XII, 29 *113*
XII, 34-35 *110, 169*
XIII, 22-25 *169*
XIV, 10 *123*
XIV, 14 *169*
XIV, 19-21 *169*
XIV, 32 *169*
XV, 6-7 *123*
XV, 6-25 *123*
XV, 7 *119, 169*
XV, 26-32 *123*
XV, 33-36 *123*
XVIII, 9 *111*
XIX, 3-14 *123*
XX, 35 *119*

1QM
XI, 4-5 *116*
XI, 14-15 *123*
XIII, 9 *111*
XIV, 6 *116, 119*
XIV, 8-10 *111*

IQpHab
II, 1-2 *110*

1QS
I, 3 *110*
I, 7, 11 *169*
I, 23-24 *109*
I, 24-26 *110*
II, 11-17 *169*
II, 14-4.26 *112*
III, 15-16 *169*
III, 15-19 *112, 119*
III, 19 *112*
III, 20-21 *169*
III, 25-26 *112*
IV, 15-17, 22-26 *112*
IV, 20-23 *119*
IV, 22 *111, 169*
IV, 23 *112*
V, 1 *169*
V, 8 *110*
XI, 7, 16 *111, 169*
XI, 9-10 *113*
XI, 10-11 *111*

4Q171
II, 5 *111*

4Q402
1 I, 4 *118*
4, 13 *111*

4Q436

10:14 *128, 154, 156, 158*
10:14-17 *155*
10:14-18 *153*
10:15 *133, 158*
10:15-18 *156*
10:16-17 *147*
10:17-18 *128, 155*
10:19-22 *159*
10:22 *154, 155, 156, 158, 163*
10:23 *132, 144*
10:25 *166*
10:26 *129*
10:26-27 *161*
10:26-31 *131, 166, 168*
10:26-31 *164*
10:29 *134*
10:30 *151*
10:31 *161*
10:35-36 *132*
10:35-39 *131*
10:36 *131*
10:39 *132*
11 *133, 143, 165*
11:1 *144*
11:1-12:3 *175, 178*
11:2 *133*
11:4 *133*
11:5 *133*
11:6 *144, 154, 167*
11:7 *158*
11:11 *132*
11:13-16 *143*
11:16 *128, 143*
11:17 *159*
11:17-19 *87*
11:26-27 *165*
11:38 *158*
11:39 *133*
11:40 *154, 158, 159*
12:1-3 *142*
12:1-4 *143*
12:2 *132, 142, 143*
12:3 *159*
12:3-4 *131*
12:7 *132*

12:14 *160*
12:15 *134*
12:16-17 *129, 131, 145, 166*
12:18 *134, 154*
12:22 *128, 143, 150, 154, 155*
12:22-23 *159, 163*
12:22-24 *154, 178*
12:23 *131, 149, 158, 159, 167*
12:25 *131*
12:28 *128, 141, 142, 143, 166, 178*
13:2 *130*
13:6 *132*
13:9 *134, 154*
13:12 *151, 158*
13:13 *128, 142, 143*
13:13-14 *143*
13:15 *131*
13:15-16 *147*
13:16 *130, 142, 157*
13:20 *147*
13:20-21 *147, 156, 178*
13:25 *134*

1 Peter
1:17 *131*
2:9 *151*

2 Peter
2:4-5 *155*

1 John
5:16-17 *170*
5:18 *170*

Revelation
2:7 *170*
2:10-11 *170*
2:16 *170*
2:17 *170*
2:23 *170*
2:26-28 *170*
3:3 *170*
3:5 *170*

3:11-12 *170*
7:1-8 *170*
11:1-2 *170*
13:8 *150, 170*
19:8 *170*
20:11-15 *131*
22:12 *131*

OLD TESTAMENT APOCRYPHA

Baruch
1:18 *123*
2:14 *123*
2:19 *123*

1 Esdras
4:36 *131*
4:39 *131*

1 Maccabees
1:49 *130*
2:18 *93*
2:19 *156*
2:22 *156*
8:1 *93*
8:12 *93*
10:18-20 *93*
14:4-46 *93*

2 Maccabees
2:2 *130*
2:18 *160*
2:19 *160*
4:2 *93*
5:16 *94*

3 Maccabees
3:15-24 *94*

4 Maccabees
1:1 *100*
2:19-20 *100*
2:21-23 *100*
7:6-15 *100*
7:18 *100*
8:6 *93*

9:10 *93*
12:11 *93*
16:8-19 *93*
17:2-10 *100*

Sirach
3:31 *92*
15:14-17 *100*
20:16 *92*
29:15 *130*
35:12-13 *92*
37:6 *130*

Wisdom of Solomon
3:14 *93*
14:26 *92*
16:24 *93*
16:29 *93*

OLD TESTAMENT
PSEUDEPIGRAPHA

Apocalypse of
Zephaniah
3:7 *150*

1 Enoch
104:1 *150*

4 Ezra
7:45-48 *100*
7:77 *103*
7:92 *100*
7:140 *100*
8:3 *100*
8:47 *103*
8:48-49 *103*
8:56-60 *100*
8:59-60 *93*
9:10-11 *93*

Psalms of Solomon
15:2-3 *131*

Testament of Job
18:1-15 *143*

DEAD SEA SCROLLS

CD
I, 4 *111*
I, 6-21 *110*
II, 14-III, 12 *109*
XV, 9-10 *110*
XVI, 1-7 *110*

CD-A
II, 7 *169*
II, 13 *169*

CD-B
XIX, 5-6 *169*
XIX, 13-14 *169*

1QH^a
IV, 13-14 *169*
IV, 17 *119, 123*
IV, 17-26 *123*
IV, 19 *112*
IV, 21-22 *119*
IV, 23-24 *118*
V, 21 *112*
VI, 8 *119, 123*
VI, 23-27 *123*
VII, 16b-29 *123*
VII, 17-26 *111*
VII, 19 *119*
VII, 24 *123*
IX, 10 *123*
IX, 20 *111*
IX, 21-22 *113*
X, 28 *119*
X, 35-36 *119*
XII, 10 *118*
XII, 18-20 *169*
XII, 28 *123*
XII, 29 *113*
XII, 34-35 *110, 169*
XIII, 22-25 *169*
XIV, 10 *123*
XIV, 14 *169*
XIV, 19-21 *169*
XIV, 32 *169*
XV, 6-7 *123*
XV, 6-25 *123*
XV, 7 *119, 169*
XV, 26-32 *123*
XV, 33-36 *123*
XVIII, 9 *111*
XIX, 3-14 *123*
XX, 35 *119*

1QM
XI, 4-5 *116*
XI, 14-15 *123*
XIII, 9 *111*
XIV, 6 *116, 119*
XIV, 8-10 *111*

IQpHab
II, 1-2 *110*

1QS
I, 3 *110*
I, 7, 11 *169*
I, 23-24 *109*
I, 24-26 *110*
II, 11-17 *169*
II, 14-4.26 *112*
III, 15-16 *169*
III, 15-19 *112, 119*
III, 19 *112*
III, 20-21 *169*
III, 25-26 *112*
IV, 15-17, 22-26 *112*
IV, 20-23 *119*
IV, 22 *111, 169*
IV, 23 *112*
V, 1 *169*
V, 8 *110*
XI, 7, 16 *111, 169*
XI, 9-10 *113*
XI, 10-11 *111*

4Q171
II, 5 *111*

4Q402
1 I, 4 *118*
4, 13 *111*

4Q436

I, 5-10 *119*

4Q504
1-2 II, 13-16 *118*
4, 11-12 *118*

PHILO

De agricultura
171 *122*

De congressu
eruditionis gratia
38 *122*
96 *95*

De ebrietate
117-19 *95*
118-19 *123*

Quis rerum
divinarum heres sit
58-60 *121*

Legum allegoriae
1.82 *122*
1.95-96 *94*
2.46 *123*
3.32 *123*
3.78 *123*
3.136-37 *122*

Legatio ad Gaium
118 *95*
148 *48*

De mutatione
nominum
28 *123*

De opificio mundi
169 *95*

De plantation
90 *122*

De praemiis et poenis
12-13 *122*

De sobrietate
55 *94*

De specialibus legibus
1.152 *95*

JOSEPHUS

Antiquitates judaicae
1.14 *87*
1.20 *87*
1.75 *98*
1.96-100 *98*
1.154-57 *98*
1.183 *98*
1.194 *88*
1.223 *87*
1.229 *89*
1.233 *91*
1.234 *89*
1.256 *98*
1.346 *98*
2.56 *88*
2.162 *131*
2.172 *90*
2.192-93 *87*
2.196 *90, 98*
2.212 *88, 99*
2.269 *90*
2.339 *131*
3.15 *92*
3.38 *90*
3.63-65 *98*
3.64 *90*
3.86-88 *87*
3.97 *99*
3.102 *99*
3.190 *98*
3.302 *89*
3.312 *88*
4 1-8 *86*
4.2 *86*
4.41 *88*
4.42-45 *88*

4.122 *86*
4.180 *98*
4.203 *89*
4.212 *89*
4.315-19 *90*
5.114 *90*
5.115-16 *88*
8.111 *91*
8.112 *131*
13.171-73 *99*
18.11-13 *99*
18.18 *99*

Contra Apionem
2.218-19 *88*
2.233 *88*

Vita
12 *99*
16 *85*
244 *85*
259 *85*
419-29 *85*

RABINNIC
LITERATURE

Mekhilta
Baḥodesh 5 *96, 101*

Mishnah
Avot 3:15 *101*

Sifre Deut
311 *101*

Talmud
Berakhot 33b *101*
Megillah 25a *101*

NEW TESTAMENT
APOCRYPHA AND
PSEUDEPIGRAPHA

Acts of John
69 *167*

84 *167*
107 *167*

Acts of Peter
7 *167*

Acts of Thomas
35 *167*

EPIGRAPHIC
EVIDENCE

Carmina Epigraphica
Graeca saeculorum
227 *45*
268 *45*
275 *45*
326 *44, 45*
332 *44*
359 *45*
360 *45*
375 *45*
400 *45*

Inscriptiones Creticae
4.168 *47, 59, 62*

Inscriptiones de Délos
4.1519 *42, 59*

Inschriften von
Priene
112-14 *59*

Inscriptiones Graecae
2.1187 *59*
4.955 *45*
5.1 *47*
5.2 *59*
5.1145 *59*
5.1208 *47*
7.190 *47, 58, 59*
12.236 *58*
12.389 *42, 60*
12.9 *58, 59*
12.899 *58*
12.1032 *59*

Inscriptiones Graecae
ad Res Romanas
Pertinentes
3.493 *59*

Orientis Graeci
Inscriptiones Selectae
248 *42*
339 *47, 59*

Supplementum
Epigraphicum
Graecum
1.366 *47, 59*
1.368 *47, 59*
2.564 *59*
11.948 *42, 47, 59*
18.143 *49*
24.100 *59*

Sylloge Inscriptionum
Graecarum 3d. ed.
708.25 *60*

Tituli Asiae Minoris
3.4 *59*

GRECO-ROMAN
SOURCES

Aristotle
    Ethica Eudemia
    1220 A39 *65*
    Ethica
    Nichomachea
    4.1.7 *40*
    5.5.6-7 *18*
    9.7.1 *179*
    1103 A17-26 *65*
    1103 A30-B1 *65*
    1103 B21-25 *66*
    1110 B27-29 *65*
    1111 B30 *65*
    1112 A2 *65*
    1113 B6-7 *65*
    1113 A10-11 *65*
    1114 A20-23 *66*
    1114 B33 *66*
    1123 B17-21 *44*
    1124 B10-12 *27*
    1126 B27-30 *33*
    1132 B31-1133 A5
       20
    1145 B25 *65*
    1155 B31-34 *56*
    1157 A22 *49*
    1158 B1 *34*
    1159 A35-36 *60*
    1162 B5-10 *56*
    1163 B2-3 *41*
    1164 B26 *27*
    1165 A2-14 *56*
    1167 A14-15 *57*
    1167 A19-21 *57*
    1169 B10 *23*
    Polotica
    1320 B10 *62*
    Rhetorica
    1.5.9 *47*
    1.13.11-12 *130*
    1.13.12 *131, 132*
    2.2.8 *95, 129*

Aulus Gellius
    Noctes atticae
    7.14.2-4 *95, 129*

Cicero
    De officiis
    1.42 *60, 68*
    1.45 *56, 60*
    1.46 *61*
    1.47 *25, 27*
    1.48 *28*
    2.11 *57*
    2.33 *57*
    2.53 *33*
    2.54 *63*
    2.63 *31, 56*
    2.69 *57*
    2.70 *58*
    2.71 *56*
    Epistulae ad
    familiars

Index of References

7.29 *37*
10.11.1 *27*
De inventione
rhetorica
1.47 *36*
De natura deorum
3.36.87-88 *68*

Dio Chrysostom
Oration
3.86 *33*
3.87 *53*
3.88-89 *53*
3.97 *50*
4.154 *61*
4.158 *46*
31 *47*
31.7 *41, 58, 61*
31.8 *41*
31.14 *41*
31.15 *57*
31.25 *36*
31.27 *41*
31.36 *58*
31.37 *31, 41*
31.39 *21*
31.50 *41*
31.53 *27*
31.65 *30, 61*
31.69 *26*
31.75 *133*
31.97 *25*
31.113 *36*
31.149 *57*

Diodorus Siculus
1.2.4 *48*
1.17.1-2 *47, 63*
1.20.5-6 *48*
1.21.6 *32*
1.31.1 *48*
1.86.3 *27*
1.86.5 *27*
1.90.2 *41, 58*

Diogenes Laertius
Vita
Philosophorum

3.96 *133*

Euripides
Helena
1234 *26*

Homer
Iliad
1.37-42 *31*
1.218 *43, 48*
1.243-44 *29*
1.292-303 *28*
1.394-95 *31, 37*
1.503-10 *29*
3.264-301 *84*
3.351-54 *25, 75*
4.42-48 *44*
4.42-49 *37*
4.48-49 *43*
4.62 *37, 38*
6.86-96 *50*
6.311 *50*
8.550-51 *50*
9.315-17 *28*
9.378-79 *28*
9.385-86 *28*
9.497-500 *43*
12.6 *44*
13.625 *25, 75*
14.234-35 *18*
14.235 *26*
15.372-75 *31*
17.147-48 *28*
18.406-408 *18, 25*
20.291-304 *35*
20.298 *50*
22.83-84 *31*
22.168-70 *43*
22.168-71 *37*
22.169-71 *44*
23.60 *26*
23.193-95 *43*
23.650 *76*
24.424-28 *32, 44*
Odyssey
1.311-13 *39*
1.318 *39*
1.378-79 *25*

2.144-45 *25*
3.58-59 *43*
3.380-83 *43*
4.328-31 *31*
4.625-74 *29*
4.694-95 *29*
4.763-65 *32*
6.208-209 *75*
7.165 *25, 75*
7.181 *25, 75*
9.269-71 *25, 75*
9.355-70 *39*
9.553-5 *50*
11.185 *38*
13.213-14 *25, 75*
14.53-54 *75*
14.388-89 *25*
15.54-55 *31*
17.240-42 *31*
17.354-55 *75*
18.194 *18*
19.396-99 *50*
24.280-86 *23*
24.313-14 *38*

Iamblichus
De Vita
Pythagorica
38 *26*

Livy
Ab Urbe Condita
Libri
37.54.17 *35*

Lysias
2.39 *31*
11-12 *39*
13 *40*
21.24 *62*
24.13 *62*
24-25 *39*

Ovid
Metamorphoses
9.700-701 *27*

Plato

Euthyphro
14B *50*
15A *44*

Pliny
Epistulae
2.9 *27*
2.13 *27*
3.4 *35, 64*
4.1 *47*

Pindar
Pythionikai
2.17 *46*
2.24 *30*
2.25-48 *30*

Plutarch
Comparatio
Cimonis et Luculli
2.3 *52*
Crassus
14.4 *59*
27.4 *59*
Demetrius
5.3 *26*
8.2 *52*
9.1 *48*
10.2 *48*
10.3 *48*
Dion
47.4 *64*
Moralia
355D *50*
485A *68*
548-68 *95*
582F *40*
786F *61*
Pelopidas
12.4 *132*
Romulus
13.5 *52*
13.5-6 *52*
Timoleon
2.1 *132, 144*

Polybius
1.7.7 *34*

1.7.12 *34*
2.11.5 *34*
2.11.6 *34*
3.15.5 *35*
3.16.2-4 *36*
3.29.8 *34*
3.30.1 *35*
10.34.1-35.3 *33*
10.34.7 *48*
20.9.7-10 *35*
20.9.11 *34*
24.13.3 *34*

Seneca
De Beneficiis
1.1.1 *40*
1.1.2 *60*
1.1.3 *51*
1.2.4 *63*
1.2.5 *64*
1.3.1 *64*
1.3.2-4 *19*
1.4.2 *20*
1.4.3 *19, 40, 51*
1.4.4 *31*
1.4.5 *33*
1.5.1-4 *56*
1.5.2 *21*
1.5.4 *22*
1.6.1 *22, 51, 56*
1.9.2 *56*
1.10.1-3 *68*
1.10.4 *31*
2.7.2 *22*
2.11.5 *64*
2.16.1 *40*
2.17.5 *40*
2.17.6 *49*
2.18.4 *67*
2.18.5 *19, 21, 23, 25*
2.22.1 *26*
2.24.1 *33*
2.29.5-30.2 *43, 95*
2.35.3 *179*
3.1.1-5 *33*
3.1.4 *26, 64*
3.6.2 *23*

3.9.3 *24*
3.7.1-2 *23*
3.11.1 *60*
3.12.2 *26*
3.14.2 *33, 51*
3.17.4 *26*
3.20.1 *68*
3.20.2 *68*
4.3.1 *60*
4.10.4-5 *56*
4.11.1 *57*
4.12.1 *23*
4.12.2 *49*
4.17.4 *68*
4.18.2-3 *23*
4.21.1 *26*
4.22.2 *68*
4.25.1 *46*
4.29.5 *141*
4.33.2 *49*
4.40.5 *26*
5.1.4 *64*
5.4.3 *48*
5.9.2 *24*
5.9.4 *19*
5.11.5 *63*
5.17.3 *68*
5.25.4 *31*
5.25.5-6 *68*
6.16.2 *21*
6.41.2 *20*
6.41.1-2 *21*
7.19.2 *33*
7.19.5 *68*
7.29.2 *33*
7.29.2-7.31.1 *64*
7.31.2 *43, 95*
Epistulae morales
41 *66*
41.1-2 *66*
41.7-9 *66*
50.5-6 *64*
50.7 *67*
50.8-9 *67*
81.30 *27, 36*
88.29 *35*
90.44 *67*
92.27 *66*

92.30 *66*
94.29 *67*
95.50 *57*
108.8 *67*
123.16 *67*
De ira
2.10.7 *67*
De vita beata
26.5 *67*

Sophocles
Ajax
520-24 *32*

Theognis
957-58 *30*
1263-66 *29*
1339-40 *30*

Thucydides
History of the Peloponnesian War
2.40.4-5 *179*
40.4-5 *63*

Xenophon
Memorabilia
3.12.4 *133*

Paternoster Biblical Monographs

(All titles uniform with this volume)
Dates in bold are of projected publication

Joseph Abraham
Eve: Accused or Acquitted?
A Reconsideration of Feminist Readings of the Creation Narrative Texts in Genesis 1–3
Two contrary views dominate contemporary feminist biblical scholarship. One finds in the Bible an unequivocal equality between the sexes from the very creation of humanity, whilst the other sees the biblical text as irredeemably patriarchal and androcentric. Dr Abraham enters into dialogue with both camps as well as introducing his own method of approach. An invaluable tool for any one who is interested in this contemporary debate.

2002 / 0-85364-971-5 / xxiv + 272pp

Octavian D. Baban
Mimesis and Luke's on the Road Encounters in Luke-Acts
Luke's Theology of the Way and its Literary Representation
The book argues on theological and literary (mimetic) grounds that Luke's on-the-road encounters, especially those belonging to the post-Easter period, are part of his complex theology of the Way. Jesus' teaching and that of the apostles is presented by Luke as a challenging answer to the Hellenistic reader's thirst for adventure, good literature, and existential paradigms.

2005 */ 1-84227-253-5 / approx. 374pp*

Paul Barker
The Triumph of Grace in Deuteronomy
This book is a textual and theological analysis of the interaction between the sin and faithlessness of Israel and the grace of Yahweh in response, looking especially at Deuteronomy chapters 1–3, 8–10 and 29–30. The author argues that the grace of Yahweh is determinative for the ongoing relationship between Yahweh and Israel and that Deuteronomy anticipates and fully expects Israel to be faithless.

2004 / 1-84227-226-8 / xxii + 270pp

Jonathan F. Bayes
The Weakness of the Law
God's Law and the Christian in New Testament Perspective
A study of the four New Testament books which refer to the law as weak (Acts, Romans, Galatians, Hebrews) leads to a defence of the third use in the Reformed debate about the law in the life of the believer.

2000 / 0-85364-957-X / xii + 244pp

Mark Bonnington
The Antioch Episode of Galatians 2:11-14 in Historical and Cultural Context

The Galatians 2 'incident' in Antioch over table-fellowship suggests significant disagreement between the leading apostles. This book analyses the background to the disagreement by locating the incident within the dynamics of social interaction between Jews and Gentiles. It proposes a new way of understanding the relationship between the individuals and issues involved.

2005 / 1-84227-050-8 / approx. 350pp

David Bostock
A Portrayal of Trust
The Theme of Faith in the Hezekiah Narratives

This study provides detailed and sensitive readings of the Hezekiah narratives (2 Kings 18–20 and Isaiah 36–39) from a theological perspective. It concentrates on the theme of faith, using narrative criticism as its methodology. Attention is paid especially to setting, plot, point of view and characterization within the narratives. A largely positive portrayal of Hezekiah emerges that underlines the importance and relevance of scripture.

2005 / 1-84227-314-0 / approx. 300pp

Mark Bredin
Jesus, Revolutionary of Peace
A Non-violent Christology in the Book of Revelation

This book aims to demonstrate that the figure of Jesus in the Book of Revelation can best be understood as an active non-violent revolutionary.

2003 / 1-84227-153-9 / xviii + 262pp

Robinson Butarbutar
Paul and Conflict Resolution
An Exegetical Study of Paul's Apostolic Paradigm in 1 Corinthians 9

The author sees the apostolic paradigm in 1 Corinthians 9 as part of Paul's unified arguments in 1 Corinthians 8–10 in which he seeks to mediate in the dispute over the issue of food offered to idols. The book also sees its relevance for dispute-resolution today, taking the conflict within the author's church as an example.

2006 / 1-84227-315-9 / approx. 280pp

July 2005

Daniel J-S Chae
Paul as Apostle to the Gentiles
His Apostolic Self-awareness and its Influence on the Soteriological Argument in Romans
Opposing 'the post-Holocaust interpretation of Romans', Daniel Chae competently demonstrates that Paul argues for the equality of Jew and Gentile in Romans. Chae's fresh exegetical interpretation is academically outstanding and spiritually encouraging.
1997 / 0-85364-829-8 / xiv + 378pp

Luke L. Cheung
The Genre, Composition and Hermeneutics of the Epistle of James
The present work examines the employment of the wisdom genre with a certain compositional structure and the interpretation of the law through the Jesus tradition of the double love command by the author of the Epistle of James to serve his purpose in promoting perfection and warning against doubleness among the eschatologically renewed people of God in the Diaspora.
2003 / 1-84227-062-1 / xvi + 372pp

Youngmo Cho
Spirit and Kingdom in the Writings of Luke and Paul
The relationship between Spirit and Kingdom is a relatively unexplored area in Lukan and Pauline studies. This book offers a fresh perspective of two biblical writers on the subject. It explores the difference between Luke's and Paul's understanding of the Spirit by examining the specific question of the relationship of the concept of the Spirit to the concept of the Kingdom of God in each writer.
2005 / 1-84227-316-7 / approx. 270pp

Andrew C. Clark
Parallel Lives
The Relation of Paul to the Apostles in the Lucan Perspective
This study of the Peter-Paul parallels in Acts argues that their purpose was to emphasize the themes of continuity in salvation history and the unity of the Jewish and Gentile missions. New light is shed on Luke's literary techniques, partly through a comparison with Plutarch.
2001 / 1-84227-035-4 / xviii + 386pp

Andrew D. Clarke
Secular and Christian Leadership in Corinth
A Socio-Historical and Exegetical Study of 1 Corinthians 1–6
This volume is an investigation into the leadership structures and dynamics of first-century Roman Corinth. These are compared with the practice of leadership in the Corinthian Christian community which are reflected in 1 Corinthians 1–6, and contrasted with Paul's own principles of Christian leadership.
2005 / 1-84227-229-2 / 200pp

Stephen Finamore
God, Order and Chaos
René Girard and the Apocalypse
Readers are often disturbed by the images of destruction in the book of Revelation and unsure why they are unleashed after the exaltation of Jesus. This book examines past approaches to these texts and uses René Girard's theories to revive some old ideas and propose some new ones.
2005 / 1-84227-197-0 / approx. 344pp

David G. Firth
Surrendering Retribution in the Psalms
Responses to Violence in the Individual Complaints
In *Surrendering Retribution in the Psalms*, David Firth examines the ways in which the book of Psalms inculcates a model response to violence through the repetition of standard patterns of prayer. Rather than seeking justification for retributive violence, Psalms encourages not only a surrender of the right of retribution to Yahweh, but also sets limits on the retribution that can be sought in imprecations. Arising initially from the author's experience in South Africa, the possibilities of this model to a particular context of violence is then briefly explored.
2005 / 1-84227-337-X / xviii + 154pp

Scott J. Hafemann
Suffering and Ministry in the Spirit
Paul's Defence of His Ministry in II Corinthians 2:14–3:3
Shedding new light on the way Paul defended his apostleship, the author offers a careful, detailed study of 2 Corinthians 2:14–3:3 linked with other key passages throughout 1 and 2 Corinthians. Demonstrating the unity and coherence of Paul's argument in this passage, the author shows that Paul's suffering served as the vehicle for revealing God's power and glory through the Spirit.
2000 / 0-85364-967-7 / xiv + 262pp

Scott J. Hafemann
Paul, Moses and the History of Israel
The Letter/Spirit Contrast and the Argument from Scripture in 2 Corinthians 3
An exegetical study of the call of Moses, the second giving of the Law (Exodus 32–34), the new covenant, and the prophetic understanding of the history of Israel in 2 Corinthians 3. Hafemann's work demonstrates Paul's contextual use of the Old Testament and the essential unity between the Law and the Gospel within the context of the distinctive ministries of Moses and Paul.
2005 / 1-84227-317-5 / xii + 498pp

Douglas S. McComiskey
Lukan Theology in the Light of the Gospel's Literary Structure
Luke's Gospel was purposefully written with theology embedded in its patterned literary structure. A critical analysis of this cyclical structure provides new windows into Luke's interpretation of the individual pericopes comprising the Gospel and illuminates several of his theological interests.
2004 / 1-84227-148-2 / xviii + 388pp

Stephen Motyer
Your Father the Devil?
A New Approach to John and 'The Jews'
Who are 'the Jews' in John's Gospel? Defending John against the charge of antisemitism, Motyer argues that, far from demonising the Jews, the Gospel seeks to present Jesus as 'Good News for Jews' in a late first century setting.
1997 / 0-85364-832-8 / xiv + 260pp

Esther Ng
Reconstructing Christian Origins?
The Feminist Theology of Elizabeth Schüssler Fiorenza: An Evaluation
In a detailed evaluation, the author challenges Elizabeth Schüssler Fiorenza's reconstruction of early Christian origins and her underlying presuppositions. The author also presents her own views on women's roles both then and now.
2002 / 1-84227-055-9 / xxiv + 468pp

Robin Parry
Old Testament Story and Christian Ethics
The Rape of Dinah as a Case Study

What is the role of story in ethics and, more particularly, what is the role of Old Testament story in Christian ethics? This book, drawing on the work of contemporary philosophers, argues that narrative is crucial in the ethical shaping of people and, drawing on the work of contemporary Old Testament scholars, that story plays a key role in Old Testament ethics. Parry then argues that when situated in canonical context Old Testament stories can be reappropriated by Christian readers in their own ethical formation. The shocking story of the rape of Dinah and the massacre of the Shechemites provides a fascinating case study for exploring the parameters within which Christian ethical appropriations of Old Testament stories can live.

2004 / 1-84227-210-1 / xx + 350pp

Ian Paul
Power to See the World Anew
The Value of Paul Ricoeur's Hermeneutic of Metaphor in Interpreting the Symbolism of Revelation 12 and 13

This book is a study of the hermeneutics of metaphor of Paul Ricoeur, one of the most important writers on hermeneutics and metaphor of the last century. It sets out the key points of his theory, important criticisms of his work, and how his approach, modified in the light of these criticisms, offers a methodological framework for reading apocalyptic texts.

2006 / 1-84227-056-7 / approx. 350pp

Robert L. Plummer
Paul's Understanding of the Church's Mission
Did the Apostle Paul Expect the Early Christian Communities to Evangelize?

This book engages in a careful study of Paul's letters to determine if the apostle expected the communities to which he wrote to engage in missionary activity. It helpfully summarizes the discussion on this debated issue, judiciously handling contested texts, and provides a way forward in addressing this critical question. While admitting that Paul rarely explicitly commands the communities he founded to evangelize, Plummer amasses significant incidental data to provide a convincing case that Paul did indeed expect his churches to engage in mission activity. Throughout the study, Plummer progressively builds a theological basis for the church's mission that is both distinctively Pauline and compelling.

2006 / 1-84227-333-7 / approx. 324pp

David Powys
'Hell': A Hard Look at a Hard Question
The Fate of the Unrighteous in New Testament Thought
This comprehensive treatment seeks to unlock the original meaning of terms and phrases long thought to support the traditional doctrine of hell. It concludes that there is an alternative—one which is more biblical, and which can positively revive the rationale for Christian mission.

1997 / 0-85364-831-X / xxii + 478pp

Sorin Sabou
Between Horror and Hope
Paul's Metaphorical Language of Death in Romans 6.1-11
This book argues that Paul's metaphorical language of death in Romans 6.1-11 conveys two aspects: horror and hope. The 'horror' aspect is conveyed by the 'crucifixion' language, and the 'hope' aspect by 'burial' language. The life of the Christian believer is understood, as relationship with sin is concerned ('death to sin'), between these two realities: horror and hope.

2005 / 1-84227-322-1 / approx. 224pp

Rosalind Selby
The Comical Doctrine
The Epistemology of New Testament Hermeneutics
This book argues that the gospel breaks through postmodernity's critique of truth and the referential possibilities of textuality with its gift of grace. With a rigorous, philosophical challenge to modernist and postmodernist assumptions, Selby offers an alternative epistemology to all who would still read with faith *and* with academic credibility.

2005 / 1-84227-212-8 / approx. 350pp

Kiwoong Son
Zion Symbolism in Hebrews
Hebrews 12.18-24 as a Hermeneutical Key to the Epistle
This book challenges the general tendency of understanding the Epistle to the Hebrews against a Hellenistic background and suggests that the Epistle should be understood in the light of the Jewish apocalyptic tradition. The author especially argues for the importance of the theological symbolism of Sinai and Zion (Heb. 12:18-24) as it provides the Epistle's theological background as well as the rhetorical basis of the superiority motif of Jesus throughout the Epistle.

2005 / 1-84227-368-X / approx. 280pp

Kevin Walton
Thou Traveller Unknown
The Presence and Absence of God in the Jacob Narrative
The author offers a fresh reading of the story of Jacob in the book of Genesis through the paradox of divine presence and absence. The work also seeks to make a contribution to Pentateuchal studies by bringing together a close reading of the final text with historical critical insights, doing justice to the text's historical depth, final form and canonical status.
2003 / 1-84227-059-1 / xvi + 238pp

George M. Wieland
The Significance of Salvation
A Study of Salvation Language in the Pastoral Epistles
The language and ideas of salvation pervade the three Pastoral Epistles. This study offers a close examination of their soteriological statements. In all three letters the idea of salvation is found to play a vital paraenetic role, but each also exhibits distinctive soteriological emphases. The results challenge common assumptions about the Pastoral Epistles as a corpus.
2005 / 1-84227-257-8 / approx. 324pp

Alistair Wilson
When Will These Things Happen?
A Study of Jesus as Judge in Matthew 21–25
This study seeks to allow Matthew's carefully constructed presentation of Jesus to be given full weight in the modern evaluation of Jesus' eschatology. Careful analysis of the text of Matthew 21–25 reveals Jesus to be standing firmly in the Jewish prophetic and wisdom traditions as he proclaims and enacts imminent judgement on the Jewish authorities then boldly claims the central role in the final and universal judgement.
2004 / 1-84227-146-6 / xxii + 272pp

Lindsay Wilson
Joseph Wise and Otherwise
The Intersection of Covenant and Wisdom in Genesis 37–50
This book offers a careful literary reading of Genesis 37–50 that argues that the Joseph story contains both strong covenant themes and many wisdom-like elements. The connections between the two helps to explore how covenant and wisdom might intersect in an integrated biblical theology.
2004 / 1-84227-140-7 / xvi + 340pp

Stephen I. Wright
The Voice of Jesus
Studies in the Interpretation of Six Gospel Parables
This literary study considers how the 'voice' of Jesus has been heard in different periods of parable interpretation, and how the categories of figure and trope may help us towards a sensitive reading of the parables today.
2000 / 0-85364-975-8 / xiv + 280pp

Paternoster Theological Monographs
(All titles uniform with this volume)
Dates in bold are of projected publication

Emil Bartos
Deification in Eastern Orthodox Theology
An Evaluation and Critique of the Theology of Dumitru Staniloae
Bartos studies a fundamental yet neglected aspect of Orthodox theology: deification. By examining the doctrines of anthropology, christology, soteriology and ecclesiology as they relate to deification, he provides an important contribution to contemporary dialogue between Eastern and Western theologians.
1999 / 0-85364-956-1 / xii + 370pp

Graham Buxton
The Trinity, Creation and Pastoral Ministry
Imaging the Perichoretic God
In this book the author proposes a three-way conversation between theology, science and pastoral ministry. His approach draws on a Trinitarian understanding of God as a relational being of love, whose life 'spills over' into all created reality, human and non-human. By locating human meaning and purpose within God's 'creation-community' this book offers the possibility of a transforming engagement between those in pastoral ministry and the scientific community.
***2005** / 1-84227-369-8 / approx. 380 pp*

Iain D. Campbell
Fixing the Indemnity
The Life and Work of George Adam Smith
When Old Testament scholar George Adam Smith (1856–1942) delivered the Lyman Beecher lectures at Yale University in 1899, he confidently declared that 'modern criticism has won its war against traditional theories. It only remains to fix the amount of the indemnity.' In this biography, Iain D. Campbell assesses Smith's critical approach to the Old Testament and evaluates its consequences, showing that Smith's life and work still raises questions about the relationship between biblical scholarship and evangelical faith.
2004 / 1-84227-228-4 / xx + 256pp

July 2005

Tim Chester
Mission and the Coming of God
Eschatology, the Trinity and Mission in the Theology of Jürgen Moltmann
This book explores the theology and missiology of the influential contemporary theologian, Jürgen Moltmann. It highlights the important contribution Moltmann has made while offering a critique of his thought from an evangelical perspective. In so doing, it touches on pertinent issues for evangelical missiology. The conclusion takes Calvin as a starting point, proposing 'an eschatology of the cross' which offers a critique of the over-realised eschatologies in liberation theology and certain forms of evangelicalism.
2006 / 1-84227-320-5 / approx. 224pp

Sylvia Wilkey Collinson
Making Disciples
The Significance of Jesus' Educational Strategy for Today's Church
This study examines the biblical practice of discipling, formulates a definition, and makes comparisons with modern models of education. A recommendation is made for greater attention to its practice today.
2004 / 1-84227-116-4 / xiv + 278pp

Darrell Cosden
A Theology of Work
Work and the New Creation
Through dialogue with Moltmann, Pope John Paul II and others, this book develops a genitive 'theology of work', presenting a theological definition of work and a model for a theological ethics of work that shows work's nature, value and meaning now and eschatologically. Work is shown to be a transformative activity consisting of three dynamically inter-related dimensions: the instrumental, relational and ontological.
2005 / 1-84227-332-9 / xvi + 208pp

Stephen M. Dunning
The Crisis and the Quest
A Kierkegaardian Reading of Charles Williams
Employing Kierkegaardian categories and analysis, this study investigates both the central crisis in Charles Williams's authorship between hermetism and Christianity (Kierkegaard's Religions A and B), and the quest to resolve this crisis, a quest that ultimately presses the bounds of orthodoxy.
2000 / 0-85364-985-5 / xxiv + 254pp

Keith Ferdinando
The Triumph of Christ in African Perspective
A Study of Demonology and Redemption in the African Context
The book explores the implications of the gospel for traditional African fears of occult aggression. It analyses such traditional approaches to suffering and biblical responses to fears of demonic evil, concluding with an evaluation of African beliefs from the perspective of the gospel.
1999 / 0-85364-830-1 / xviii + 450pp

Andrew Goddard
Living the Word, Resisting the World
The Life and Thought of Jacques Ellul
This work offers a definitive study of both the life and thought of the French Reformed thinker Jacques Ellul (1912-1994). It will prove an indispensable resource for those interested in this influential theologian and sociologist and for Christian ethics and political thought generally.
2002 / 1-84227-053-2 / xxiv + 378pp

David Hilborn
The Words of our Lips
Language-Use in Free Church Worship
Studies of liturgical language have tended to focus on the written canons of Roman Catholic and Anglican communities. By contrast, David Hilborn analyses the more extemporary approach of English Nonconformity. Drawing on recent developments in linguistic pragmatics, he explores similarities and differences between 'fixed' and 'free' worship, and argues for the interdependence of each.
***2006** / 0-85364-977-4 / approx. 350pp*

Roger Hitching
The Church and Deaf People
A Study of Identity, Communication and Relationships with Special Reference to the Ecclesiology of Jürgen Moltmann
In *The Church and Deaf People* Roger Hitching sensitively examines the history and present experience of deaf people and finds similarities between aspects of sign language and Moltmann's theological method that 'open up' new ways of understanding theological concepts.
2003 / 1-84227-222-5 / xxii + 236pp

John G. Kelly
One God, One People
The Differentiated Unity of the People of God in the Theology of Jürgen Moltmann

The author expounds and critiques Moltmann's doctrine of God and highlights the systematic connections between it and Moltmann's influential discussion of Israel. He then proposes a fresh approach to Jewish–Christian relations building on Moltmann's work using insights from Habermas and Rawls.

2005 / 0-85346-969-3 / approx. 350pp

Mark F.W. Lovatt
Confronting the Will-to-Power
A Reconsideration of the Theology of Reinhold Niebuhr

Confronting the Will-to-Power is an analysis of the theology of Reinhold Niebuhr, arguing that his work is an attempt to identify, and provide a practical theological answer to, the existence and nature of human evil.

2001 / 1-84227-054-0 / xviii + 216pp

Neil B. MacDonald
Karl Barth and the Strange New World within the Bible
Barth, Wittgenstein, and the Metadilemmas of the Enlightenment

Barth's discovery of the strange new world within the Bible is examined in the context of Kant, Hume, Overbeck, and, most importantly, Wittgenstein. MacDonald covers some fundamental issues in theology today: epistemology, the final form of the text and biblical truth-claims.

2000 / 0-85364-970-7 / xxvi + 374pp

Keith A. Mascord
Alvin Plantinga and Christian Apologetics

This book draws together the contributions of the philosopher Alvin Plantinga to the major contemporary challenges to Christian belief, highlighting in particular his ground-breaking work in epistemology and the problem of evil. Plantinga's theory that both theistic and Christian belief is warrantedly basic is explored and critiqued, and an assessment offered as to the significance of his work for apologetic theory and practice.

2005 / 1-84227-256-X / approx. 304pp

Gillian McCulloch
The Deconstruction of Dualism in Theology
With Reference to Ecofeminist Theology and New Age Spirituality
This book challenges eco-theological anti-dualism in Christian theology, arguing that dualism has a twofold function in Christian religious discourse. Firstly, it enables us to express the discontinuities and divisions that are part of the process of reality. Secondly, dualistic language allows us to express the mysteries of divine transcendence/immanence and the survival of the soul without collapsing into monism and materialism, both of which are problematic for Christian epistemology.

2002 / 1-84227-044-3 / xii + 282pp

Leslie McCurdy
Attributes and Atonement
The Holy Love of God in the Theology of P.T. Forsyth
Attributes and Atonement is an intriguing full-length study of P.T. Forsyth's doctrine of the cross as it relates particularly to God's holy love. It includes an unparalleled bibliography of both primary and secondary material relating to Forsyth.

1999 / 0-85364-833-6 / xiv + 328pp

Nozomu Miyahira
Towards a Theology of the Concord of God
A Japanese Perspective on the Trinity
This book introduces a new Japanese theology and a unique Trinitarian formula based on the Japanese intellectual climate: three betweennesses and one concord. It also presents a new interpretation of the Trinity, a co-subordinationism, which is in line with orthodox Trinitarianism; each single person of the Trinity is eternally and equally subordinate (or serviceable) to the other persons, so that they retain the mutual dynamic equality.

2000 / 0-85364-863-8 / xiv + 256pp

Eddy José Muskus
The Origins and Early Development of Liberation Theology in Latin America
With Particular Reference to Gustavo Gutiérrez
This work challenges the fundamental premise of Liberation Theology, 'opting for the poor', and its claim that Christ is found in them. It also argues that Liberation Theology emerged as a direct result of the failure of the Roman Catholic Church in Latin America.

2002 / 0-85364-974-X / xiv + 296pp

Jim Purves
The Triune God and the Charismatic Movement
A Critical Appraisal from a Scottish Perspective

All emotion and no theology? Or a fundamental challenge to reappraise and realign our trinitarian theology in the light of Christian experience? This study of charismatic renewal as it found expression within Scotland at the end of the twentieth century evaluates the use of Patristic, Reformed and contemporary models of the Trinity in explaining the workings of the Holy Spirit.

2004 / 1-84227-321-3 / xxiv + 246pp

Anna Robbins
Methods in the Madness
Diversity in Twentieth-Century Christian Social Ethics

The author compares the ethical methods of Walter Rauschenbusch, Reinhold Niebuhr and others. She argues that unless Christians are clear about the ways that theology and philosophy are expressed practically they may lose the ability to discuss social ethics across contexts, let alone reach effective agreements.

2004 / 1-84227-211-X / xx + 294pp

Ed Rybarczyk
Beyond Salvation
Eastern Orthodoxy and Classical Pentecostalism on Becoming Like Christ

At first glance eastern Orthodoxy and classical Pentecostalism seem quite distinct. This ground-breaking study shows they share much in common, especially as it concerns the experiential elements of following Christ. Both traditions assert that authentic Christianity transcends the wooden categories of modernism.

2004 / 1-84227-144-X / xii + 356pp

Signe Sandsmark
Is World View Neutral Education Possible and Desirable?
A Christian Response to Liberal Arguments
(Published jointly with The Stapleford Centre)

This book discusses reasons for belief in world view neutrality, and argues that 'neutral' education will have a hidden, but strong world view influence. It discusses the place for Christian education in the common school.

2000 / 0-85364-973-1 / xiv + 182pp

Hazel Sherman
Reading Zechariah
The Allegorical Tradition of Biblical Interpretation through the Commentary of Didymus the Blind and Theodore of Mopsuestia

A close reading of the commentary on Zechariah by Didymus the Blind alongside that of Theodore of Mopsuestia suggests that popular categorising of Antiochene and Alexandrian biblical exegesis as 'historical' or 'allegorical' is inadequate and misleading.

2005 / 1-84227-213-6 / approx. 280pp

Andrew Sloane
On Being a Christian in the Academy
Nicholas Wolterstorff and the Practice of Christian Scholarship

An exposition and critical appraisal of Nicholas Wolterstorff's epistemology in the light of the philosophy of science, and an application of his thought to the practice of Christian scholarship.

2003 / 1-84227-058-3 / xvi + 274pp

Damon W.K. So
Jesus' Revelation of His Father
A Narrative-Conceptual Study of the Trinity with Special Reference to Karl Barth

This book explores the trinitarian dynamics in the context of Jesus' revelation of his Father in his earthly ministry with references to key passages in Matthew's Gospel. It develops from the exegeses of these passages a non-linear concept of revelation which links Jesus' communion with his Father to his revelatory words and actions through a nuanced understanding of the Holy Spirit, with references to K. Barth, G.W.H. Lampe, J.D.G. Dunn and E. Irving.

2005 / 1-84227-323-X / approx. 380pp

Daniel Strange
The Possibility of Salvation Among the Unevangelised
An Analysis of Inclusivism in Recent Evangelical Theology

For evangelical theologians the 'fate of the unevangelised' impinges upon fundamental tenets of evangelical identity. The position known as 'inclusivism', defined by the belief that the unevangelised can be ontologically saved by Christ whilst being epistemologically unaware of him, has been defended most vigorously by the Canadian evangelical Clark H. Pinnock. Through a detailed analysis and critique of Pinnock's work, this book examines a cluster of issues surrounding the unevangelised and its implications for christology, soteriology and the doctrine of revelation.

2002 / 1-84227-047-8 / xviii + 362pp

Scott Swain
God According to the Gospel
Biblical Narrative and the Identity of God in the Theology of Robert W. Jenson
Robert W. Jenson is one of the leading voices in contemporary Trinitarian theology. His boldest contribution in this area concerns his use of biblical narrative both to ground and explicate the Christian doctrine of God. *God According to the Gospel* critically examines Jenson's proposal and suggests an alternative way of reading the biblical portrayal of the triune God.
2006 / 1-84227-258-6 / approx. 180pp

Justyn Terry
The Justifying Judgement of God
A Reassessment of the Place of Judgement in the Saving Work of Christ
The argument of this book is that judgement, understood as the whole process of bringing justice, is the primary metaphor of atonement, with others, such as victory, redemption and sacrifice, subordinate to it. Judgement also provides the proper context for understanding penal substitution and the call to repentance, baptism, eucharist and holiness.
2005 / 1-84227-370-1 / approx. 274 pp

Graham Tomlin
The Power of the Cross
Theology and the Death of Christ in Paul, Luther and Pascal
This book explores the theology of the cross in St Paul, Luther and Pascal. It offers new perspectives on the theology of each, and some implications for the nature of power, apologetics, theology and church life in a postmodern context.
1999 / 0-85364-984-7 / xiv + 344pp

Adonis Vidu
Postliberal Theological Method
A Critical Study
The postliberal theology of Hans Frei, George Lindbeck, Ronald Thiemann, John Milbank and others is one of the more influential contemporary options. This book focuses on several aspects pertaining to its theological method, specifically its understanding of background, hermeneutics, epistemic justification, ontology, the nature of doctrine and, finally, Christological method.
2005 / 1-84227-395-7 / approx. 324pp

Graham J. Watts
Revelation and the Spirit
A Comparative Study of the Relationship between the Doctrine of Revelation and Pneumatology in the Theology of Eberhard Jüngel and of Wolfhart Pannenberg

The relationship between revelation and pneumatology is relatively unexplored. This approach offers a fresh angle on two important twentieth century theologians and raises pneumatological questions which are theologically crucial and relevant to mission in a postmodern culture.

2005 / 1-84227-104-0 / xxii + 232pp

Nigel G. Wright
Disavowing Constantine
Mission, Church and the Social Order in the Theologies of John Howard Yoder and Jürgen Moltmann

This book is a timely restatement of a radical theology of church and state in the Anabaptist and Baptist tradition. Dr Wright constructs his argument in dialogue and debate with Yoder and Moltmann, major contributors to a free church perspective.

2000 / 0-85364-978-2 / xvi + 252pp

www.ingramcontent.com/pod-product-compliance
Lightning Source LLC
Chambersburg PA
CBHW062011220426
43662CB00010B/1290

"Mission drift" is an often overlooked and underestimated dynamic of hybrid organizations. Dr. Israel K. Kombaté's study of seven parachurch agencies regarding their handling of mission drift challenges identifies factors and dynamics that all faith-based organizations will profitably take note of. I congratulate the researcher and author of this significant study.

Bernhard Ott, PhD
Professor Extraordinarius in Missiology, University of South Africa
European School of Culture and Theology, Korntal Campus
Gesellschaft für Bildung und Forschung in Europa (GBFE)

It seems inevitable. Most have witnessed the painful process. A faith-based mission organization slowly but steadily drifts away from its original Christian mission and identity. Rudderless, it loses its way and sinks into the abyss of secularism and irrelevancy. Now, however, thanks to Dr. Israel K. Kombaté's fine study, *Dealing with Mission Drift in Parachurch Agencies*, the factors leading to this drift and the means by which to combat it have been analyzed and described. This illuminating study of seven parachurch organizations is marked by solid theological reflection, substantial empirical research, and interaction with an impressive array of missiological scholarship. The result is a must-read for pastors, missionaries, and leaders of Christian NGOs seeking to retain a robust, biblically informed commitment to the holistic mission that Jesus calls us to embrace.

Robert P. Menzies, PhD
Adjunct Professor, Asia Pacific Theological Seminary, Philippines
Director, Asian Center for Pentecostal Theology

Every Christian organization and mission face the potentially exterminating power of mission drift. Dr. Israel K. Kombaté's insightful research exposes the reasons for drift, clarifying the internal and external factors that move missions away from their founding identity and purpose to something entirely other. His skilful work not only delineates the immeasurable danger of drift but by carefully examining that process in multiple organizations he has melded a solid tether between the capacity to understand the consequences of drift and the means to prevent it.

His study serves as a prophetic harbinger presenting the possibility to remain mission true through the lens of a well-developed holistic theology where love for Christ and our neighbor expresses itself in the refusal to bifurcate gospel proclamation and the restoration of human dignity.

Rev. Steve Pennington, PhD
Vice Chancellor,
Pan-Africa Theological Seminary, Lomé, Togo